D0911953

the good news for Working Mothers

Betty Holcomb

A Touchstone Book
Published by Simon & Schuster
New York London Toronto Sydney Singapore

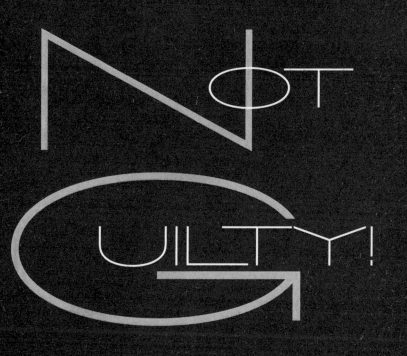

TOUCHSTONE
Rockefeller Center
1230 Avenue of the Americas
New York, NY 10020

First Touchstone Edition 2000
TOUCHSTONE and colophon are registered trademarks of
Simon & Schuster, Inc.

Designed by Brooke Zimmer
Set in Sabon
Manufactured in the United States of America

1 3 5 7 9 10 8 6 4 2

The Library of Congress has cataloged the Scribner edition
as follows:

Holcomb, Betty.
Not guilty!: the good news about working mothers/Betty
Holcomb.
p.   cm.
Includes bibliographical references and index.
1. Working mothers—United States. 2. Mothers—
Employment—United States. I. Title.
HQ759.48.H66   1998
331.4'4—dc21   98-16527
CIP

ISBN 0-684-82233-4
0-684-86725-7 (PBK)

To Rachel and Daniel Waldholz,
in hopes that they realize their dearest dreams,
in both love and work.

To Mary Holcomb and Irene Johnson
for providing insight into what it means to be
a strong woman.

Contents

Acknowledgments

Coming to the end of this project, I now fully appreciate why so many authors say that their books could not have been written without the help of others. For me, there are a number of people to thank.

First of all, I thank my children, Rachel and Daniel, for their patience and excitement as they watched this book grow from a few pages to several hundred. There is also deep appreciation to Michael Waldholz for reading the early drafts of many chapters. My sister, Priscilla Holcomb, offered unwavering, unconditional support and encouragement, which was invaluable to me. Elisabeth Werby and Pamela Redmond Satran also gave generously of their time and thoughts to help shape the ideas in this book.

Judsen Culbreth, editor in chief of *Working Mother* magazine, gave me the time and encouragement to develop this project and proved to be one of the most family-friendly bosses a mother could ever wish for. If ever there was a flexible workplace, she has created it. Catherine Cartwright, a senior editor at *Working Mother,* contributed some research to this book, as well as her good humor and encouragement. My agent, Flip Brophy, proved to be patient, encouraging, and compassionate. Leigh Haber offered great encouragement and support. Jane Rosenman provided wise counsel, many insights, and careful editing to make this a better book, even on the tight schedules that we finally faced.

Many others also reviewed portions of the manuscript, gave generously of their time, and provided research as well as insights and support. To them, I also extend many thanks: Fran Rodgers, one of the smartest and most dedicated advocates of working parents in America today, both inspired parts of this book and generously agreed to read it in its rough stages. Faye Crosby offered intellectual and moral support as she reviewed several chapters and patiently listened as the project developed. Her Center for Feminist Conversation proved to be fertile ground for sowing some of the key themes in this book. Cynthia Fuchs Epstein also encouraged me and contributed many insights. Janice Steil contributed insight and precision to the chapter on changing families. Dana Friedman, Ellen Galinsky, and Arlene Johnson have all been generous with their time over the past decade, helping me to gain a fundamental understanding of the issues in the workplace. Many others also offered enormous help, including Lois Hoffman, Alison Clarke-Stewart, Alice Kessler-Harris, Judith Vladeck, Donna Lenhoff, Judith Lichtman, Helen Blank, and Edward Zigler.

I also thank the hundreds of working moms across the country who shared their stories with me. In the end, this book is for them, for their children and my children, in hopes that it will make some small contribution to making their lives easier.

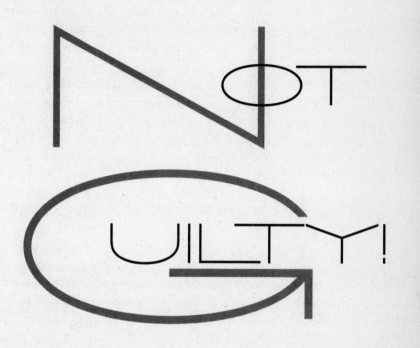

Preface

This book was born the day I walked up the steps to my daughter's first child care center, wondering if I was doing the right thing.

As I mounted the dark and dreary staircase to Basic Trust Infant and Toddler Center on Manhattan's Upper West Side, I was nearly certain that all the horror stories I had heard about day care would be true. The paint in the stairwell was peeling; the gates on the door were locked tight. It almost felt like a prison, hardly a place I'd want to leave my three-month-old infant. I had arrived here only out of desperation, when I could find no other alternative.

Yet once I crossed the threshold, a new world opened for me—one that called into question everything I had ever been told about child care. Although the stairway and the setting were institutional, nothing else about this center was. And the "strangers" who would look after Rachel soon turned into extended family and confidants. At the time, I did not know that Basic Trust was a national model, a very special place in America in 1984. As a new mother, I did not realize the staff were unusual—trained as they were in early childhood development. I only knew that the moment Rachel and I walked in, we both felt at ease.

With its well-worn couches, toys, and books, this place was like home—except that the adults in charge seemed to know a lot more about babies than I did at the time. I sank down in the couch to watch and knew that my idea of child care would never be the same. Rachel, even at a mere three months, was clearly enthralled. Although she could not yet crawl, she thrust her whole body and arms out toward the other two babies on the floor, eager to join in the fun.

Rachel did thrive at Basic Trust, or "B.T.," as we and the other families called it. But my doubts and questions about Rachel's care dogged me for the next two years, often inspired by friends, neighbors, and relatives. "Isn't it a long day for her?" was one of the most frequent queries. "Couldn't you find anyone to come to your apartment?" was another. And over and over again, people would say, "Too bad you have to work."

There were many days, of course, when I'd rather have been with my new baby. Indeed, I didn't leave her in anyone else's care even once in the first three months. As a first-time mother, I couldn't bear the separations. And even though I loved B.T., I delayed starting her in the program until six months after my initial visit. As luck would have it, I found a part-time caregiver, a Brazilian woman named Cacilda, the very week I needed to resume work. She came to me highly recommended from a family I knew. Cacilda was an experienced mother herself, a grandmother, in fact, who relaxed me about leaving Rachel for a few days each week. She cared for Rachel at home until I was ready for B.T.

But there were also plenty of times when I knew that both Rachel and I were better off when I had a few days for writing and she had a few days at B.T. She was attached to the other babies and to the caregivers, and she was happy. We sang the songs she learned there; we played the games at home. We got to know the other families there, through monthly gatherings and potluck parties.

The same year that Rachel started B.T., I began to get my education about the difficulties mothers were having in the workplace. An editor at *Savvy*, a monthly magazine aimed at working women, asked me to write about the new generation of moms juggling professional jobs and families. Back in 1985, such women were still rare. *Savvy* wanted a practical story, tips for moms on how to survive on the job after the baby was born. So that is what I served up, and what the magazine printed at the time.

But what stayed with me over the years was something else: the anger and pain I heard in women's voices as they described the choices they had to make between work and family. The feelings came pouring out in interview after interview, as if they had just been waiting for someone to ask. They wanted to talk about the hostility they met in nearly every quarter, but most especially on the job. A vice president at a New Jersey–based brokerage house, for example, confided that her boss threatened to fire her for taking an extended lunch hour to see her five-year-old son in the hospital. "My son had a fever of one hundred and five. He had pneumonia, and I was afraid to take the day off. All I did was take an extra hour for lunch. And my boss wanted to *fire* me," she said. She spoke, like so many women, only on the condition of anonymity, for fear of reprisal. The lesson she learned was a simple one: she began to lie to her boss. "After that, whenever I had a family problem, I just told them I was with a client."

In the decade or so since then, life has unquestionably improved for many working moms. New laws provide for some time off when a child is hospitalized, a growing number of companies offer flexible work schedules, and a few even help parents with the cost of child care. But such support is still painfully rare. And there is still plenty of indignation in women's voices. "I laugh at all the articles that tell me how to make a slick presentation to my supervisor to win a flexible schedule. It's just not going to happen where I work. The big bosses just won't allow it. Or if they do, it's done on the sly, for just one person at a time. Their attitude is 'You had the baby; it's your problem!' " a radio producer confided in the fall of 1995, a full decade after my *Savvy* article. The irony is that this producer was telling me this even as she prepared a piece for listeners on how to win a flexible schedule at work. She was interviewing me as an editor at *Working Mother* for the piece she was taping for later that day. The story did run, and to a market of millions of listeners in one of the nation's largest cities. "It's a joke, isn't it?" she said.

As the editor at the time for *Working Mother* magazine's annual list of family-friendly employers, I didn't want to agree. I didn't want to feed her cynicism. But I knew in my heart that all too many women shared her frustration. I knew from the letters and faxes and interviews and even from my own friends and my own life that mothers still faced capricious bosses and hostile work environments. I knew how hard it was to find a place like Basic Trust, a child care center where children can thrive. Mothers told me how they worried over the compromises they were forced to make, both on the job and at home.

In the years since I first climbed the stairs to that child care center, I have also come to understand just how complicated the issues are for working parents. I have come to understand the issues on both a personal and professional level. In those thirteen years, I've had another child, a son, Daniel, who is seven as this book goes to press. My experiences with him are so utterly different from what they were with Rachel. I've changed jobs, changed towns twice, and had to switch child care arrangements several times. I learned that it didn't get easier as the kids got older, it just got different. Now I am involved in the public schools, have to make after-school arrangements and search for summer programs, and worry about what to do when the schools shut down for snow. Rachel is pushing into adolescence and Daniel is rebelling against elementary school.

For most of those years, however, I was one of the top editors at *Working Mother* magazine. That perch gave me access to leading experts on child care and child development, the changing workplace, and family and women's issues. I've been at ground zero of many of the great debates over women's changing roles in the past decade, from the uproar over the "mommy track" to Zoe Baird's nomination for U.S. attorney general to Marcia Clark's custody fight. I've talked to hundreds of moms, read their letters, and analyzed their responses to surveys about their lives. Most of all, I've listened to them.

And I admire them. They are creative and resourceful as they patch together their daily approach to integrating work and family life. At times, I am astounded by their energy and persistence as they invent brand-new ways of living and working. "Shortly after my son's birth, I decided to go back to school to earn my paralegal certificate. Not because I had such an interest in the law, but because I needed a stable job with good benefits," Lisa Marshall, from Elk Grove, Illinois, wrote in response to a recent *Working Mother* survey on women and ambition. "I don't mind saying that I'm very proud of myself, as well I should be," she said. She acknowledged that it was also a demanding life. "Sometimes it amazes me that I manage to get up every morning, get my son and I dressed, fed and off to school and work, let alone anywhere close to on time and looking presentable."

Yet the question that puzzled her most is the one that is central to this book. "Men pride themselves on their ability to earn a good living in order to take care of their families. Why is it that woman must be made to feel guilty about doing the same thing?"

This is the book I wanted to read after I had Rachel. It is angry and it is an affirmation. Those are the sentiments I hear in women's voices today. I see that, still, there is nothing simple about becoming a mother.

Introduction

For women, the times were heady, full of promise. It's almost hard to recall the optimism now, when the catchphrase "having it all" first took hold in popular culture. It was the early 1980s, and America seemed ready to embrace working mothers. Aided by new equal rights laws, including the all-important Pregnancy Discrimination Act, young women were charging into law, medicine, and business. There was no sense yet that they would bump up against a glass ceiling, or be sidelined on the "mommy track." Day care was finally getting a clean bill of health; even Dr. Spock, who had once dismissed day care as "baby farms," conceded it was acceptable for Mom to work outside the home. Madison Avenue, always attuned to America's fantasies and wishes, invented a new image to express the dreams of this unique era: the confident young mom with a baby on one arm and a briefcase on the other began to appear regularly in television commercials and magazine advertisements. Women seemed poised to attain what men had always taken for granted: success on the job and a family life, too.

But the romance didn't last long—it never has with working moms—and by the early 1990s, Supermom was dead and buried, replaced by a new image: the frantic, fatigued woman who worked only because she had to. The idea of women "having it all" was dismissed as hollow, unrealistic. A new catchphrase, the "second shift," coined by sociologist Arlie Hochschild, expressed the new pessimism. "Having it all" simply meant doing it all—a shift on the job, then a second one at home. At the time, Hochschild hoped to move what she called the "stalled revolution" for women's rights ahead, by pointing out the unfair burden of labor that women shoulder at home. She proposed an ambitious agenda to make it truly possible for women to have both a job and a family. So did Betty Friedan and a host of other women's activists.

But instead, a new and darker image of working moms gradually gained ground. In congressional testimony, glossy magazines, news stories, and Op-Ed pieces, moms with successful careers were reviled as selfish and materialistic, putting their own ambitions ahead of their children's needs. In 1991, the hip metropolitan magazine *New York Woman*, which was usually an outspoken advocate of working women, went so far as to compare the children of professional women with victims of domestic violence. The illustration to the feature story, which ran under the cover line "Trophy Kids: Children of the Rich and Busy," portrayed a doleful child, wasting away for lack of attention, while her mom worked. Career success even became pivotal in a wave of widely publicized child custody cases. Tragically, some women lost their children when judges ruled them to be "too career oriented."

Throughout this onslaught, some child care experts did defend working moms, of course. Many argued that it was not so much the quantity of time a mom spent with her kids but the quality of that time that mattered to kids' emotional health. In other words, children did just fine, whether Mom worked or not, as long as she was a sensitive, responsive, and caring parent. That conclusion is, it turns out, exactly what the research now shows.

But by 1997, even that defense of working moms had crumbled. Arlie Hochschild, the sociologist who had made women's predicament so vivid in her book *The Second Shift,* now came forth with a sensational new book, *The Time Bind,* which made a provocative new argument. Many parents, she argued, turned to work as an *escape* from their children, rather than as a way to earn the money to care for them. The *New York Times Magazine* was the first to excerpt the book, in April, making it a cover story, "Work: The Great Escape." The headline inside claimed that "Americans say they want more time with their families. But the truth is, they'd rather be at the office."

Within weeks of the book's hitting the bookstore, the "buzz" among New York's media was intense, and working parents took a serious hit. "Quality time" was now a topic of widespread derision, the notion that kids automatically suffered when mothers worked revived passionately. On May 12, the cover of *Newsweek* declared quality time to be a "myth" that might salve a mother's conscience, but did nothing for kids' emotional health. In fact, working parents were "cheating" their kids, by failing to give them enough love and attention. The same week, *U.S. News & World Report* ran its cover story "Lies Parents Tell Themselves about Work, Kids, Money, Day Care and Ambition." That story, like so many others that came to dominate the 1990s media, did include men as well as women. That was a subtle sign of how times were changing, an acknowledgment that many men, as well as women, now struggled as they tried to blend work and family life.

But the picture inside revealed the real target of this new wave of media coverage. An affluent young woman, laden with department store packages, smiled over the headline "Lie #1: We Both Work Because We Need the Money." Clearly, this glamorous young white woman was on a shopping spree, buying luxuries for herself. There were no kids in sight.

For women thick-skinned enough to shrug off this criticism, however, there was another disturbing story gaining momentum that was harder to dismiss. Starting in 1994, a spate of reports began to warn of new dangers in child care. Day care might just stunt a child's brain growth. It was possible, according to stories that ran in *Newsweek* in February of 1997 and in coverage offered by other respected media outlets, that poor-quality child care could affect the physical growth of the brain. Many working moms took anxious note. "That idea was truly scary to me. I even showed that article to my child's day care director," says Shayne Parker, mother and human resources manager at Lucent Technologies in New Jersey. With a child under the age of one, she'd paid close attention to all the negative coverage of working parents in 1997, and it'd sent a chill through her. "These stories make you second-guess yourself. To me, the message of all this media coverage was really saying that I should be at home."

That is no small admission from Parker. As a specialist in work and family benefits, she knows the research on working mothers quite well. She knows kids can thrive when mothers work. She sees her own twelve-month-old daughter doing fine at the local day care center. "She's very social. I think more social than she might be if she were home with me. She'll walk right over to people and hold their hands. She's confident and interested in people." Still, the media coverage fuels doubts about working. "I mean, I'm not going home, but these stories are really scary. There are certainly days when I wonder why I am doing this. They make me worry and even feel somewhat guilty."

And so it is for so many others of the millions of mothers who both want and need to work outside the home. Each day, in large ways and small, they find their choices scrutinized, their motivation under attack, the well-being of their children constantly called into question.

Indeed, they find themselves dead center of a renewed debate over the place of work in women's lives once they have children. Increasingly, women find it dangerous to say that they "want" to work after they have children. The only acceptable reason for taking a job is "economic necessity." And even then, a woman had better not be too ambitious about her work, or she risks being branded a poor mother. "If as a mother, I suggested that my career drive is more critical than ever now that I have children, society would not see me favorably. The support just isn't there," says Karen Metcalf Wehman, mother of two and a marketing professional in Indianapolis, Indiana. She says she is well aware by now that working mothers are blamed for "causing the breakdown of the traditional family and family values with our 'me first' attitudes. I am so tired of trying to defend my rights as a working woman and a working mother that I know I do sound caustic at times."

The idea that children inevitably suffer when mothers work, that women's interests and children's interests are at odds, has gained wide acceptance. So has the notion that women are inevitably exhausted and depleted when they try to combine a job and family duties.

But these ideas are just plain wrong.

It's time to recognize that today's families do not suffer because women entered the workforce and stayed there once they had children. Forty years of research confirm that real life is far more complicated than that. The mere fact that a woman works outside the home is simply not much of a predictor of children's welfare, for better or worse. Instead, the impact of Mom's job on herself, her children, and her mate depends on the quality of her job, her control over her work, and whether she really wants to work at all—just as it does for men.

The purpose of this book, then, is to challenge the collective change of heart about women's expanded roles, and the assumptions of the current public debate about blending work and family. It's time to take on the most common and destructive myths about employed moms, track their origin, and dispel their harmful power. Above all, it's time to reassure moms who both need and want to work that they are doing the right thing for themselves and their families.

That is not to argue blindly that working outside the home is the best choice for every woman. Many women, just like many men, would love to win the lottery and quit work. The downsized workplace is less appealing to workers of both sexes. Nor will this book suggest that combining a job and family duties is easy. Only a fool could dismiss the problems that women with children still face on the job and in the home. Nor will it minimize the joys and satisfactions that many women find in being home with their children.

But it is time to acknowledge that the lingering stereotypes about who makes a good parent and who makes a good worker are not just a harmless nostalgia for simpler times. Taken together, wrongheaded assumptions about mothers and work form the backbone of a powerful bias that hurts both women and their families. They create an unrelenting assault on women's psyches, pocketbooks, and rights in the workplace. Most important, they fuel discrimination on the job and undermine support for expanding and improving child care in this country.

The idea that women should not and do not want to work once they have babies, for example, drags down women's wages and hurts their chances for promotion. Many managers confess they still harbor such outdated views of women, and see them as unreliable and uncommitted workers and so pass them over for plum jobs and assignments. The attitudes persist despite the fact that the vast majority of moms today now return quickly to the job after a baby is born. Studies also show women do better in performance reviews than men.

The idea that children are always better off at home, in the exclusive care of their mothers, also serves to stigmatize child care. The distorted view leads the media to exaggerate the problems of abuse in child care and fuel parents' worries about the kind of care their children are getting. Research also shows that public ambivalence about whether infants can thrive in other-than-mother care undermines public funding for child care. "Our society's bias that women ought to be at home with kids keeps us from looking carefully at child care in this country and improving its quality," said pediatrician T. Berry Brazelton in the spring of 1994. Brazelton himself conceded that he had been slow to come around to a positive view of mothers working during the first year of a child's life. "It's hard for all of us to let go of this ideal of mothers at home."

What women need now is a more balanced appraisal of the costs and benefits of working. Above all, they need the reassurance that they are doing the right thing for themselves and their families. The current, distorted cultural lens makes it hard to get a clear picture of their own accomplishments and the true sources of their discomfort.

"We hear all about the stresses, but not the joys of working," says Cynthia Fuchs Epstein, distinguished professor of sociology at the Graduate Center of City University of New York. "One of the problems women face is that there is no one out there saying, 'Sure, it can be hard, but it's worth it. Go for it!' Instead, they're constantly asked to explain themselves and told, 'It's too hard.'"

As in the past, the current backlash against working women did not happen entirely by accident. In some cases, the needlessly negative images of working moms are the product of organized interest groups. Over the past decade, a loose network of social conservatives, motivated by both religious and secular beliefs, has churned out a steady stream of research indicting working mothers and child care and extolling the virtues of traditional male and female roles. Articulate and well organized, these activists have had a notable impact on public opinion and policy.

But the renewed negativity could never have taken root were it not for a collective anxiety about women's changing roles. And no wonder. Nothing signals more profound change than the working mother revolution. This change affects everything, from who does the dishes and cares for the children to who sits in the executive suites. Suddenly, all the premises of power and personal identity are on the table. Men and women must grapple with what it means to be a father or a mother, a worker or a parent. For many, such questions even touch on their deep-rooted feelings about what it means to be male or female.

So it's almost inevitable that mothers' roles are once again the lightning rod for debates on key social issues. And it's no surprise that Americans return, again and again, to the assumptions of the past. Decades of research on stereotypes show just how difficult it is to change notions about gender, especially when the economy and home life are constructed around them.

Prejudice about what it takes to be a proper worker and what it takes to be a proper parent springs from habits of thinking, from values so ingrained they seem like the immutable laws of nature. One of the Big Three automakers recently resorted to hiring a cultural anthropologist to identify the attitudes and rules that favor men with stay-at-home wives on the job. Without such a guide, few managers can even see the prejudice that hobbles so many workers and drains productivity.

It's also true that some of the myths have staying power because they carry some core truths, often those closest to our hearts. Who could disagree, for example, with Penelope Leach's assertion that babies benefit from a strong, loving bond with their moms? Who can dispute that many parents today are hungry for more time with their kids? The trouble is that the answer served up to women leads them down just one path: women should be at home.

Most women today are too busy careening through life each day to stop and analyze the truth of the many messages that come their way. Those who work outside the home often absorb the idea that they are guilty of some wrongdoing almost by osmosis, from newscasts, teachers, relatives, bosses, child care advice books, and even neighbors. You can hear it on their lips as they compare notes about their jobs and their families. Debbie Clay, an office worker in Maryland, says she carried her guilt like a "ball and chain" after her first child was born.

For many others, the idea that something is terribly wrong in their lives resonates—and with good reason. Just navigating through the day can be a trial in a society that provides few supports and little encouragement.

This need not be the case, of course. There is now plenty of evidence to show that when women and their families get the right kind of support—control over the hours they work and high-quality care for their kids—they thrive. Women with challenging and rewarding work, with some control over the hours and way they do their jobs, rank highest in their life satisfactions. Their lives may not be perfect—trying to mesh work and family duties is never without its stresses. But neither are they miserable. "The point is that working parents' lives might be somewhat frazzled, no matter what the circumstances," says Fran Rodgers, chief executive officer of Work/Family Directions, one of the nation's leading authorities on work-family issues. "But they don't have to be as frazzled as they are today. A lot of their stress arises from the fact not enough has changed in the world around them."

But rather than finding help, women often find themselves under siege, hammered by a media that focuses on the downside of their lives, a political environment that scapegoats them for the problems of today's families, and a workplace that refuses to meet their needs. It's hardly surprising that many sound doubtful and tentative about working outside the home. In such a negative environment, it's also easy to see why many women today feel more comfortable saying they "have" to work, even though polls show they enjoy their jobs and find satisfaction and esteem in paid work outside the home. "If you say to people, I 'have' to work, I don't have a choice, then it's okay. But if you say you like to work, then it's assumed, by a lot of people, that you can't be a good mother. It's treated as if you don't like being with your child," says Elizabeth Raynor, mother of two and a manager at Barnett Banks in Jacksonville, Florida.

The truth is that many women find an outlet in work not available elsewhere, just as men do. Three out of four women surveyed by *Working Mother* magazine in 1993 said they "liked" or "loved" their jobs. Nearly 84 percent said that "using their skills" was an even greater motivation than money. It is, as Freud said, that people need both work and love; women do not want to choose between the two. "Part of me comes alive when I see a patient improve," Charity Goodwin-Johansson, a physical therapist in Pittsboro, North Carolina, told work-family researchers. "If I didn't have that kind of excitement in my life, I would suffer and so would my children." In a Gallup survey a year later, women with jobs as various as desnouting hogs and teaching physics said they enjoyed their work. "I like what I do. It's challenging and even kind of exciting because it's not predictable. I'm not always cranking out the same thing every day," Cheryl Benek, a software designer in Pennsylvania, told writer Carin Rubinstein in follow-up interviews to the Gallup poll. "For me," Benek said, "work is part of who I am."

Yet American women now live in a world where it is safer to discuss their angst than their anger, to feel powerless rather than exercise their collective power, to focus on their problems and defeats rather than their joys and successes.

It is time to free women up to speak honestly about their lives, to hear about the pleasures as well as the frustrations that come with being a working mother in America today, to change the climate from one that encourages women to feel powerless to one that celebrates their power, from one that sanctions only talk of their guilt to one that acknowledges their joy.

Above all, it is time to recognize that many of their problems are not personal ones that can be solved privately, but the result of barriers created by a society designed for families of another era. Once the real dialogue begins, women will be free to break the last barriers to full equality. When they do, the world will be a better place for them, their children, and men who want to be more involved with their children.

1

Supermom's Daughters

The Birth of a New Pessimism

WHEN AMY LANGSTON hit her senior year at Harvard University, she tried to imagine what it would be like to have both a job and a family. It was not a pretty picture. "I read about these women getting up at four-thirty A.M., who then clean for an hour, then make everyone's lunches, and then go to work. It worries me. I wonder, 'How could I do that?'"

So when the spring issue of the student newsletter arrived on campus with an article entitled "The Right Sacrifice," Amy paid it close attention.

"I used to believe that it was possible to have it all," wrote the author. "But those delusional days are over." Even with a prestigious Ivy League degree on the way, and even before she had conceived a child, the young author saw her career compromised by her desire to be a mother. For women, juggling work and family was all a "matter of choosing the right sacrifice."

A simple black-and-white line drawing of a young woman dressed in a long, flowing gown illustrated the story. She stood at a fork in a road marked "career" on one side and "home life" on the other. Her dress and demeanor unabashedly called up the Victorian era, that time a century ago when women were exhorted to maintain a separate sphere from that of men. She faced the path marked "career." But she hesitated, because an angelic, idealized cherub tugged at her skirt, pointing her toward "home."

The essay voiced not a trace of anger that women feel compelled to choose one path or the other. Instead, the author, Sheila Warren, then a sophomore majoring in economics, called on her classmates to face reality. "If I want to bring my kids up the way I was brought up, then I have to be around, like my mother was around. Plain and simple."

Oddly, the article never fully explained just what the "right sacrifice" might be. But it certainly conveyed, from its headline to its illustration, the timeworn message: Women need to make a choice. You can be a good mother or you can be a good worker. One path precludes the other.

Buried in the same issue of the *Lighthouse* was evidence of a revolution in the making. This one had great significance for the way work and family issues would be handled in the coming years. This news was about how attitudes were changing among young men. The editors had polled ninety-three undergraduates—an admittedly small sample. But what they found was startling: some 83 percent of the men said they were "willing to interrupt their careers to help raise their children." Certainly, this was a departure from earlier generations. Harvard men of the past went on to seats of power, to run the nation's corporations and politics, to set the standards for today's workplace and family life. Most chose careers that left little space for family and practically none for children. The new poll revealed a stark departure from that old way of life.

But this intriguing result from the poll was barely noted. The editors revealed it in the small-type footnotes that ran under a chart. The chart itself focused on another, far less surprising result: young men were far more likely than women to predict they would be "very successful" in their careers.

Why would a student-run newsletter at a university full of the nation's most ambitious young women publish "The Right Sacrifice" in 1996? "The topic grew out of an anxiety we'd heard other women express and we ourselves are feeling," Katherine Fausset, editor of the *Lighthouse* at the time, explained in a phone interview. "I'm thinking I'll have to make a choice between a career and children."

Like Amy Langston, Fausset worried that the life of a working mom would be one of unending drudgery—and one that consigned children to neglect. "I'm not really expecting my husband is going to split things fifty-fifty with me. I'm not really expecting that on-site child care is going to be prevalent. I'd really like those things to happen, but I don't think that they will. So I'm going to have to make a choice," said Fausset.

That message resonated for Langston, who had already spent considerable time thinking about her future prospects. Growing up in western Virginia, she put a high value on marriage and children. "At home, everyone thinks it's crazy that I'm not engaged yet," she said. At times, she felt out of place at Harvard. "People here are so career oriented. It's the first time I've ever met people who said they didn't want to have children," she confessed. When she expressed her feelings about the importance of family on campus, she was often teased. "One of my roommates used to tell me I'm just going to end up making peanut butter and jelly sandwiches."

As a senior soon to launch herself in the world, she had yet to resolve the tension she felt over how to pursue both work and family. "I'd like a job in which I could be a woman," said Langston, "but a lot of jobs don't feel like I could be a woman in them. I couldn't be a happy investment banker. I'd have to work so many hours. I'd abandon a whole part of me."

So "The Right Sacrifice" struck a chord. "The feminist message is that you can have it all," said Langston, "but that's just not realistic. Not every man, not every workplace, will be supportive of me once I have children." The answer to her dilemma? She needed to create her own personal solution, she believed. There was little chance, she said, that the institutions around her would change. "It's up to me to find a spouse who supports me and a workplace that is supportive. It's just a matter of being realistic, whether I like it or not."

Amy did not know that Sheila Warren had cranked out the article in ten minutes flat, off the top of her head. "It just kind of came out," Warren said. "I don't really even know where it came from."

But there it was. By the spring of 1996, the pessimism about women's expanded roles had infected even some of the young women at Harvard University. With their education, talent, and ambition, women like Langston, Fausset, and Warren might well have expected to storm the nation's boardrooms and executive suites, the halls of Congress, and even the White House. With their credentials and connections, they could arguably expect future employers to do most anything to meet their needs and secure their talents. That very spring, a Harvard recruiter boasted to the *New York Times* that the university had to be selective about admitting students, since it was "grooming the next generation of national leaders."

Yet here they were, pausing before they even got out of the gate, uncertain whether to join the race at all.

Their resignation was striking even to a casual visitor. "These young women seemed to be losing a belief you can have both a career and a family. That's very disturbing to me," said Fran Rodgers, one of the nation's leading business consultants on family issues, after she gave a speech on campus.

Rodgers knows better than most just how tough life can be for working moms. Over the past two decades, she's been inside scores of the nation's largest corporations and seen the fierce resistance that can arise in response to even the simplest innovation, such as flextime, in today's world of business. Work/Family Directions now takes thousands of calls each day from workers inside these companies, offering them help with family problems that spill over into the workplace. She knows the conflicts men and women still face as they try to succeed as both parents and workers. And that is why the attitudes of many young women worry her. "Each generation has to play a role in making the world a different place, in making institutions into new places. But you need to start out with a full tank or you'll never make it. I worry about a new generation starting out so discouraged.

"They seem to have the idea that women have been trying to do this long enough, so if it hasn't happened yet, it's just not realistic," Rodgers says. "What they should be concluding is that if it hasn't happened yet, if women are still having trouble balancing a job and a family life, then maybe the issues just haven't been taken seriously enough."

HABITS OF THINKING

It's instructive that Sheila Warren's essay tumbled out of her, without much thought. That is no criticism of Warren or her essay. Rather, "The Right Sacrifice" stands in its own little way as an artifact, a testimony to the power of cultural stereotypes.

Young women do not live in a vacuum, of course, but in a culture that has created a particular lens for viewing women's options. The vision draws, as it must, on collective memories and experiences. So it's not surprising that the illustrator for Warren's essay turned to images from the Victorian era, the time when home and work first diverged to become "separate spheres." It was then that Americans first decided, by both informal custom and formal law, that much of women's work would go without pay and men would earn a wage to support their families. Domestic chores would be part of women's "wifely duties," put on a pedestal, bathed in the sunny appeal of a cheery domesticity. In this cultural shorthand, children become cherubs, women wear flowing robes and follow the path laid down in nature. Such an image is especially apt in the current period of backlash against women, encouraging even the most ambitious women to make the right and noble "sacrifice."

The distinctions between men's and women's work have blurred over the past century, of course. But the cultural vision of what it takes to be a good mother remains largely unchanged. A woman of the Victorian era could easily embrace the rules for today's moms.

Good mothers work only because they "have" to; the best are home full-time.

This picture leaves much out of the frame, of course. There are the employers with the power to change the way Americans work, the policymakers who could fund child care and improve its quality, the school boards who could create before- and after-school programs for kids. These actors stand in the wings; the pressures that shape women's choices are treated as if they were immutable. Calls for broad-based social change are dismissed as unrealistic, too expensive. Even changing the ground rules for personal relationships is deemed to come at too high a cost, as if women might be asking for "too much" or trying to do "too much." One therapist revealed that young women feared they might "poison" their marriages by "an overinsistence on equality."

So it is not surprising that women's expanded opportunities now feel more perplexing than exciting to most Americans. How can a woman go to work without decent child care? How can she manage the domestic chores and a job at the same time? How can she succeed on the job when the workplace remains largely hostile to parents' needs?

Young women today enter the adult world with a keen awareness of these problems. Unlike the baby boomer women who were buoyed by the naive optimism of the women's movement, these women harbor few illusions about the stubborn resistance to change on the job and at home. "Full equality still seems an elusive goal and there is palpable frustration" among young women today, writes Harvard economics professor Claudia Goldin, who has studied the historical records of college graduates in this century. Her research has turned up no generation yet able to strike a reasonable balance between family and career. Women choose to become "career" women and succeed on the job, or to be mothers and forgo a career. "Is it no wonder that today's college women assert they have no role models?" Goldin asks.

They know that nearly every major institution in America, from the schools to the workplace, still operates as if every family had a homemaker mom and breadwinner dad. In such a world, women's sacrifices come to seem inevitable. Warren, for example, has yet to take her first professional job, but in her college essay, she lays out the ground rules for advancement in many workplaces. "If I want to succeed, I mean really succeed, in my career, then I have to throw myself into it, heart and soul. I have to be the one working overtime so I will be eligible for the promotion. I have to bring home work if need be. I have to travel if that's what it takes. No matter what career I decide upon, I have to give it my all." With profitable companies still laying off employees even in good economic times, many would agree with her. Workers today "know the first to go will be the ones the boss thinks are not giving 150 percent," Alice Freedman, a consultant with Fran Rodgers's firm, told *USA Today* in April 1997.

For young women, such a vision of the workplace sets off urgent, personal questions that have become the stuff of late-night heart-to-hearts. How ambitious should they be? How will their work affect their children? How involved will their husbands be in child care? "Young women tell me they talk about these issues in their dorms at night," says Ellen Snee, the student advisor who arranged for Fran Rodgers to speak at Harvard. "They are really struggling over the issue of how to have a career and a family."

All too often, the conversation is infused with, and confused by, assumptions about gender. Amy Langston worries aloud, for example, about how to find a job that she can be a "woman" in, as if jobs define gender. With that frame of reference, there is certain to be no easy path for having both a career and a family. The core stereotypes of what it means to be female in America—nurturing, soft, and caring—clash with the notions of what it takes to make it on the job. Executives are often described as hard-driving, tough, and competitive. That makes work and family mutually exclusive on a deep, psychic level. To be successful at work is to fail as a woman and, most especially, as a mother.

These distinctions are no small matter. The rules that prescribe what it means to be a man or a woman, male or female, carry the most special meaning of all to most people. Gender, after all, sits at the core of each person's identity, as one of the most visible and defining human characteristics. Some psychologists call gender a person's "master identity," since it colors virtually every aspect of life, every social interaction. And nothing bothers people more than violating the conventions of gender.

Yet that is exactly what working mothers do, each and every day, in large ways and small. And that fact creates a world full of dissonance and anxiety for many. At times, working mothers find they must even hide who they are. "I've learned not to mention the fact that I have a son," says a single mother and successful stockbroker in Atlanta, Georgia. "It's better at work if the fact that I'm a mother is invisible. Otherwise, the guys automatically assume that I am not going to be as productive or interested in my work."

And so it is that the debate over women's roles roils with emotion, lighting up both public and private discourse. Powerful new think tanks devoted to "family issues" churn out policy papers and studies of the effects of women's expanded roles, children's welfare, and the state of child care in this country. Politicians claim "family values" as they try to grab votes and inspire the loyalty of special interest groups.

In such an environment, it's hard to hear women's—or men's—authentic voices as they struggle with their options—or lack of them—in today's world. Their words can inspire a new image of motherhood today, one that puts work and family in harmony rather than at odds. "I think women today are trying to redefine what success is. I am not going to sacrifice my family for my career, nor am I going to sacrifice my career for my family," says Anne Brown, controller for a small firm in Dayton, Ohio. She is active in her church and her children's schools, and she works full-time. "I call it blending work and family, not juggling. Some days, I go to my job, then to my son's school, then back to work. No one at work questions me. It's accepted because they know I do a good job."

Women in jobs once reserved for men also defy the old stereotypes. Just listen to Dottie Bryant, a truck driver for Safeway grocery stores and mother of two children, talk about her work. On the road, she says, "the moon is full and you can see Venus, too. The night is very bright and beautiful. I love this part of trucking. I love driving a tractor-trailer. The good things always outweigh the bad things. The day I retire, I'll climb down out of a tractor cab," she says, "and tell everyone, 'It's been good for me.'"

But Americans often fall back on the old shorthand, the old habits of thinking, the stereotypes of gender that lead women to shed their ambitions and their voices. The idea that women must still make the "right sacrifice," as the Harvard essay suggests, simply follows the path of least resistance.

But scratch the surface and a much richer and more complicated reality lurches into view as Americans feel their way through a massive transformation of men's and women's roles. In a phone conversation after she published "The Right Sacrifice," Warren expressed a more textured sensibility, a range of feelings that did not come through in her printed essay. When pressed to define what the "right sacrifice" might be, for example, she was deeply confused. "I don't know what the answer is. Some days I'll think that I can't possibly give up my career to stay home and then I'll see a baby carriage and I'll think I will.

"I want to keep working after I have kids," she quickly added. But she had no model for that path; her own mother didn't work. "What I want to do and what I will do are probably different."

Settling on an answer seemed to calm her. "I'm not embittered about it. I don't view it as martyrdom or anything like that. It's very difficult choices, but I don't think it's a woman-only thing."

So her boyfriend felt the same way? Well, not exactly, it turned out, and that disturbed her a little. "He wants to be active in his children's lives," she said. "But when he sees himself as a father, I don't think he thinks about the implications for his career or the complications of it. He just sees it as something that exists in his future. He will be a father."

This difference riled her up again. For Warren, the "complications and implications" of having a child were daunting. She was especially worried about how her children might turn out if she worked full-time. She said she didn't know much about what the research said about the children with working moms; she relied on what she saw with her own eyes. Some friends back in high school with working moms had a "lousy home life because their parents were too busy. All of the more stable people here have very stable home lives with mothers who were at home."

Warren did not know that decades of research showed that the mere fact a woman works predicts very little about children's well-being. In many cases, a job will have far less significance in a child's life than, say, a family move, marital problems, or a parent suffering from depression. Conversely, a mother's job can stabilize a child's life; a steady income can dispel the chaos brought on by poverty. That point had been made over and over again in the national debate over welfare reform, swirling all around Warren and her classmates that very year. And, of course, millions of working-class women have raised successful and well-adjusted children over the years. Everyone knows that, when they stop to think about it.

Still, it's not surprising that Warren found herself framing the questions the way she did, pitting women's ambition against children's well-being. Plenty of other experts, as well as reporters and editors, all of them seasoned veterans, had been sounding themes quite similar to those in "The Right Sacrifice" for several years. From *Good Morning America* to *USA Today,* from the *Louisville Courier-Journal* to the *Austin States-American,* the media proclaimed that this "Superwoman" or "Supermom" was dead—and that this trend was for the better. Better for children and for women themselves. If nothing else, the pursuit of a job and family was simply exhausting. "I think a lot of us women are going to limp into the 21st century if the majority of us keep trying to do it all," a psychologist told the *Detroit News* in May of 1996.

It's almost surprising the pessimism didn't reach Harvard sooner. The negative views of working motherhood have been gaining momentum across America for years. Indeed, Amy Langston says her views of what it meant to be a working mother had taken root long before she ever picked up the *Lighthouse.* "My own mother was home, so I didn't have the experience of a working mother myself. My only real knowledge is through things I read," she says. "I guess I get these ideas from reading my mother's magazines. I read about these women who are exhausted. My fear is of spreading myself too thin. I worry that if I work when I have children, I'll just

be too tired. There won't be anything left for my children or for me."
In a phone interview, *Lighthouse* editor Katherine Fausset confessed,
"Just hearing the two words together—'working' and 'mother'—
makes me feel tired."

Neither could put her finger on a particular magazine, television
show, or news report. It was just a feeling that they had absorbed.
And no wonder.

2 Homeward Bound?

The Feminine Mystique circa the 1990s

B Y THE MID-1990S, the idea of "having it all" rang hollow to most women. Across America, the fact that working moms were struggling was no longer even an open question. The catchphrases "second shift," "mommy track," and "glass ceiling" now served as shorthand for the serious obstacles women still faced at home and on the job. At work, women were often stymied by discrimination and dead-end jobs; at home, they were still in charge of the kids and the house. "Having it all" was now a fate reserved for women so unlucky they "had" to work. Feminists were under attack for glorifying work and luring women out of the home. It was their fault that so many women had to do double time.

So what was the solution?

Starting in 1990, reporters and producers began to thunder back the answer. Women, and most especially those irascible baby boomer women who thought they could "have it all," were in retreat. The media began to insist that "career" and "professional" women—doctors, lawyers, and other female professionals in "high-powered" positions, often identified as earning "six figures"—had simply changed their minds about work. Juggling work and family was too hard; the answer was to drop the work "ball" and go home.

In other words, the very few women who had broken into serious careers, those who were making good money and challenged the conventions of the male-dominated workplace, had been routed. They were on their way home. And if they weren't home yet, surely they would join the ranks of homemakers soon.

Young women such as Amy Langston and Katherine Fausset did not have to look far to find "evidence" of the supposed trend. Only weeks after "The Right Sacrifice" appeared at Harvard, *Parents* magazine published a poll of 18,000 moms, announcing, "It May Be Quitting Time!" The news show *CBS This Morning* publicized the poll, reporting that the new trend showed that many moms "would rather be homemakers than wage earners." As with so many stories, this one portrayed the life of full-time homemakers as pure relief from the rigors of the career world. "I think it is so stressful for the typical young mom to balance career and family," *Parents* editor Ann Pleshette Murphy told CBS viewers. Given that Murphy herself was the mother of two and had a demanding job as the editor of a major magazine, she certainly could be seen as an authority on the topic. "To be home full-time is hard. I mean, we all know that. But to do both is particularly stressful." She insisted most moms "don't see the value in working full-time. Only four percent said they would work full-time if they had a choice."

Neither she nor CBS anchor Paula Zahn noted the fact that about 40 percent of *Parents* readers actually work full-time these days, even though most still have children under the age of two. The truth is that women aren't quitting, as the CBS broadcast implied. Indeed, the true watershed of the past two decades is the phenomenal growth in the number of mothers with very young children who now work year-round at full-time jobs. Their ranks doubled between 1972 and 1992, from 16 to 32 percent, a fact lost in this broadcast. That is still a minority of moms with infants, but it's an unmistakable trend, one that has persisted through good economic times and bad—and one that is most certainly evident in the demographics of *Parents* readers. During those same years, the number of working moms with children under the age of three also doubled, rising to 60 percent. The majority of women now return to work at least part-time before their child's first birthday, an astonishing shift from two decades earlier, when only about a third of moms worked at all before their children reached school age.

Even more intriguing, the U.S. Department of Labor released a study in 1995 revealing that men's and women's career patterns are now beginning to mimic each other. "It used to be that you'd see a dip in women's participation in mid-life, as they raised children," Katharine Abraham, commissioner of the U.S. Bureau of Labor Statistics, told reporters and women's activists gathered for a seminar in May of that year. "But an increasing proportion of women now work full-year, full-time, even after they have children." That fact, she said, should lay to rest the idea that women are less committed to work than men. "When you look at the statistics on who is most likely to work, you find that married women, and especially married mothers, are one of the groups most likely to be employed." Women with school-age children are even expected to work, and most do. Between 1975 and 1994, the percentage of women in this group zoomed from 50 to 75 percent.

Yet the idea that women had changed their minds about work persisted. "The idea that women can thrive as moms in high-powered careers is often an illusion. So say women who are cutting back on careers—or leaving them altogether," *USA Today* declared. Its story, which ran just a few months before the *Parents* poll, asserted that "successful career women" frequently learned that "their professional achievements weren't worth the hassle of juggling two jobs: office and home."

Feminists—not the business leaders who stubbornly refused to change the workplace or the spouses who refused to share domestic duties—frequently took the heat for women's distress. Just as the young women at Harvard blamed the women's movement for creating unrealistic expectations, so did more seasoned journalists, analysts, and experts. "Professional women" are abandoning their careers because they are "frustrated by the simplistic solutions of the feminist formula that said you could have it all," *Newsday* insisted. Women's problems in seeking success as both parents and workers were now treated as the natural fallout of trying to do "too much."

Martha Stewart gleefully proclaimed the trend a "backlash against the '70's and '80's, when women went off to work in great numbers and forgot about their kids. People are trying, once again, to set a standard that'll be more conducive to raising good children and maintaining a nice house." By 1996, she had built an empire on that fantasy.

A new raft of books and media stories claimed many moms of the 1990s had embraced the home front with new gusto. "Home-making is glamorous again," proclaimed the publicists for *At-Home Motherhood: Making It Work for You,* in a press release. "Working mothers want your job!" Like many other stories at the time, this one cited a poll by the national market firm of Yankelovich, Clancy and Shulman that found a growing number of women wanted to quit their jobs, if only they could afford to.

Women who stayed home became the "lucky" ones, even branded "status symbols" by the *Wall Street Journal.* In 1994, baby boomers who had pursued careers were declared the products of "mindless careerism" by none other than an editor of *Working Woman.*

By mid-decade, a whole new genre of stories had emerged focusing on young women identified as the "daughters of Supermom." This was the generation of daughters who grew up with baby boomer moms, and they served up a harsh critique of what it was like to have a working mother. "Exhaustion, guilt and divorce" were the likely outcomes, reporter Joanne Lublin wrote on the front page of the *Wall Street Journal* in late 1995. Children felt hideously neglected. "I've always wished my mother could have been more of a mother," lamented one. Many working moms were "never home," according to one of the subtitles in the article. Now-grown daughters detailed how lonely they felt when their moms worked. As a result, these young women vowed to quit work when they had children.

The fault, as usual, was with the women's "choices." The social climate, the difficulties women faced on the job, were barely mentioned. What a different message Lublin would have sent if those issues had been addressed, if she had put the workplace on trial instead of the women. What a different reaction readers would have had if she had placed the struggles of Generation X in the context of women's continuing struggle for economic survival, if she had asked the "supermoms" to talk about the price they were forced to pay at a time when there was no talk of "work-family conflict" or even working mothers' stress. "There was no understanding of what these women were going through, the challenges professional women faced then, of what it was like for these women when they were raising kids," says Freda Hurst, psychologist in New Jersey and one of the key sources for the story. "There were no allowances for women with children. For me, the issue came up when I was pregnant and up for tenure. Back then, if you took time off, you lost out on tenure. It was simple as that."

Indeed, many women of that generation were afraid to put photos of their children on their desks for fear of signaling biased bosses and coworkers that they weren't committed to their jobs. Many hid their pregnancies under bulky clothes and waited to announce the news at work until the latest possible moment, for fear of getting fired. Without a law barring pregnancy discrimination, they had virtually no protection from such treatment. Indeed, it was routine for many employers to lay women off the moment they showed.

This story, like so many others that bashed "Supermom," also put the basic tenets of the women's movement on trial. The word "feminist" was not used; instead, the offending mothers were identified as baby boomers. By then, "baby boomer" had clearly become a stand-in, a code term that meant "feminist," since that generation came of age with the women's movement. Indeed, Lublin's piece was quite open about the significance of choosing these women. "Many of today's professional women rebelled against their own stay-at-home moms, entering or re-entering the job market in record numbers during the late 1960's and early 1970's," she wrote.

In a telephone interview about a year after the front-page story came out, Lublin recalled the story was inspired partly by the idea that baby boomers constituted a "breakthrough generation" who "thought they could have it all." As one of them herself, she was interested in finding out how their children had fared. She recalled that the story, which was syndicated around the country, garnered strong reactions. "Some people thought I was undercutting the women's movement," she said. "But I thought it was my job to get around the stereotypes, to tell the truth."

Whether intended or not, stories like Lublin's did fuel the growing backlash set off by a new generation of antifeminists who claimed the women's movement ignored and derided motherhood. "Feminists expect children to fit the nooks and crannies of women's lives, the way children have traditionally fit the nooks and crannies of men's lives," charged Elizabeth Fox-Genovese in her highly publicized book *Feminism Is Not the Story of My Life*. "When motherhood is demoted from the center of women's lives to a parenthesis, children are demoted as well."

Her book and many other conservative tracts of the 1990s contend that a feminist "elite" has simply "lost touch with the real concerns of women." It was a theme sounded just a few years earlier by economist Sylvia Ann Hewlett in her two books *A Lesser Life* and *When the Bough Breaks: The Cost of Neglecting Our Children,* which also received widespread media attention in the late 1980s and early 1990s.

Feminists are rightfully stung by these accusations. "When people attack feminists for not caring about motherhood, I am always a little sad," says Judith Lichtman, executive director of the Women's Legal Defense Fund. Her group led the fight for the Family and Medical Leave Act, giving mothers—and fathers—the right to take time off work to care for a new baby or sick child. Far from relegating children to the "nooks and crannies" of working women's lives, Lichtman and other feminists have struggled to have the importance of raising children recognized by employers. She was in the forefront of battles for the Pregnancy Discrimination Act and other laws that protect mothers who work. "Most of us see how motherhood becomes a central issue in women's lives. We've understood that there are very complicated questions at the heart of it."

Most important, of course, is whether women's choices should be *limited* by motherhood, as they have been in the past. Indeed, motherhood has stood at the center of the struggle for equal rights and many of the victories especially important for mothers most in need of a paycheck. Far from hurting working-class mothers, sex discrimination laws have historically *helped* them care for their children, by ensuring them the right to earn a paycheck to house, clothe, and feed their kids.

Although few Americans are aware of it, the very first case brought under sex discrimination laws to make it to the U.S. Supreme Court was one brought on behalf of mothers with young children who had applied for work at Martin Marietta, a defense manufacturer at the time. Managers at the company argued that moms made unreliable workers because of their child care responsibilities, and held to the blanket policy even when mothers declared themselves ready and able to do the jobs. The women won, putting companies across the land on notice that many moms wanted and needed to work to support their families.

Indeed, Lublin and other journalists looking at how baby boomers have fared could have placed the struggle for equal rights in a much broader context. Far from forcing women to act like men, the women's movement has sought to broaden men's options as well and to make it possible for both men and women to be good parents and good workers. "One important part of our vision is to include men in family life. We wanted a law that would give societal permission for men to be involved with their children. Otherwise, women would be permanently saddled with both work and family responsibilities and men be permanently shut out of family life," says Lichtman.

Media stories also ignored the fact that it was feminists who first forecast women's current difficulties in integrating work and family if society did not change along with women's roles. "Can Women Really Have It All?" *Ms.* magazine asked in a March 1978 cover story. "By now, it seems that every woman is supposed to want Everything.

And Everything means the three-ball juggling act: job, marriage and children," Letty Cottin Pogrebin wrote. A mother herself, she knew how difficult it could be to reconcile the demands of family and career when there was no support at home or in the workplace.

At that time, Pogrebin worried over what she called a "new cult: Having It All," which she believed to be the invention of Madison Avenue. It was an obvious disservice to women, she argued, to market the idea that all women had to do was "find the right formula, figure out a timetable that makes most efficient use of the crucial years (roughly age 20 to 35)," and they could succeed both on the job and at home. This false notion, she contended, was the invention of a marketing and advertising community eager to speak to women's changing sensibilities as feminism took hold on Main Street.

But she warned, as did other feminist writers of the time, that no one could possibly manage to raise kids and have a satisfying job without serious social change. "Without equal parenting and more societal responsibility for child care, without equal responsibilities and increased flexibility in the workplace and home, there is virtually no person who can do it."

Many feminist scholars had also devoted themselves to making child care and housework visible and valued in a society that dismissed and devalued such work. The early and "radical" feminists also fought for relief for housewives left bereft and impoverished after divorce, setting up local offices to aid these women and fighting to see that legislation was passed to help "displaced homemakers" who wanted to get an education and find work. Yet now, writers and editors seemed to have a collective lapse of memory about the fate of those homemakers. Now they urged women to stop working and waxed romantic about life at home.

In early 1997, *Esquire* took this new mystique to its most regressive and damaging level. What young women really longed for, the magazine suggested, was not a career at all, with children or without. What women wanted was quite simple: a man to take care of them. In a story that quickly gained attention in New York's influential media circles, author Katie Roiphe wrote in a confessional tone about her secret desire for a "man in a gray flannel suit." She hungered for "a lawyer with a creamy leather briefcase going off to work in the mornings and coming back home in the evenings to the townhouse he has bought for me." Many "independent strong-minded women of the nineties" shared her dream, she insisted. This fantasy man would relieve her of the need to even try to balance a career and family life; he would be "a man who pays the bills, who works when you want to take time off to be with your kids."

Roiphe's core thesis was the most clichéd of all stereotypes of women, that there is a "traditional feminine desire to be protected and provided for." It is almost ridiculously predictable at a time of backlash. She could have made a far more intriguing point if she had asked young men how many of them might also yearn to be taken care of, to dispense with the realities of earning a living. Most certainly, there would have been many, especially among the cutting-edge, New Age young men in New York's literary circles.

But instead, *Esquire* served up Roiphe's ideas as sassy, honest commentary, representing the true desires of younger women, the daughters of Supermom. Roiphe could be marketed as a New Age heroine of sorts, a budding young writer unafraid to stand up to the noisy feminists and reveal the central emotional truths of young women's lives.

Other writers had already begun to insist that women were simply coming to accept the natural limitations of their gender. "Yes, Motherhood Lowers Pay!" thundered a headline on the *New York Times* Op-Ed piece by conservative thinker Danielle Crittenden in August of 1995. "This is an issue to take up with Nature, not Congress." In 1993, the *Washington Times* had profiled a physician who described her decision to quit working as a "worthy sacrifice," adding, "We are the gender that gestates."

So, AS ONE reads and listens to the changing tone of the media coverage and family experts since 1990, it is hard to miss the birth of a new mystique about motherhood, one that is quite ominous for women's progress. In the most extreme versions of the story line, moms who drop out of the workforce are not just exhausted and stressed. They are celebrated. Motherhood is once again promoted as a "calling" for women, a job that is done best when it is done full-time. Chucking it all is now chic.

"Each age defines the good mother anew, in its own terms, with its own requirements, ideals, prohibitions, mythology," says Shari Turner, associate professor of psychology at Boston University. She characterizes the current standards as "formidable and self-denying and utterly unattainable."

That, at least, is the conclusion one must draw from the media coverage that glorifies women who leave the workforce to embrace motherhood as a full-time profession. The new mystique was obviously not aimed at all women, however. Unlike the 1950s media, reporters and producers now seem willing to concede that there are plenty of women who need to work. The new Zeitgeist afoot in America even insists that some women—the poorest women of all—*should* work. Keeping them on welfare proved too large a burden to the upper classes, their dependency deemed too expensive. Welfare moms and poor women quickly became an easy target, a scapegoat to blame for the nation's social ills. Under new welfare laws, they would be forced to work, even when there was no one to care for their children during the day. In some cases, they would be recruited to take jobs caring for other people's children, even when they had no one to care for their own.

Indeed, the target audience for the new mystique is a very special one. The profiles of reformed career women who quit senior jobs described only one particular group of women, and it happens to be the very same one that could lead the final phase of women's—and men's—liberation in America. Armed with college degrees and the hard-won equal rights laws of the 1960s, they now occupy a critical spot in American business and culture. They are in the pipeline to real institutional power. Some even hold the title of senator, executive vice president or chief financial officer at major companies, or senior partner at major law and accounting firms. They serve as examples and role models to young women; their progress and problems serve as a powerful barometer of women's prospects.

Interestingly, this generation of women also serves as the first to envision widespread structural change in America's key institutions, from the schools to the workplace. With experience, talent, and clout at many companies, they are the first to experiment with such "family-friendly" policies as flextime, professional part-time work, job-sharing, and other innovations that make it easier to succeed as both parent and worker. So far, they have made the biggest strides in industries where their skills are in high demand and short supply, such as high-tech firms and the research and development units of major pharmaceutical companies. And their progress signals major change not just to younger women, but also to men who hope to break out of the straitjacket of the old role of breadwinner. Surveys show that many more young men are hungry for family time, if only social attitudes and economic incentives would allow them to be more involved at home.

Yet just as women reach this critical juncture, just as the topic of new ways to structure the workplace begins to make the agenda in corporate boardrooms, the media trumpets women's supposed retreat and disillusion with work.

Roiphe was careful to say in her *Esquire* essay that all this was just a "fantasy." As such, she seemed to be asking women to excuse any damage her words might do.

But one could only hope that no working woman would. By 1997, it was way past time for women—and most especially women with children—to speak out against such media stories. As Betty Friedan had written so powerfully in *The Feminine Mystique* three decades before, it is exactly such fantasy that stands to harm women, muffle their voices, dim their prospects for equality and independence. Women of earlier decades were ushered out of the workplace on the strength of such bias. Alice Kessler-Harris, chair of the Rutgers women's studies department and author of *Out to Work*, has unearthed women's magazines in the 1930s featuring such stories as "You Can Have My Job: A Feminist Discovers Her Home." The idea that women look to men to support them, that they will quit their jobs the moment they have a baby, sits at the core of workplace discrimination. The revival of these themes was touched on by Susan Faludi in her now-famous book *Backlash*.

But the full-scale mystique had just barely hatched as Faludi's book hit the bookstores in 1991. Three years later, the media coverage became so widespread as to alarm the executives at Catalyst, a nonprofit organization based in New York City, which works to spur women's progress in the workplace. In an unprecedented bulletin to the nation's major corporations, Catalyst announced that "a renewed backlash" against women was under way, in a new barrage of "media stories that perpetuate myths or distort the facts relating to women in the workforce. One myth that continues is that women are leaving the workforce in droves to go home and have babies." The group pointed out that just the opposite had proved to be true— more than 80 percent of all women now returned to work quickly after the birth of a baby.

Still, the stories persisted. "There's a brigade of liberated women who relinquished career for home and hearth, replacing the man's world they fought so hard to conquer with the love their mothers left behind," *New Jersey Monthly* announced in January of 1997.

That the new mystique required young women to forsake many ambitions and dreams did not seem to matter. That false news of women's retreat from the workplace could hurt women's earnings and opportunities was rarely explored. The stories just kept on coming.

IN THE 1990s version of the mystique, the women in retreat had done better than any generation before them. Jill Johnston, a Detroit lawyer, for example, reported that she turned down a dream job to stay home with her children. "I turned my back on the temptingly tangible and esteem-enhancing benefits of a great job so that I could be there to cook dinner for my husband and help my kids learn their multiplication tables," she wrote in an essay for the *Wall Street Journal*'s editorial page. Johnston was a particularly interesting example, given that her children were school age, and there is now broad consensus that once kids hit school age, it's acceptable for mothers to work. But Johnston asserted even women with older children should be home and they should also minister to their husbands—a clear indication that a woman's work is far less important than her husband's.

The reasons for her choice, she insisted, had nothing to do with barriers in the workplace. "Say what you will about sexism and old boy networks. It's not a glass ceiling we encounter," Johnston wrote. She asserted, in fact, that "I make no sacrifice, merely a trade-off between richly but differently rewarding options." In the end, it is women who are to blame—or to be congratulated—for making the "right" choice. "I have met the obstacle and she is me."

Her essay expressed the new mystique ever so compactly, in the space of a couple hundred words. It all boiled down to the fact that women don't want to work, they choose not to work, after they have babies. Feminists were just plain wrong to bellyache about unfairness on the job or to pretend that men and women might want the same things. Women simply weren't as invested in career success as men were, not once they had a baby.

Finding such a piece on the *Wall Street Journal*'s editorial page had become predictable by then. But even in the early 1990s, such reasoning was hardly limited to pundits of the right. "Not many years ago, Americans promoting family values and personal responsibility seemed to be mostly conservative Republicans, TV evangelicals and a twice-married man with estranged children named Ronald Reagan," the *Kansas City Star* noted. "But no more. Today an updated and refined sense of family values has moved to the very center of political and social discourse." The reason? The change was "driven most of all by the dilemmas of moms who aren't in the kitchen—working women trying to balance the income, fulfillment and obligations of work with the pleasures and responsibility of domestic life." The combination had turned deadly, the *Star* insisted, driving more women to drop out.

"Six-figure" salaries and BMWs became staples of the first wave of coverage, a quick way to pigeonhole high-achieving women as materialistic. A professional-dropout mom was the first example in *Time* magazine's cover story on Americans' yearning for the "simple life." Marsha Bostick of Columbus, Ohio, quit her $150,000-a-year job to be home with her children. "I found myself wondering, 'How wealthy do we need to be?' I don't care if I have a great car, or if people are impressed by what we own. We have everything we need," she told *Time*. Her children "needed more parental attention if they were going to get the right sort of values," she concluded.

"We used to have a BMW and live in Del Mar; now we have a 1988 Chevy Nova and we live in Rancho Penasquitos. But we are happy," Heidi Strudler, a former pharmaceutical sales representative, told the *San Diego Union-Tribune* in late 1993. No matter that the vast majority of working women—75 percent—still earn less than $25,000 a year and their paychecks are used just as men's are—to put food on the table and a roof over their heads. The image of a vast army of career women who abandoned their materialistic ways in favor of hearth and home kept popping up in these stories.

Over and over again, these stories insisted, *career* women had discovered motherhood to be the most rewarding work of all. Such a change of heart was cheered on by the likes of then–first lady Barbara Bush. "Quite a few career-oriented, professional women, doctors and lawyers, have suddenly realized they weren't very happy with their children being brought up with someone else. So with enormous support from their husbands, they have decided they will stay home, pull in their belts—until the children get a little bigger," she told *Redbook* magazine.

In the most extreme versions of the mythology, the decision to quit working was not just a retreat, but a renunciation, the rebirth of a fallen woman. At times, it even took the tone of a religious conversion. "Sheri Neilson was sunning herself on the beach in Ixtapa when her life flashed before her eyes and she began to cry. Neilson was on the career fast-track as a hospital administrator and she and her husband and daughter had money to burn on expensive vacations and other frills—but she wasn't happy," the *San Diego Union-Tribune* began. "She quit her job to be home. She no longer spends $100 on an outfit for herself and the beach in Ixtapa has become a distant memory, but now that she is home, she is content." Three years later, the business section of the influential *New York Times* ran a story declaring that motherhood was a "revelation" to many women. "When you hold that baby in your arms, that's it. Your life takes on a completely different meaning. All of this Me, Me, Me, I need to do this for Me starts melting away. You begin to realize you really can impact the world and society just by this one little baby in your arms," declared one executive who quit a demanding job in advertising.

Over and over again, the women in these stories insisted that the awakening to motherhood was a "surprise," as if most women never anticipated that motherhood was a major life event. The truth, of course, is that most women make career choices and life plans with the well-being of their children constantly in mind. Even young women who have yet to get pregnant think about how having a child will change their lives. Danielle Bensen, a radiologist in the residency program at Yale University in 1996, reported that she switched her career path from surgery to radiology because she believed she'd have more control over her hours as a radiologist and it would be easier to raise children.

But in the stories promoting the new mystique, "career" women were cardboard caricatures, women who never bothered to consider the impact of having children on their lives. The birth of a baby then became the life-changing event, forcing them to reconsider their misguided allegiance to a career. The fact that most new parents go through an intense adjustment to their new identity, the fact that most everything about life changes the moment a man or a woman becomes a parent, was not part of these stories. The fact that children bring serious new financial obligations and concerns was also ignored. Instead, the fierce new attachment brought one revelation and only one: work was no longer important to these previously deluded women. "I was very surprised at how quickly I shifted to wanting to be with them, instead of going to work," Marian Gormley, the mother of twins, told the Knight-Ridder News Service in a story syndicated across the country.

As with the *Parents* poll, the return to the home is also frequently portrayed as an antidote for women's stress. "Responding to Stress: Women Shift Values from Workplace Back to Home" was a *Los Angeles Times* story. "A growing number of professional women are quitting their jobs and choosing a life at home with their children over the pressures of trying to manage a career and motherhood," the *Dallas Morning News* told its readers a few months later. This idea is particularly odd, given that reams of research show that women who are home full-time with young children tend to suffer more stress disorders, ranging from depression to anxiety, than other groups of Americans. Women's dissatisfactions with life at home have also been widely documented, starting with Betty Friedan's classic book, *The Feminine Mystique.* In the late 1980s, one survey found women still preferred work to homemaking. About 56 percent of all full-time homemakers interviewed said they would choose to have a career if they could do it all over again. By contrast, only 21 percent of employed moms said they'd quit their jobs to stay home. Such findings cross class and race lines; women working as wait-resses, as domestic workers, and on factory assembly lines reported the same commitment to their jobs as white-collar women.

The reasons are not hard to fathom: life at home with young children puts women in situations least likely to promote mental health—they have little control over their time, they have less power over decision making in the family, and their work is held in low esteem by the society around them.

These truths are implicitly acknowledged in articles that run in women's and parenting magazines, advising women on how to make peace with the role of full-time homemaker. While Ann Murphy promoted women's retreat from the workplace as an antidote for the stress of working, for example, her own magazine also published pieces advising women on how to survive the stress of being a stay-at-home mom. "Could quitting your job jeopardize your healthy marriage?" a May 1990 article asked. Although the main article was entitled "Home Full-Time and Loving It," the article conceded that "the stay-at-home mom may feel less than equal now that she is no longer earning a salary" and her husband may "begin to resent the burden of being sole provider for the family." A woman at home may also "miss interacting with her peers, enjoying their positive rein-forcements for her accomplishments and appearance." The fallout of all these feelings? Such a woman may "fall into distinct negative patterns of thinking about her self-worth, her identity, her auton-omy and the balance of power between herself and her partner."

Yet if women struggle with their own self-esteem when they stop working, the new mystique assures women that their husbands will not. "The stay-at-home mom is fast becoming the newest status symbol of the conscientious 1990s," the *Wall Street Journal* proclaimed in a front-page news story in 1993. One male stockbroker told the newspaper that he made enough money so his wife could be home full-time. "It's not something you brag about," he said, "but it's a source of pride."

Women, on the other hand, had supposedly abandoned aspirations to make money. "Forget the Porsche!" read the front-page headline of *Advertising Age*. "'90's Moms Want Time for Family." The breathless lead to this story insisted that a growing number of high-powered women were "slamming the brakes on their careers" to make time for motherhood. "It's as if these 'superwomen' are jumping into phone booths, changing from business suits to casual clothes and emerging as power moms."

No Evidence for "Trend"

Like the stories that preceded this one, *Advertising Age* acknowledged that "the trend is just a blip right now." But a "blip" or what the *Washington Post* would call an "intriguing dip" in women's labor force participation was all that reporters needed to set them tracking women's supposed retreat from having it all. Indeed, the strangest aspect of the flood of stories about women's retreat home was their factual inaccuracy. The first trickle of stories began in late 1990, when the Labor Department reported the number of working women had flattened, with a slowing economy. None of the data showed a clear trend—the number of working women declined by just a little over one percentage point, as did the number of men. Nor did any of the available data clearly link the slight decline with family concerns. But the birthrate increased at about the same time, so reporters and television producers made the connection for themselves.

The *New York Times* led the pack in November of that year, announcing that "Women's Push Into Work Force Seems to Have

Peaked, for Now" on the front page. The *Times* was rather restrained compared with the flurry of stories that followed. Reporter Louis Uchitelle noted that change was small and might well be temporary, due with the slackening economy. But he also quoted experts who suggested that a lack of child care and a rising birthrate might be at issue—in other words, motherhood might be behind the trend.

It was not long before that misguided idea came to be reported as fact. "Women Change Career Paths: More Choose to Stay Home with Children," *USA Today* announced on its front page in May of 1991. As a part of a "stunning trend," the newspaper told its readers, women were abandoning the workforce by the "thousands" to go home and care for their kids. The data available to reporters at the time did not provide a sophisticated breakdown of which workers had dropped out of the labor force. "No studies exist to explain who is staying home and why," *USA Today* reported, but "anecdotal evidence suggests a shift in values is taking place, at least among women who can afford to quit work."

As things turned out, the big dropouts of that era weren't moms. The great bulk of the women who left the workforce at the time were younger and childless. As the data would later show, many had enrolled in school, probably in search of better jobs once the recession was over. Young women seemed to understand, even if the media did not, that their future prospects depended on their own earning power. That being the case, even *USA Today* seemed to have trouble marshaling evidence to support its "homeward bound" thesis. The first example in the story was not a mom who had actually quit working, but one who predicted "it was more than likely" she'd be "stopping work altogether" after she had a second child.

By late 1991, at least some reporters and editors had begun to grow skeptical of the flood of coverage of women's retreat. That summer, *Washington Post* reporter Richard Morin took his fellow reporters to task, in a story headlined "The Trend That Wasn't: Are Moms Leaving Work or Did the Dip Deceive?" Morin chastised even his own paper for promoting the "myth of the dropout Mom," pointing out that the forecast of moms going home didn't have any solid factual basis. The "demographic molehill" of women at home, he noted, was "buried by the mountain of women who continue to move into the labor force." *Working Woman* ran a similar story a few months later.

BUT THE story wasn't about to die. It had the force of cultural assumptions and values and even institutional power behind it. Even after it was beaten back, the idea would surface again and again, speaking to the deeply embedded—if wrongheaded—assumptions of the psyche that insisted that mothers belonged at home. And the story was told most often in the place where it hurt working women the most—the business press.

Publications such as *Fortune* and the *Wall Street Journal*, *Barron's* and *Business Week* are required reading for many middle managers; their subscriptions are frequently paid for by their employers. This specialized media provides critical information on business conditions and trends. Reports in these outlets also track trends among workers, and the agenda for social issues in the workplace. A report that women are dropping out of the workplace, that they lose interest in work the moment they have a baby, can color managers' attitudes and influence the way they treat the women they supervise. "The *Wall Street Journal* is like the Bible for men in my office. It's so influential with them," says Jill Doherty, a middle manager and human resource specialist in Wisconsin. "When there's a front-page story on women or affirmative action, they take it as the gospel. They talk about it. It's a big topic for conversation in the office where I work."

Unfortunately, many of the stories often served to reinforce attitudes that could hamper women's progress once they had children. "Noticed many pregnant women in your office the past few years?" *Fortune* writer Joseph Spiers asked at the beginning of his February 1992 column. It was the kind of visibility most working women still hoped to avoid, since pregnancy in the workplace was nearly always equated with a lesser commitment to work, and getting passed over for promotions and raises. But Spiers was willing to explore the idea in print, and share his ruminations on the pages of one of the nation's leading business magazines. "It's what the number crunchers call anecdotal evidence—you see something that looks like a trend, yet can't 'prove' it." But Spiers, like others, didn't wait for hard evidence before sending the message out to the executives and managers of the nation's business community. "Babies are back, the rise in the percentage of women entering the labor force has stopped growing, and young women seem more interested in starting families earlier than their older sisters."

This trend was important for business to watch, he insisted, because tomorrow's consumers would be "homebound," with fewer discretionary dollars to spend. "What modern woman would want to be tied down by bottles and diapers," he went on to ask, when she could have the exhilaration of "doing leveraged buyouts?" It was an absurd question on many levels, since few women had even made it to the table of high-profile business deals—and most likely, few would ever see the two experiences as comparable. At the time, women on Wall Street were struggling to find a way to make a decent living and have a family life.

But these issues were not mentioned in Spiers's column. Again, he trusted the "anecdotal evidence" and was willing to connect that to labor statistics to assert that "quite a few" women had decided that having a baby was better than having a high-profile job on Wall Street. "Especially notable," he added, was the sharp rise in the birthrate among college-educated managers and professionals over thirty, "and particularly those married to college-educated husbands." These women, he insisted, would surely work less as their husbands' earnings rose. To bolster this argument, he cited market research from Yankelovich, Clancy and Shulman, one of the nation's leading market research firms. This survey, he said, demonstrated that women were "not as committed to their careers, and so will work fewer hours, travel less and take less work home." At the time, however, statistics showed that college-educated women were the group of women *most* committed to their jobs after they had a baby, with the highest rate of returning to the job after maternity leave.

But no story of women's supposed retreat was more outlandish or audacious than the one that appeared on the cover of *Barron's*, one of the nation's most prominent business publications, in March of 1994. The entire cover was devoted to the headline "Workin' Women: Goin' Home!" The illustration? None other than old photographs of housewives from the 1950s, smiling as they waited on their husbands and children. Inside, a lengthy story spun out the saga of a "demographic sea change" forecast by Wall Street economist Richard Hokenson. "The two-paycheck family is in decline," he declared. "The traditional one-paycheck family is now the fastest-growing household unit." By the year 2000, the magazine counseled marketers and business leaders, supermarkets may well be chock-full of stay-at-home moms. "At present, women of child-bearing age are flocking back home. The trend line is sharpest among women 20 to 24."

Hokenson's prediction rested largely on his assumption that more women could afford to stay home as inflation eased in the early 1990s. He used statistics from the Bureau of Labor Statistics—the same ones that had caught the attention of the *New York Times* and *USA Today* a few years earlier—as evidence to show that the incipient trend was already under way. He expected it to mushroom soon, since, by his calculations, the "average woman's real wages have remained so low that it doesn't seem probable that she would want to work. After paying for child care—not to mention lunches, bus tickets and a working wardrobe—she may well find herself laboring for free." With lower interest rates, many families would refinance their mortgages and women would stay home with the kids.

"Thus, it is not impossible that the Liberated Woman of recent years could meet the fate of the Gibson Girl—prototype for that larger-than-life female who invaded the all-male professional world at the beginning of the century and, over the course of two generations, disappeared," wrote Maggie Mahar, *Barron's* staffer and author of this piece.

But there is little, if any, evidence to support this thesis. Most certainly, there was no sign of a drop-off in employment among mothers. Employed women with children were one of the few groups whose ranks kept growing, even through the deep recession of the 1990s. And all indicators show that many women will surely continue to work, as men do, out of both choice and necessity. Women are now earning more than half of all college degrees, and married women now bring home at least as much as men do in the majority of American families.

Further, the decline in two-paycheck families, the Bureau of Labor Statistics found, was due to a rise in single-parent homes, not an increase in traditional families. The long-term trends in the workforce also ran counter to Hokenson's forecast. Between 1974 and 1994, there was a 46 percent increase in two-earner households—and a 38 percent decline among married-couple households where Dad was the sole provider. If anything, women's work patterns were beginning to look more and more like men's—with fewer and fewer interruptions.

Most intriguing of all, both Hayghe and economists at the Census Bureau noted a drop in men's employment during the early 1990s. During the deep recession, more men than ever became full-time parents, nearly 20 percent.

That is not to say that Hokenson and the media did not have their fingers on the pulse of a psychic change in America, driven by a shifting economy and a renewed debate over core social values. By the early 1990s, the business climate had most certainly changed the workplace. The effects of global competition, new technology, and an economic downturn all conspired to make many companies less hospitable to many workers. "Downsizing plays a critical role in all of this, even at companies we call 'family-friendly.' These layoffs of workers have been going on for about five years now, and it makes people afraid to stand out. They don't want to ask for time for their families. They're afraid if they do, they'll become a target in the next downsizing," says Barney Olmsted, head of New Ways to Work, a consulting firm based in San Francisco that advises businesses on how to set up alternative work schedules. She is not surprised to hear that other consultants use two words to describe the work environment of the early 1990s: "economic terror." It has, Olmsted says, become "much more difficult for workers to concede that they have any kind of personal life."

Most certainly, there was plenty of data to show that the workplace had become far less appealing to all workers, male or female. In

1992, research from Yankelovich, Clancy and Shulman revealed that both men and women were growing increasingly dissatisfied with the world of work: 42 percent of the men and 43 percent of the women said they'd quit working if they could afford to. The following year, the Families and Work Institute reported that stress was the number one issue in the workplace, for both men and women. But it was women's stress that grabbed the headlines. "There are plenty of men who would like to quit their jobs if they could," said Anne Clurman of Yankelovich at the time. "Many media stories miss that important fact." Indeed, men are not encouraged to drop out and go home.

That message is reserved for women. And it is one that is amplified when women's progress is perceived to be a threat to men. "When women stayed generally in women's professions, they never heard they couldn't manage it all. But now that they have a chance at real power, that's exactly what they are hearing," says sociologist Cynthia Fuchs Epstein.

NONETHELESS, *Barron's* plunged ahead, on the strength of Hokenson's forecast, along with some interviews with a dozen or so women who had quit working to stay home. As usual, the anecdotes from the story reinforced the idea that a mom at home meant a stronger, better family life. "My mother worked, my husband's mother worked; we want our child to have more parental guidance at home," said one. "I think if I stay home, we're less likely to divorce—more likely to keep the family whole."

The *Barron's* story reverberated through the culture, sparking many other stories about mothers who decided to quit work to stay home, as well as a renewed debate about whether moms wanted to work at all. *Fortune* quickly weighed in on the side of *Barron's*, sending a message to corporate America on its June cover that year: "Women Chill Out."

"Conventional wisdom has it that young females continue to throng to the workplace. Wrong: The rush is over," the story began.

The media coverage began to grate on many. "There wasn't a single shred of evidence to support Hokenson's thesis, but his prediction started a whole wave of stories," argued Cheryl Russell, editor in chief of the *New Strategist* and author of several reports on trends among the baby boomers. "Mothers weren't going home; they weren't becoming housewives. Instead, women were going to school—probably to get better jobs."

Howard Hayghe, economist at the U.S. Bureau of Labor Statistics, was dumbfounded by the flood of phone calls following up on the *Barron's* story. As a longtime specialist on women in the workplace, he had become one of the point men for the Labor Department when such stories broke. Soft-spoken and evenhanded, he was always careful with his data, taking the time with any reporter who wanted to probe a story deeply. But he knew by the volume of calls from reporters on short deadlines that Hokenson's thesis was not going to yield thoughtful coverage. And as a student of working women's progress, he knew only too well the sort of damage such a story could do to working women. "Making a prediction like that can make employers see men as more committed, and women as more likely to quit their jobs. That makes it less likely that employers will want to hire women, advance them, or give them raises. It's just not helpful to working women." Why, indeed, should companies invest in workers who are likely to quit the moment the baby arrives? "I felt a lot of the reporting at that time was simply irresponsible," he says.

Consultants who specialize in work-family issues confirm the power of wrongheaded assumptions. The idea that women aren't as committed to their work springs largely from the idea that all women are likely to quit once they have children or, at least, scale back their dedication to the job. This is so, even though women, in fact, have better attendance records than men. One survey of 1,500 male and female workers with children also revealed that moms tended to give more, rather than less, at work than men with children did. "Contrary to popular stereotypes, we found that women put more effort into their jobs than men, even though they have more responsibility for household responsibilities," says William Bielby, the sociologist at the University of California who conducted the research. Both facts may stem from their sense that women with children often feel pressure to counter the stereotype that they are less committed to working than men are. "We have to get past this idea of work and family as a zero sum game," says Arlene Johnson at the Families and Work Institute in New York City. "Work does not automatically suffer at the expense of family."

If anything, studies show that it is the family that now takes a hit at the expense of work. Overtime, changing shifts, relocations, travel, and the everyday stress and strain of today's workplace are three times as likely to disrupt family life as family demands are to disrupt work, according to research conducted by Johnson and her colleagues.

Hayghe grew so concerned at the tone of the media coverage that he took the time to dispute the *Barron's* story in print, in an article in the Labor Department's *Monthly Labor Review*. "The data on families," he noted, "do not support the notion that women are leaving the labor force." Indeed, in his review of the statistics, he was startled to see a sharp increase in the number of families where *fathers* were unemployed. And, he added, the "one-paycheck" families that Hokenson had spotted were most likely not a return to the days of *Ozzie and Harriet*. Two-thirds of the growth in single-paycheck families was due to the growing number of families headed by single moms.

If, in fact, some professional women had decided to be home full-time with their kids, it wasn't much of a change from the past. Many were married to professional men, and lived in a social class where many moms had traditionally been at home. "The difference with these women today is that they were lawyers before they had children," said Hayghe. Again and again, he told reporters "the real trend" was that so many more women of all social classes—including those who could probably afford to stay home—now remained in the workplace after they had children. That trend was especially notable, given the lack of support that so many faced both in the workplace and at home.

HAYGHE's rebuttal of the *Barron's* story did spark a wave of corrective media stories for a few months. *USA Today* reporter Margaret Usdansky wrote a story headlined "A Trend Without Substance: For

Women, No Rush Back to Homemaker," which was picked up by scores of major newspapers around the country.

But the heartfelt ambivalence about mothers in the workplace still rose to the surface. More than anything, the *Barron's* story revealed the deep confusion that still governed in the collective psyche, a reflection of the deep-seated anxiety that still reigns over women's roles. Although the facts said that more mothers were in the workplace, the psyche couldn't accept it. The headlines were at war with each other, contradicting one another, sometimes even in the same newspaper, sometimes even in the same week.

In June of 1994, the *Detroit News* announced, "Superwoman has had enough. After two decades of balancing children and careers to secure a place in corporate America, more working mothers are finding there's no place like home." But in August, that same paper ran Usdansky's story under the headline "Are Women Leaving Jobs for Home? Not Likely."

The *Sacramento Bee* subsequently picked up the stories from the *Detroit News*—but ran them in the opposite order. Thus, Sacramento readers first read on August 15 that Hokenson's theory was all wrong. But on August 21, the *Bee* announced that he was right, that moms were "jilting" the workplace to go home. Similarly, the *Salt Lake Tribune* printed a series of stories contradicting each other. The *Tribune* ran a story titled "Young Women Making Career Out of Staying Home." A month later, however, the paper picked up Usdansky's *USA Today* story under the headline "Gender and Jobs: Facts Derail the Myth That Women Are Fleeing the Career Track."

When the *Syracuse Herald-American* covered the *Barron's* story, the headline in the business section noted that Hokenson had found that the percentage of women who work had dropped for the first time in thirty years. After the first few paragraphs, the article noted that "several economists and trend-trackers said the *Barron's* theory doesn't hold water. One was quoted as saying that Hokenson's theory amounted to 'wishful thinking.'"

The theory that most mothers would somehow, some way, find their way home was difficult to put to rest. A full year later, well after

Hayghe printed his analysis of the labor figures and six months after the Catalyst directive, *Fortune* still continued to lend credence to Hokenson's theory. Mothers would continue to drop out of the workforce, Joseph Spiers wrote in his October 1995 column, "because families with two full-time workers are opting out of their stressful lifestyles." In January of that year, *USA Today* had run a cover story, "In Balancing Act, Scale Tips toward Family," citing Hokenson's work. *USA Today* editors seemed to have forgotten that they had dubbed Hokenson's work a "trend without substance" a year before.

It was, as the Syracuse editors had noted, the wishful thinking, the fantasy, the stereotype, that kept the most dogged reporters on the trail of women's retreat. And there were a handful of experts willing and eager to support the thesis. For them, the fantasies and wishes were potent tools, the vehicle that helped sell their ideology and their products.

3
Marketing the Mystique

For Profit and Ideology

IN LATE SUMMER OF 1996, Dominique Browning was at the helm of an ambitious undertaking. As the new editor in chief of *House & Garden* magazine, she was now presiding over the $40 million relaunch of the venerable, ninety-two-year-old monthly.

Widely known in New York's journalistic circles as talented and dedicated to her career, Browning certainly had the credentials to run any magazine: she'd once been literary editor of *Esquire,* executive editor of *Texas Monthly,* and, most notably, assistant managing editor of *Newsweek.* As her bio proudly boasts, she was the first woman ever named to the executive level of any newsmagazine.

In interview after interview in the national media, however, she conceded that her new position was surprising. "I am totally unrecognizable in the home furnishing world," she confessed in news reports that month. But, she added, "I've read these magazines for years. My girlfriends and I call them girls' pornography."

And, Browning added, if she was new to the home scene, she was simply joining the rush. Americans are, she explained, "turning to our homes for comfort, refuge and joy. We're returning to our homes, to our children, to our gardens."

How fitting, then, that *House & Garden* publisher David Carey presented her with a $700 vacuum cleaner as part of the celebration of the magazine's relaunch.

It may have even been a defining moment for the decade.

With home now the center of the universe, women might find status and pleasure in owning a really good vacuum cleaner, one crafted with precision and care. Or perhaps in owning a state-of-the-art cappuccino maker or cultivating a very special garden, full of fussy perennials. The dream now was to become an unharried woman of leisure, a woman who would have the time to decorate the home marketed by the likes of *House & Garden*.

One had to wonder if Browning would ever get around to using that vacuum cleaner, however. She admitted in interviews that her own home had fallen into a bit of chaos, because of the demands of work. Most certainly she made a hefty salary; rumor put it over $300,000. The best guess was that she hired someone else to vacuum that house. It was, however, just the sort of appliance that one could imagine in the hands of Martha Stewart. *Martha Stewart Living* had recently devoted an entire article to instructing its audience on the correct way to mop a floor. That was necessary because young women who grew up with baby boomer moms, those unfortunate daughters of supermoms, lacked such skills. "I did homework. My mother did the dishes. There was not a lot of training going on related to domestic skills," Susan Wyland, editor of *Martha Stewart Living,* said in an interview with *New York* magazine. "My mother thought I'd have more important things to do." *New York* clarified that Wyland was "one of those children of the seventies—whose mothers worked and brought home Chicken Delight and were taught by a newly liberated *McCall's* magazine to make friends with their dust balls."

No more dust balls in the 1990s. Not with fancy vacuum cleaners to whisk them away.

• • •

BY THE early 1990s, Madison Avenue had decided to cash in on the psychic shift under way in America. Women's distress and disenchantment with the inflexible workplace could be harvested for profit. And it was only appropriate that the magazine publishing giant Condé Nast would enlist such an impressive talent, a truly accomplished baby boomer woman, to show career women how to channel their ambition and energy into buying sprees for the home.

It was also appropriate that Browning described the new phenomenon as "girls' pornography." Magazines like *House & Garden* were sumptuous fantasies, meant to seduce women. The idea that accomplished women like Browning have permission to describe themselves as "girls" once again, and that they seek secret and illicit pleasure in domesticity, was at the core of the potent new mythology. By the time Browning arrived on the scene, some ninety magazines—thirty launched in 1995 alone—focused on home decoration, providing an escape from the responsibilities and conflicts grown-up women faced. That this escape was sensuous to its target audience of well-educated liberated women of the 1990s made it, like all pornography, more enticing. And, of course, the message that adult women were really dependent girls at heart, girls who loved to play house, spoke to the deep-rooted cultural assumptions about women and femininity. It was the same fantasy that informed Katie Roiphe's *Esquire* magazine essay about marrying a "man in a gray flannel suit."

Ironically, of course, the new mythology about home and family was simply a vehicle for encouraging a new wave of aggressive consumption. *Child* magazine itself was born of an appeal to reach the most affluent, well-educated parents of all and convince them to buy high-end baby gear. The relaunch of *House & Garden* was declared by the *Wall Street Journal* an "ambitious bet that the materialistic urges of nesting yuppies will make for a new hit magazine." The bet paid off. Six months after the relaunch, *House & Garden* sold 330 pages of advertising, exceeding its original sales goals, according to a spokeswoman for Condé Nast.

The success arrived, of course, because the new marketing campaigns spoke straight to women's hearts. The rich images of home as a haven speak both to women's dreams and to their discontent. "Making a home is an act of love," Browning told the *Los Angeles Times*.

That was a powerful message in a culture gripped by economic change. Indeed, the new feminine mystique had credibility with the media because it was hatched from a brew of the powerful social and economic forces unleashed in the early 1990s, and nursed along by those with a vested interest in selling it to Americans.

MADISON Avenue and social conservatives alike came to understand how the power of idealized images of hearth and home, of cherubic children and warm kitchens, could be used to inspire and mobilize their constituencies. Advertisers and politicians also understood how emotional images can overwhelm factual reality. Both decided to put "family values" at the center of their campaigns to reach their constituencies.

They consciously adopted this strategy even though work took up an ever-greater portion of most women's lives and energy. Even as the new *House & Garden* hit the newsstands, the Women's Bureau of the U.S. Department of Labor was compiling new data showing that women's work patterns were beginning to mimic those of men. Not only that, but over the next decade, the growth of women in the labor force was expected to surpass that of men.

But the glorification of home life was still appealing to many Americans. It was such a soothing message for Americans suffering through one of the worst recessions since the Great Depression, shaking many families to their core. Those lucky enough to keep a job were expected to put in longer hours, even take on the work done previously by two workers. Stretched to the limit, nearly everyone wanted a break.

The message that home provided a refuge from the workplace grew especially appealing to women with children. They were not about to quit, but the glossy images served up in magazines like *House & Garden* and *Martha Stewart Living* were easy to get lost in. The world in these magazines was an updated, stylish version of

Ozzie and Harriet, a comforting vision of Mom at home, enjoying the kids, instead of fighting a hostile workplace.

That dynamic is quite evident in interviews with Marcia Hines, an entrepreneur in Kansas City, who has seen just such a shift in mood among some of her friends over the past five or six years. "They aren't quitting their jobs. They can't afford to." Instead, she says, they engage in what she calls a "psychic retreat," scaling back their expectations on the job and putting more emphasis on their home life. "I see almost a swing back toward being more traditional, making more of their homes, cocooning."

The change is so notable to Hines because it is so dramatic. In 1989, ten of them gathered in her living room to create the "Burned Out Business Women's Association" of Kansas City. Although the name reflected their exhaustion, Hines says, it also revealed their humor and a good dose of "free-floating anger" they'd come to feel. "We were all dealing with the same problems. We'd go to work and fight the issues women have to fight on the job. We felt that we had to struggle to be taken seriously, that we were often shown a lack of respect. Then we'd come home to take care of the family. Getting your husband to help was another job. Men either want to be verbally rewarded or told exactly how to do everything at home. That was so energy-draining. We'd just fall into bed, exhausted. We began to ask ourselves, What could we do to help ourselves get through this?"

The group came up with a number of practical ideas, including proposals to make the workplace more flexible, such as flextime, professional part-time work, job-sharing, and telecommuting. Their ideas most certainly struck a chord, making headlines from the *Kansas City Business Journal* to the *New York Times.* "We got a lot of press without really trying. I think it was because we hit a raw nerve in women's psyches," Hines recalls. "Women were reading what we had to say and saying, 'Yeah! Yeah! Yeah! Things have to change.'" She and some of her friends even wound up on national television talk shows and corresponding with women around the country.

Still, the reaction was not the one Hines and her friends wanted the most. "We got no response from employers," she says. And without that, her friends fled into romanticizing home life. "They just sucked back into that ideal, because of all these problems. Some of them began to talk about how their own mothers had been home, making their own chicken soup." Hines herself still soldiers on, lobbying for change in local businesses. She launched a management consulting business with a friend, helping employers create flexible work policies and other family-friendly practices. "But I see a lot of women give up. They don't want to raise the issues, and be seen as nags or whiners. So they just turn away from trying to change things."

THE NEW SALES PITCH

The marketing community, always vigilant to Americans' shifting sentiments and tastes, began to discern this new mood by the early 1990s, in attitude surveys and focus groups. Both men and women said they'd be willing to trade part of their paychecks for more time with their families, if only the rules for success allowed them to do so. Family life became the new priority, the new value, the new fashion, for the new decade. "The power wife-mother is our latest status symbol, more important than a mink coat," Laurel Cutler, an executive at the advertising and marketing outfit of FCB in San Francisco, told the *New York Times* in early 1995.

Social conservatives also believed the new mood could be turned to their advantage. A new band of think tanks devoted to framing family issues popped up and began to churn out policy papers for the media, to galvanize their core constituency. They welcomed what they called a new "realism" about women and work, and did their best to promote the idea that women had no interest in serious careers once they had children. "The media elite have finally caught up with the rank and file," William Mattox of the Family Research Council, one of the social conservatives' leading advocacy and research groups, asserted in late 1992. "It took the superwoman myth crashing for the media elite to catch on to the fact that full-time, full-throttle careerism was simply not the vision all women had for themselves."

At the Institute for American Values in New York City, David Blankenhorn was equally cheerful about the changing attitudes about working moms. "Women have come to see that a job is just a job, not a path-breaking thing to do, not an act of self-assertion, not a political act," he said in 1994. "Working women are now consciously saying, 'I want the shift toward home more than it is now.' The idea of doing both, of working and raising children, is not as attractive as it once was."

This was not the entire truth, of course. While women were frustrated, they also took increasing pride in their roles as breadwinners and providers for their families. Bigger paychecks, better opportunities for advancement, flexible hours on the job, and child care topped the wish lists of working women in wide-ranging surveys by the U.S. Department of Labor. Promoting a retreat of women from the workplace was beside the point of most women's experience. If anything, work was more central to more women's lives than it ever had been. "There is a rising sense that we have to do something to create a woman-friendly family and a family-friendly workplace," asserted Marcia Gillespie, editor in chief of *Ms.* magazine. Marcia Hines and her friends in Kansas City underscore this point. "Women need the money they earn to survive. And the problems they face touch on equality and fairness in the game of life," Hines says. "What they want is a level playing field, both at home and at work."

But addressing the real concerns of real women would take time, money, and serious effort. In the end, it is far easier to profit from women's discomfort than to relieve it. This is something that the deans of Madison Avenue understand quite well. They are in business to track changes in the collective American psyche, to anticipate trends, in pursuit of more sales.

IN 1991, Yankelovich, Clancy and Shulman released new results of the *Monitor,* one of the country's oldest and most respected surveys of social attitudes. The number of women who said they would quit working permanently if they could afford to jumped from 38 to 56 percent in just one year. "I think it shows something big," Susan

Hayward, then executive vice president at Yankelovich, told *American Demographics*.

She warned reporters not to interpret it as a sign that many women would actually quit their jobs. Like most men, most women simply couldn't afford to do that. Nor did labor statistics show any dramatic trend. Instead, the poll might be seen as evidence that the workplace of the early 1990s had grown less hospitable to workers, especially women with children. "Hayward sees it as a new demand that work lives bend to accommodate home lives," *American Demographics* explained.

But within days, the *Monitor* results quickly fed the appetite of reporters tracking women's supposed retreat from the workplace, and Hayward became one of the most widely cited authorities on the nontrend. Some of the nation's most prestigious newspapers joined the chorus. The *Washington Post* proclaimed, "Work Losing Romanticized Aura of the '80's; Polls Show Shift toward Emphasis on Motherhood and Home," quoting Hayward extensively. Two months later, the *Post* returned to the story, claiming, "More Women Trade Paychecks for the Pay-Offs of Full-Time Parenting." The dramatic lead to the story was syndicated across the country: "After years spent knocking down barriers to get into corporate America, a growing number of professional women in Washington and beyond appear to be choosing a life at home with their children over another day at the office." Reporter Liz Spayd cited the Yankelovich survey as evidence of a "larger shift in values from material wealth to a greater involvement in family life."

In interview after interview, in stories that ran in hundreds of newspapers across the nation, Hayward asserted women had undergone a startling and sudden change. The fact that working women with children had always felt torn and unsupported was not acknowledged. Instead, the new mystique held that women had undergone a dramatic transformation as the new decade dawned. Last year, they were careerist; this year, they discovered motherhood. "Women are no longer willing to put work at the center of their lives. It's become one of a number of competing priorities," Hayward told the *Chicago Tribune.* "We've been striving to reach things and accomplish things that turned out not to deliver the promise," she told the *Seattle Times.* "Other things on the back burner, like children, turned out to deliver more."

The interview in the Seattle newspaper was one of many that managed to reinforce the two most damaging stereotypes about working moms, all in one stroke. First, there was the assumption that women with serious jobs put their children on the "back burner," which obviously makes them bad mothers. What good mother would do that? Second came the idea that good mothers make poor employees, because they make work a lower priority than men do.

These damaging observations were broadcast directly to a critical segment of the business community. In May 1991, *Human Resources News,* a publication that goes out to the people who set personnel policies for the nation's major corporations, reported on Hayward's poll, announcing that "the attitudes of working women are starting to change." The bulk of the article was devoted to detailing Hayward's assertion that women were less committed to work. "In 1990, for the first time in 20 years, the proportion of women who favor a career for mothers dropped below 50 percent," read a large-type summary in the middle of the page. "The proportion of working women who would consider leaving the workforce is also growing," the story added. Nowhere did the article note that the income from the growing number of moms in the workforce was more necessary than ever to their families' well-being. Nor did the newspaper mention research that showed that women who did remain in the workforce after having children tended to have good performance records. Like the rest of the media coverage, this story simply added to the false notion that working moms were less committed to their jobs than men were.

Hayward's research continued to be mentioned, again and again, for years to come, in stories that tracked women's supposed departure from the workforce. The infamous *Barron's* cover story used the Yankelovich study as "evidence" that Wall Street economist Richard

Hokenson was right to predict an exodus of professional women from the workforce. So did scores of other reports that popped up in the media throughout the 1990s.

The fact that this poll tracked only *feelings* instead of *behavior* was glossed over, or not even mentioned at all.

But feelings are, of course, at the heart of marketing, and so Madison Avenue sat up and took notice of the research. At the same time, other data revealed a lucrative new market in the works. A baby boomlet was under way, fueled by the fact that women in their thirties were now finally starting their families. This new generation of parents were better educated and more affluent than any who had preceded them, and they were having fewer children per family. And that meant they had more money and more interest in buying the best for and doing the best by their babies. Ironically, of course, the market that focused on family was created in large part by the fact that more women were working outside the home than ever before. On average, two-income households had more disposable income than those that depended on just one earner.

As a result, sales of baby products, child advice books and magazines, and toys boomed. The Juvenile Products Manufacturers Association reported that sales of products for infants up to the age of two climbed 8 percent between 1990 and 1991, to $2.5 billion. That included such items as strollers and high chairs, but not clothing, toys, or disposable diapers. Sales of those items were worth billions more, and demand was growing. Entirely new lines of baby food, diapers, and baby strollers hit the market. All this at a time when most of the economy was flat.

Today, in fact, the marketplace looks quite different than it did just a decade ago. New parents have a remarkable array of baby equipment to meet their every need or desire, from car seats that turn into infant seats to items that can childproof every corner of the home. Suburban moms now drive minivans, one of the most remarkable success stories of the car industry in years. The Baby Gap, kids' reading rooms at Barnes & Noble and Borders, and CDs for the under-six set all speak to the new emphasis on kids and family. Even sexy movie stars like Sarah Jessica Parker talk about their desire for babies and a home life. Demi Moore posed naked for photographs while she was pregnant—an idea that would have been verboten in the go-go 1980s.

As manufacturers and marketers sought ways to create new niches and new markets that spoke to the importance of family, publishers jumped in to help them. During the late 1980s and early 1990s, media aimed at parents exploded. "A third generation of baby magazines is being nurtured as publishers experiment with new techniques to reach parents and lure advertisers. The boom is being driven by a burgeoning array of products from marketers—especially in health care, food and clothing—that target new parents," noted *Advertising Age* in 1989. In 1993, *Ad Age* reported that while consumers were cutting back in some areas, "children will be one area where the wallet likely will remain open."

All of this, of course, gave editors and writers plenty of space to fill with advice to new moms. And fill it they did. From *Parenting* to *Child* to *Working Mother,* they offered new moms advice about how to raise baby. University public relations offices, happy to promote their faculty, eagerly provided experts to expound on child development and child rearing. Mothers were encouraged to invest themselves in every aspect of a baby's development, from teaching a baby's eyes to track an object to offering enough stimulation to ensure proper brain growth. Raising an intelligent child became almost a fetish. "Your Child's Brain Power: Are You Doing All You Can to Boost It?" *Child* magazine asked its readers in January of 1995. Like other articles in the media, this one advised anxious new parents that they could boost their child's IQ by as much as twenty points by playing the right games and buying the right toys. Whole new lines of toys and new toy store chains emerged, led by Zany Brainy, Noodle Kiddoodle, and Teachsmart, to capitalize on the parents' anxieties.

Women were encouraged to consume for the home and family with new gusto, selecting from a range of products their mothers never even imagined. Americans spend about $20 billion a year on toys alone. They are expected to fork over another $200 billion on home renovations and gardening by the year 2000.

Thus, the message created by Madison Avenue was that it was fine for women to spend money, even spend it with abandon, on home and family. But they should not aspire to make money or control money or their own economic destiny. Earning the money, especially the good money, was left to men.

And that was exactly the scenario that so appealed to a network of social conservatives who were gaining influence at the time. They, too, rode the wave of economic dislocation and dissatisfaction with the workplace to mobilize their constituency and promote the new mystique.

FODDER FOR THE CULTURE WARS

For social conservative David Blankenhorn, the Yankelovich poll was simply more evidence that a new "familism" was afoot in America, a turning away from the workplace and a return to family. Barbara DaFoe Whitehead, a social historian who collaborated extensively with Blankenhorn in the late 1980s and early 1990s, concurred. She and Blankenhorn cofounded the Institute for American Values, a conservative think tank based in New York City. "In the 1990s, the bubble has burst. More people are seeing the wisdom of what their grandmothers would say: Work isn't everything; families are important; and there's a very real conflict between the two," Whitehead told the *Washington Post* in a story that ran under the headline "Polls Show Shift toward Emphasis on Motherhood and Home."

Whitehead was just beginning to make her name in the early 1990s, but went on to become one of the leading voices in the "culture war" waged by social conservatives. A few years later, she published a widely discussed and hotly debated article in the *Atlantic* under the title "Dan Quayle Was Right," which laid many social ills on the decline of traditional family values. She and Blankenhorn managed to assemble a working group of academics and experts who were willing to talk to reporters and policymakers, pushing this agenda. Many were quoted in articles about women's new disdain for work, and the new "familism."

William Mattox, a rising star at the conservative Family Research

Council in Washington, D.C., also found the Yankelovich poll a useful tool as he pushed his ideas out into the media. It was fodder for an opinion piece in the *San Diego Times-Union* entitled "A Growing Number of Mothers Drop Jobs for Duty at Home."

This trio—Blankenhorn, Mattox, and Whitehead—are the sources cited most frequently in hundreds of media reports that both chronicle women's supposed retreat from the workplace and then ponder the predicament of today's families. Sophisticated and well-spoken, they now play key roles in leading the "culture wars" and "family values" debates. They got their start running focus groups together in Baltimore, and have since established their own orbits, but all still dedicate significant time to arguments that support traditional gender roles. They have worked hard to create what they believe to be a new perspective on social issues—one that serves as a counterweight to feminists and liberals. And they've gained a wide audience, with plenty of influence, from the Beltway to Main Street. Few voices have done more to shape the popular conception of the problems that bedevil today's working parents.

They've succeeded largely because they have their fingers on the anxiety that drives the debate over women's expanded roles—and they don't challenge the stubborn and ingrained habits of thinking, the well-worn "commonsensical" explanations of men's and women's behavior. Instead, they offer up the formulas that come to mind first—the stereotypes of gender, the shared assumptions about men and women, fathers and mothers, parents and workers, that Americans have held for the past century. "Women are in charge of the home; men are the junior partners and they like it that way," Blankenhorn says. "Men are sold on being involved, but not sold on things being fifty-fifty. Men see their primary responsibility as breadwinning and protection." They don't call for widespread social change, but simply a change of "values" or a change in "culture."

Blankenhorn lambastes feminists for trying to "remake" men and trying to "make men into women." He dismisses the idea that men need to do half the domestic chores, for example, as downright silly. "The feminist movement has focused on the need to resocialize men, as if there's a deficit in men if everything isn't split fifty-fifty.

Trying to resocialize men is counterproductive. If a man is a bread-winner, and he's there in the evenings, that's a pretty good model," he says. "If men are earning more, working more, and feeling more responsible for the breadwinning, that can work out fine. Fathers are different than mothers. Trying to quarterback who's taking respon-sibility for everything all the time is not important."

He dismisses studies that show that women put in twice as many hours at home as men as unimportant. In the focus groups and con-versations he has, he says, those are simply not important issues. "When I'm home, I pull out the skillet. The idea that men are being dragged kicking and screaming into the kitchen is not true," he says. The bottom line, he insists, is that women are "in charge of the household. Women say, 'I run the train and I let him run the house-hold sometimes.'"

These three thinkers all lay claim to their own original research and eventually developed separate and independent platforms for promoting their ideas. But they spent some of their early days together, exchanging ideas and sharing research. Mattox laughs at his first memory of Blankenhorn. "We met at a conference of the Children's Defense Fund, if you can believe that," he says. These days, Mattox is often at odds or even at open war with the Children's Defense Fund, one of the most liberal advocacy groups in Washing-ton. At the time, both Blankenhorn and Mattox joined a fight to defeat a major child care funding bill. That initial battle led them to explore ways to redefine the political issues affecting families, and they began with the focus groups in Baltimore. "We wanted to hear from parents outside the Beltway," Mattox recalls. "And those groups confirmed a lot of my hunches." Most especially, he says, parents in these groups thought there had been an "overglamoriza-tion of the work world" and there was a "perception of cultural decline," which was destroying American families. It is what Blankenhorn and Whitehead call "kitchen table" talk. The real prob-lems for today's families, they say, are the shows broadcast on televi-sion and the values taught at school. "Parents used to feel supported by social institutions and the media," Blankenhorn says. Television shows of the 1950s, for example, showed a family life that supported

Americans' core values. As for child care, he says, "most" Americans "have always been hostile to day care." Although he is quick to assert that he "is not promoting a return to the 1950s" or a return to traditional gender roles, it's often hard to see how his formulas for life in the 1990s point in any other direction.

In the early 1990s, William Mattox's outfit, the Family Research Council, was just gaining a foothold in Washington politics, thanks to its new director, Gary Bauer, a conservative who had served as a domestic policy advisor in the Reagan White House. By 1996, Bauer had become a force in national politics, able to take presidential nominee Robert Dole to task on the front page of the *New York Times* for not being responsive enough to social conservatives. He teamed up with another conservative power, James Dobson, a psychologist, evangelical Christian, and radio personality, and together they made the Family Research Council into a formidable voice in national politics and policy. Indeed, it was Dobson, who keeps a low profile, who gave the Family Research Council a crucial boost in the late 1980s. Dobson brought the financial power and grassroots help of his Colorado-based Christian organization, Focus on the Family, with him. Dobson had already established himself as a force on public policy affecting children and families. He served on a task force related to White House Conferences on the Family and on several committees related to juvenile justice in the 1980s. His group claims millions of members across the country, publishes newsletters and magazines, and supports the agenda of the Christian right, especially strong opposition to abortion.

But it was child care and issues of work and family that interested Mattox, and during his tenure at the council, he made his mark, trying to create what he calls a "new paradigm" for thinking about today's families. His research and ideas have gained wide currency today, and are often used in the cause of bashing working mothers. Author and academic Sylvia Ann Hewlett, for example, used Mattox's ideas in part to justify an argument that children suffer everything from obesity to depression because of a "family time famine," a term coined by Mattox in the late 1980s to describe what happens when both parents work. Mattox claims that his analysis is "gender neutral," but at heart, he also concedes that he "believes deeply in gender differences."

In fact, Mattox's paradigm hardly sounded new to anyone familiar with women's history. His attacks on "careerist" working moms have become common fare in Washington, D.C., where he regularly testifies against child care bills and other initiatives that are so key to working women with children. He attacked the family leave bill as a giveaway to "fast-track careerists" who cared more about their jobs than being with their babies. One of his most influential papers, published by the right-wing Heritage Foundation, argues that women have become too much like men, falling prey to workaholism and ignoring their children. His arguments are reminiscent of those made some sixty years ago, when women were ushered out of the workplace at the height of the depression to make way for men. Feminist historian Alice Kessler-Harris of Rutgers University has documented how commentators of that era argued that "truancy, incorrigibility, robbery, teenage tantrums," and other social ills were all the direct result of "the absence of women at the job." Indeed, his "new" paradigm sounds suspiciously dated.

NEW GROUPS FEED THE MYSTIQUE

Reporters and producers would not necessarily run with the story of women's retreat based simply on the ideas of social conservatives, of course. They needed the stories of individual women—the anecdotes that bring a story to life and prove the point. Journalists most often found these through a new breed of support groups that emerged in the 1980s, created specifically to help women who quit their jobs to be home with their kids.

Two national groups in particular feed the media's appetite for these stories: Mothers-at-Home, based in Vienna, Virginia, and Formerly Employed Mothers at the Leading Edge (FEMALE), based in Elmhurst, Illinois, just outside Chicago. Formerly Employed Mothers at the Leading Edge itself became a compelling barometer of the changing national sentiment. When it was founded in 1987, its acronym stood for Formerly Employed Mothers at Loose Ends. But in 1991, with increasing coverage in the media, they renamed themselves Mothers at the "Leading Edge." "As we entered the decade of the 1990s, we did feel that women were changing. We were embarrassed by a name that suggested that spending more time with our children meant we were at 'loose ends,'" explains Linda Rush, FEMALE's spokeswoman. "The name no longer fits the mind-set of our members."

Mattox and Blankenhorn frequently cite the existence of such support groups as evidence of women's collective change of heart about working. In the *Washington Post* that year, a reporter cited the "explosive growth" in these groups; a few years later, both the *Washington Times* and *USA Today* referred to the "proliferation" of such groups. The membership rolls of these groups remain tiny, however, compared with the ranks of working moms. Mothers-at-Home claims about 15,000 members, and FEMALE just 4,000—even though both have been around for a decade. Neither has grown rapidly, despite their perennial mention in both national and local media. By comparison, there are now 3 million mothers who work full-time before their babies have a first birthday—and their ranks have doubled in the same period. That is still the minority—about a third—of all moms with infants. And surveys do show that most new parents would prefer a paid leave to care for a new baby, so that both they and their children have time to recover, adjust, and spend time together. But the fact is that more and more mothers are working—and many more are working full-time, year-round. In fact, today's married mothers are twice as likely to work full-time as those of two decades ago.

But if these groups are hyped, it is not by accident. They are not only cited by social conservatives, but they work hard in their own right to gain visibility in the media. Mothers-at-Home now publishes a regular newsletter, *Welcome Home*, puts out press releases and policy papers, and even has several paid part-timers on its core staff. Each year, the group generates stories around the country with its press packets, full of story ideas for Mother's Day coverage. In 1997, for example, the group suggested reporters pick up on the idea "A Happier Mother's Day 1997. More Mothers Discover that Being

Home Is an Affordable Option." The group's two public relations specialists, Heidi Brennan and Marian Gormley, are quoted repeatedly in articles that tout the new "trend" toward home.

Formerly Employed Mothers at the Leading Edge also has designated public relations representatives at the national level, and encourages its local chapters to contact their local newspapers and television stations. By the mid-1990s, both groups had wide exposure, appearing everywhere in the media, from *Good Morning America* to *Parents* to the *Wall Street Journal*. They appear in stories aimed at the mass media and the business community, justifying both the "news" and marketing rationale for reporting that women are turning homeward. "Marketers are just now catching on to the fact that people have stopped glorifying work as the be-all and end-all of life and portraying that may not be the way to capture women's hearts," Marian Gormley, spokeswoman for Mothers-at-Home, told the *New York Times*.

The idea behind these groups is to promote a positive, updated vision of women who are at home with their kids. They eschew the terms "housewife" and "homemaker" and emphasize that they are well-educated women with plenty of vitality and smarts who take pride in their role as full-time moms. "The term 'housewife' evokes an image of a woman who does not have much on the ball, someone who is passive with men and her husband and who is highly focused on keeping her house up," explains Mothers-at-Home spokeswoman Brennan. "We don't know if she ever existed. But we certainly don't like the term. We aren't home to take care of our houses. We're here to take care of our children." The founders of Mothers-at-Home even published a book entitled *What's a Smart Woman Like You Doing at Home?* to rebut common assumptions about moms at home—and to help women form their own answers to such demeaning questions.

And these groups have certainly had a salutary effect for their constituency. They've truly improved the image of mothers at home; some polls even show that self-esteem among this group of women has begun to grow after decades of decline. They also provide practical and emotional support to women who would otherwise be isolated as they rear small children. Of the two groups, FEMALE has been far more supportive of moms who work—the leaders of the group consciously kept the word "employed" in its name, and have told the press repeatedly that many of its members work part-time and are often searching for family-friendly workplaces rather than full-time motherhood. The group has also consciously kept out of the media mommy wars.

Mothers-at-Home, on the other hand, has taken a more aggressive role in promoting full-time motherhood as a "career" for women, insisting that it is the best way, perhaps the only way, to raise well-adjusted children—and frequently bashing working moms in the process. In 1991, the group published *Discovering Motherhood,* an eighty-page book full of essays that profiled women's renunciation of careers to embrace full-time motherhood. From essays entitled "Maternal Instinct" to "I'm Glad I Can Be Home," this book sends the message that children are "shortchanged" or somehow suffer when moms work. "I don't have any daughters, but I wonder if my future daughters-in-law will someday feel free to stay home with their children. I will feel sorry for them—and for their children—if they don't. There is great value for the whole family if Mom can stay home," writes one contributor. The group is now listed in a media directory of "women experts" put out by the conservative Independent Women's Forum (IWF). The IWF has become a powerhouse of the right, creating a wave of media coverage, Op-Ed pieces, and speakers for forums across the country as a counterweight to feminists. Heidi Brennan is listed as a "public policy analyst" under a section headed "Workplace Issues: Family Leave and Child Care." So is Marian Gormley, the other official spokeswoman for Mothers-at-Home.

Brennan explains that the two groups have no formal links, and do not work closely together. "Marian [Gormley] and I are small potatoes compared to some of the women in the IWF," Brennan points out. "Most of the members of that group wouldn't even know who we are." Yet the synergy of these groups and conservative activists continues to build momentum for the media coverage that insists that mothers belong at home. Heidi Brennan was, for example, quoted in an essay in the conservative monthly *Commentary* that bashed mothers with serious careers for putting their children "last." The piece was written by Mary Eberstadt, an associate researcher with Blankenhorn's Institute for American Values. This piece was also excerpted on the *Wall Street Journal*'s editorial page, a favorite outlet for social conservatives.

William Mattox used that page to personally praise his own wife for quitting her own professional job to stay home with their children. His wife, he said, was setting a powerful example for their daughter, Allison. "I owe a debt of gratitude to my wife whose esteem-building job as a mother at home rarely receives the public esteem it deserves."

Surely, many women would welcome more appreciation for what they do at home. But Mattox wrote the piece for Take Our Daughters to Work Day in 1994, a not-very-veiled message about women's proper place. That day, after all, was created to counter stereotypes about women's abilities and prospects and to show girls there are many opportunities for them in today's workplace. Instead, Mattox used the day and the platform provided by the *Journal* to reinforce old stereotypes, the very ones that hold women back in the workplace. And he chose to do so on the pages of one of the nation's most influential business publications, one which reaches the nation's business leaders. Nearly every CEO or chairman of the nation's top corporations is a man with a wife at home full-time, and study after study shows that his personal experience affects the way he does business. Indeed, many management consultants spend long hours trying to educate senior managers about work-family conflicts because so many are unaware of the problems parents face on the job.

But anyone who tries to counter the growing mystique quickly discovers just how difficult that is. Even when the evidence is presented, it may be hard to find people willing to listen.

A NEW MESSAGE

By the winter of 1995, Ellen Galinsky and Dana Friedman, then the copresidents of the Families and Work Institute in New York City, believed they had finally marshaled the definitive evidence to put the debate over women's roles to rest. Both women were pioneers in the field of work and family research and consulting, and they knew they were onto something big.

Galinsky had blazed an impressive trail as an early educator, as a member of the faculty at Bank Street College in New York, and as a leading consultant to corporations on work-family conflicts. These days, she is called to the White House, to corporate boardrooms, and to speaking engagements around the country to discuss her wide-ranging research on work and family conflicts. Friedman, who started out as a child care lobbyist for the Day Care Council in Washington, D.C., pioneered the first major business conferences on work and family issues for the Conference Board, a prestigious business think tank serving large corporations. She, too, has garnered a reputation for innovative research and insights into work and family issues and remains one of the most respected authorities on work and family issues in the nation. The two women joined forces to found the Families and Work Institute in New York City in 1994, and have produced some of the most groundbreaking studies to date on women, work, and family.

In 1995, however, they came up with findings that they knew would generate more headlines than usual. In a carefully constructed poll, conducted jointly with Louis Harris and Associates and sponsored by the Whirlpool Foundation, Galinsky, Friedman, and their colleagues at the institute amassed some compelling facts on women's expanding roles.

Most notably, the survey showed women to be the breadwinners that they are—about 55 percent told pollsters that they provided half or more of their family's income. Of those, nearly 20 percent were the sole support of their families. The research merely confirmed data already available from the U.S. Department of Labor. But Galinsky now had significant resources at her disposal, including a public relations firm to run a press conference in New York City, make advance calls to the media, and deal with reporters and television producers after the report was released. On May 11, the institute released the study, entitled "Women: The New Providers," to a packed room of reporters at the Intercontinental Hotel in New York.

"This study calls for an end to the debate over whether women should or shouldn't work," Colleen Keast, an executive of the Whirlpool Foundation, told the *New York Times*. The poll showed women to be not only breadwinners, but also at ease with the role. Many asserted that earning money and helping to pay the family bills is one way women care for their families.

In the five days following the press conference, the story was picked up by hundreds of newspapers and scores of television and radio outlets around the country. The public relations firm that handled the survey calculated that the story had made more than 1 billion media impressions—a virtual saturation of the media, covering the major newspapers as well as small ones, from the *Wall Street Journal* and the *New York Times* to the *Anniston* (Alabama) *Star* and the *Marysville* (Georgia) *Appeal-Democrat*. "We had done other stories with the same message that never got much attention. I guess there was a social readiness to hear this message. It was treated as hot news," Galinsky reported a year later. "Suddenly, there was just a cultural readiness to hear that women were no longer working for pin money, that they were really breadwinners."

And, indeed, many of the stories did confirm just this message. "Women Indicate Satisfaction with Role of Big Breadwinner," the *Wall Street Journal* reported in its "Workplace" column. "From Pin Money to Paychecks—Women as the New Providers," reported the *Christian Science Monitor*. "Women Are Becoming Equal Providers: Half of Working Women Bring Home Half the Household Income," the *New York Times* announced. "New Provider, Thy Name Is Woman," the *Saint Paul Pioneer Press* crooned.

But Galinsky had not had time to look through all the clippings the public relations firm had collected for her—or to carefully evaluate those billion media impressions being made out there in the real world. What the folders and folders of newspaper clippings did show was a persistent deep ambivalence, even in the face of the impressive evidence and clear message sent out by Galinsky and her colleagues. Even large, sophisticated media outlets disagreed over how to interpret the very same story. Could it really mean that women were comfortable being both parents and breadwinners? The *Philadelphia Inquirer* seemed to think so, and ran its story under the headline "Study Denies that Women Are Torn between Their Career and Family," adding, "Most Women Won't Give Up Either Role." Indeed, the first sentence of the story insisted that women thought both roles were equally important. But when the *New York Daily News* picked up the same story a few days later, its big, bold headline proclaimed, "Women Put Family First." The *Janesville Gazette* in Wisconsin agreed with the *News*: "Family Still No. 1 Concern for Women."

The *Los Angeles Times* and the *Miami Herald* also had a difficult time reaching consensus on what the study meant. The editors at the *Times* settled on the headline "Working Women Play Key Role at Home, Study Finds," while the *Herald* ran the same story under the headline "Women's Role as Provider Grows Stronger."

The *San Francisco Chronicle* picked up a story from the *New York Times* and ran it under the headline "Women Earn Half of Families' Incomes," true to the original story written by *Times* reporter Tamar Lewin. But the *Chronicle*'s editors added several important nuances to the story with such subheads as "Husbands' Jobs More Secure" and "Most Prefer Part-Time"—suggesting, of course, that maybe women's incomes weren't so key to the family's well-being, after all.

The ambivalence at *Newsweek* ran far deeper. The headline in the family section noted that a new study showed that women were indeed providers, but the first example in the story indicated that women weren't very happy about that. Indeed, "the last thing Cheryl Jones wanted to be was the family breadwinner," the story began— a conclusion that ran directly counter to what Galinsky found. And like many others in the media, this story beat up on baby boomers as materialistic careerists. "Unlike many baby boomers, driven to prove they could juggle a full-time career and motherhood, Jones, 37, made relationships her priority."

Three weeks later, *Newsweek* ran another short article on Galinsky's research, apparently just to make sure that readers didn't conclude from her findings that it was a good thing that women were now breadwinners. "About That Good News—Was That Cause for Celebration?" the headline asked. The short item in the front of the magazine—one of the best-read sections of any magazine—reassured *Newsweek* readers that the study demonstrated that "being the top breadwinner is not what interested most women." Indeed, *Newsweek* now insisted that most moms would prefer part-time work. And, the magazine went on to note, just in case its readers might worry that some women were getting too far afield of their natural calling, there was plenty of evidence to the contrary: "In previous studies, women have made child and elder care their top concerns."

Other media outlets—at least 100 newspapers around the country—picked up a column by syndicated columnist Mona Charen that attacked Galinsky's study as simply wrong, saying that it defied "common sense." Charen, a former aide to President Ronald Reagan, turned to William Mattox for an assessment of the study, who cheerily concluded that Galinsky's research didn't "reflect the reality of choices parents are making." He noted that many moms of very young children work part-time, which is certainly true. But what he and Charen didn't add to that analysis is that the number of moms who work full-time has doubled in the past two decades. Charen declared that even this compelling study could not stop the debate over whether mothers should work.

In the end, even the editors at the liberal *New York Times* revealed they were having trouble digesting the facts that Galinsky had assembled. In an editorial on the Whirlpool poll entitled "Mom the Provider," the editors plumbed the cultural ambivalence about women's expanded roles: "Everyone knows there are women at work. But working women, especially those with families, are still seen as supplemental." This study revealed a reality that most Americans still didn't see, they continued. "Imagine it: in all those suburban streets, half of the houses, half of the computers, half of the new pairs of Nikes and mountain bikes and orthodontists' bills, paid for by mother. Why haven't we noticed the magnitude of this contribution?"

But rather than embracing this revelation, the editors seemed intent on muting it, making it palatable to themselves and others who were uncomfortable with women's expanded roles. "Maybe we haven't noticed" because "women themselves do not count the cash as very important." They were quick to add that "women still value a caring and generous nature above all other human qualities." The rest of the editorial dwelled on this point, as if to reassure the *Times* readers that women could still be women, even if they earned a serious paycheck. Finally, they concluded, "it seems mom is still doing just what she has always been expected to do: look after the house and the children. She still holds the values associated with the hearth: honesty and an open heart. Only now she has begun to pay half the bills."

So it was that even the sophisticated, erudite, and liberal editors of the *New York Times* felt it necessary to reassure readers that women's new earning power wouldn't disrupt or disturb social relations too much. It didn't matter if Mom had a job, after all, they seemed to be saying, or that she might earn as much as or more than Dad, as long as her primary role survived intact: she would remain in charge of hearth and home. Perhaps the headline that ran in the *Charlotte Observer*'s story on Galinsky's research best summarizes the current attitudes toward working moms: "Study Affirms Our Ambivalence about Women and Work."

THE WORK done by Galinsky and Friedman did, of course, help to expand public acceptance of and consciousness of women's new roles. The very idea that the words "mother" and "breadwinner" are mentioned in the same breath at all is heartening. For all too many years, working-class moms, especially those from the African American community, have toiled in relative obscurity, treated as invisible and disposable, their paid labor discounted and undervalued. Their struggles to see that their children are safe and well cared for go largely unnoticed.

As Galinsky sensed, there is now more of a "social readiness" to acknowledge the reality unfolding all around us, to put words to it and bring it to consciousness, as women share more of the earning and men share more of the child rearing. Today's media is more attentive, now that women of all social classes and ambitions work outside the home—including more of the editors, reporters, and producers who decide what stories to cover. The very fact that the news pages of the *Wall Street Journal* now include a regular "Work and Family" column stands as testimony to the social transformation under way. The author of that column, Sue Schellenbarger, is a working mom herself.

But part of the collective psyche still resists reality, still finds it hard to move ahead, to shed the old ways and embrace the new. Susan Mitchell, a psychologist and author of *The Official Guide to American Attitudes,* still hears fairly regularly from news reporters who ask whether there is a new trend afoot—whether women are quitting work in large numbers to stay home full-time with their children. So does Robin Hardman at the Families and Work Institute. "It's still one of the most common questions we get."

Sometimes, Mitchell says, she is able to persuade reporters with the facts. Sometimes, she is not, and reporters and producers go with their gut, unaware of or uncaring about the fallout from such stereotypes. "These backlash stories make me so angry," Mitchell says. But she puts her finger on the force that drives them, the underlying anxiety that both men and women feel in the face of breathtaking change. "Of course, women feel a push-pull about family life. It's very hard to go through the radical change from a patriarchal family that we had before to a question-mark family that we have today, a family where everyone is bargaining new roles.

"Of course, women are torn. Everybody's torn. But women are not going home," she insists. "What women want, according to the statistics I see, are options. They want a reasonable life. They want life not to be so damn difficult."

Some conservatives hope to harvest the collective discomfort, to galvanize it and use it as a brake on the pace of change. "Nostalgia has become a political act. That is why it is attacked so angrily on the left," wrote David Gelertner in the conservative *Weekly Standard* in May of 1996. "People will accept this society the Left has made only so long as they can't imagine anything better. The America of half a century ago needed a utopian future. We need a utopian past." The article proposed nothing less than a museum dedicated to nostalgia, to help Americans regain their moral compass.

That social conservatives' calls resonate for many is to be expected. The way they have framed the debate makes a return to the old roles sound downright appealing. They offer the home and family as a refuge and haven from a materialistic world, a place where no one challenges the old order of things, where men can be men, and depend on women to play a supportive role. There is no conflict here, no need to challenge social convention. The end result is rather startling, however. It is quite remarkable that women are now treated to the likes of Dominique Browning, an outstanding journalist, in hot pursuit of the perfect vacuum cleaner.

Most everyone can agree that having a pleasant home and family is one of life's great satisfactions. But it's important to recognize that the outdated assumptions about men's and women's roles do more harm than good. And embracing the so-called traditional roles for men and women does little to improve the prospects for today's families. Indeed, the embrace of nostalgia, the pretense that women don't want to and should not work, serves only one important function. It preserves the status quo. It saves everyone the effort of changing the nation's institutions, of coming up with real answers for today's real families.

Most notably, it preserves the notion that motherhood and work don't mix, that "career" women are a breed apart from other women. And that myth persists much to women's detriment.

4

What About Your Kids?

Stigmatizing Ambition

MARCIA CLARK, the high-profile prosecutor in the O. J. Simpson case, was bound to go on trial herself sooner or later. As a visibly successful woman in a male profession and the mother of two young boys, she was an irresistible target for public scrutiny. Once her estranged husband sued for custody of their sons, the media circus began.

And working moms across the country held their collective breath. Would Clark's career success translate into losing her children?

At the time, the boys lived with Clark and spent alternate weekends and two evenings a week with their father, Gordon Clark. In court papers, Gordon claimed Marcia was so wrapped up in the Simpson trial that "on most nights, she does not arrive home until 10 P.M. and even when she is at home, she is working." A computer engineer, Gordon claimed he was home by 6:15 P.M. every day and better able to care for their sons. The boys were "starved for attention," he claimed, since Marcia "is never home and never has any time to spend with them." Marcia Clark refused to discuss the case in public, and managed to seal the court papers and proceedings in the case.

Ironically, even as her husband charged she was neglecting the boys, Clark took heat in the courtroom for giving the boys too *much* attention. The day the custody dispute burst out into the public, she told Judge Lance Ito she couldn't stay for an evening court session because she had to get home to her sons. Clark's child care problems translated into instant headlines around the country, sparking commentary about mothers' ability to handle the demands of the workplace. "Like all moms, Marcia Clark can't have it all," the *Detroit News* summarized.

Clark thus became the latest and most visible example of a highly accomplished woman to draw fire as both mother and worker. It wasn't so long before that Zoe Baird lost her bid to become the first female attorney general of the United States because of her underground child care arrangements. In nationally televised hearings, U.S. senators peppered Baird with intrusive and demeaning questions about her mothering abilities, suggesting that she cared more about her career than her children. Senator Joseph Biden wanted to know exactly what time she left her home and returned each day and whether she gave her children enough attention. Kimba Wood, another impressive talent, also lost the nomination because of child care arrangements. In the end, a childless woman, Janet Reno, won the job.

And, of course, there is Hillary Clinton. A Yale lawyer with her own record of stellar career success, a woman known to be articulate and outspoken, she and President Clinton's political advisors have struggled throughout her husband's presidency to find an image palatable to the American public, one that is both maternal and intelligent. How could a smart, aggressive "career" woman be a good mother and wife? The acrimonious debate over her proper role even spawned a satiric newsletter, *The Hillary Clinton Quarterly,* which chronicled and poked fun at the ongoing public ambivalence.

But no mother in the public spotlight at the time was fighting the same high-stakes battle as Clark. Only she stood to lose her children because of her success at work. And most moms watching the drama knew that losing the boys was an all-too-real possibility. They had already seen it happen in other widely publicized custody disputes. Only a few months before Clark's case burst into the headlines, another female lawyer, Sharon Prost, then an aide to Utah senator Orrin Hatch, made the front page of the *New York Times* as she surrendered primary custody of her two sons to her ex-husband. The judge in that case ruled Prost was "simply more devoted to and absorbed by her work and her career than anything else in her life." Around the same time, Ruth Parris, a realtor in Hilton Head, South Carolina, appeared on NBC's *Dateline* with Jane Pauley, describing how she, too, lost custody of her only son when a judge pronounced her "too career oriented."

What was really on trial was women's ambition, the social acceptance of women's expanded roles. How far could women really go on the job once they had children?

Americans had come to reluctantly accept the idea that many women might work when they must. Poor and working-class women could be excused for taking jobs outside the home, if they did so "out of economic necessity." But "good mothers" were always expected to limit their aspirations at work. A real mom simply does not want a real career. Instead, she is happy with part-time work or other marginal or temporary jobs. The idea is that lower-level, less ambitious jobs do not get in the way of women's maternal duties.

Just the opposite is true, of course, as any working-class woman can easily testify. Jobs at the margin pay less and tend to be less flexible, which can make having a decent family life even harder. If anything, surveys show working-class mothers to be particularly upset about lack of advancement opportunities on the job. "As heads of households or women married to men who aren't making that much, women need the pay and benefits to keep their families stable. They are tired and angry at being stuck in low-wage entry-level, dead-end jobs while men around them advance," said Chris Woods, a labor organizer for the AFL-CIO, at a conference on labor issues in the fall of 1996.

What all women want, of course, is the chance to succeed both on the job and at home—especially now that work is such an integral part of most women's lives. "I don't view my ambition as a detriment to my family or a separate pursuit from being a mother. It's just part of me being who I want to be as a whole person. Motherhood should not be an alternative to a successful career, but should be part of it," says Pamela Carter Bryant, a registered nurse who works in Mission Viejo, California.

And contrary to popular wisdom, having a baby can inspire new aspirations. "After I had a baby, I thought, 'Well, if I'm going to work, I need to get satisfactions and rewards from working or else I'm not going to take the time away from the kids. If I'm going to be in the workforce, I'm going to make it worthwhile. I'm going to do it right.' I had a greater desire to excel," says Anne Brown, the controller and mother of two who lives just outside Dayton, Ohio. After her first child, she did something she had delayed for years: she took the exam to become a certified public accountant, a necessary step to getting ahead in her work. "Up until then, I'd been somewhat ambivalent. Having a child meant I had to be clear about why I was working."

For many women, of course, the soul-searching does not lead to such a simple conclusion. They are ambitious, but they see no clear way to succeed on the job without a serious cost to their families. Most women are, after all, still the primary parent and, as such, keenly aware of the ways many careers can disrupt family life. "I have thought a lot about my life and where I want to be. Trying to be the best mom and trying to be the best at my job are constant battles," says a thirty-one-year-old mother of a toddler who lives on Long Island and works as a sales representative for a major drug company. "It is so hard to do both, without sacrificing something." That is because her company requires all executives to spend some time at its headquarters, which for her means a major relocation. "I ask myself, why not make the moves necessary to become a vice president? For men, it seems to be a no-brainer. Picking up the family and moving wherever is commonplace. Why is this such a hard thing to do if you're a woman?" The answer, of course, is that women tend to be the ones who resettle families and see how hard it can be for kids to adjust to a move. There might be other ways for the company to groom people for advancement, but at the moment, there is no other road to making vice president.

"I feel I could bring a lot to upper management," she says, almost wistfully, and there are times when the need to put her ambition on hold bothers her. "I do wonder where I would be if I had chosen to take the career-advancement path." When she feels confused, she says, "I just look at my son and think about how fast he is growing and how lucky I am to even be able to make the choices."

Increasingly, however, women are asking why it's necessary to make a choice at all. Their ambition is to lead a rich and full life, one that includes both family and work. "I want to be rewarded and recognized at work for my competence and professionalism," says Anne Brown. "And I want to be a mother."

Nonetheless, Americans still routinely sort working women into two camps, those with ambition and those without. Those with children are regularly stereotyped as lacking ambition. The *Harvard Business Review,* the nation's most influential business journal, even condoned the practice a few years back, by publishing an article suggesting such distinctions be adopted as formal workplace policy. In 1989, the *Review* printed an article that argued that employers should identify women as either career-track women, with ambitions to move ahead at work, or "work-and-family women." The ambitious women would be groomed for advancement, while the "work-and-family women" could be granted flexible hours—in return for lower pay and fewer promotions. The idea seemed so natural, so much a part of the culture, that Felice Schwartz, the author of the article, was genuinely surprised and puzzled by the ensuing uproar over her proposal. Her idea, which came to be known as the "mommy track," generated cover stories and debates for months. To this day, William Mattox at the Family Research Council describes it as an important turning point in changing public opinion about working mothers.

Schwartz did not understand that she was freezing women into permanent categories, limiting their choices once they became moms. "This 'mommy track' was simply formalizing the discrimination women already experience on the job," says Joan Bertin, a New York–based attorney who has gained national recognition for her litigation around issues involving motherhood and work. Indeed, it is only in the past decade that women have won the right to hold a job after they are pregnant and to return to it after they have a baby. In the past, the assumptions that mothers didn't want to or couldn't work ran so deep that women were routinely harassed, demoted, or let go the moment they announced they were pregnant. Motherhood was the ultimate signal that a woman was not suited for the workplace.

The truth is that neither men nor women are permanently "ambitious" or always "career" persons. For both men and women, ambition ebbs and flows, depending on economic needs, the opportunities on the job, and the way family life is going. Most certainly, ambition may recede for new parents—and not just for women. Fathers actively caring for a new baby often express the same ambivalent feelings about work that new moms do, and for the same reasons. "It's emotionally wrenching to come back to work, because you're so focused on that child. For months, I could imagine that I didn't want to stay here," says a male attorney at a major New York law firm after a month's paternity leave.

What surveys show is that both men and women want the workplace to change, to allow people to be both the best workers and the best parents they can be. Yet by and large, employers remain resistant to that idea for both economic and psychic reasons. A senior partner in a law firm, for example, confessed to sociologist Cynthia Fuchs Epstein that he had noticed more young male associates wanted to spend less time in the office and more time with their families, and that he considered that "a very serious economic problem," one that was "irritating" to him. Even more irritating to him, a growing number of young attorneys were quitting the firm rather than put up with the long hours.

Like so many other employers, however, he did not see this as a call for change. The firm was not about to change the rules for making partner or to adopt flexible schedules. Instead, he interpreted the problem as an affront to his firm and the old rules for success on the job. "You've worked with somebody and brought them along and have brought them into this and then all of a sudden, they're gone," he said.

He was hardly unique, of course, which is why it is women who are scrutinized and challenged, rather than the workplace. It is women, rather than the tenets for success, that go on trial. At a minimum, many women feel social pressure to hide their true feelings about work. "I am ambitious. I want the same things most people want from a career—recognition, challenge, achievement, intellectual stimulation," says Karen Metcalf Wehman, a marketing professional in Indianapolis. But she says she's careful not to be too vocal about those feelings, since a mother's ambition is so frequently translated into a lack of interest in her children. "I do feel stymied by society's attitude toward working mothers."

Indeed, the question of women's *intentions* about work become crucial once they become mothers. And that is because women are still seen as mothers first, and workers second. Their paid work must not interfere with their maternal duties. Most certainly, they should not *want* to work or hope to get ahead on the job. "Men are still seen as providers, working to support their families, an unselfish act. Women, on the other hand, are seen as selfish because they are stepping out of their social role. They are not seen as providers, so working is seen as something they do only for themselves. Working then becomes a selfish act," says Faye Crosby, professor of psychology at Smith College and author of *Juggling: The Unexpected Advantages of Balancing Career and Home for Women and Their Families.*

The idea of "career" women as indulgent persists, of course, in big ways and small. In the fall of 1996, for example, syndicated talk show host Rush Limbaugh asserted that women spend their paychecks on pedicures, makeup, and haircuts—rather than the mortgage, groceries, and college tuition. And if that is the case, the question naturally arises, How can women "leave" their children to earn the money for things the family doesn't even need?

Indeed, social conservatives find it useful to question women's motives for working. So-called family values champions William Mattox, David Blankenhorn, and Barbara DaFoe Whitehead often distinguish between "career" women and "working" women. "Whitehead drew a distinction between those who work primarily for fulfillment and financial independence and those who work primarily for the money, especially in non-professional groups," reporter Paul Taylor explained to readers of the *Washington Post*. Such distinctions are in fact quite useful for these social conservatives. They make them sound instantly compassionate for all the women who "have" to work and for all those children who suffer when Mom has to go to work, and give them the freedom to chastise and criticize all those "fast-track careerists" who don't care about their kids. The charges against working moms are then reduced to pat phrases that speak to these common stereotypes. Arch-conservative Republican congressman William Dannemeyer, for example, has charged that American society has been "devastated" by working mothers who "put careers ahead of children and rationalize material benefits in the name of children."

Marcia Clark challenged such categorization. She represented a new wave of women, women who refused to choose between visible career success and their families. Even more remarkably, Clark did so in the limelight, standing before the nation, without remorse.

Indeed, Clark's ambition was well known and widely documented in the media. A few years before, she had taken an office job in the district attorney's office, one that required fewer hours. But she missed the action of the courtroom, and moved back to prosecuting cases, a far more demanding job. "Her ambition has cost her sympathy," wrote Jane Mayer in the *New Yorker*. Most certainly, it was an issue that spoke to many editors, reporters, and producers, as they pondered their own demanding schedules and the often unpredictable hours required by their jobs.

For that reason, Clark's case touched a deep chord across the nation, signaling a new juncture for women. From *Newsweek* to online chat rooms, from lunch breaks at work to the checkout lines at the supermarket, Americans could be heard debating the relative merits of Clark's performance both as mother and worker. Even before the custody fight, of course, nearly everyone had an opinion of Marcia Clark, as a woman who challenged social convention. Her hair, her clothes, her manner of speaking, her style in the courtroom, were thoroughly examined and debated. "My mother calls her 'Marcia' and talks about her with the same familiarity she uses to catch me up on the doings of the daughter of an old neighbor," wrote Susan Reimer in the *Baltimore Sun*. "As in: 'Did you see Marcia's hair is different?'" Clark-watching was practically a national sport, a collective effort to come to terms with women's progress.

And women's behavior was on trial once again, rather than the institutions and assumptions that constantly forced them—as well as a growing population of men—to make choices between work and family. "She was appointed chief prosecutor because of her tenacious work habits. Now, those same work habits may cost her custody of her children," wrote Reimer. "If the O. J. Simpson trial is a forum for America's deep racial animosities, it is now the place where this country will try to sort out its gender confusions, too. While Marcia Clark is trying the 'Murder of the Century,' she must help us decide how we feel about tough-as-nails women who work late."

Put in that light, it's hard to see how any judge could be sympathetic to Clark's desire to keep her children. Would anyone want to award custody to a workaholic woman who was "tough as nails"? Would such a woman provide the warmth and security that young children need? Framed the way it was, with Clark the caricature of a hard-nosed "career woman," an Ayn Rand who cared only for her success, it seemed unlikely.

At the time, one reader of the *New Orleans Times-Picayune* argued that "women should think twice about getting pregnant if they're going to pursue careers."

As it turned out, Marcia Clark retained primary custody of her boys. The judge in this case deemed Clark to be a perfectly acceptable parent, with a track record of caring for her boys. While the Simpson trial imposed an incredible demand on her time, it was a temporary one.

In the end, one had to ask why Gordon Clark didn't simply step in and take care of the boys during this period, if he had the time, rather than put his sons in the middle of a heated and public custody dispute. It is a telling fact that it was Marcia's behavior and not his that drew the most public scrutiny.

Yet it's also easy to understand why this case generated sympathy on both sides. It was a dramatic case that went to the heart of the deeply felt conflicts that bedevil today's working parents. There is no doubt that some jobs, at some times, place unreasonable demands on both men and women, making it hard to be an involved parent. It's also true that the rules of success at many jobs, whether one wants to be chairman or just get a decent raise, often require employees to at least pretend their first priority is the workplace. "You are often judged by how much you show your face in the office—how much time you put in on weekends, how late you stay and how early you come in," says Arlene Johnson, from the Families and Work Institute.

That is all the more reason why the spotlight should be on the demands of employers, on the way most workplaces measure success, not on women's behavior. Even more important, it's time to challenge the core assumption that sat at the center of the debate over Marcia Clark's case and so many media stories that blast working parents. The idea that children inevitably suffer when Mom works just isn't borne out in the research.

A MATTER OF TIME?

It's understandable, however, that so many Americans believe kids are hurt when mothers work outside the home. The belief stems from assumptions that seem logical enough on the surface. First of all, there is the idea that everyone has a finite amount of energy, enthusiasm, and patience. If that is the case, it follows that women might get "used up" on the job, and have little energy left for their kids at night.

By such logic, it also seems reasonable to assume that the more successful the woman, the more she might neglect her children. Professionals and managers often put in more than forty hours a week and carry more responsibility. Preoccupied with a demanding job, it's easy to imagine that women in high-powered jobs simply don't have the mental or physical energy to raise kids properly. That concept, in fact, was the defining theme of the *Newsweek* cover story in 1997 that attacked working parents. The magazine's cover featured distorted photographs of a dual-earner couple, compressed and stressed, standing on the face of a clock. They were literally slaves of time, mechanical stand-ins for the hands of the clock, set apart from their son who looked to them for attention and love. Gordon Clark summoned up such images when he charged that his sons were "emotionally starved."

The earliest studies on effects of mothers' working, conducted in the 1950s and 1960s, flowed from just such a primitive formula. Women's time at work was simply translated into "maternal absence." There was no attempt to acknowledge the fact that a working mother was still a permanent and guiding presence for a child, that she forged her bond with her child over the course of a lifetime. Nor was there any attempt to investigate how differences between jobs, a family's need for income, the contributions a father might make to child rearing, the different sorts of relationships that arise between mothers and children, the values a mother brought to child rearing, or a child's temperament might change the impact of mom's employment.

Further, researchers did not bother to investigate the possible *benefits* of a mother's work outside the home. The most obvious payoff, the stability and security that a steady paycheck provides a family, was not part of the discussion. The idea that working women might serve as positive role models for their children was not on the agenda.

Instead, studies were undertaken with the assumption that children must suffer some deficit when moms work, and the research simply set out to find and report it. When the evidence wasn't there, social scientists relied on Freudian theory and studies of children who were permanently separated from their mothers to argue that kids did need Mom at home. "In the early days, studies were financed with the idea of demonstrating the evils of employed mothers. The idea was to find dreadful consequences," jokes Lois Hoffman, professor of psychology at the University of Michigan for several decades. She is now retired, but still conducting and publishing her studies on working moms. Hoffman has, more than most anyone, changed the assumptions among researchers and the direction of research on maternal employment.

Hoffman's work now spans four decades, and was initially driven by simple scientific curiosity. "I didn't really set out to study maternal employment per se," she recalls. "I was interested in studying work, and the effects of the mother working on the household division of labor and the power structure between husbands and wives." She herself took time off work to be with her children when they were younger and describes it as one of life's greatest pleasures. "I had my first child in 1960, after I had been working for many years. I was quite excited about staying home and playing with my babies," she says. Because Hoffman was a promising researcher, her mentor convinced her to keep on working, which she did, after 7:30 P.M. "One thing my children will tell you is that bedtime was always seven-thirty, no matter what. That's when I did my work. But until then, I was a full-time mom and it was a beautiful time. I was thrilled and it was a delightful time. I think men should have the opportunity to be with their babies."

And even with her own intense bonds with her babies, she was not willing to accept the simplistic notion that children are automatically hurt when mothers work. Common sense told her that human relationships are far more complicated than that, that the effects of a woman's work could not be boiled down to any simple formula. By the time she published her first studies in the early 1960s, she had discovered that kids not only survived, but often thrived, when mothers worked, given the right set of circumstances. But the social climate at the time made it practically impossible for her to communicate that message to the general public. "Even when I reported positive effects on maternal employment, they didn't always come out in print," she says. "I remember one instance very clearly when I wrote a nice scholarly review of the literature for an encyclopedia. But when the article came out in print, it was changed. The editors had totally, utterly changed the substantive content to show that children of working mothers suffered."

For many years, Hoffman says, she simply refused to talk to

reporters at all. "I told my secretary to tell anyone from the media I was out of the country. At that time, in the early 1960s, nearly all the reporters were men. They would come and I would talk very sincerely about the effects of maternal employment and I would tell them about my research. Then I'd read the articles and see that they had already written the article in their heads before they interviewed me."

The integrity of Hoffman's analysis, however, did command the attention of her colleagues and eventually helped to move the research to a more sophisticated level. Her first book, *The Employed Mother in America,* which she coauthored with psychologist Ivan Nye, went through several printings and gained wide attention in the academic world.

Most important, she was the first to insist that there was no *one* outcome for kids, an idea she has continued to emphasize over the years. "The data reveal primarily that the dual-wage family is not a single pattern and parental attitudes seem more significant than the mother's employment status," she concluded in 1989. The messages took a while to reach the public, however. In 1990, the National Academy of Sciences was still trying to make that point. In 1995, a paper from the Families and Work Institute continued to hammer home the same theme.

Over the years, Hoffman also managed to tease out a number of key factors that predict how children fare when mothers work: the parents' attitudes toward the mom's work, the quality of the parents' marriage, the level of support that Dad offers, and the social supports available to Mom. The most dramatic effect she discovered was a "modest increase" in the participation of men in child care and household chores. "There's very big changes in American families because of mothers working, but they aren't the ones that the researchers initially set out to find," says Hoffman.

She also suggested the children of working moms may indeed be different from other children in several important ways. Some studies show that girls with working moms score better on social adjustment tests, do better in school, and even have more professional accomplishments. This may be because their moms serve as important role models; some studies show that girls with employed moms tend to name their moms as the person they admire most.

Certainly, many employed moms see themselves as positive role models, showing their children that women can be competent and productive as both parents and workers. "My husband and I talked about me continuing to work before I got pregnant and we decided it was best for myself and our family. I have always valued employment, and not just for the money," says Gail Luttrell, an insurance adjuster with Chubb Insurance in Louisville, Kentucky, and mother of two children. "Both I and my family benefit in so many ways, the fact that you are contributing to your family, your company and community. I am proud to be using the brain God gave me and the education my parents paid for." These are the values she hopes to instill in her daughter. "I raise her to value both employment and children. I don't want her to have to choose."

Hoffman found kids with working moms also tended to be more independent than those raised by full-time homemakers. This only makes sense, since working parents often need their children to do more for themselves. Further, many see the development of independence and self-reliance in their kids as a positive trait. By contrast, full-time moms at home may have a stake in their children's dependency. "Homemakers may see the child's movement toward independence as a threat to their major role and source of self-esteem," she noted in a 1989 paper.

Studies also show that kids raised by working moms tend to be more flexible about male and female roles, which many moms see as a plus. Most kids today can expect to be part of dual-earner couples when they grow up, and thus will need both domestic and job skills to survive. That is why many women consciously work to teach their children that real women do earn a paycheck and real men do the dishes. "Our boys see both of us working outside the home and sharing things at home. They see Dad doing the wash. I think that's very important nowadays. I don't want my boys to be raised to think women do all the cooking and cleaning," says Barbara Brazil, a human resources assistant for the Kent, Washington, school district. Such daily lessons, she and other moms believe, will prepare her kids better for the adult world.

OVER THE years, many psychologists and sociologists have spent considerable time refining the core questions that Hoffman raised. How do parents' attitudes toward Mom's working outside the home mediate the impact of her job? If a man feels threatened, for example, by his wife's paycheck, how does that play out in the marriage and with the kids? What about Mom's feelings about work—does it matter how she sees her role? Does the nature of a mother's job outside the home matter? "We are starting to ask far better questions about the strains and gains of men's and women's changing roles," says Nancy Marshall, from Wellesley College's Center for Research on Women. "We have begun to look more closely at the *quality* of women's various roles. When a woman enjoys her work and has a lot of autonomy in her job, for example, she's a lot more likely to be happy in life than if she has a boring, repetitive job. It sounds so simple when you stop to think about it. But it's taken researchers a long time to sort through all of our cultural biases and reach some sophisticated answers about family life today."

By now, there are literally thousands of studies probing these issues, with many more produced every year, homing in on the most critical issues. Some of their findings are surprising. "The way both men and women—but especially women—view traditional sex roles is significant. If women are committed to a more nontraditional view, that it is okay for Mom to work, that men and women should share chores, then it's more positive for the kids," says sociologist Marshall. When a mother feels it's inherently wrong to work, studies show, she naturally feels unhappy in the role and tends to share her discomfort with her children. One landmark study by Ellen Hock at the University of Ohio shows, for example, that moms who feel guilty about working tend to communicate their worries to their children by continually asking their children if they are all right. The very fact that Mom is raising the issue communicates her anxiety and makes her kids feel anxious.

The way a woman feels about her particular job and the extent of control she exerts over the terms of her work are also important. Not surprisingly, women who work jobs where schedules frequently change, with a lot of mandatory overtime, and with little control over the content of the work or the way work is done, tend to feel less satisfied in their jobs—and bring that stress home, just as men do. "I feel good about working right now because I've made progress in my career and I'm making decent money," says insurance adjuster Luttrell. "I can see my feelings would be completely different if I wasn't making much money and wasn't making any progress professionally."

Luttrell's point is key, yet one that is often ignored in debates over women's employment. Work and family life are not static, but moving targets, and the costs and benefits of working change over time as circumstances change. Vicki Brett-Gach, a middle manager with a bank in Ann Arbor, Michigan, for example, confesses she periodically goes through moments of doubt about working full-time.

"Those feelings come and go," she says. At the time of the interview in late 1996, life is good. Her job is satisfying; both her children are thriving. She and her husband are building a new home, and she has an outlet for her artistic talents both in the creative work she does at the bank and as president of the county council for the arts. "My children are fine, and right now my life is just wonderfully fun. I think if you enjoy your work, working and having children is really the best of both worlds," she says. "I have a very nice position and I like my work. I value the friendships at work and I'm proud of the work I do there. And I have a wonderful family. It's ideal."

She quickly adds, however, that it's "not always easy" blending work and family. Her most difficult moments arose right after her second child was born, in the first weeks back on the job after a three-month maternity leave. "I had lots of mixed feelings when I came back. I just wanted my daughter near me. I missed her. I kept thinking if only I had a few more months off, I'd be happier. Or that working part-time would be better," she recalls. In the midst of her angst, she opened the *Wall Street Journal* to the front-page article that declared stay-at-home mothers the "status symbol of the 1990's." One mother in the article compared day care to "meat factories."

"It's hard enough to leave your child, without adding that extra measure of the media telling you that your kids are worse off," she says. "I had to think a lot about my decision." Indeed, sociologist Marshall's studies identify social approval and social support as a key ingredient in making life happy for employed moms. The fact that women repeatedly hear that they are doing something wrong undermines their confidence and adds to their stress. Many studies show that period Brett-Gach describes, the first year after the birth of a baby, as a time that can be particularly raw. The weight of new responsibilities, the lack of sleep, the adjustment to the new identity as a parent, and staging a return to work can conspire to make women especially susceptible to criticism. Women having special problems, dealing with a colicky baby, for example, or recovering from a difficult birth, may feel even more troubled by the message that the only good moms are those at home full-time.

Seasoned mothers offer reassurance. "I had such angst with my first," says Lynn Asinof, a reporter at the *Wall Street Journal* and mother of two. "Now I realize how obsessive I became, because it was all so new and I didn't know anything. Now I realize I don't even have that much control over how the boys turn out. Not the way I thought I did. I was much more relaxed with my second, and I think that was good for both him and me."

That is not to discount the legitimate concerns that women—and men—feel about not having enough time with their children today. "Mothering is a serious business. Good mothers are always thinking about what's good for their children," says Hoffman. Some guilt is, of course, a healthy signal that something is amiss and needs to be changed. If the hours at work are consistently too long, if a baby is consistently protesting when left with a caregiver, it's natural to feel concerned. "But there's also a message out in society that goes beyond that rational consideration. There's less of it today, but still, there's a social message that blames women unnecessarily for their children's problems. Women have to learn to screen out those inappropriate messages."

BENEFITS OFTEN OVERLOOKED

But the most startling aspect of research on working moms is how rare it is to find anyone asking how a woman's job *enhances* children's lives.

First and foremost, of course, there are the economic benefits. This is a telling omission, given that the financial benefits are seen as the *primary* benefit men give their families. Today, the majority of working moms—about 60 percent—are married to men earning less than $15,000 a year. Clearly, their paychecks make a significant difference in the quality of their children's lives. "Even if I didn't have to work, I would," says Kelly Hogan-Lewis, a registered nurse and mother of four in Wilton Manors, Florida. Hogan-Lewis is now divorced, but she worked throughout her marriage. "My salary made a thirty-six-thousand-dollar difference in our lives then, giving us the chance to own a house, live in a better neighborhood. All four of the kids have college prepaid because I was earning money." Now that she is a single mom, her children are totally dependent on her income. And just as important, she believes, they were protected from enormous upheaval and unhappiness when her marriage broke up. "My work provides a stability in our family life, for me and the kids."

Fascinating new research in economics shows, in fact, that the more control women have over family finances, the better their kids do. Studies in Europe and in developing countries show that when a mother is in charge of income and spending, kids are better fed and clothed than when a father is. The research focused on spending patterns in families receiving social benefits from the government, something akin to welfare in the United States. "We don't have comparable studies for a wealthy country like ours, but economists are taking these studies very seriously because they are an indication of what happens when women control the family resources," says Shelly Lundberg, economics professor at the University of Washington. "When mothers controlled the resources, children did better on several measures of well-being, including their height and weight, the nutritional adequacy of their diet, and overall survival."

Lundberg argues the study is no reflection on men's ultimate ability to care for children. Instead, it shows how traditional male and female roles color men's and women's behavior. Most cultures still assign women primary responsibility for children's well-being, and when women get the purse strings, they use money for their kids, not themselves. Women are trained to take children's needs seriously, sometimes as even more important than their own. That is not always true for men.

Yet women are still chastised for being selfish and self-absorbed when they work. The message is often delivered casually, in the course of daily conversations, yet with a sense of moral authority drawn from the conviction that kids are hurt when mothers work. "Someone at work asked me, 'Don't you ever yearn to stay home with your children?' She talks about what nice experiences she had being at home with her children when they were younger, how her children still tell her how much they loved the fact that she baked them warm muffins," says Brett-Gach, the bank manager in Ann Arbor. When she told her coworker that staying home was "kind of a moot point for us financially, we simply couldn't afford it, she told me, 'Well, we just made the decision to be poor.'"

At the time, Brett-Gach was speechless, stung by the accusation that she cared more for money than for her children. "Later, I thought, 'I'm not sure it would be the best decision for my children to choose to not have health insurance I get on my job, or to not be able to afford a house in a safe neighborhood, with good schools, and not have a retirement fund.' I resented the fact that she acted like I wasn't taking good care of my kids because I work." Like many women, Brett-Gach says, she works so she *can* take care of her kids.

THE TIME BIND REVISITED

There is another critical strain of research on working moms. It is especially important because it calls into question the popular wisdom that working women are simply too exhausted to be good moms. "Psychologists used to assume that taking on a new role, such as the role of worker, would add conflict and stress to women's lives," says psychology professor and author Faye Crosby. Social scientists conceived of life as a giant zero-sum game; if people gave at the office, they had nothing left to give at home. Thus, the more ambitious and attached a woman was to her career, the more her children were likely to suffer.

Yet starting a decade ago, that thesis began to look mighty shaky. What the hard data show is that "work often adds new satisfactions and rewards, enriching women's lives instead of detracting from them." In many cases, women draw more energy from combining work and family than they do from choosing a more narrow path.

Indeed, adding a new role can create what psychologists call a "buffer," a boost to mental health. The new role—as wife, mother, worker, community activist, whatever a woman chooses—often serves as protection against depression and anxiety. If a woman has problems at home, for example, such as marital conflict or a difficult phase with her children, her job can provide some balance, an alternative source of joy and satisfaction. Many women say that working even adds to their energy, making them feel more generous, patient, and involved at home. "When I'm driving home from work, I start thinking about my kids and it really gives me pleasure," says Elizabeth Knoll, an editor for an academic publisher and mother of two. "Children and home life require a whole different part of you than work, and that's important to me. I love my work. It's part of who I am. I would feel like a fake if I pretended I was doing it only because I had to. But I also see that I could easily turn into a brain on a stick, a bookworm or a career woman. That would have been grim. No one has children because they make life easier. But I would have been a lot less happy if I weren't able to have both. Just as work is sometimes a relief from the children, then the children are a relief from work."

Still, Crosby understands that the idea that doing more can translate into more energy is counterintuitive—especially given the cultural prejudices that place women at home. She can still remember her own surprise when she stumbled on the evidence that having more than one role might *relieve* stress, rather than exacerbate it, back in 1978. "I was studying what made people satisfied at work and at home. And I had massive amounts of computer printouts in my hands," she recalls. "Back then, you just put asterisks next to the significant results, a place where you could find some sort of possible cause-and-effect relationship. And what those asterisks revealed was that the more roles a person had—worker, parent, spouse—the happier and more satisfied that person was in each role."

And that, she says, riveted her attention and aroused her curiosity. "It was absolutely contrary to everything I'd ever read about the strain women suffered when they expanded roles. I kept asking myself, 'How could this be?'" It took Crosby nearly a decade to come up with an answer, culled from studies of her own and the work of others. "It was really a ten-year process of rethinking what I and so many others had thought."

In the end, what she concluded, and what is widely accepted among psychologists and sociologists today, is a simple enough proposition. Conflict between different roles—especially between those of worker and parent—is not inevitable. A job may reduce stress via several routes: it can provide economic independence, a sense of accomplishment, and a wider range of activity in life than is possible at home. "I thought while I was home I would be able to keep my house clean, cook tons of neat meals, and my children would love me more!" says Roxane MacLellan, a medical technologist in Colorado Springs, Colorado, who recently decided to revive a twenty-year-old dream and return to school to become a veterinarian. For years, as a military wife, she'd made her career secondary and felt pressure to be home once she became a mother. At first, she looked forward to it, but over time, she found that "cooking meals and cleaning house were the last things I wanted to do and my children were bored and wanted to play with other children. I love my children and husband, but I needed to get back on track and pursue my dreams. I had buried my dream because of my perceived role of what it meant to be a good woman, wife, and mother." Now, she says, "I see I can be all of those roles without sacrificing who I am."

And contrary to the stereotypes that divide women into camps of "career women" and those who have "just a job," or mommy-trackers versus those with ambition, it turns out that such findings apply to all working women. Although many commentators and even scholars assume that working-class women would quit their jobs if only they could, that is not what studies show. Instead, women in blue-collar and working-class families take just as much, if not more, pride and pleasure in their jobs. "Their wages often make more of a difference in their families' lives than the wages of women in middle-class families. In many cases, their jobs simply change the situation of their families the most dramatically. A lot of lower-class women can say, 'We were able to buy a house, able to set up a fund to send a child to college,' " says psychologist Hoffman. "I think this is quite interesting. It runs counter to what the people in my field and in the media assume, which is that morale is higher among middle-class mothers, and especially professional women."

By contrast, studies show that full-time homemakers in blue-collar families are more likely to be depressed. "When you talk about women working or not working, you have to compare the experience of work to the one of being at home. And working-class and lower-class women often report they have a sense of more control and effectiveness when they work. And they enjoy the social stimulation," says Hoffman. Indeed, studies of working-class women in textile mills in New England in the 1970s revealed just how much these women valued working. "When you read interviews with these women, you hear in their voices just how much they like working. They'll say, 'My boy's in college, he wouldn't be in college without me.' " In other words, they saw the concrete benefits of their jobs for their children.

PHONY FAMINE?

Nonetheless, social conservatives have worked hard to promote the idea that children suffer enormously from a lack of parental time and attention when both parents work. Indeed, it was none other than William Mattox of the Family Research Council who first popularized the notion of a "time famine," through a widely circulated article, touted and publicized in the early 1990s by several influential outlets. "There were three major incarnations of my paper on the family time famine," he recalled later, one published by the Heritage Foundation, the nation's leading conservative think tank, one published by his own Family Research Council, and the third by David Blankenhorn's Institute for American Values. Focus on the Family, James Dobson's group, also published a version of the article.

And, it turned out, it was nothing short of a scathing indictment of working parents. "Parents today spend 40 percent less time with their children than did parents in 1965," he asserted, drawing on data collected by John Robinson, a sociologist at the University of Maryland. In actual hours, that translated, he said, into a reduction from thirty hours a week to just seventeen a week. Mattox offered no original research, but rather pieced together the work and ideas of other scholars and conservative thinkers. Indeed, the root cause of many childhood problems was attributed to "unbridled careerism" by Karl Zinsmeister, a resident scholar at the conservative American Enterprise Institute: "Now it appears workaholism and family dereliction have become equal opportunity diseases, striking mothers as much as fathers." Zinsmeister, an ardent opponent of day care and mothers' working outside the home, turned up at forums organized by arch-conservative Phyllis Schlafly to beat back day care legislation, served on the board of Blankenhorn's Institute for American Values, and frequently testified before Congress on family policy.

Zinsmeister captured one of the key themes in the paper—that parents were simply too busy working to properly love or even adequately supervise their children. So did other authors that Mattox quoted, both scholars and reporters in the lay press. His plaintive picture of kids in middle-class homes was drawn from an article by Suzanne Fields, a conservative columnist with the *Washington Times*: "The child who grazes, standing in front of a microwave eating his fried chicken, biscuits or refried beans, won't starve, but he may suffer from an emotional hunger that would be better satisfied if only Mom and Dad were there to yell at him for every pea he slips onto the knife." The themes most certainly echo Gordon Clark's charges; one subtitle of Mattox's piece was simply "Starved for Attention." Mattox also quoted from the work of both of his friends at the Institute for American Values, David Blankenhorn and Barbara DaFoe Whitehead.

The article garnered significant attention in both the media and among policymakers, much to Mattox's delight. "Even Judy Mann of the *Washington Post,* a liberal who disagrees with me on just about everything, agreed with me on this," he says. The version published by the Heritage Foundation was entered into congressional testimony, when Mattox appeared there to oppose the Family and Medical Leave Act.

Economist and author Sylvia Ann Hewlett also latched on to the idea of a "time famine." Both Mattox and Blankenhorn recall sharing Mattox's work with her at the time, and Hewlett helped popularize the idea with her book *When the Bough Breaks: The High Cost of Neglecting Our Children,* published in 1991. In a forty-state publicity tour for the book, in appearances on both local and national television shows, and in interviews with newspapers, she laid out the charges succinctly. Teen suicide, poor achievement in school, and even obesity among kids can be linked to the fact more moms now work outside the home. She claims to have found an "astonishing level of neglect among middle-class and affluent youngsters" that could be traced at least in part to "stressed-out working mothers." She was still making the case against employed moms in 1996, in an article in *Parade,* the Sunday magazine supplement that reaches millions of Americans in their local newspapers.

The idea that children suffer from a "time famine" caused by their parents' overwork and materialism is now part of American culture. Mattox's figure—that working parents spend 40 percent less time with their kids—was often quoted as accepted fact, without even the need for attribution, in many media outlets. "Parents and children are spending 40 percent less time together than they did a generation ago," the *New York Times Magazine* reported. *Fortune* magazine asserted that "with more and more women joining the workforce, and many workaholic parents of both sexes," parents and kids spend just seventeen hours a week with their kids—the figure popularized by Mattox.

Yet Mattox's source for this figure, sociologist John Robinson at the University of Maryland, simply disagrees with Mattox's analysis. One of the nation's leading experts on the way Americans spend their time, Robinson has access to extensive diaries from regular folks who have been asked to track the way they use their time, hour by hour. He knows that the idea of a "time famine" is a popular one, but one he cannot substantiate in his research. "There's certainly a common misperception that families have less leisure time in general than they used to. But from what I can tell, the change is in the way people spend their time, not the overall amount of time they have," says Robinson. Over the past two decades, he argues, five of those thirty hours that Mattox cites as lost family time have actually been eaten up by the favorite American pastime—watching television. "I think the common perception that people have less time arises from what I call 'over-choice'—there are so many things out there to choose from, so many more activities and ways to spend leisure time. With so many choices, life appears more hectic and complicated."

Employed mothers might well beg to differ with Robinson—and agree with Mattox. There is very little doubt that they are one group of Americans with more demands on their time than most other people, especially when their children are very young. "The conservatives touch a nerve when they talk about a speedup," says Stephanie Coontz, family historian at Evergreen State College and author of *The Way We Really Are*. "Women certainly do feel pressure." Studies show, for example, that mothers with professional jobs in corporate America put in an eighty-hour week—thirty-three hours on child care and housework, in addition to forty-seven hours on the job. Professional men are also strapped for time, but not so intensely. They put in two more hours on the job—forty-nine hours—but only eighteen on child care and housework.

These figures challenge the thesis that Mattox and other conservatives advance—that children are hurt when mothers work. Rather than seventeen hours a week, women are putting in nearly twice that many—in addition to their full-time jobs.

If anything, it is women who pay the price for any time famine that may exist. Indeed, the great irony of the debate over whether mothers should work is that so many studies show that women are the ones making the sacrifices, both in terms of time for themselves and in earnings on the job. "Women are the shock-absorbers for change in our society. As we have changed family life, women have been the ones to absorb the change—mostly at their own expense," says Fran Rodgers of Work/Family Directions. Moms give up time for themselves—not time for children. They often take shortcuts in housework and meal preparation and reduce their own leisure time to see that their children's needs are met. "I'm very careful about my time. I have to decide who's going to get it and how much of it," says Louanne Allison, a manager for GMC Trucks, outside Detroit, and mother of two. Her days often start at 5:30 A.M. "I do prepare everybody for the day. I make sure the baby's fed, dressed, and ready to go, that the supplies are in the diaper bag. Most of the time, I do it because I *want* to. I want to know that everything's getting done and everybody's taken care of." In the late afternoon, she is often the one who makes sure her older child makes it to tumbling, Girl Scouts, and catechism. All that, she says, doesn't leave much time for herself. "Family, work, and church take up most of my time," she says. "We do like to get videos, and we do like to go for walks. But there really isn't much time just for myself."

That is the most startling finding of the latest research on the way Americans use their time. Indeed, the debate over "family values" inspired a closer look at the specific time that parents spend with their children. "The family values people and some others believe that child rearing is a full-time, twenty-four-hour-a-day job. But when you look at what it takes to raise a child and how people spend their time, it gets a lot more complicated," says sociologist Keith Bryant of Cornell University. That is why he and colleague Cathleen Zick decided to comb through time-use diaries and take another look at the sorts of activities that parents and children do together.

"To look at the impact of a mother's job on children, you have to look not only at the amount of time, but the composition of that time," says Zick, a family economist at the University of Utah and a leading expert on the ways working moms spend their time. "It's not surprising that employed moms spend less time in direct child care—

and so do employed men. But it's the composition of the time that matters in terms of child outcomes."

In plain English, children are known to benefit not just from having unlimited time with their mothers, but from having fun together, feeling listened to, feeling important and cared about when they are together. "You can't say certain parents are better just because they are there. A parent who works might spend more time talking or playing with her child," observes Steven Nock, a psychologist at the University of Virginia who studied several hundred couples in the late 1980s to ferret out any differences between families where moms worked and those where they didn't. Zick concurs. "We found that what really mattered were parenting styles, how Mom and Dad interact with their children, not the specific amount of time."

No serious researcher denies that real conflicts exist between work and family duties today, but the point is that they are not inherent to women's expanded roles. They are not inevitable. Instead, they result from the hostility working moms face on every front. And the old and false stereotypes about what makes a good worker and a good mother serve to encourage some of the darkest treatment women face as they try to earn a decent living and raise their children. They may not aspire to be as successful as Marcia Clark. But what they find is that they may not even be able to hang on to their paychecks once they become mothers.

5

Mothers Not Welcome Here

How the Myths Fuel Discrimination

MARY Q., a manager at Tiffany's, the world-famous jewelry store on Manhattan's Fifth Avenue, claims she got quite a greeting when she told her boss she was pregnant back in 1991.

"Oh, shit!" was how she recalls her boss's instant reaction to the news. In the courtroom, five years after the incident, her supervisor testified he never said that.

Mary Q.'s attorney would not allow her to discuss the case outside the courtroom, but in court, she indicated she was not too surprised by this alleged expletive. After all, she testified that her boss had made his views of mothers rather plain just a few months before she announced her pregnancy.

"Are you really serious about your career, or are you just going to go home and get pregnant?" she claims he asked her during her annual performance review. Given that comment, she chose not to tell him she was already expecting a baby at the time. Instead, she assured him that she was "very serious" about her career. In court, her boss also disavowed that comment.

Mary says, however, that her immediate supervisor was not the only manager at Tiffany's to hold stereotypical views about mother-hood and work. She says another executive took it upon himself to tell her that he believed it best for mothers to be at home, like his own wife. Mary replied that she did not have the luxury of this choice, and that she considered her income part of caring for her child. In court, this manager conceded that he may have talked to Mary about the importance of mothers bonding with their babies.

Seven months after Mary announced her pregnancy, and just a few months after the birth of her first child, Tiffany's notified her by mail that her $40,000-a-year job had been eliminated. The reason? A corporate reorganization.

Mary spent the next five years trying to get her original job back, first by pursuing the matter within the company and later by suing Tiffany's for pregnancy discrimination and for retaliation against her when she protested the discrimination. She claimed that while her title had been eliminated, her duties had simply been reassigned to childless workers. Tiffany's did eventually give her another posi-tion, but two levels below her original one, with less pay and fewer benefits. She lost stock options, a week of paid vacation, and some pension credits.

Tiffany's put up a vigorous defense, arguing that Mary lost her job only because of a necessary corporate reshuffling. And the jury in the case exonerated the company of pregnancy discrimina-tion. But the jurors did conclude that Tiffany's managers retaliated against Mary for filing a legal complaint of discrimination, and awarded her nearly $100,000 in punitive damages. Louis Satriale, the attorney representing Tiffany's, said company officials decided not to comment on the case. "It's all a matter of public record," Satriale said in the fall of 1997, "but that's all I was instructed to say about it. At this point, it's just not productive to discuss it any further."

But as Mary Q.'s case came to a close in the courtroom, another quiet drama about motherhood and work was taking place a half mile away. But these conversations took place out of public earshot, in the well-appointed offices of a New York City law firm. The partners here were devoting a small part of their monthly business meetings to casual speculation about which of the female associates were likely to become pregnant anytime soon. Three were in line to be partner, all in their early thirties. "One has already moved to the suburbs, so I'm betting she'll get pregnant first. No one moves to the suburbs unless they're thinking about kids," one of the partners joked during a conversation outside the office. "When she does, she'll probably quit her job. She's not going to be able to handle the commute and having kids." The partners decided to postpone any decisions about partnership for these young women until they saw how things shook out in the women's private lives. "Probably none of these women will make partner," this lawyer confided. "Once they have kids, they'll want to quit anyway."

High-achieving women in the financial field are well aware of the penalties women routinely suffer once they have children. "After I asked for maternity leave, I learned I wasn't going to get my bonus. I checked around with friends and learned that was pretty standard practice the year women take a maternity leave," says one investment banker who worked first for a major brokerage house in New York and then for a leading bank in the Southeast. A bonus is no small matter for her or her colleagues—it amounts to about half of her annual compensation. "I'm the breadwinner in our family, so this could really hurt," she adds. But she didn't want to challenge the decision for fear of being branded a troublemaker and blackballed in the banking world, she says, as she sips coffee at the Plaza Hotel in New York City.

But in checking with female colleagues, she says she quickly learned the name of someone who could help her if she ever decided to sue. And she kept the name handy, just in case.

Many talented and successful women include the name on their Rolodexes. It's one that few of their male colleagues have ever heard of: Judith Vladeck, an attorney who specializes in employment discrimination cases. It is a name the women trade with each other, in confidence, out of earshot of senior management. Some fear repercussions if their employers learn they have paid Vladeck a visit.

"Women on the Street know her name. We'd see it in the *New York Times,* winning one lawsuit after the next for women. We'd bring those stories into work and show them to each other. 'Did you see that article?' we'd say. 'This is my woman. I may need her some-day. She can make these guys shake!'" asserts a Wall Street trader who won an out-of-court sex discrimination settlement against one of the nation's leading brokerage houses.

Vladeck is not surprised to hear that she is well known among professional women in New York City. In the past few years, she says, hundreds of senior women from the world of high finance, from banks, insurance companies, and major corporations, have arrived here in her offices near Times Square, seeking counsel.

But that fact is not making Judith Vladeck happy. By now, she has earned national recognition for her decades of work on sex dis-crimination cases. A graduate of Columbia University's law school back in 1947, Vladeck has been on the front lines, both personally and professionally, as women have broken into the professions and corporate life. But now that a few have arrived in the pipeline to real power in the business world, they are learning some hard truths.

"Whatever picture you paint, it can't be bleak enough," Vladeck insists, in her low, gravelly voice. She pauses before speaking, choos-ing her words carefully. "Most young women think the war is over and now women can do anything they want. But that is total, absolute hogwash. Women should be told the truth. If they're going to . . . go into the professions or corporate America generally, into financial services, into law, into medicine, and have a child—or, per-ish the thought, have more than one—they're going to suffer."

Vladeck delivers this pronouncement with utter assurance, based on the women who walk into her offices in midtown Manhattan each day. "The assumption will be that they have taken themselves off whatever their career track might be." And, she adds, "they will pay a price for that.

"Let me tell you about a case that walked through my door in just the past few weeks," she says. "I had a woman with a high-risk preg-nancy because she was going to have twins. She delivered the babies, returned to work quickly. Her first day back on the job after maternity leave, she was put on probation and told her job was in jeopardy. Can you imagine that, a few weeks after you've delivered twins?"

The reason is obvious to Vladeck, from her years of representing such women. "Having a baby is used as an excuse not to give women opportunities," says Vladeck. "Women are still stereotyped. The assumption is that they have made a choice, that having children ends their commitment to their career.

"Women postpone having children because of these attitudes," she adds, only to learn that even putting off motherhood doesn't help. "Even if they take just six weeks to be with their babies, they come back and find their jobs are given to somebody else, that a job opening that should have been theirs was given to someone else, that their job was eliminated when they went on maternity leave. I've seen it in every area, in every kind of workplace."

Janice Goodman, another well-known employment rights attorney working just a few blocks away in midtown Manhattan, nods when she hears Vladeck's assessment. Goodman has also spent the better part of three decades litigating sex discrimination cases and, like Vladeck, has a national reputation for her savvy negotiations on behalf of women. And she is not seeing as much progress as she'd hoped for. "I hear and read that there are premier corporations that have policies to help women and even help with child care. But I haven't seen that happening," she says. "Of the cases I see for sex discrimination, the majority are for pregnancy discrimination, and I don't see any change in attitudes over the years." She sighs. "Some days, I feel like I'm just litigating the same cases over and over again.

"With senior women, managers, and directors, the most prevalent thing that happens is that they get sidetracked in their careers," she says. "I've seen a whole bunch of traders on Wall Street, for example. They'd go out on maternity leave—that was no problem. In fact, some of the leaves can be extremely generous—three or four months at full pay.

"But when they come back from leave, important clients have been taken away from them. Before the leave, they would have the Chryslers and the GMs and the Hewlett-Packards. But when they come back, all they get are the mom-and-pop grocery stores. That change in clients makes a big difference in their compensation package and where they go as a career path. You're not going to get advanced if you have ma-and-pa grocery stores as your clients. Those clients don't make the trades that bring in the money.

"The concept is sort of the same in big corporations. After maternity leave, women come back and the employer says, 'We've "reorganized."' A woman may have had twenty people reporting to her in the past, but when she comes back, it's only one person."

Goodman pauses for a moment, thinking about the women she's seen in recent years. "I've watched these women and they're really devastated. This is supposed to be a happy time in their lives. They've had their babies and they intend to go back to work. It's devastating to have it happen at that time," she says.

So it was for one woman, one of Judith Vladeck's clients, who spent more than a decade working at one of the nation's best-known Wall Street firms before she had her first child. Sworn to secrecy, she spoke off the record. Not even Vladeck knows that she's talked to a reporter. "At first, I felt life was so rich. I can remember when I came back to work, I felt so lucky. I remember walking around thinking, 'I've got this wonderful baby, wonderful husband, and wonderful job. I feel so enriched.'"

But within months of maternity leave, life at work began to sour. It began when she stopped going out for drinks after work. She was passed over for a long-awaited promotion, despite the fact that she was still making her budget and bringing in plenty of new clients for the firm. She protested being passed over, but resolved to be patient. But it did her no good. Her supervisors now assigned her second-rate clients with smaller accounts.

A Wall Street veteran, she knew her career would dead-end if she couldn't get better clients sent her way soon. Without big trading accounts, she couldn't bring in the big money and her career would soon be in free fall. She lobbied her bosses, wrote memos, documented what she believed to be discrimination against her. She also consulted Vladeck, who advised her to put everything in writing. Still, things did not change. "By then, they started telling me that I had a 'combative personality' because I was pressing the issue. I told them I thought I'd been patient enough. For two years, I'd made my numbers while men got promoted and I didn't," she says. "It had all changed after I had my baby. And when I stopped acting like one of the guys, when I stopped going out for drinks with them. I had spent sixteen years on the Street, but I now had a commitment to my kids. I wasn't going to stay late and go out drinking just for the sake of staying late and schmoozing with the other traders."

In the midst of the career difficulties, she had her second child, and she decided to make a change herself. "I could see they weren't going to promote me or give me any good clients. So I went to my boss and I said, 'Instead of promoting me, I'll take a four-day work-week,'" she says. "I figured it was better to keep my job and get a better lifestyle than to struggle with these guys." In May, she was granted the new schedule. Five months later, she was laid off. "I knew it was going to happen. I wasn't even dumbstruck. I'd been through all the bad feelings six to eight months before. First you cry about it, then you say to yourself, 'This is my life. I have to take it in my hands and change it,'" she says.

The day her boss fired her, he told her it was because business was slow. By then, she was ready for him. "I let him know I was going to hold him accountable for the way I'd been treated since I had my kids," she says. Her anger is still palpable. "I wanted to put some acid in his stomach, so he'd suffer a little." She told him she was going to sue.

Within weeks, she won an out-of-court settlement. It was generous enough for her to set up her own business, which she now runs out of her home. Many of the women she keeps up with on the Street think she is lucky to have her own business and be close to her kids. None of them know that she won the start-up funds from her former employer. "I can't talk about the settlement. So they think I just wanted a lifestyle change," she says.

Attorney Janice Goodman is cynical about the willingness of most major employers to change. "If they [big companies] wanted to change, they'd give these women their jobs back," she says. "But that's the one thing you can't ever seem to get. When you call, their attorneys say, 'Well, what do you have in mind? Do you have a figure?' They never admit they did anything wrong, but they're willing to settle financially. They pay off these women, and that cost is just factored into the cost of doing business."

Nancy Shilepsky, an employment rights attorney with the Boston firm of Dwyer and Collora, also handles plenty of sex discrimination cases. "I joke with other attorneys that out-of-court settlements are simply a licensing fee to discriminate," she says.

Vladeck concurs. "If these companies really cared about making an environment more hospitable to women, they would change these male shops. The message has to come from the top. They have to send the message that this has to change. But they obviously don't care. It's a matter of economic indifference," she says. She, too, contends that the companies simply figure in out-of-court settlements as an ongoing business expense.

As attorneys who represent workers in discrimination cases, these women do, of course, tend to see only the underside of corporate life. And Vladeck knows as well as anyone that women have made some truly significant gains in the workplace. She knows firsthand how things have changed. She recalls how difficult it was when she was pregnant with her second child in the 1950s, and she worked with her husband. "My husband shared a suite with other lawyers. They thought a pregnant woman in a professional office was extremely inappropriate. They got together and asked him if I could confine my visits to the office to nighttimes and weekends."

She went along with it. After all, in those days, she knew she was lucky to work as a lawyer at all. She'd gotten her slot at Columbia's law school during World War II, and she was constantly reminded why. "There was such a shortage of men going to law school that women could get in. But I remember the dean of the law school saying we didn't belong there. Many of the teachers were horrible. They'd say, 'Why are you here, anyway? You're taking a seat away from a man. You're just going to get married, anyway, and quit working.'"

The women who walk into Vladeck's offices today have the weight of the law on their side—the civil rights laws of the 1960s, the Pregnancy Discrimination Act of 1978, and most recently, the Family and Medical Leave Act of 1993. With such protection, more are willing to challenge ill-treatment. Says one woman of her firing, "I wasn't upset when it actually happened. I had anticipated it. By the time my boss delivered the news, I knew I had a good case against them. I had documented my case every step of the way. I was more interested in putting him on the hot seat, to let him know I was going to hold him accountable."

Women are also more confident generally, even more willing to declare themselves "ambitious" after having children. Some 92 percent of the 1,250 women surveyed by *Working Mother* magazine in the fall of 1997 called themselves "ambitious" or "highly ambitious." That is a dramatic turnaround from earlier generations, who feared such a label would brand them unwomanly.

And as is widely reported, women now hold more than a third of all management jobs and are more widely represented in the professions of law, medicine, financial services, and corporate America.

But there is a growing body of evidence that reveals a more complicated truth about where women stand today—and lends credibility to the darker picture painted by Vladeck and Goodman. The oft-cited statistics on women making strides in middle management, for example, tell only part of the story. These women, it turns out, are still clustered in jobs that tend to pay less and offer less opportunity for advancement, such as human resources and public affairs, according to a raft of studies emerging over the past decade. And the pay gap among managers is wider than in other categories. Female managers make just 59 percent of what their male counterparts do.

Their progress into the upper ranks also remains stalled, despite the fact there are more of them and they are better educated and more experienced than any previous generation. That is the news from report after report issued in the 1990s, from the Federal Glass Ceiling Commission to Catalyst, a nonprofit think tank in New York that monitors women's progress in the workplace.

Sociologist Barbara Reskin at Ohio State University has identified what she calls the persistent "authority gap" for women. "The growing numbers of women who have the title of manager are concentrated lower in chains of command than men are and tend not to supervise men," she says. Those who participate in decision making tend to be relegated to gathering the information and making recommendations to male managers with more authority. She and other researchers note that women are often not given the same resources as men to succeed on the job—they often lack control over the budget and the power to hire employees. "When you get into the management ranks, it's so male," says one executive woman who works for a major automobile manufacturer. "I constantly find myself the only woman in meetings with thirty or forty men. I analyze the data and make a recommendation to get the money to get the job done. I can do it, but it's a constant struggle. The men take care of the men." She did not get a raise or a bonus after her first baby. "A few years later, I realized how much that hurt. I was at the bottom of the pay scale for my level. They are not comfortable with women, let alone mothers. I know I am productive. I have the numbers to prove it. I got a promotion last year, but no raise."

Most disturbing of all, the pay penalty that women suffer once they become mothers grew considerably worse in the 1980s, even though women with children tended to be better educated and more attached to the workforce than those who preceded them. "Family status continues to be quite important in explaining the lower pay of working mothers. It accounted for a large part of the gender gap in 1980, but an even larger part in 1991," says Jane Waldfogel, an economist at Columbia University who has studied the impact of motherhood on women's wages. Childless women's wages reached almost near parity with men's; women without children now earn about 90 percent of what men do. Mothers, by comparison, earn just 75 percent of what fathers do. This fact could not be explained by a difference in experience or skills.

Nor is it because mothers choose to scale back their hours and work less when the baby arrives, Waldfogel says. Rather, it is the combined impact of both the practical barriers and bias that mothers face. Many lose seniority and wages, for example, because their employers do not offer maternity leave. In fact, only about half of all working parents in America today can count on getting even an unpaid maternity leave. Fewer still receive any paycheck at all, unless they hoard vacation and sick days.

And as the stories from attorneys and court records show, women face a fierce and persistent prejudice once they become mothers. The number of pregnancy discrimination cases filed with the federal Equal Employment Opportunity Commission steadily rose in the 1990s, from 3,000 in 1991 to 4,191 in 1995. Many hear the same refrain as Lisa Bailey, who was fired from her job as a receptionist for a small company in Virginia in 1994. In court papers, she said she was told that she was "no longer dependable since she had delivered a child," that "her place was at home," and that "babies get sick sometimes and Bailey would have to miss work to care for her child." A lower court judge even condoned this treatment, but in October 1997, the Virginia Supreme Court ruled that Bailey had grounds for a lawsuit. The case was eventually settled out of court; Bailey received a monetary settlement, but her employer refused to concede to any wrongdoing. The difficulty so many women face after having a baby is the very sort of scenario that Waldfogel and other researchers believe contributes to the pay gap between mothers and other workers. Women have trouble maintaining their earnings. "On balance, men get a premium for getting married and having children, and women are penalized," says Waldfogel. By 1991, the biggest gap in earnings was the one between moms working full-time and dads working full-time; the average mom earned just sixty cents for every dollar that a dad made. In other words, the simple fact of having kids hurt women's earnings—and boosted men's.

Other research confirms this bias. Studies by Linda Stroh, a professor at the University of Chicago, took a hard look at the pay and career progression of 1,029 male and female managers in Fortune 1,000 companies. The men and women in her study were matched for education, experience, and commitment to work, demonstrated by such things as their willingness to relocate for the job and to travel. Even with identical work records, women's pay still lagged behind men's. "Discrimination is one of the only logical explanations," she concluded.

Many mothers may not be aware of the profound and growing gap between men and women, however, since most still work in largely segregated settings, with no means for comparison. The top four occupations for women remained exactly the same in 1995 as they were in 1975: secretaries, administrators, cashiers, and book-keepers. Next came nurses and nursing aides. Even more profound, many jobs are still labeled "female" at many, if not most, companies. "When we looked at individual companies, we found sex segregation to be even more pronounced than when you look at occupations," says sociologist William Bielby, who has served as an expert witness in many prominent sex discrimination cases. In one in-depth study of 500 California companies in the early 1980s, he and a colleague found that 90 percent of all jobs were segregated—that is, a particular job, such as clerk or secretary, was held only by men or only by women. Not surprisingly, the higher-paying jobs were often associated with traits and activities thought to be male, and the lower-paying jobs associated with traits often stereotyped as female, such as caregiving and nurturing. "It's often said that women make rational choices about working, that they prefer certain jobs, even though they are lower-paying," says Bielby. "But that kind of argument can't explain the nearly total segregation that we've found repeatedly in so many companies."

In one class-action suit against Home Depot, depositions collected from male managers indicated that such stereotyping seemed simply commonsensical to many of them. Home Depot eventually settled the case without admitting any wrongdoing. However, one manager said women "feel comfortable being in a cashier position" and that the "male gender is not necessarily equipped" to do word processing on computers or filing in the vault departments. Another said that one of the reasons that women are disproportionately represented in cashier positions is that the company wants people it hires to "feel comfortable in the positions which they do."

Bielby, like other researchers, finds that women's "family responsibilities" are frequently cited by managers as a reason not to put women in certain jobs or on certain shifts. "Choice always explains some of the differences, but that argument is vastly overstated. If you look at surveys of what men and women value on the job, and you use a truly representative sample, what you find is that they value the same things—job security, the opportunity to get ahead, and decent pay."

He adds, however, that people often shape their behavior to meet employers' expectations. "In the cases against grocery store chains, the employer will say, 'We dug up some applications; women never apply for night crew or stock clerk.' But that kind of information doesn't take into account what men and women do because they perceive it to be the employer's preference. We've found that if a woman wants to maximize her chances of getting hired, she'll apply for jobs where she sees a lot of women. If she sees women are mostly cashiers, she'll apply to be a cashier."

It is when women push the envelope, when they seek a job in the professions or in a male-dominated field such as construction, that they feel the most heat. Challenging deeply held biases about the way women should act, and most especially the way mothers should act, they often face the harshest treatment and suffer the gravest penalties. Even today, they are treated the way Vladeck was back in the 1950s, as if they are taking jobs away from men, especially when the economy weakens.

The Bar Association of the City of New York, for example, recently funded a study of women's status in major law firms and found women falling behind. Women had moved slowly but steadily upward throughout the go-go 1980s as many firms expanded. Some big Wall Street firms had even quadrupled in size and made room for women. But in the early 1990s, as hard times hit, women's prospects dimmed considerably. Indeed, the percentage of women making partner dropped from 15 to 5 percent in just two years.

If not in a backlash, the nation's employers remain remarkably resistant to change. "I tend to describe myself as an optimist," says Charles Rodgers, chairman of WFD Consulting, the research arm of Work/Family Directions. "But I'm not optimistic about women's representation in the senior ranks. Many people think that it's just a matter of time before women make it to the top jobs. But I think the barriers into the pipeline to top-level jobs are more persistent than people think."

And when it comes to the very top jobs, women's stalled progress is truly confounding. In 1970, they held 3 percent of the most senior jobs at Fortune 500 corporations. Today, it is only 5 percent, despite women's increasing experience, education, and demonstrated interest in the jobs.

As one looks at the data and listens to women themselves, it's hard to miss one critical fact in all of this. More than anything, the meaning and impact of motherhood shadows every woman, narrowing her options. Even those without children may be made to feel the heat; the mere fact that they are of childbearing age may compromise their career prospects. As a mom, a woman may find it impossible to prove herself to senior managers. The core myth, of course, is that women automatically and voluntarily scale back their commitment to work the minute they have a baby. And like many other false assumptions about women, this one remains stubbornly resistant to change.

A SOCIALLY SANCTIONED BIAS

Many forms of sexist behavior—making lewd comments or unwanted sexual advances, for example—are off-limits in most workplaces by now. But treating women differently on the basis of motherhood is another matter entirely. Speaking up about what it takes to be a good mother is an American pastime, on and off the job. New mothers are often the targets of unsolicited advice, scolded even by strangers on the street about dressing a baby too warmly or not warmly enough, advising them to put a hat on their infant or take it off. Most certainly, many of those doling out the advice do it out of what they believe to be the best of intentions.

That license carries over to the workplace, where many managers feel little compunction about sharing their bias about what it takes to be a good mom, telling women that motherhood and work don't mix—even if the result is to deny a woman a raise or a promotion, or to eliminate her job altogether.

Ironically, at the same time, many Americans see motherhood as the *explanation* for women's failure to advance on the job, even though that is not the case. "One of the most common reasons men—and women, for that matter—gave for women's failure to advance was that they would quit after they had a baby," says Joanne Totta, executive vice president of the Bank of Montreal. Totta oversaw a four-year effort at the bank to eliminate barriers that held women back. When she started out, women made up 75 percent of the workforce, but held only 9 percent of the most senior jobs. When bank officials made a systematic effort to find out why, managers told them, in written surveys and focus groups, that women of childbearing age were frequently passed over for promotions, raises, or high-profile jobs because they were simply seen as a bad risk. "The attitude seemed to be, 'Why should I invest in training these women—they're just going to get married, get pregnant, have babies, and then quit.'"

This supposed truth of the psyche persisted against the evidence. When Totta reviewed women's employment patterns at the bank, she learned that 98 percent of those who went out on maternity leave returned to their previous jobs within a few months of childbirth. Women also tended to have longer tenure with the bank, staying for several years longer than men at every level, except senior management. Junior-level women, for example, stayed at the bank nearly fourteen years, compared with seven and a half for men. "Even I was surprised at the high rate of retention," Totta recalls.

The Bank of Montreal is unusual and exemplary in that its top executives bothered to thoroughly investigate this stereotype and its impact on women's chances for advancement. In the fall of 1995, Catalyst reported that "the stock answer" corporate executives give to the question of why women leave big companies is to stay home and raise a family.

That women's childbearing status is still kept constantly in mind and works to devalue women is not even an open question for sociologist Cynthia Fuchs Epstein at the Graduate Center of the City University of New York and author of *Deceptive Distinctions*, which probes the enormous impact of sexual stereotyping on women. "In professional life, as in the rest of society, women are often regarded as potential mothers if they are childless but of child-bearing age," she notes in her research.

As such, their commitment to the workplace is under constant scrutiny and their value to their employer open to constant question. After conducting in-depth interviews with men and women at eight leading law firms in New York City, Epstein discovered that many senior partners were reluctant to groom young women for top positions, to introduce them to lucrative clients, or to otherwise mentor them and help them succeed. As one lawyer put it, "If they don't think the person is going to be here for the long haul, they're not going to waste so much time with them . . . like there's a woman . . . she's going to get married, and she's going to leave. Why should we invest in her?"

This general unwillingness to invest in, mentor, and develop young women, she concluded, was one of the major reasons why women's advancement into partnership positions slowed or stopped altogether in the early 1990s. Tougher economic times at even the most prestigious firms created an unprecedented competition among young lawyers vying to be partners, she noted, making it harder than ever for any new associate to make partner. Without help from senior partners, women fell far behind men.

Similar problems were turned up by the Harvard Women's Law Association, a band of Harvard law students who decided to publish a guide to the nation's major law firms, based on questionnaires sent to senior women in the firms. They published their findings in 1995, much to the chagrin of Harvard's administration, which refused to kick in funding for the publication of the guide. Even a casual perusal of the book reveals the same prejudices at work that Epstein so painstakingly documented. "Many noted that mothers, by definition, are subject to pernicious stereotypes which label them as 'less committed to the firm, regardless of the hours they work or the work they deliver.'"

But it's not just professional women who suffer from such stereotypes. Several major lawsuits won against grocery store chains in the far West revealed that the same issues shadow women in all sorts of jobs, as Bielby notes. Managers at Lucky Stores, for example, cited women's "family responsibilities" as a reason not to put women into management-track jobs. The managers assumed that the jobs would simply be too demanding for any women with children.

Researchers and policymakers have become ever more concerned about why such bias still persists, given women's increasing commitment to work. Nearly every study of their attitudes shows that women work for the same reasons men do: For the money, first of all. But also for the satisfaction of using their skills. And four out of five return to work after the birth of a baby.

So a growing cadre of academics and consultants have grown more intent on finding out why it's so hard to change attitudes in the workplace.

NEW SCIENCE ON BIAS

Over the past decade, a new generation of scholars, led mostly by young women who came of age with the feminist movement, have begun to peel back the layers of Americans' most deeply held beliefs and shed light on the thinking process that justifies bias on the job. In effect, they have begun to illuminate the contours of discrimination, to understand what it is, when it occurs, and why it is so resistant to change. The new science of stereotyping also helps to explain why gender bias is especially powerful, and so embedded in the culture as to seem nearly invisible, why the catchphrase "glass ceiling" is such an apt description of the resistance women still face in the workplace.

And their work is especially relevant to mothers, who have special status in American society. In their dual roles of worker and parent, they are caught in the cross fire of mutually exclusive stereotypes. "Because I'm a mother and a wife, it is assumed that those roles might get in the way, that I won't be able to devote as much time to my job as a man would," one mom told investigators for the Wisconsin Glass Ceiling Commission.

Such attitudes cost women plenty of money. In Wisconsin, only 186 women were making more than $100,000 in 1990. That, as compared with 8,992 men. The hope of the new research is to turn that around and put women on an equal footing with men.

OLD PROBLEM, NEW VISION

Scientists have long explored the profound impact of cultural stereotypes in American life. As far back as 1922, psychologists were able to demonstrate that Americans were willing to systematically ascribe certain traits to people based on race, gender, or ethnicity. In pioneering studies, psychologists conducted their first, rudimentary surveys, presenting Americans with checklists of adjectives, and found Americans readily able and willing to define those traits as either male or female, black or white, and so on.

Over the years, they also learned that stereotypes about gender run particularly deep. "People place gender ahead of most everything, even race or age," says Kay Deaux, distinguished professor of psychology at the Graduate Center of City University of New York. Sociologists and psychologists launched many studies of how girls and boys, men and women, absorb messages about what is male and what is female, and about how to make career choices based on those values. By the 1970s the women's movement had the entire culture talking about the way women were channeled into jobs related to caregiving, such as nursing, teaching, and social work, and men into jobs related to physical strength, such as construction work.

By now, no social scientist disputes the power of such stereotypes. Even in the 1980s, studies showed that Americans continued to take gender into account in critical decisions on the job. Given two résumés of equally qualified male and female candidates, for example, most still would choose the man for a management position.

But until relatively recently, most psychologists did not understand just why stereotypes were so ingrained and difficult to change. Prior to the 1970s, scientists described them as simply a "shared set of cultural beliefs," enforced by a system of subtle and not-so-subtle rewards and punishments, an unspoken social contract of sorts. Men earned higher wages, for example, largely because of a shared belief that men were the breadwinners for their families and therefore needed a higher salary than women. Women earned less out of a belief that they could depend on a man to support them.

But in the 1970s, cognitive psychologists studying how people recall and retain information opened up an entirely new way of studying prejudice. The origins of bias, it turned out, might lie in a perfectly rational response to daily life. Each day, in each new situation, people have to quickly judge each new person or situation, to decide how to respond to it. They do so by sorting their experiences into categories—or stereotypes—based on previous experience or knowledge. "It's a cognitive shorthand, if you will," says Deaux, one of the pioneers of this new research. "It saves us time and effort. It makes life manageable. We'd be overwhelmed if we had to start doing a calculus of everything we know about men or women every time we encounter something new."

Not surprisingly, gender—one of the most noticeable and emotionally salient differences in life—becomes an integral part of many stereotypes. For example, if most executives are male, the ideas of maleness and leadership in the workplace meld together into a single category. At times, when people encounter a situation that runs counter to this shorthand, they may not know how to evaluate the new information. In fact, studies show that most people reject or simply forget the exception to their rule.

"Stereotypes are remarkably resistant to change. What we know from the research is that you remember the things that fit into your template in your mind, the system of beliefs that make up the stereotype. You remember the things you believe, and the things you don't believe, you simply don't remember," says Deaux.

In one pioneering study Deaux conducted, for example, managers in a steel plant recalled that women had inferior work records to men's, when they based it simply on memory, without consulting their written records. Their recollections did not jibe with their previously written evaluations, however, which showed that the men and women had performed at about the same level. "They remembered the women who made mistakes and the men who did well because it fit their expectations," Deaux says.

For psychologists interested in gender discrimination, this new view opened up a promising new avenue of research. Unlike the social scientists who preceded them, they had separated the content of stereotypes from the process of stereotyping. The new view held that everyone, even the most well-meaning among us, is prone to categorize others. At what point does that stereotype turn into bias? What information do people use to create a stereotype, how do they refine or reject a general category, and under what circumstances do they rely on it wholeheartedly? Why would one supervisor see gender as the most important piece of information about a person?

No psychologist was more excited by the possibilities of this new theory than Susan Fiske, then a graduate student in psychology at Harvard. She had come of age in the early 1970s, at the height of the women's movement, and questions of differences between the sexes absorbed her interest.

She used the new perspective to produce a Ph.D. thesis at Harvard that laid out basic new tenets of gender discrimination—ideas that would shortly become the winning arguments in a landmark sex discrimination lawsuit against the accounting firm of Price Waterhouse that went all the way to the U.S. Supreme Court. In both the laboratory and fieldwork, she began to identify the conditions that most often promote stereotyping in the workplace. First and foremost, she noted, people who are part of a distinct minority, those who make up 15 percent or less of a workforce, are most likely to be stereotyped. Their "solo or near-solo status" becomes the thing people notice most about them, and not surprisingly so. A woman in an all-male workplace certainly stands out. "The difference becomes the focus of attention," says Fiske.

And, in the absence of written rules and policies, the woman's gender becomes her defining trait—and she will be evaluated by gender, rather than performance. In other words, the men in a predominately male workplace are likely to fall back on their stereotypical thinking—that women are less committed to the workplace, for example, and therefore a poor risk in management. That is especially true, Fiske found, if managers have very little information or interaction with the woman. "We all fall back on our gut feelings in the absence of other information," Fiske notes.

In practical terms, these conditions described the common experience of women executives in most American businesses. Holding fewer than 5 percent of the most senior jobs, their gender becomes a defining characteristic. The idea that women and other minorities were seen as "tokens" had gained some currency at the time, through the work of sociologist Rosabeth Moss Kanter, author of *Men and Women of the Corporation*.

But Fiske defined the conditions so precisely and so concretely that they became useful in a court of law. She used the written and oral evaluations made by managers in performance reviews to show when a person's gender became the salient factor in deciding whether to offer a raise, promotion, or other benefit in the workplace. Women might be described as "nurturing" or "not tough enough," for example, even when they produced good bottom-line results. This type of documentation not only opened a window on bias in the workplace, but provided a technique for attorneys to produce a written and oral record of managers' decision-making process in order to build a case.

The work of Fiske and others also demonstrated how simple policies and procedures could blunt the effects of prejudice. Managers who were forced to gather specific information about job candidates and measure them against specific job descriptions and criteria for promotion were less likely to make decisions based on stereotypes—even if they initially typecast women. Rather than assuming a woman did not want to or could not lift heavy items, for example, a manager might administer a test of strength.

Fiske was drawn to her subject out of a hope that it could be useful to real women, that she could contribute ways to better understand and stem discrimination in the real world. And that is exactly what happened when she was asked to serve as an expert witness on behalf of Ann Hopkins, a woman charging Price Waterhouse with sexual discrimination.

Few cases could have been better suited to showing the truth of Fiske's assertions. As the only woman among eighty-eight candidates for partner, Hopkins was certainly in a distinct minority, putting the spotlight on her gender. Further, the firm used vague criteria for evaluating her performance. Although Hopkins had more billable hours than any other candidate, had sterling recommendations from many clients, and had brought in $25 million worth of new business, she was told she failed to make partner because she had a difficult personality. In particular, managers at the firm told her she was too "macho"; one coworker even suggested that she might make partner if she learned to "walk more femininely, wear makeup, have her hair styled, and wear jewelry."

As an expert witness, Fiske was able to use such statements by senior partners to show exactly how stereotyping led to discrimination against Hopkins. Not only was Hopkins solo, but the partners relied on the vague criteria of "personality" for evaluating her. With eighty-eight candidates to evaluate, the partners also failed to take a comprehensive look at Hopkins's record. They relied on sketchy negative reports, when there was also evidence that Hopkins got on very well with many clients. In the end, then, her fate rested on her gender. The Price Waterhouse partners judged her fitness as a woman, rather than as a partner in an accounting firm.

Fiske's testimony was novel. In the past, attorneys had relied on statistical evidence or outright evidence of hostility to prove discrimination cases. Attorneys for Price Waterhouse asserted that her research did not constitute science at all, but rather "women's intuition," "soft ideas," "gossamer" reasoning. But Judge Gerhard Gessell found Fiske's work illuminating. During the trial, he peppered Fiske with questions and read widely in the psychological literature before siding firmly on the side of Hopkins. "Gender-based stereotyping played a role" in Price Waterhouse's decision not to make Hopkins a partner, he asserted. Elsewhere in his opinion, he noted that the "subtle influence of sex upon a person's perceptions may vary with each observer and play both an unconscious and conscious role in influencing actions taken." When Price Waterhouse appealed the decision, the American Psychological Association stepped in to defend Fiske's work as legitimate science, in a friend-of-the-court brief.

Hopkins's case was decided in 1992. Since then, three conditions have become widely recognized in the courts to fuel discrimination—and they are three conditions that exist at the top of every workplace in America. Most important, the research shows that people tend to suffer discrimination when they comprise 5 percent or less of a particular group—as is the case for women in the senior ranks of most companies. "One of the biggest problems for women is that they still don't have a critical mass in corporate America," asserts Vladeck. "There are still so few of them; some are scared if they're even seen in discussion with other women. Yet one woman standing alone is very vulnerable. After all, no one is perfect. Everyone has their flaws, and I worry that they are going to get picked off, one by one."

Charles Rodgers, chairman of WFD Consulting, the management consulting arm of Work/Family Directions, echoes the concern. "Can you generate any real change without more women in senior management?" he asks. "I don't think so. The notion of critical mass is important. A woman on her own doesn't want to raise the issues, to fight the battles. There are so many ways you can get sabotaged."

Discrimination is also more likely when companies lack formal procedures for hiring and evaluating employees and when people making decisions have little information about a person to work from. In such situations, people do what would seem to be the most reasonable thing—they fall back on their gut feelings, which are often stereotypical.

One woman described how the informal process works at Wisconsin companies. In that state, many executives like to hunt and fish in their spare time; it's an "outdoor man's corporate culture," according to that state's glass ceiling commission, with golf, hunting, fishing, and ball games at the center of conversation. And if you don't fit in that culture, one executive woman says, "you just don't move up; you don't hear about job openings. There are no postings for higher-level jobs." Without access to the inner circle, there is simply no way to even find out about a job opening. And she adds, "The openings aren't posted because they have someone in mind. The boys are used to working together and they are just plain comfortable together."

SOLUTIONS ARE SIMPLE

Happily, the research also offers a fairly simple antidote for such discrimination. And it's basically the stuff of most affirmative action programs and the job rules that most unions insist upon. Women—and other groups of workers who are underrepresented in certain jobs and may fall prey to stereotypes—need to be actively recruited, job openings need to be publicized, and companies need to have written criteria for evaluating and promoting workers. Additional measures, such as diversity training, can also help managers grow more aware of their own tendency to stereotype and how to avoid it. With such training, many managers are persuaded to shed their prejudice and approach each woman on the merits of her performance.

In some cases, of course, such procedures don't work. Some managers are so attached to the prejudices that they resist such training—they often poke fun at it and continue to act on their gut values. Social psychologists call this "prescriptive" use of stereotypes. And the very newest research shows the people most likely to do that are the ones who subscribe to traditional gender roles for women, those with a strong sense of "gender ideology"—that is, the belief that men and women have different roles and responsibilities and these roles should not be violated.

Interestingly, these beliefs may be delivered in a way that is seemingly benevolent. "It's what I call the 'women are wonderful' effect," says psychologist Deaux. "Women are described as nurturing and sensitive and caring—especially women who are mothers." The trouble is, as Deaux notes, "those aren't the skills that are generally valued in the workplace." Indeed, women may suffer penalties, even lose their jobs, in the face of such "benevolent" stereotypes. They find themselves struggling, as Marcia Clark did, to succeed in roles that so many Americans see as contradictory. How can a soft, nurturing mom prosecute a murder case? Women with less stamina than Clark often find themselves out of a job or overlooked for a promotion—unless employers take aggressive action to change the minds and hearts of managers who so deeply subscribe to outdated roles for women.

VEIL OF SECRECY

The scope of women's problems is shielded partly because of the way the legal system works. Women who win out-of-court settlements are usually sworn to secrecy, paid off by the companies that spurned them. Their court documents are sealed, and they could be sued themselves for publicizing their case and their fate. Those who will talk about the problems they've faced often do so furtively and fearfully, and only with strict assurance they will not be identified.

Their silence keeps them apart from each other. They don't learn the common threads of their experiences. Many think it is only their industry, or their company. They are surprised to learn that other women have suffered through nearly identical treatment, sidelined or fired from major companies. Their cases are thus rarely brought to public attention and their remedies rarely involve collective action.

Their isolation is also amplified by changes in the law. In the past two decades, in the face of an increasingly conservative political climate, sex discrimination attorneys have lost some of the key tools once used to promote broad-based change for women. Most notably, class-action lawsuits are harder to bring and to win. Given this situation, Judith Vladeck sees only one solution. "I don't think women have yet realized their only real hope in our lifetime is to work collectively. Together, women can be quite formidable. I told dozens of women in the last year that until they organize themselves and speak up, there will be no progress. My contribution to the cause is to rent a hotel room and put out a call to the few hundred women I've spoken with. Once they start talking, they'll find out their experiences are endemic. They might begin to understand their common predicament and work to change it."

That was the solution used by the women of another era, who fought to get equal rights laws on the books. But today, mothers find their problems are harder to solve, because at times, they are even harder to name. The most difficult barrier, many find, is the very structure and nature of work itself. To succeed, they must conform to the rules designed for families of another era. At times, that comes with a very high price tag. It is a price men are never asked to pay.

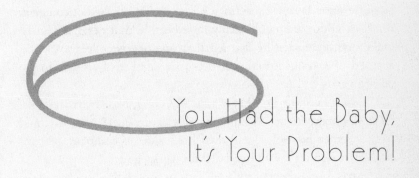

You Had the Baby, It's Your Problem!

Justifying the Inflexible Workplace

BARRY HARRIS sat in stunned silence. A top executive at SC Johnson Wax, one of the nation's premier marketers of household products, he was taken aback by the anger now pouring from some of the company's senior women. In a three-day session led by an outside management consultant, he suddenly gained a window on a reality that coexisted with his own, one that had been invisible to him during his fifteen years at this family-owned Midwestern business. He learned what it was like to be a woman at this company.

During this particular exercise, the men had been instructed to remain quiet while the women spoke, a common practice among diversity trainers. Thus, Harris was now regaled with stories of the offensive comments women endured when they announced a pregnancy, of the way their opinions were disregarded or dismissed in meetings, of the inquisitions they faced when they had to take a lit-

tle time off to take a sick child to the pediatrician. He learned how
they struggled to find last-minute child care to cover breakfast and
late-afternoon business meetings, which he himself had often called
on short notice and could easily have been held at other times. To
make matters worse, he learned that one of his colleagues stood
accused of making sexual overtures to a number of women in the
company.

"I was ignorant of what was really going on," Harris recalls.
"The whole experience was unbelievably depressing." After listening
to the women honestly detail their life inside his company, he concluded, "I wouldn't want my daughter working here."

Harris found the women's revelations especially shocking, since
he prided himself and SC Johnson Wax on treating employees
well. The company's Racine, Wisconsin, headquarters boasted a
state-of-the-art child care center, still a rare occurrence in corporate
America. Employees and their families were welcome to use the on-
site recreation center, with its Olympic-sized pool, basketball courts,
gym, and workout rooms. SC Johnson Wax also had a good health
plan and paid its employees well. All this in an era when many companies were cutting back benefits and downsizing. He believed he
was an enlightened boss of the 1990s, working at an enlightened
company.

And with good reason. Even outside these walls, SC Johnson
Wax had a hard-earned national reputation for being a great company for women to work for. The corporation was a regular on
Working Mother magazine's much-acclaimed list of family-friendly
employers.

Indeed, Harris expected this diversity-training session to be a
huge waste of time, given all the attention the company had already
put into making the workplace more hospitable to women. Even
worse, it would chew up three precious days during his division's
busiest time of year. He had budgets to prepare, deadlines to meet—
a fact he made clear to others at the outset of the sessions. "I remember him saying it was a complete waste of time, that he had better
things to do," says Deborah Lake, SC Johnson Wax's director of
diversity, who planned the workshop.

Harris remembers he went to the meetings only because "I had no choice. I was told by top management I had to be there."

No one surprised Harris and his male colleagues more than Joanne Brandes, a senior attorney in the law department and one of the most highly respected and well-liked women in the company. Her story made it clear that SC Johnson Wax, even with its on-site child care center, remained largely hostile to women with children. The rules for success—and at times, even basic survival at the company—were written for one type of worker and one type of worker alone: a man with a stay-at-home wife. With full-time support at home, men in such traditional marriages could and did devote themselves fully to work. They need not worry about child care or any other pressing family responsibility. Their daily needs, from dinner to clean laundry, were taken care of. They could call meetings on a moment's notice, put in overtime, and travel as needed.

Anyone else who wanted to succeed at SC Johnson Wax had to squeeze into that mold, no matter what the costs—or bail out. The pressures of that reality were totally invisible to Harris until Joanne Brandes spoke up. The costs had not even been so clear to Brandes herself prior to the session. If anything, she felt luckier than most women. Her job as a corporate attorney was both financially and personally rewarding; her daughter was thriving; she had a good marriage. She had managed to fit in, to succeed and have a family as well. She had not admitted, even to herself, just how frustrating the journey had been. The sudden clarity of vision startled and overwhelmed her.

"I still remember it very, very well. It was one of those very few life-changing kinds of events that stays with you," she says, even though the events unfolded a few years back, in 1993. "I can still remember the feelings I had as I sat in a circle of women, in the middle of the men. Suddenly it didn't matter what these men thought anymore. I didn't need to please them to get ahead. I thought, 'I've worked very hard to get where I am. My sacrificing is going to stop right here.'"

That new attitude was born when she saw, for the first time, how Harris and the other senior men viewed women. Until this moment, the men had been busy in another room, responding to a diversity trainer who asked them to list the reasons they believed explained why so few women made it to the senior ranks in this company. The men's answers, scrawled on huge sheets of paper, were now tacked to the walls around Brandes. The fault, these men said, lay with the women themselves: Women weren't "tough enough"; they were "too emotional" and "too indecisive" to be leaders. "Mother, cook, and nurse" were the jobs these men most associated with women. They believed that women were unwilling to travel, relocate, or put in extra hours because of family obligations.

The men saw themselves, on the other hand, as natural "leaders." "Strong" and "military" were two terms they equated with masculinity. A few gloated over the power men still had over women. Harris had gleefully proclaimed he was pleased to be old enough and senior enough to know he would never have to report to a woman. That comment had drawn smiles from the men just a few moments earlier. But now he dared not acknowledge he was the one to write those words. He was hearing firsthand from the women themselves about the sort of anger and pain his prejudice could cause.

Brandes was among the most eloquent. She was moved to speak, she says, once she saw the false assumptions about women laid out so clearly, so succinctly, in one place, by the men in her own company. "I was shocked and disappointed to see these attitudes, these stereotypes, written out like that, in black and white," she recalls.

But there was one simple statement that bothered her far more than the rest. "Women don't sacrifice enough to get ahead," it said.

Sitting in this circle of men, she realized she had sacrificed something far too dear, something these men couldn't even see: having a second child.

"All kinds of things rushed through my head, all the things that women have to do to get ahead. Extra education. Extra work. But most of all, I realized that I had sacrificed a child."

Up to that moment, Brandes had kept this fact at a comfortable emotional distance. She had never planned to have just one child; it had just evolved as an almost inevitable trade-off in a busy life. As one of the first women aiming for senior management, she thought it only realistic that she would have to work harder to prove herself, even do better than most of the men she worked with. And until now, she believed she was at peace with it. "I knew I was a pioneer, and I never expected it to be easy," she says.

But as she looked around the room, she noted that all the senior men had had children as they moved up. Not one of them had even considered paying such a high price for career success. "Having my first child was the happiest experience of my life. But I put it off until I was in my thirties," she says, for fear of sending the wrong message in the workplace. Even then, after she had established a stellar record on the job, she suspected the news would not be welcome at work; she waited until her sixth month to tell her boss. After the news was out, several colleagues confirmed her suspicions. "One said, 'Oh, Joanne, and I thought you were going places!' as if I had ended my career right then and there," she says. So she delayed the second pregnancy. "I kept putting it off and putting it off. I was worried about the reaction at work. And now I am over forty, and it is too late to have a second.

"And why had I put it off? It was amazing to me at that moment realizing that I didn't have another child because of this, because of these stereotypes about women," recalls Brandes. But the revelations from these men made it clear to her that this workplace would never change if she didn't speak up. These men needed to understand that the real reason there were so few women with children in top management—or even men with working wives—was because the workplace was so unbending, so inflexible for people who didn't fit their mold.

"I began to talk about how I had felt forced to make choices all the time. I had to try to fit in," Brandes says. "I talked about all the women I knew in the company that struggled with these issues, how many other women thought they couldn't have children and still succeed." She told how women throughout the company lived in an underground culture, playing guerrilla warfare against a set of rules that ignored or was downright antagonistic to the demands of their daily life. She let the men know how women swapped tips with each other on how to break the news of a pregnancy in the workplace, shared ideas on how much maternity leave would be tolerated without jeopardizing advancement and how to paper over child care issues that got in the way of work.

She went on to explain that, once they did have children, many of the women were immersed in a constant struggle to find, keep, and pay for child care. She herself had come to learn of the difficulties working parents faced only after her daughter, Julia, was born. "I was shocked when I looked around. I found it hard to find anything I was comfortable with, and I had a lot of resources. I didn't know how women who earned less than I did could manage." That concern had led Brandes to campaign for and eventually establish a company-sponsored child care center. For these men, that center served as a symbol that women's problems had been addressed. Brandes's own climb up the corporate ladder was further proof that working moms could succeed in this workplace.

But for Brandes, the opening of the child care center simply opened a window on how much more remained to be done. Now identified as a champion for working moms, she was often sought out by other women with children in the company—or even those thinking about having children—for advice and consolation. She knew some women still got a hostile reaction when they announced a pregnancy, that others felt humiliated having to beg for a few hours off for a pediatrician's appointment. "Women still didn't know if it was possible to have a family and a serious career at Johnson Wax," she recalls. "The demands of the job kept forcing them to put their children last."

Soft-spoken and intelligent, Brandes delivered her words with all the care she had acquired as a lawyer and with all the feeling she had as a parent who wished for another child, according to several of the other participants. "She was very effective. To many male managers, I'm sure they thought that she was not a person who had made obvious sacrifices for her career. She had not been asked to leave Racine, to relocate, as many of them had. They probably thought she had an easy time of it, compared to them," says Betsy Owens, brand manager and one of the most senior women in the revenue-producing side of the business. "I wasn't as vocal as I wanted to be. I found the sessions to be scary and risky. But, I think, for some of the women, like Joanne, it was a do-or-die situation. They felt they had to speak up about how it feels to be female at this company."

Owens herself was grateful that an honest dialogue had begun. She had moved to Racine from Boston just a year before and been trying to decide for herself when to have her first child. She worried constantly that having a baby might jeopardize her prospects for advancement, but she hadn't shared that concern with anyone, not even Brandes. She still felt like a newcomer at SC Johnson Wax. "There were few women in senior positions, no female role models for me. It was strange to me. I had sailed through Harvard's business school, never thinking about my sex. But now I found I had to be thinking about my gender all the time, and whether or not it might impact my success."

Some of the men sitting in the room that day began to understand that difference as well. "It opened up my eyes," Harris says. "I began to realize that I had spent the last ten years of my life going to meetings with the same ten people, trying to solve problems with the same ten people, all like me. They had no idea what it was like to be a woman in this company."

Neal Nottleson, chief financial officer and senior vice president, was also deeply touched. "You had to be deaf and dumb not to be touched by Joanne's story. You really felt guilty that collectively we had forced someone to make a choice like that.

"I was taken aback," Nottleson says, "by many things the women said. I've worked with many women in my career. I was amazed at the depth of feeling the women had about these issues."

At the end of the training sessions, he went home and shared an insight with his wife. "'The women I work with must really resent you,' I told her. 'You've given me a real advantage.' In fact, I realized that I have had an advantage my whole career. I have had the advantage of a wife at home, doing things for me that would have taken me away from my work," says Nottleson. "I hadn't thought about that so explicitly before."

For Nottleson, an understated and quiet man, this is quite an admission. And it is not one that he makes lightly. There are tears in his eyes as he recalls the sessions.

Deborah Lake, director of diversity, knew it would take a jolt to reach the top men at SC Johnson Wax. "When it came to family issues, most senior managers assumed everything was okay. If somebody wasn't getting ahead, they assumed it was because the person wasn't smart enough or working hard enough," she says. "For the most part, women weren't talking about these issues. The attitude of most women was 'I'm happy to have a job. I have to shut up and make it work somehow.'"

Lake did not share her own story that day. As a leader of the sessions, she wanted to draw out these senior managers, to get them talking. She only nodded when Brandes began to talk. But, as she revealed in later interviews, she knew exactly what it felt like to try to play by rules that simply didn't fit. When she first started out in the sales force, she had a three-year-old son. "It was very difficult in sales, as a new person and as a woman. There was a lot of traveling, and my boss kept reminding me how important it is to be places on time. I knew I was being scrutinized because I was a woman with a child," she remembers.

Her boss insisted that she meet him at 7:30 A.M. in Indianapolis, an hour's drive from her house. That very day, her son was set to start a new child care program. "He didn't want to go, so I had to leave him crying and sobbing and rush off to meet my boss. I am crying the whole way, but I had it timed perfectly," she recalls. Right until she found the cars in front of her stopped dead, halted by a car wreck up ahead. Yet even with the accident, she made it to her boss just ten minutes late. "My manager greets me with his arms crossed and an angry look, as if I have just committed the worst sin in the world," she recalls. "He told me I should have been there at least fifteen minutes early, ahead of the appointed time. Nothing in my family life should interfere with keeping an appointment."

Lake didn't protest. Instead, she apologized. "I needed the job. I needed to succeed," she says.

. . .

BY THE close of the diversity sessions, Harris says, he was truly a changed man. He volunteered to become an in-house "facilitator" to run future workshops like this one, aimed at moving women and minorities up. He vowed that his division, one of the largest in the corporation, would aggressively hire and promote more women and minority workers. In 1996, this busy executive is still eager to recall those sessions, which, he says, gave him lasting insight into what it's like to be a woman in corporate America today.

Things have changed at SC Johnson Wax since then. More women—and more women with children—are in the senior ranks. Harris himself instituted a strong affirmative action program for his division. Most important of all, the company launched more ambitious programs to make jobs more family-friendly. Many divisions began aggressive campaigns to encourage more flexible schedules, telecommuting, job-sharing, and other innovations that make it easier to blend work and family.

Unfortunately, Barry Harris and Neal Nottleson remain the exceptions to the rule in the business world. Only a few visionary leaders have emerged who are willing to wrestle with the fundamental issues and practical barriers that women—and a growing number of men—face as they try to integrate their work and family lives.

Most any working mom can tick off the obvious dilemmas. Rigid schedules, long hours, no time off to care for sick children, little vacation time to be with families, lost pay and seniority because so few firms have a decent maternity leave—or even guarantee women their jobs back after childbirth. Mandatory overtime, rotating shifts, and abrupt changes in schedules also wreak havoc with family lives. A recent study by the Families and Work Institute shows that the demands of the job are three times as likely to disrupt employees' home lives as the other way around.

The problems are not limited to big corporations, of course. They are only more visible there, since larger companies have begun to allow consultants and reporters to come in and take a close look at how working parents are faring. Thus, most major studies and reports on work-family issues to date tend to focus on the several dozen major companies already committed to change.

But the fact is that the problems are pervasive in the workplace of the 1990s. Women who work as cashiers, nurses, teachers, clerical and support staff, and social workers face the very same barriers each day as they try to earn a decent living and raise their children. "It's not any better in universities, nonprofit foundations, or small businesses. The real problem is the nature of work and the way work is organized," says Fran Rodgers from Work/Family Directions. "We have to redefine some of the core assumptions about work as the workforce changes. The problem is the way we work."

The most obvious dilemmas have begun to garner attention in the media and public policy circles, as a growing number of parents wrestle with the bad fit between paid work and raising children. Tina Miller-Silverman, a flight attendant for USAir, for example, made headlines in 1995 after she was fired for refusing a last-minute overtime assignment on an air shuttle between New York and Boston. She was given no warning, just commanded to board a flight in New York City and fly to Boston, even after she protested she had no one to care for her five-year-old daughter at home in New York City. It took Miller-Silverman, who had twenty-five years of experience with the airlines, over a year to win her job back via union negotiations. In arbitration, she claimed that one of her supervisors had told her, "You have to choose between your child or your job."

But such stories rarely probe why such "choices" are endemic to the workplace. The fact is that they are the predictable fallout of a workplace created to serve only one type of family. They spring from a long-standing, but now outdated, assumption about who should work for pay and who should reap the most benefits from that paid work. In some cases, the rewards and penalties are the result of conscious decisions made in the past to favor the old-style male provider. "You've got to understand the workplace is gendered, that it is built for people, mainly men, who have certain expectations about what their role in life is. The workplace is created for the breadwinner who can pay all his attention to the job," says Lottie Bailyn, professor at the Sloan School of Management and author of *Breaking the Mold: Women, Men and Time in the New Corporate World.* "Back in 1963, when I first started studying these issues, I thought all we had to do was point that out to people, make the values and myths visible to people. But now I see it goes much deeper than that. And change comes slowly because we are dealing with such deep attitudes."

The bias is enforced by history and custom, and underwritten by powerful economic sanctions. Two of the nation's most important employment programs, for example, Social Security and unemployment benefits, were invented to serve what lawmakers at the time explicitly described as the "ideal family," one in which Dad was sole provider and Mom stayed home to raise the children. At the time, the prospect of married women working was seen as a threat to family life, men's jobs, and the very social fabric of the nation. As a result, the highest Social Security benefits still flow to workers who follow traditional male patterns of full-time, year-round continuous careers over a forty-year period. Anyone who deviates from that model earns fewer Social Security credits, and thus, a lower retirement check. That is true of women who are fired or quit their jobs for lack of child care or maternity leave. Most private pension plans and union-negotiated benefits flow from the same assumptions.

Other perks and benefits were also created with a traditional male provider in mind. The best and most lucrative benefits—stock options and bonuses, for example—are reserved for employees who put in the most hours, travel, and even regularly uproot their families and relocate for the job. Many employers do not offer health insurance or disability or vacation pay to anyone but full-time, salaried workers. Until 1990, professional workers at the Du Pont Company had to quit their jobs and come back as hourly employees if they wanted to work less than a forty-hour week, the standard workweek set down by law and union bargaining in the early part of this century. That policy is still in effect at many large companies.

The very structure of many career paths is also constructed for workers with old-style families. The "move up or out" mentality at many businesses—the partnership tracks at law and accounting firms, for example—makes it difficult for women with young children to succeed. It means that employees are required to put in long hours on the job in their twenties and thirties, the very years most women start their families. A forty- to fifty-hour workweek is considered "part-time" at many big-city law firms; young associates often boast about working until midnight or even pulling all-nighters as a sign of their devotion to their career.

At times, such hours are necessary to meet a deadline, of course. But many professionals acknowledge that the behavior demanded to get ahead can verge on the ridiculous. There is the concept of "face time," for example, among many white-collar workers, who say they must show their faces in the office at certain hours, whether they are doing anything productive or not. It is widely known to be a charade, part of a game to win bigger paychecks. "I never leave the office before seven or eight," says one attorney who is a junior partner in a major law firm, because he knows the senior partners notice when people leave. To keep himself there that late, he says, he often spends two hours in the middle of the day at a local health club working out.

Such behavior is not unusual among New York's ambitious young male attorneys. Indeed, research reveals a virtual underground war between men and women at the firms about the use of their time for family needs. "Many women complain that they try to use their time efficiently so they can go home and have dinner with their families but their male associates waste time earlier in the day, or perhaps spend their lunch hours at the gym and then start working in earnest in the afternoons and evenings. They further suggest that the men do this intentionally, so that senior partners will regard them as especially industrious when they are working late into the night," a study conducted for the local bar association found.

Like so many other practices and policies that sustain the old-time breadwinner dad, this one hurts women's pocketbooks. Even as the men were rewarded for going along with the charade, women were punished for making their commitment to family visible. "Women's failure to make partner was frequently attributed to their failure to meet the 'time demands' of the legal profession because of family obligations—such as getting home for dinner," the study found.

Few Americans hold New York lawyers up as models for life, yet the rules for success in the world of law are only a slight exaggeration of those in many other fields. The assumption that workers can and should put their work ahead of everything else in life sits at the core of most workplace rules, from attendance policies to accounting practices, shaping the very nature and structure of work for most Americans.

Above all, success is "linked with the willingness and ability to work long hours, have few dependent care responsibilities, make work the central focus of life and have a nonworking spouse," concluded an ongoing study of more than 3,500 senior managers by the executive search firm of Paul Ray Berndtson and the Cornell University Center for Advanced Human Studies.

This study is particularly illuminating because it highlights the attitudes of highly paid executives who are deeply identified with their work. The managers in this study stand at the top of their companies, making an average of $158,000 a year. To move up or even hold a place in the executive ranks, they reported, they had to spend more time at work than they wished to, travel more than they wanted to, and spend less time with their children than was desirable. Not surprisingly, 95 percent of them were white men.

But the real story in this study is that nearly two-thirds of these top-ranking executives also reported they were *happy* with their jobs. In fact, most said that work was their top priority and three-fourths described their lives as "close to ideal." Thus, few saw any reason to change anything about the workplace. They were having a good time. "One of the problems I run into as I try to change the workplace is that the executives are just having too much fun. They love their work, they love to travel, they love the perks and power that come with the job, the cars, the fancy meals," one human resources executive who works for a major company confides as she attends a seminar sponsored by the Conference Board in New York City on work and family issues. "I find it hard to get them to pay attention to what I say about work and family conflicts. They don't see conflicts. They can't understand why anyone would want to live differently than they do."

Indeed, study after study shows that many managers find it nearly impossible to absorb new ways of thinking about the way their employees work or the way work is organized. Even if they are not all having such a good time, many have risen through a system and feel validated by it. They are not eager to accept new ways of doing things. When Merck, the pharmaceutical giant, first tried to introduce flextime policies, for example, many middle managers had trouble digesting even this fairly simple innovation of allowing workers to adjust starting and stopping times. One senior manager told outside consultants that "my employees can use flextime as long as they're here from nine to five." Another asserted that committed workers arrive early, stay late, and put in hours on the weekend. Another went so far as to monitor whose cars were in the company parking lot early, late, and on weekends.

Such a boss can make life miserable for working parents, of course, even driving them to quit. "The supervisor is where the rubber hits the road at work," says Ellen Galinsky of the Families and Work Institute. "A boss's attitudes can make or break the work environment." That is because middle managers usually have wide discretion in deciding whether or not to grant a day off or to authorize a new schedule, even when a company has a family-friendly policy on the books. And the research shows the least flexible bosses tend to be men with stay-at-home wives. "It's very hard for people who've never had the experience to understand what it means to try to succeed when the rules don't fit you. Most people in power don't understand what it's like for the women beneath them," says Fran Rodgers from Work/Family Directions. They've never had to wake up a child running a fever and try to figure out whether to show up at work or stay home. They've never had a caregiver quit on short notice. They've never had to pay for child care or worry about whether their child was in safe hands while they worked. "Even the most well intentioned have trouble understanding these issues because they don't live with the issues personally. It's kind of a blind spot for them."

A few actively resist the new realities, even when the evidence is presented to them. Faith Wohl, now executive director of the Child

Care Action Campaign, cut her teeth on work and family issues when she worked in the human resources department at Du Pont. She started her campaign for flexible work schedules back in the mid-1980s by making formal presentations about the changing demographics of the workforce to senior managers. "I remember one executive pounding the table and saying, 'I don't believe these studies.' Even the facts couldn't persuade him that the reality for most workers was quite different from his own," recalls Wohl. After many years of what amounted to guerrilla warfare within the corporation, Wohl and a handful of other advocates managed to get the company to adopt a wide array of policies to help working mothers, including on-site child care at several factories. But Wohl, who went on to an appointment with the federal government to help create more flexible schedules for government workers and then took over the helm of the Child Care Action Campaign, concedes it's still tough to win such policies. "You have a lot of arguments as you try to change things, I can tell you that," Wohl says.

At their most generous, many managers still see flexible schedules and child care as peripheral issues to their main business. Such innovations are treated as "soft" issues, nice ideas with some public relations value but irrelevant to the bottom line. Indeed, family-friendly benefits such as on-site child care, schedules that vary from the standard nine-to-five day, job-sharing, and part-time work for professional workers are frequently described as "accommodations," "alternate work schedules," or even "favors" for workers who can't fit the standard mold. And that perception, women know, has serious consequences. "My biggest challenge is overcoming the fact that if you ask for a flexible schedule or part-time work, you are immediately perceived as non–career-oriented or not serious about your work. There's the belief that you can't work part-time or have flex hours if your job is too important or interesting," says a female manager at a large company.

For those in blue-collar, pink-collar, and clerical ranks, the rules for success are imposed mechanically, via attendance policies, time cards, time sheets, and even old-fashioned time clocks. For years, New York Telephone workers suffered an automatic demerit for most absences, no matter what the cause. Every worker was "stepped," or disciplined, for each absence, even maternity leave—and with too many "steps," a worker could be fired. "We never had a case of a worker disciplined for maternity leave. But, I guess, the system did communicate that taking a leave was misbehavior of a sort, a deviation from the standard. One consultant who looked at the policies described the company as so strict that it resembled a paramilitary organization," says Donna Dolan, union respresentative for the Communications Workers of America, which represents many workers there. By the early 1990s, the union had begun to win many family-friendly benefits, including generous child care benefits. But control over a worker's time remains a tough issue to negotiate. Indeed, both unions and management remain largely ambivalent over the issue of flexibility. For organized labor, the idea of allowing workers to vary their hours represents a threat to hard-won bargaining agreements that govern hours and seniority. For management, flexible hours suggest a loss of control over workers. "It's hard to win fights over scheduling," Dolan says.

For working parents, the issue of time arises over not only the number of hours they must put in, but also control over when they put in the hours. The ability to shift even a few minutes of the average day can make a critical difference in a parent's life. But working mothers report there is often resistance to even small adjustments. "By the time I drop my kids at the sitter's in the morning, I barely make my train to work. If I miss it, then I am fifteen minutes late to work. Instead of agreeing to extend my hours fifteen minutes per day, they would rather type it as chronic lateness," an administrative assistant at one company says. "My managers don't know and don't want to know about flexible hours."

Indeed, women interviewed for this book often reported encountering an outlandish arrogance when they suggested new approaches to work. "When I proposed sharing a job with one of my colleagues, my boss just laughed at me," says a Chicago attorney who worked in municipal government. "He said, 'I've never heard of such a thing. I'm not going to even entertain the idea.'" He tossed aside the lengthy proposal she had prepared on the subject, detailing how the arrangement would work and citing examples of its value to other companies. Several months later, she quit. On the official record, she is another mother who left to be home with her baby. And, in fact, she did happily spend a few months at home with her infant son. But within a few months, she went back to work for another employer who was willing to grant her a more creative schedule.

The arrogance is fed by the insular nature of the lives that many executives lead. Most pass their days with people just like them, men with stay-at-home wives. Prior to diversity training, Barry Harris says, he hadn't even noticed that there were so few women in the top jobs or that those few who were tended to be childless or have just one child.

Many also socialize with people just like them, a powerful reinforcement of their values and beliefs. Indeed, Harris says, his social life grew distinctly less comfortable once he went through the training sessions and began to lead them himself. "I've lost some friends because of this," he says. "They observe the changes in my behavior and it makes them uncomfortable."

He recalls one instance in particular. "I attended an orientation session for a group of twenty-eight students interested in working for the company a few months after my own diversity training," he says. "When the students asked how women and minorities were faring at Johnson Wax, one senior executive 'joked' there'd been plenty of progress. I remember he said, 'We just had an opening at the senior level and we filled it with a white male.' I could see the comment was painful to young women in the group. One young woman's face was crestfallen. I knew I should have spoken up at the time, but I didn't." Two days later, however, when the same "joke" was told at a small meeting of senior managers, Harris did protest that it was in poor taste and not in the company's best interests. The response? "One of my colleagues said, 'Gee, I think Barry needs to be taken out for a drug test. He seems to be losing his mind.'"

Harris sighs after he tells the story. "This is a big challenge, you know, to get managers in their fifties to *want* to change the workplace. They think the workplace is just fine the way it is."

Given such attitudes, it's not surprising that the data on the workplace of the 1990s shows a disturbing trend. Even as the work-force grows increasingly diverse—about 60 percent now have working spouses or are single parents—the ranks of management do not. In fact, the management posts of the nation's biggest and most influen-tial companies are even *more* likely to be men with stay-at-home wives than they were a decade ago. Over the past decade, Charles Rodgers and his wife, Fran Rodgers, have put together a database cov-ering hundreds of thousands of workers. In 1995, they discovered that about 64 percent of managerial men had nonworking spouses.

No one knows exactly why this is so, but most consultants who have studied the trend speculate that this is because many jobs have grown even more time-consuming as companies downsize, making it even harder for workers with child care duties to get ahead. "We seem to be winnowing it down to the men who have wives at home," says Charles Rodgers.

THAT FACT now seems obvious to just about everyone except the executives themselves. "They don't experience their lives as being privileged. When you go around a company, everyone but the senior white males will say there is an old boys' network. Then when you talk to senior men, they don't see it," says Fran Rodgers. "They feel they're out there competing to get ahead themselves. They'll say things like, 'If there's an old boys' network, I want to be a part of it.' They don't realize what their everyday fabric of experience does for them."

Working moms often joke about this phenomenon, but their anger is never far beneath the surface. "It took Bristol-Myers five years to come up with a maternity leave policy," says one. "If women had been on the planning committee, it sure would have happened a lot faster." A mid-level manager from Barnett Banks thinks life there might be different if her CEO had to deal with the same problems she does. "Allan Lassinger does not wake up in the morning wonder-ing what will happen if his child is sick that day," she says. Barbie B., a secretary for a major pharmaceutical company, says, "Lots of employees here want flexible schedules. The human resources department made a whole case for flexible hours, especially compressed workweeks, and showed how the company would benefit. But top management squashed it. They don't know what it's like to have a child come down with an asthma attack. They leave all that to their wives."

All of this matters, of course, even for workers who don't aspire to chief executive officer. Everyone must play by the same rules to win a raise, a promotion, or even an interesting assignment on the job. And that means that the practices and policies of the workplace—the very structure of work itself—drive mothers' wages down, and, for that matter, the wages of any man who makes his children a top priority.

More than half the women who opted for a flexible schedule in one study of seventy companies reported they were passed over for promotions. About a fourth said their salaries remained flat for three years, while their coworkers got raises. Losing out on even a 2 or 3 percent raise each year can hurt a family, obviously. It amounts to a pay cut at a critical time in family life. Raising children takes money, from paying for the baby food to being able to afford to live in a town with decent public schools.

THERE IS very little doubt among consultants that the main reason such benefits are so stigmatized is that they are still seen as benefits for women only. Attitudes about "gender roles may penalize both men and women. These include the assumptions that women should take primary responsibility for children and family matters, and that men have to work, while women have a choice," concludes Deborah Schwartz of the Families and Work Institute, in research she conducted for the U.S. Department of Labor. Women's conflicts with family care are considered largely illegitimate in the workplace. Over and over again, women say they have been told, "You had the baby; it's your problem!" as if life could be so easily divided into separate spheres, one for work, one for family, one for men, and one for women.

Historically, of course, the workplace has responded to "personal" issues. Vacation, health insurance, retirement, sick pay, and other benefits related to male workers' traditional roles have gained acceptance over time. Faith Wohl, who fought so successfully to create a more hospitable atmosphere for parents at Du Pont, notes that companies were quick, as well, to institute paid leave for the reservists who fought in the Gulf War, but balk at the idea of paid maternity leave. "You hear the term 'work-family conflict' when it's about a woman's problem, but 'work-family issue' when it's about men," Fran Rodgers jokes. Certain kinds of conflicts have always been more easily accommodated in the workplace—time off for medical appointments, for example—because they were problems that afflicted male breadwinners. "When I have a pediatrician's appointment, I have learned to tell my boss that I have a dental appointment for myself," says one mother who works at a small company in New Jersey. At times, women also use family obligations as a cover for leaving an inhospitable workplace. Work-family expert Dana Friedman says that over the years, she has come across more than a few cases of women telling employers that they were quitting for "family" reasons, rather than confronting a boss about harassment or poor working conditions. "It's often expected. Employers don't question it, so it avoids a confrontation," she says. Of course, such lies serve only to reinforce the stereotypes of women and camouflage the true extent of the needs of today's workers.

That is a shame, since a growing number of surveys show that both men and women desperately need more flexibility on the job to attend to their children's needs. Surveys of the Du Pont Company's employees, for example, show that conflicts between work and family duties are nearly as likely to arise for men as for women. About 47 percent of the female managers and 41 percent of the male managers said they would not relocate for the job. Among employees in manufacturing jobs, about 45 percent of the men and 39 percent of the women said they had refused to put in overtime because of family obligations. And 12 percent of the men and 15 percent of the women said they'd turned down promotions for family reasons.

The change among men is palpable to James Levine of the Fatherhood Project, who runs corporate seminars on how workers can strike a balance between their duties on the job and at home.

Since about 1990, he says, he's been more apt to see men in such seminars, a distinct change from previous years. That is not to say that he is swamped by men. "This is no revolution, but it's a beginning," he says. "We're seeing lots of men who want to come and talk about conflicts between work and family."

Some of the nation's more progressive employers recognize this trend; Bausch & Lomb, Merrill Lynch, and American Express even asked Levine to run special seminars for working dads. "We didn't market or advertise, but we started getting these calls, asking us to do seminars just for fathers." And, Levine adds, these men have many of the same concerns that working moms do—especially how they can keep their careers on track and still have time for family. "There's generally more permission for women to talk about these things, and women have figured out who to talk to in the office among themselves, discreetly." Men, on the other hand, often feel isolated because "work-family stress is still largely perceived as a woman's problem and men are afraid they'll be seen as unmasculine if they talk about these things."

A few men who took the traditional route to success speak with deep regret about their choices. "My epiphany came because there was finally no question that my family had to come first," says one senior corporate manager, after his daughter was diagnosed with schizophrenia. "Faced with her illness, I realized I had sacrificed time with her when she was growing up, and I could never get it back." Indeed, he expects she'll never be entirely free of her illness, as she was when she was a young girl. But while he missed those years, he is now intent on caring for her. These days, he frequently leaves work early and comes in late to help care for her. And he now understands how the pressures on him to be a successful "provider" drew him away from intimacy with his daughter. "I'm going to be fifty-five this year, and now I've begun to see that all the little decisions I made along the way—to miss her birthday party or piano recital—in the name of succeeding at work added up to a big loss for her and for me."

Although he still does not share his daughter's story with coworkers, he is now an ardent advocate of a flexible workplace—

and of values that allow both men and women to succeed at home and on the job. "Men have to admit there's a lot of ego tied up in working long hours," he says.

Both men and women manage, of course, to work around the existing rules. Some women are able to organize their lives successfully enough to fit that mold, but often at great personal expense. Many hire in-home help, use high-end child care centers, or both. "I think that my child care situation is different than most. My level in the company and my income set me apart. I am not second-guessed—there is an assumption that I will reliably handle my duties whatever comes. No one talks down to me or makes me feel guilty. I get more support than lower-ranking women in the company. I know several secretaries who always lie to their bosses and say they were sick when they must stay home with a sick child. Also, I can afford to buy the best care for my children. When my kids had chicken pox, my child care expenses were five hundred dollars over usual for in-home care during the illness. It is much more difficult for less senior women in the company," a senior female manager in a large company told outside consultants from Kwasha Lipton, a New Jersey–based management consulting firm.

Indeed, that is a crucial question. What about the women—and men—who can't afford such child care? Should their paths to upper-level jobs and more income be blocked because the structure of work favors employees who can give the most time to the job?

THAT QUESTION would not even have to be asked, of course, were it not for the stubborn resistance to updating work practices and policies to fit the new realities of employees' home lives. And the biggest irony is that so many businesses could be so much more successful if they would only adapt to today's changing workforce. There is now plenty of evidence that when companies create a more hospitable atmosphere for parents, it helps profits. When IBM, for example, surveyed its top-performing employees, child care and other family-friendly benefits ranked second only to salary as a reason to stay with the corporation. Officials at Corning, the ceramics company, reported that family-friendly policies, including on-site child care and flexible schedules, along with programs designed to advance women, reduced turnover among women managers by half.

Indeed, companies find that the failure to address the needs of today's workers costs them money. By most estimates, it runs from one to three times a worker's salary to recruit and train a replacement. Amoco, for example, estimates that its new family-friendly policies—such as elder and child care—saved the company $2.2 million in reduced turnover and lower absenteeism in just one year.

If anything, the latest research shows that the old ways of working are simply counterproductive. They often drive up the cost of doing business and hurt families along the way. Just consider the story of one woman, a vice president for a bank in Miami, Florida. She had worked out a flexible schedule, with the blessing of a supervisor she had for several years. She came to work a half hour early and left work at 4:30 P.M. That simple change of a half hour allowed her to pick her daughter up from an after-school program and take her to ballet, religious classes, and Brownies. But in 1994, the bank suddenly abandoned its formal flextime policy. "The new hours were nine to five, and I was told I was lucky it was only nine to five, and I didn't have to stay until six," she says. But that translated into a pile of stress. "I now have to tear out of the office by five, drive like a madwoman to pick up my child in day care, or risk charges of fifteen dollars for every ten minutes I'm late." Even worse, it means her daughter is often the last child there.

The new hours made it harder to reach the bank's customers. "I deal with South American clients, mostly in Brazil, and they're three hours ahead. By the time I get in at nine now, it's noon there and they've gone to lunch," she says. In addition, the bank's operations center, which processes the transactions, opens early and closes early, so she ran into problems completing a transaction in a timely fashion once her hours moved back.

After several months on the new schedule, she wrote a lengthy, well-reasoned memo to her supervisor to protest the change in her hours. She argued that flexible schedules not only helped employees, but also boosted productivity. She then enlisted other employees to sign it. "Women got very excited that I was speaking up. At first, they were afraid to sign it with me. But finally, a few said, 'If you sign it, since you're an officer, I'll sign it.' "

In the end, however, the women's fears turned out to be well founded. "The president of the bank made it known that she was unhappy about the memo. A lot of secretaries were pulled in and told that this was not a good thing to do," she recalls. The standard nine-to-five day remained in effect in 1997. Not only that, but women at the bank were effectively silenced. "No one wants to challenge anything now."

Such a scenario is far from rare. "When you go into a company as an outsider and talk to people, you find out that employees have lots of ideas about how work could be organized differently. It might be that a job can be done with less travel and more use of the telephone. Or it might be that a job could be shared with somebody else. Or it might be that the hours could be more flexible," says Charles Rodgers. "All you have to do is talk to the people who work there. The solution at most companies is just creating an environment where people can suggest things and get a reasonable audience."

Indeed, when managers are persuaded to take a hard look at business practices, they are often surprised at what they find. Rodgers recalls, for example, the work he did at another bank, where many employees in the customer service department wanted part-time schedules. The bank refused to grant the requests, and as a result, turnover remained high in the department. "The bank's logic was that employees needed to be on call, available to customers all the time," he says.

But when he surveyed the bank's clients, he discovered a more bothersome problem. Their number one complaint was high turnover among the bank's staff—they had grown weary of explaining their needs to a constantly changing cast of customer service workers. What they wanted most was a stable person on the account, even if that worker turned out to be a part-timer. Having someone available forty hours a week, on a standard nine-to-five schedule, simply wasn't as crucial as having an employee familiar with the account.

Bank officials would not, of course, have ever discovered this problem if Rodgers had not forced them to question their core assumptions about the nature of work. And that is why the most innovative companies have come to see that the best way to make the workplace more hospitable to parents is to retrain managers, teach them to think in new ways, and give them the tools to succeed at creating a more hospitable workplace. The attitudes run so deep, the policies are so entrenched, that it's difficult to promote any serious change without a frank discussion of the biases that lurk beneath the surface.

7

Will Only Mommy Do?

The Power of Scientific Myths

IN 1986, after a decade of reports showing day care to be a positive experience for children, working moms suddenly started getting an earful of bad news. One of the nation's leading authorities on child care proclaimed it risky for infants to be away from their moms for more than twenty hours a week. This esteemed psychologist proclaimed that babies separated from their moms might turn out to be troubled later in life, and be more likely to act out in school and have poor relationships as adults. The announcement made headlines across the nation for weeks, and was followed up in magazine articles and books that put day care under a new cloud of suspicion. A little over a decade later, the debate still rages, fueling periodic media coverage and keeping the questions about infant care alive.

But few moms knew this message was based on what other scientists believe to be unreliable tests and outdated assumptions.

Many, already ambivalent about returning to work a few months after giving birth, took the news to heart. Debbie Clay, for example, who lives in suburban Maryland and works in Washington, D.C., was deeply disturbed by what she was hearing. Her anxious words tumbled out in a phone call to the offices of *Working Mother* magazine. She wanted to find out more about the academic studies cited in the magazine that refuted the news and reported that babies could thrive in high-quality day care. As she spoke, it was clear that she was seeking just one thing: reassurance about the well-being of her four-month-old son.

"There isn't a day that goes by when I don't ask myself if I'm doing the right thing by going to work. I wonder if he will be okay," she said. "In order to keep our home, we really need my salary. But I worry about him every day."

Her doubts persisted, despite her confidence in the woman who watched her son. "She's very good. I know she is. I've seen the way she is with children. I checked out all the references she gave me. I know people who have used her for years," Clay said. "But still, I worry that he's getting second-best. From what I've read, you can never replace the feeling a mother has."

Clay's distress was born of the fierce new love she felt for her son, to be sure. She adored holding him; she missed him while she was at work. Her personal preference would have been to quit working, but that was not an option for the family.

But her natural anxiety spiraled nearly out of control as she read books and magazines. Like many new moms eager to learn about their new roles, she had become a voracious consumer of child-advice books, and what she had absorbed was a nearly hysterical concern about the fate of infants in day care. "I worry he's getting hurt emotionally, that he won't recover from the hours away from me," she said. "An awful lot of child care books indicate that the early years—some say the first three years, some a year, some two years—are so crucial to how a child is going to turn out as a person. So many of these books make it look like if you mess up then, it's a permanent disaster."

Although she didn't know it, Clay was quoting almost verbatim from the work of psychologists who subscribe to "attachment theory," one of the most influential and controversial schools of thought in modern psychology. Indeed, no research has had a more profound effect on the notions of what makes a good mother in the past forty years. Each year, attachment researchers publish literally thousands of papers in academic journals examining the way tiny babies build relationships with the adults in their lives, most especially their mothers. Those research articles are often promoted to the media by university public relations offices and the findings publicized in magazines, newspapers, and television and referred to in many widely read child-advice books. "It's become virtually an industry unto itself," insists Diane Eyer, a psychologist and author of *MotherGuilt*, a book that explores the influence of attachment theory in modern culture.

What attachment theorists have demonstrated—with searing clarity—is the power of human affection. In their earliest studies, conducted in the early 1950s, they learned that babies could literally die of emotional starvation. Infants could be fed and kept warm and clean but without a stable, loving relationship, they would lose interest in eating, playing, or looking around.

From these first studies, the attachment theorists went on to study the growth and development of human relationships, particularly those between mothers and infants. According to this theory, the patterns set early in life determine the pattern of relationships for life. That means infants who receive enough attention and affection from a loving adult right from the start are most likely to succeed socially and emotionally. Without such a bond, they are likely to be troubled and neurotic—even to suffer serious character disorders and depression.

These core concepts of attachment theory now dominate most child-rearing advice and define what is best for children's emotional health. And what is best, according to most of this research, is an ever-present mother during the earliest years. "This theory has made a stay-at-home mother the gold standard," says Eyer. "Everything is measured against this mythical, nonexistent, perfect mother."

Indeed, it is the attachment theorists who first proposed that even a brief separation from Mother could trigger lifelong emotional problems. Starting in the 1950s, this idea took hold and persisted until the mid-1970s, casting a dark shadow over any woman who dared to work outside the home. Child care researchers even found it hard to study the effects of other-than-mother care—they were accused of hurting kids by separating them from their mothers.

"Anything that suggested separating an infant from his mother for even an hour a day was considered damaging to children," recalls Bettye Caldwell, one of the nation's leading experts on early childhood education, who has long fought to improve child care in this country. When she opened a child care center in 1964 serving infants in Syracuse, New York, the reaction from both the public and her colleagues was intense. "I got hate letters, remarks from other professionals that I was hurting children instead of helping them," she says. "I was the target of censure, criticized for taking children away from their mothers."

Prominent pediatricians, such as Benjamin Spock, relied on attachment theory as the basis for recommending that mothers stay home with children during their early years. Even into the late 1960s, Spock's book included the "working mother" under the section devoted to "special problems" in child rearing. And day care merited a scathing indictment in the early editions of his book. "A day nursery or 'baby farm' is no good for an infant," he advised in his bestselling *Baby and Child Care* in 1968. "There's nowhere enough attention or affection to go around."

Such ideas were so sacrosanct that virtually all states refused to even license day care for children under the age of three into the early 1960s. And even as recently as the late 1960s, the Child Welfare League vehemently opposed any out-of-home care for children under the age of three. The league's formal position papers held that everything should be done to see that children were reared at home by their mothers, including counseling for the mother, if necessary, to help her understand the importance of being home full-time with her children.

It was not until the early 1970s that new day care research—and

the vibrant new women's movement—began to challenge the
supremacy of attachment theory. Research coming out of the new
federally sponsored Head Start programs and research sites such as
Bettye Caldwell's showed that child care could promote positive
development in children when it was done right. The new body of
research findings was so convincing that even Dr. Spock felt compelled to revise the 1976 edition of his book to say that it was okay
for Mom to work and Dad to pitch in with child care duties. "The
zeitgeist then was to see day care as a positive," recalls Alison Clarke-
Stewart, psychology professor at the University of California and
one of the nation's most distinguished day care researchers, "at least
for poor children."

But Americans have never been of one mind about child
care, their ambivalence often fueled by views about women's proper
roles. "The truth is that it's not science driving these debates about
child care," says Michael Lamb, a research psychologist at the
National Institute of Health who has studied child care for several
decades.

Instead, it is the American "ideology" of gender roles, the belief
that women belong at home, that drives this debate, often with
ammunition gathered from attachment theory. "The ideology that
women belong at home has great power in American culture. Americans act as if it is the most natural pattern, the only one that occurs
in nature or in human history. But in truth, human babies and young
children have long been cared for by people other than mothers."
The real "anomaly," he notes, is the peculiarly American insistence
that women be isolated in their homes, taking care of only their own
children.

The continuing power of the mythology, he suggests in a new
book on child development, may arise partly from the fact that men
with power—financial, political, and intellectual power—in American society are simply reluctant to talk about something they perceive to be a women's concern. "Child care is still perceived of as a
women's issue, even by scientists," Lamb says.

•   •   •

STILL, IT was probably only a matter of time until the debate over day care revived. Like all great debates over social issues, this one was triggered by many sources. By the 1980s, the majority of mothers were back in the paid workforce at least part-time before their babies' first birthday. That was a startling development in a nation that still had virtually no formal system of child care or even an organized way to find the care that existed. Care for children under the age of two was the fastest-growing segment of child care, yet it was provided largely via an underground economy, without any quality control or even a sensible way for most parents to find it in their neighborhood. Unlike mothers in most every other industrialized country, moms like Debbie Clay had no right to a paid leave to care for their newborn babies.

Legions of women before Clay had faced this dilemma, of course. Working-class women—and most especially women of color—had been subjected to excruciating choices about child care since the dawn of the industrial revolution. But now the need for safe, high-quality care for even the tiniest of infants had arrived as a terrible problem in middle-class America. "Sheer demographics began to drive the issue," recalls Helen Blank, a longtime child care advocate with the Children's Defense Fund. Child care issues were now the stuff of regular media coverage.

It was against this backdrop, in 1986, that Jay Belsky, one of the nation's leading psychologists, made his stunning announcement.

When Belsky, an aggressive and outspoken scientist, began to talk to the media, the effect was akin to throwing a lighted match into a vat of gasoline. The impact was explosive, dramatic. The debate still rages between Belsky and his colleagues today, and still fuels media coverage and questions among parents.

This is remarkable, given that right from the outset, Belsky conceded the risks were small, the evidence for them was scant, and further studies were needed before any firm conclusion could be drawn. Nonetheless, he made his case in such powerful forums as the *Today* show, the *Wall Street Journal,* and other national media, sending a scare up the spines of working moms. "Some of us are saying there are some risks out there for kids, and we have to decide which risks we are willing to take and which ones we are not," he told *New York* magazine at the time. "I don't want to be hysterical," he added, "but if I had to give a recommendation to somebody who could afford to stay home without terrible consequences, I would tell them to do it."

Belsky came under immediate fire from his colleagues, who attacked both the methods and conclusions of his research as flawed and outdated. Some branded it as downright irresponsible, since the evidence was so slight and so likely to fuel worry. Normally sedate scientific meetings grew heated, with angry words and even tears exchanged behind closed doors after the official presentations. Professional newsletters carried personal attacks. "It's the most heated debate going on in my field today," Ed Zigler, head of the prestigious Bush Center for Child Development at Yale University and one of the nation's foremost experts on child development, proclaimed in mid-1987.

Such heartfelt controversy among the nation's leading authorities on child development sparked extensive media coverage that had to be unsettling to any caring parent. "There's good reason to believe this whole generation of infants who are spending ten hours a day in groups are going to have trouble relating to another person in a close relationship like a marriage," Byrna Siegel, then a child psychologist at Stanford University Medical School Center and author of *The Working Parents' Guide to Child Care,* told *New York* magazine.

So it was that by the time Debbie Clay got around to having her son, the concerns over infant care had reached a new and feverish pitch. Even the staid *New York Times* put the topic on its front page, under a series headlined "The Good Mother." The articles raised questions serious enough to make even the most confident mother have a second thought. "Do working mothers imperil their children's inner security and future happiness? Does day care at an early age put children on a slow track for life?"

If mothers weren't worried enough by Belsky's statements, sensational new headlines began to add another worry by 1994: a child's brain growth might be permanently stunted without the proper stimulation in the first three years of life. In a widely heralded report on the state of America's children, the prestigious Carnegie Corporation warned that poor-quality child care could have lifelong repercussions.

By 1997, such claims made the cover of *Time* magazine, in a special report, "How a Child's Brain Develops and What It Means for Child Care and Welfare Reform." Once again, moms were counseled that "there is some evidence that children benefit if their mothers stay home with them until they are one year old." And what if Mom went off to work and put her child in someone else's care? Now permanent brain damage loomed on the horizon.

Early childhood advocates hailed the new studies as evidence that the attachment research had been onto the truth all along. "Psychiatrists and educators have long recognized the value of early experience. But their observations until now have been largely anecdotal. What's so exciting is that modern neuroscience is providing the hard, quantifiable evidence that was missing earlier," Matthew Melmed, executive director of Zero to Three, a nonprofit organization devoted to highlighting the importance of the first three years of life, told *Time* magazine for a cover story on the topic in early 1997. It was true that new technology had given scientists a window on the way the brain grows, from infancy to adulthood. "Because you can see the results under a microscope or a PET scan," Melmed said, "it's become that much more convincing" that the first three years of life are the most critical ones. Such statements are striking, given the remarkable lack of evidence that a child's experiences in day care predict much of anything about who he turns out to be as an adult.

If anything, the steady stream of research on child care over the past three decades has time and again revealed one notable fact: day care produces no consistent long-term effects on children's emotional health, for better or worse. Indeed, kids who attend day care programs even as infants are virtually indistinguishable from other kids as they grow up. Further, studies show that when it comes to intellectual and social skills, child care can be a plus. "Personally, it's unbelievably frustrating to me that the message never gets through that we've found no adverse effects on babies. There should be some closure here, but it never seems to occur," says psychologist Alison Clarke-Stewart, who has devoted her twenty-odd-year career to day care research.

But closure never arrives in the great American day care debate. Indeed, the current studies on children's brain growth have only invigorated the debate over child care and given new power to the observations by attachment theorists. The power of early experiences to determine a child's life course is now written larger than ever among child care advocates and scientists.

That has happened even though the highly touted research has yet to be linked with child care experiences. Instead, the studies of brain growth show effects only in extreme situations, in the face of extreme trauma or deprivation. Animals that are blindfolded for an extended period, for example, lose their sight. "The effects of total deprivation on the brain are not a particularly new idea in science. Nobody would deny that if you raise any organism without any stimulation that you would have those effects," says researcher Michael Lamb from the National Institutes of Health. "But there's no reason to believe that even substandard day care even begins to approximate those conditions. These studies have absolutely nothing to do with the effects of child care on brain growth." What has happened is that scientists now have the tools—machines that can peer inside the brain—to observe normal brain growth, and to see how much happens in the first ten years of life. And it is true that there is remarkable growth in that period, much of it in response to stimulation from the outside world. Yet no one yet knows just what it takes to stop that growth, aside from extreme deprivation.

"It's a leap of pure speculation to relate this research to child care," Lamb asserts.

But that is exactly what happened at *Time* magazine. "This story came to be because there seems to be an obvious fit here between what we know about the brain and what we know about the importance of the first few years of life," says James Collins, the *Time* staffer who wrote "The Day Care Dilemma," which linked the brain research and experiences in day care. "Of course, I think it's very hard to know what's true here, what works and what doesn't, in terms of child care." But Collins and his editors thought the story an important one to do, in light of public policy issues and debates at the time. With massive new welfare policies unleashed across the land, the face of day care was about to change. "We just wanted to look at the new research in light of welfare reform and government policy and what child development people are saying. Under new government policies, a lot more mothers may be forced to work and this research seemed to suggest some issues about the quality of day care. I would agree that it is somewhat speculative. The research is new. But it did seem to confirm what child development people have been saying and it seemed like a timely story."

But for mothers who read the story, the message was immediate and disturbing. "My sister called me and said, 'See, I told you, day care is bad. It can stunt babies' brain growth,'" said one child care advocate, who asked to speak off the record. "It's a little scary, isn't it, that that's the message people get from these stories."

Meanwhile, other prominent child care experts saw the research as an opening for advocacy. Ellen Galinsky of the Families and Work Institute and Matthew Melmed from Zero to Three, to name two, trumpeted the brain research as reason to increase child care funding. Indeed, when *Newsweek* followed *Time*'s lead and published a special edition on infant development in the spring of 1997 that focused heavily on the brain research, Zero to Three sent copies of it to its media contacts.

But the most significant aspect of the interest in both attachment theory and the brain research is how it reveals the bedrock American belief in the power of a person's earliest experiences. All the hoopla just reinforces the cultural view, advanced by the attachment theorists and Freudian theory, that a person's earliest experiences have life-shaping power. This is not a universal belief, held in every culture. "Western social scientists seldom recognize that belief in the crucial importance of the early weeks, months, and years of life is not shared by most people on this planet today," Lamb notes. Indeed, many Asian cultures discount the importance of human experiences before children reach the age of reason—that is, age six or seven.

Indeed, a growing number of psychologists, even those steeped in attachment theory, now concede just how difficult it is to sort through the myriad experiences in human life and decide which are the most influential. Many now think that attachment research gives far too much weight to a baby's experiences in the first year of life—and to a mother's ability to set a child's course for life during those years.

THE REASONS for this are obvious to just about everyone, with the notable exception of new parents still insecure in their new roles and deeply involved with their new babies.

A child's personality, a family tragedy, divorce, a move to a new town, financial instability, are all far better predictors of a child's emotional problems than whether or not he or she was in child care as a baby. "Attachment research sometimes seems to read as if life ends after the first year, and nothing important happens after that to influence a person's emotional health," Sandra Scarr, one of the nation's most prominent developmental psychologists, observed in the early 1990s, as the debate over the risks of day care continued to rage. Just as important, studies show that a child's genetic makeup and temperament play a powerful role in life. Shyness, for example, appears to be at least partly inherited and apparent from birth. Not only that, but a shy baby is easily startled and uncomfortable with too much commotion. These facts will color all of his experiences in life.

In addition, there is plenty of research that shows the power of a child's larger social arena. Schoolchildren perform better when a teacher expects them to, for example. And then there are the nettlesome impacts of poverty and opportunity, which can exert a powerful influence on a child's sense of well-being and confidence. "There are a zillion things that influence us in life," says Diane Eyer, a vocal critic of attachment research. "One child might be growing up in a neighborhood where bullets are flying, another in the peaceful suburbs. One may have alcoholism in the family, the other may not."

Yet today the message that child care is toxic for small children still hangs in the air. Today, it is the best-selling authors Penelope Leach and Burton White who still argue that children may suffer lifelong emotional harm if a mother works in the first year of life. It's a message that many mothers absorb almost like air, because it fits so neatly with the cultural assumptions and practical realities of their lives. In some cases, it tips the balance in favor of quitting work to stay home with the kids.

For millions of other moms, however, who have no choice about whether to work, the message is far from soothing. These ideas were so disturbing to Debbie Clay that she even decided to call Burton White after she read his book, *The First Three Years of Life,* a staple on the shelves of many new parents. White, a child psychologist and director of the Center for Parent Education in Newton, Massachusetts, is well known among early educators as a critic of mothers who work before their children are three years old. "I actually called him up and said, 'Do you know how this makes working women feel?'" Clay recalls. His response, as she remembers it, was not reassuring. "He said, 'I'm just telling it like it is. Children need their mothers at home in the early years.' He made me feel terrible, but I admired his honesty. He didn't sugarcoat anything. Yet I was left with this feeling; for those of us who don't have an option to stay home, it puts a real hurt on you. You just feel you're giving your child second-best and at times it's very damaging."

Most moms don't bother to call the child care experts in person. But many report that, like Clay, they are bothered by what they read and hear from experts about the impact of child care on a child's emotional development. "I spent the first two years of Zach's life struggling over these issues," says Kristen Storey, a human resources manager who works for the University of Michigan in Ann Arbor, Michigan. "I wondered, 'Is he going to feel close to me or his caregiver? Am I giving him the kind of attention he needs? Am I robbing him of something he needs by going to work? Am I damaging him in some way?'"

By the time Zach entered kindergarten, Storey had no doubts that he was thriving. "I started looking at my son, instead of thinking about all these messages about women being at home. Once I looked at Zach and put those other messages out of my mind, I relaxed. He's a very happy, well-adjusted little boy. I've always gotten good feedback about him from everyone. He has lots of friends. He wasn't deprived or lacking or showing any weird behaviors—he's fine."

Storey's passage is hardly an uncommon one. Most women—and men—travel a path from insecurity to confidence as they adapt to their new responsibilities and roles as a parent. "My thinking has evolved amazingly. I'd be much less angst-ridden today if I had to go through choosing day care again," says Lynn Asinof, the reporter for the *Wall Street Journal* and mother of two elementary school boys. Over the past twelve years, she's used nannies, day care centers, nursery schools, au pairs from Europe, after-school programs, and a variety of other child care arrangements. "When you start out, you haven't the faintest idea what you're looking for, how to process the information you get, and a lot of us haven't even figured out what we believe about child rearing. It's very hard to make the first choice about child care, when you're not terribly secure in what you're doing yet.

"But after you've been through it twice, you understand kids are resilient, that they do survive. I don't think my closeness with my children has been affected in any way by the kind of child care they've had. A lot of other things have affected our relationship—birth order, for example. The way you deal with the second child is way different than the first. With the first, you're thrilled to just sit and watch the baby sleep. The experience is so new. But by the second, you have no time for that," she says, laughing. "And you realize your child will survive."

But none of this is obvious when a mother first begins to look for child care for her first child. "Every new parent comes fresh to the role, and it's a new issue to them. They go through the same soul-searching that would have happened five, ten, or twenty years ago, about whether to work," says Clarke-Stewart. "This is especially true of new mothers, of course, because mothers have been responsible for the care of infants. Even if in principle you favor child care, there's still the specific hardship of finding a care arrangement that you think is good enough."

And more than anything, focus groups and surveys show, parents feel responsible for and worry about their children's psychological well-being. "In our focus groups, we've found that parents believe they have the most impact on their children's emotional development," says Lynnette Ciervo, director of communication for Zero to Three in the winter of 1997. "That's not the case with intelligence. A lot of parents think their children are born with that and there's not much they can do to increase their children's brain power. But they see emotional development as their responsibility."

Which, of course, only stands to reason. And most certainly, part of the reason that attachment theory has such power in American culture is that its core tenets speak to such heartfelt truths about human relationships. Who can disagree with the idea, for example, that children who experience love and caring early in life are off to a better start? Who can doubt that the kind of relationship a child has with his mother is key in shaping a child's confidence and self-esteem?

FEW AMERICAN women have ever heard of John Bowlby, the father of attachment theory. But few modern thinkers, outside of Sigmund Freud, have had a more profound effect on their lives and the choices they make once they have children.

Bowlby, a British psychiatrist, was the first to see the startling phenomenon of infants withering away from lack of emotional bonds. He made his observations in British orphanages after World War II. The babies he watched had their physical needs satisfied, but were rarely cuddled or given the opportunity to develop a bond with the changing army of nurses who cared for them. Without a stable, loving relationship, they retreated into a shell. The official diagnosis: failure to thrive, a condition that could be fatal if no one intervened.

Bowlby's studies changed the way the Western world looked at raising children. In a widely circulated report for the World Health Organization published in 1951, he concluded that infants were at high risk of lifelong emotional difficulties if deprived of a mother's care. Bowlby believed that many forms of neurosis and character disorders were the product of a baby's separation from Mom. Like most psychologists of the time, he considered mothers to be the central figure in a child's emotional development. It was only in extreme cases, such as a mother's death, that another adult might stand in her place. If she were available, he insisted, a mother must provide "constant attention day and night, seven days a week and 365 in the year," or put a child's mental health at risk.

The report fit neatly with the cultural biases at the time, which were drawn from psychoanalytic theory and held that the bond between mother and infant was sacred, the principal source of a child's confidence and security. Any fissure in that bond, popular wisdom held, could lead to serious emotional problems in adult life. As a psychiatrist, Bowlby himself had a strong allegiance to Freudian theory. His initial interest in infants was motivated by his work with children who had suffered debilitating separations from their parents.

His studies gained all the more attention because they came on the heels of fascinating animal research conducted by American psychologist Harry Harlow, which showed the importance of emotional bonds among primates. In Harlow's studies, conducted in the 1940s, baby rhesus monkeys put the desire for love and affection even before their need to eat. When given a choice between a surrogate mother who would offer physical comfort or one that would feed them, the monkeys chose physical comfort over food. "It was an astounding finding at the time," says Merry Bullock, developmental psychologist and senior scientist at the American Psychological Association. "Until then, scientists assumed that food and sex were the most important motivators for primates. Harlow's work demonstrated the profound need for physical touch." Bowlby himself repeatedly cited animal research as evidence of a fundamental human need for infants to bond with their mothers.

Though Bowlby's studies of infants focused on care in institutions that were the equivalent of orphanages, they remained the only systematic observations of tiny babies in out-of-home care for several decades. In essence, his work was interpreted as a tacit indictment of day care—an institution that most Americans already distrusted.

In 1944, for example, *Parents* magazine noted, "There are still a large number of women who when they hear 'child care center' automatically think 'regimentation' or 'abandonment.'" *Parents* went on to paint a picture of what worried moms of that era. "Will he grow hollow-cheeked and bony because you are not there to say, 'One spoonful for Mommy, one spoonful for Aunt Clementine and now another for Uncle Archie,' over his cereal bowl? Will he be left to cry in a corner because all the bigger children grab his toys and you are not there to act as an avenging angel?" At the time, *Parents* reassured moms that a child care center could be a positive experience. "The center realizes that it is its job not only to provide for the child's physical development, but also contribute to his emotional growth, his intellectual enrichment and his social adjustment."

But Bowlby's searing portraits of babies withering away for lack of human affection fed parents' natural anxieties and worries, making the pictures of children growing "hollow-cheeked and bony" in day care totally credible. Pediatricians, psychologists, and other child care experts began to issue ominous warnings about lasting emotional damage to children if moms worked outside the home.

"The women of my generation really got battered by every institution in our lives," says employment rights attorney Judith Vladeck, who launched her legal career in the early 1950s and then had three children. "All the guilt. You can't imagine it now, coming at you from every direction. Of course, it's better now." Vladeck recalls that one of her sisters-in-law was "shocked" when she decided to continue working and that "older women were horrified that we were 'abandoning' our children when we worked." At one point, when Vladeck decided to run for public office, total strangers would ask her about her child care arrangements should she get elected and have to travel. "I created a fiction. I would say, 'Oh, my mother will take care of them.' That was the only acceptable answer. Otherwise, I would have been a fallen woman, neglecting my children."

That message, of course, fit the governing ideology of the time, that women needed to be home. It is the era now so famous for the television show *Ozzie and Harriet*, which reflected the cultural ideal of Mom at home and Dad as provider. Women who had worked in the factories during World War II yielded their jobs to returning soldiers, sometimes under intense pressure. "The pressures on women who wanted to stay in their jobs was enormous," recalls Mildred Jeffrey, a longtime union activist who worked for labor leader Walter Reuther at the time and went on to become governor emeritus at Wayne State University in Detroit. "Women were transferred to the worst jobs and forced to work long hours, to get them to quit. I remember talking to one woman who told me it was so hot where she'd been placed and the hours so long, she thought she was going to faint. She said she couldn't take it anymore; she was going to quit. And I told her she had to stay there, no matter what, even if she fainted. I told her they just wanted her to quit and go home, that was the point, and she had to hang in there."

Jeffrey also recalls just how hard it was to get child care at the time. "I remember when I needed child care, it was suggested to me that I put my child in foster care while I worked. That was the idea of what child care was back then."

Bowlby's work simply spoke to the times, reinforcing the social message that women's highest calling was to nurture their babies, that the mother-infant bond was sacred and all-important.

Over the decades, attachment researchers began to look beyond that one bond and to explore the patterns of intimate relationships across the life span. The idea of "maternal deprivation" has softened, and nearly every serious scientist concedes that children can grow up happily and well-adjusted even when a mother goes off to work. "Many psychologists have moved away from the early idea Bowlby had that a mother's presence is like vitamins. And many have moved away from the idea that a child's entire emotional well-being and personality are set in those early years," says Arlene Skolnick, sociologist and author of *Embattled Paradise,* a study of modern family life. "In fact, within the academy, those ideas have become quite controversial. But those ideas are still out there among the popular child development experts."

Burton White, Penelope Leach, Sylvia Ann Hewlett, and syndicated radio-talk-show host Laura Schlessinger, to name a few, still trumpet the supposed dangers of other-than-mother care. "To put it bluntly, after more than 25 years of research on how children develop well, I would not think of putting a child of my own in substitute care—especially a center-based program—before they reach the age of three," White wrote in his *First Three Years of Life*. His only exception: families that could not raise their children because of a debilitating condition, such as alcoholism or drug abuse. Otherwise, he argued, parents risked compromising their children's lifelong development. It was during the first three years that humans developed the "full range of social and intellectual skills that now appear to be necessary for subsequent development," he said. And those skills could easily be compromised, he contended, if a child entered day care in those years.

Sociologist Skolnick is not surprised to hear of emotional calls about the effects of day care to the editors at *Working Mother* magazine. "This is a constant message to women. I was at a meeting not so long ago of very high-powered career women, and a psychologist got up and told them all how their children would be damaged by their working outside the home. She said, 'You women are not going to like what I am going to say, but you are going to do serious damage to your children by working. Your child needs you to be there and nobody can substitute for you and nothing that you do in life can possibly match up to the importance of your being home with your child. That happens to be the scientific truth.'

"I remember the guilt level in the room was intense; the women really reacted strongly," Skolnick recalls. "I was upset because it was a setting where there was no opportunity for me to get up and give the other side. These women were just left with this unnecessary guilt."

And even though more women work today, many of the professionals they see and depend on for advice may believe that it is wrong for them to do so. The ideas of attachment theory still hold sway, for example, among many pediatricians. As recently as 1990, a poll showed that the majority still believed it was wrong for a mother to work full-time before an infant's first birthday. Male pediatricians took a dimmer view of women working than their female colleagues—about 77 percent of the men thought it harmful, compared with 50 percent of the women. About 63 percent of the men doctors also said it was harmful for Mom to work before a child was three years old. "A growing number of pediatricians feel that the holding, cuddling, touching, and feeling that is so important in the first six to eight months can't be done by a surrogate," Henry Harris, M.D., a spokesman for the American Academy of Pediatrics, told *Working Mother* magazine at the time. "Generally speaking, caregivers don't enrich as much as mothers do," he said, with the effect that kids "grow up deprived of a nurturing environment."

As this language shows, whether one subscribes to attachment theory or not, Bowlby's perceptions still shape much of the debate around child care. The idea of separation and loss still colors much of the conversation; it's common to hear that working moms are "abandoning" their children in day care—even though they see their children every day. It is a language that speaks directly to the heart. "If you are the only people your baby loves, you are probably right in thinking it would break his heart to be left with anyone else, tomorrow," counseled child care guru Penelope Leach in her parent handbook, *Your Baby and Child*. A substitute caregiver, she went on to say, would have to "ferry" a baby across the "chasm of your absence." This is certainly not an appealing image to new mothers. In fact, many glean just one message from Leach and other childrearing experts.

"What I got from Penelope Leach is that she tells you basically to give up your life for your child, or your child will be screwed up. You read magazine articles about kids who grow up with Mom working and have problems. I remember just when my son was born, an article came out in the *New York Times,* some longitudinal study about mothers who stayed home versus those who worked. It was sort of a flash in the pan, but it raised concerns about how kids would turn out, and I remember we mothers in the neighborhood all stood outside our houses and talked about it," says Constance Bauer, a lawyer in Chicago who returned to school to become a social worker after her first child was born. "I don't really believe that children are harmed when their mothers work. My mom and I are extremely close. My mother worked and I don't feel I was deprived or have emotional scars to show for it. Still, I think the message is out there that it's better for kids if women are home. You hear it both subtly and explicitly. So I always have this vague sense of guilt about working, that somehow it might damage my son."

BUT IT IS not just the bedrock emotional message that makes attachment theory so powerful in American culture. Equally important is the fact that this research carries the aura of "hard science," the authority of indisputable scientific fact. And that is due largely to the work of one of Bowlby's brightest protégées, Mary Ainsworth. It was Ainsworth, an American psychologist at the University of Virginia, who gave attachment researchers a key tool to measure the power of the bond between mothers and infants.

Steeped in Freudian theory, Ainsworth wrote her Ph.D. dissertation in 1939 on an infant's need for a strong bond with Mom. That bond, she believed, inspired confidence in an infant, what she called a "secure base" that allowed a baby to feel at ease in the world, to trust and explore both the physical and psychic territories of human experience, rather than to feel fearful and anxious. In 1950, she married her husband and moved to England. There, she teamed up with Bowlby and together they studied babies in British orphanages. Four years later, she moved to Africa, where she studied the interaction between mothers and babies and grew ever more intrigued with Bowlby's ideas. In the decades that followed, she and Bowlby maintained a close relationship and together helped shape the main ideas of attachment theory, focusing on the conditions that seemed to feed or retard human relationships.

It was in the 1960s and 1970s, however, that Ainsworth made her most profound contribution to attachment theory, by seeming to solve one of the most vexing problems facing researchers who wanted to study tiny babies. The most widely accepted barometer of a child's emotional well-being was still a healthy attachment to Mom. But how could scientists make any judgment about the emotional life of humans too young to talk and barely able to control their bodies?

Ainsworth delivered the answer in the form of a twenty-minute laboratory test that has come to be known as the "Strange Situation." The test is brilliant in its simplicity—all an infant needs is a good set of lungs. A mother and her child, between the ages of twelve and eighteen months, are brought into a laboratory. A stranger enters, and the mother departs briefly. The infant usually shrieks in horror. The mother returns, and upon reunion with Mom, the baby's behavior is observed and he is sorted into one of three categories. Those who are easily comforted by Mother are said to be "secure" and have strong, healthy attachment. Those whose moms have trouble calming them are described as "anxious." Those who turn away from or otherwise avoid contact with Mom at the reunion are labeled "avoidant." These categories, Ainsworth believed, were predictive of later mental health. As children grew older, Ainsworth discovered, those with secure bonds were judged to be happy, curious, and confident. Those in the other categories tended to have problems getting along socially and also tended to be more easily frustrated and withdrawn. "It was a real breakthrough in psychology. All of a sudden, we had a handle on how to measure the infant-mother relationship," says Jay Belsky.

By the late 1970s, the "Strange Situation" had become one of the most widely used tools to assess the effects of child care. And it was studies that relied on the "Strange Situation" that led Belsky to sound the alarm about infant care in 1986. He reported on a study he conducted himself as well as several others that used this twenty-minute test as a barometer of children's well-being.

And that, it turned out, was one of the main reasons that so many of Belsky's colleagues were infuriated with him when he released his findings to the media.

THE HEART OF THE DEBATE

Indeed, many of his colleagues thought the "Strange Situation" was a strange barometer to use in looking at the effects of child care. While it offered a snapshot of the bond between a mother and a child, it might not reveal much more than that. And children who had already been in day care might respond differently from others—they might, for example, be more comfortable with strangers and separations from their moms than other babies. If so, they might not seek their mothers so quickly upon reunion—and would be classified as less secure by the "Strange Situation."

But more important, many scientists argued that the Ainsworth test revealed little about a child's actual experience in child care. Wouldn't the content of different programs, the responses of caregivers, and other differences make for wildly different effects on kids? Did it matter if caregivers had training? Using the "Strange Situation" as the sole barometer of children's adjustment would never answer such questions.

"We don't honestly know all that much more about the specific effects of day care today than we did when Jay started raising the issue. But the trend in the data shows that the effects depend on a lot of things, including the child's relationships with his teachers and peers," says psychologist Carolee Howes. "The thing is, we were pretty certain even then that there was no simple formula about predicting what's best. You couldn't say not to put a child in child care for more than twenty hours a week before the magic age of one. There just wasn't conclusive evidence for that."

A better use of attachment theory, Howes and others argued, was to look at the quality of the relationships a child forged in the child care situation. Studies emerging from Europe in the mid-1980s showed that tiny infants could develop sustaining attachments to several adults in addition to their mothers. Some scientists began to argue that a child would have better mental health with strong bonds to several adults by the end of the first year. A wider universe could give a child a sense of broad security and trust in the world beyond the family. "The idea that a baby can and should feel emotionally secure only in the presence of its mother seems like a rather perverse development to encourage," Sandra Scarr, then chair of the University of Virginia's psychology department, asserted at the time.

Scarr and other critics of the "Strange Situation" also argued that simple biology played a larger role in a child's emotional development than is allowed by attachment theory. By the time Belsky made his pronouncement, scientists had learned more about how memory and awareness develop. Some studies showed, for example, that an infant's long-term memory didn't kick in until the fourth month of life—and thus babies weren't likely to have the ability to remember and prefer their moms to other caregivers before then. The genes seemed to act almost like time-release capsules, sending messages about how and when a baby would develop mental and physical capabilities. A growing number of research scientists began to describe even the tiniest of babies as a rather sturdy lot who could adapt to a variety of child care arrangements without serious harm.

All in all, Belsky's critics argued, he was wrong to choose studies that relied heavily on the "Strange Situation" to indict infant care. He could have cast a wider net, going beyond attachment research, as a way of investigating the effects of day care. "I just don't think the 'Strange Situation' is a good prism for looking at child care," says Alison Clarke-Stewart. "The question of how children are affected by their experiences in child care is so much more complicated than this one test can show."

That appraisal is now borne out by the evidence. Indeed, much research now shows that Ainsworth's test has very little predictive power. In other words, a child classified as "secure" at a year might show up as "avoidant" a few months later. "Over time, it's quite common to get different results with the same child. In fact, there's a better-than-average chance that a child will behave differently six months later," says scientist Michael Lamb. Why? "Because the child's feelings depend on what's going on in the relationship at the time. If the mom gets divorced, or is preoccupied because of a move to a new house, or is fatigued because she is pregnant again, she may not be as responsive to the baby and that might show up in the test," he explains.

Indeed, Belsky's other independent studies at the time, which did not rely on the "Strange Situation," showed that a child's illness, marital discord, or family financial problems, not child care, were strongly associated with a child's acting out in school or suffering emotional turmoil. "The debate over Jay's findings was very ugly and harsh and I don't want to comment on it on the record. I don't want to get into personal attacks. But I believe that what Jay did was a dis-service to the women of this country. He offered no perspective on his conclusions. He put child care in the same category as drive-by shootings in poor neighborhoods," says one prominent child care researcher.

For his part, Belsky argued he was simply trying to shine a light on problems that might otherwise have been ignored. "I broke the eleventh commandment: Thou shalt not speak ill of day care," he said. Even a full decade after the initial debate, he sounded bitter about the response of his colleagues. "I was accused of everything from hating women to wanting to put women back in the home to being anti–day care," he said in a telephone interview in 1995. "It was almost Soviet-like attacks, verbal crap, intellectually bankrupt." He added that there was an "ideological need to dismiss me" among what he called "the day care mafia," colleagues who bitterly disputed his conclusion.

According to Belsky, that "mafia" included two of the nation's most respected psychologists—Sandra Scarr, who was then on the faculty of the University of Virginia and subsequently held such posts as president for the Society for Child Research and Development, one of the most widely respected professional organizations for developmental psychologists, and Deborah Phillips, one of Scarr's protégées at the time. Phillips went on to be staff director for the prestigious Board on Children and Families at the National Research Council in Washington, D.C.

Phillips, Scarr, and a handful of other researchers, including Clarke-Stewart, argued that Belsky was the one who tended toward ideology, who was willing to release a study that tainted child care and chilled the hearts of working moms, all on the basis of weak evidence and research methods that were under fire. "All I remember is that I spent a lot of time on the phone with reporters trying to calm people down, to tell mothers that they weren't going to hurt their babies by putting them into day care," recalls Kathleen McCartney, professor of psychology at the University of New Hampshire. "I got a lot of hysterical calls."

Even in the heated passion of the day, it was clear to nearly everyone that the debate was sparked as much by controversy over women's changing roles as it was by the evidence in the research.

Indeed, Belsky himself went so far as to include a caveat about his personal life in his published report on infant care—a rare occurrence in scientific journals. "I feel it is important to make several facts clear about my circumstances. I am the father of two darling and demanding young sons who spent their entire infancies in the primary care of their mother and who did not start preschool (on a three-half-day-a-week schedule) until they were two and a half and three years of age. Because I am not sure that this family reality of mine does not influence my reading of the scientific evidence, I share it here," he wrote in *Zero to Three,* the journal for the National Center for Clinical Infant Programs. And although none of Belsky's critics ever publicly raised the issue of his personal choices, he continues to frame the debate as one informed by personal bias. "Many of my critics, my most vocal critics, were all women who had chosen career paths and chosen infant day care. They had a stake in this. They were susceptible to intellectual bias and emotionally unable to acknowledge their personal stake in this," Belsky asserted in the 1995 phone interview.

The tenor of the debate grew so personal and so fierce that the dean of the field, Ed Zigler, finally intervened. "It was in the papers every other day. And here were all these mothers going to work every day, worried sick about their babies. It just wasn't right. I know all these researchers, so I called them all together in a room and told them, 'You're driving parents in this country crazy. We need to figure out what there is we can say we know and what we don't know and issue a joint statement.'"

The feuding scientists convened in Washington, D.C., in 1987 and from that meeting, the controversy was finally channeled into one of the most elaborate and visible studies of infant care ever conducted. As follow-up to this early meeting, the National Institute of Child Health and Human Development launched a study at ten sites around the country to settle the questions about infant care, once and for all. Known as the Early Child Care Research Network, the project followed 1,300 families and their child care arrangements for three years, to try to sort out the long-range effects of child care.

That research project included Belsky and many of his critics, all trying to hammer out a consensus about what is best for babies. The acrimony still shows, as the 1995 interview with Belsky so vividly reveals. "We agreed that we would all agree on everything before we released anything. But we barely agree on anything easily," Belsky said. Privately, several other of the key scientists acknowledge that feelings still run high. "This has been the research project from hell," says one of the principal investigators, who would speak only on the condition of anonymity. "There have been a lot of tears and anger expressed."

In the spring of 1996, the researchers issued their first definitive results. As earlier studies have so often found, this new one found that child care "neither adversely affects nor promotes the security of children's attachment to their mothers." In other words, Belsky's concern turned out to be ill-founded, after all. "I wish this message would finally get through," sighs Clarke-Stewart.

Above all, the study showed that it's hard to discern any effects of child care for better or worse, unless a child has a poor relationship with his mother. In such cases, bad experiences in child care can exacerbate a child's troubles. Such children may indeed have trouble socializing and doing well in school as they get older. Yet this effect shows up only when a child has an unresponsive or insensitive mother—in addition to bad experiences in child care. Kids who have a good home life, however, suffer no lasting effects from a poor experience in child care. While most mothers wouldn't choose to put their kids in a mediocre or bad situation, this news should be reassuring after all the publicity about the damage day care can do to kids. "What this study shows is simply that the family is the most important influence on children. That should be reassuring to most parents," says Deborah Phillips.

That is not to say that all of child care in America deserves a clean bill of health. Far from it. Study after study shows that much of the child care in this country still fails to meet even minimal health and safety standards. The most rigorous study to date showed that half of the care was mediocre to substandard. "Some of the debate over child care is just plain silly," says Zigler from Yale. "We all know that some care is so bad, you can see it with your own eyes, and that certain things tend to make it better."

INDEED, the main reason attachment theory finally grew so controversial is that it seems to have taken scientific research on child care on a side trip, ignoring the real experiences that real children have in child care. "There was really a shocking lack of attention to trying to define the specific conditions that create high-quality care," says Michael Lamb. "We've just begun to ask the right questions." That includes looking at how the caregivers interact with the children, how many caregivers are on hand, and what the adults and kids do together all day.

To date, the researchers looking into these questions have turned up some simple truths. Children do best when the adults caring for them are sensitive to their needs and desires. That is most likely to happen in small groups, where there are enough adults on hand to give individualized attention for at least part of the day. Consistency is also important; children grow distressed if the adults in their lives are constantly changing. And kids are happiest when there are a variety of interesting activities to do during the day.

And one of the key findings of child care research is that good things tend to happen together—when one or two of these qualities exist, the others are likely to be there as well. That means that if a child care center has cheerful, attentive caregivers and a good assortment of toys, it's also likely to provide a healthy and safe environment. The opposite is also true: if you find one woman trying to care for five infants at once, it's unlikely you'll find a safe or stimulating environment.

And while parents often scour child care advice books about the ingredients of high-quality care, it's usually, as Zigler says, quite easy to spot. Consider a scene at Johnson & Johnson's on-site child care center. A ten-month-old baby is fussy. She seems hungry but can't quite settle with her bottle. But Joan Bechtle, one of the caregivers on duty, takes care to soothe her. Bechtle rocks her and talks in a soft voice. "You are so tired, aren't you, Lindsey." Within a few minutes, Lindsey lets the nipple go and drifts off to sleep in Bechtle's lap. Bechtle's affection for the infant is obvious. "Lindsey isn't quite over her cold yet," Bechtle informs a visitor. "She needs a little extra cuddling."

Such a bond between a young child and a caregiver is probably the most important ingredient of good child care. "Mostly, when it comes to child care, when we are asked about the effects of child care, we still have to say, 'Well, we don't know because we haven't spent enough time asking the right questions,'" says psychologist Carolee Howes. The most honest answer, she says, is, "It all depends on the child's family life, the specific child care situation, and the child's relationships with peers and teachers in child care."

That last point has been the focus of Howes's research for more than a decade, and she has learned just how powerful the bonds—or lack of them—can be to a child in a day care situation. Howes has discovered that "children do form very particular relationships" in day care, often choosing one adult as their primary caregiver. When that doesn't happen, they have a tough time and tend to act out both physically and emotionally. The children who forge successful bonds tend to be happier and more socially adjusted. This only makes sense, since affection is so much at the heart of taking proper care of children.

But it often takes seeing such a relationship up close for parents to trust that such care exists. Sharon Jacobs, a compensation consultant for a nonprofit health care company in Philadelphia and mother of two daughters, remembers her first trip to the Parent-Infant Center in west Philadelphia when she was pregnant with her first child. "It was very sunny, with large classrooms, and the teachers were very good with the children. Most had college degrees," she recalls. "It was all so well organized; the staff was happy and you rarely heard a baby crying. That's tough with ten babies, but they were just very attentive to the children's needs. It was clear to me that they knew a lot more about children than I did as a new mother."

That is not to say that it was easy to leave her new baby at the center the first day. "The first day, they wanted me to just leave her for a short period. At that point, she couldn't even hold her head up. I saw all these kids crawling on the floor and I thought, 'Oh, God, will somebody step on her?'

"After I dropped her off, I was emotionally off-center. And to add insult to injury, when I came back to my car, there was a parking ticket. My husband had arranged for us to go have lunch together that day, which would normally be a treat. But I remember not hearing a word he was saying. I couldn't wait to race back and pick up the baby."

She recalls how fiercely protective she felt of her new daughter after she picked her up. "I didn't want to put her down; I couldn't let go of her the rest of the day. I just remember wanting to be really close to her." But over the next few weeks, she saw that her daughter was doing fine. "I remember that the director told me that she would form a bond with a caregiver, will seek someone out. And, in fact, that's what happened." In fact, Jacobs has one vivid memory of the time her daughter spent at the center, and it is a telling one. "Whenever I came, someone was always holding her."

THAT THIS would be so, however, was not at all clear to Jacobs beforehand. "My pediatrician told me quite candidly that mothers should be home for the first year," Jacobs recalls. "It was better for bonding with the baby. So, I worried a lot."

These days, she passionately believes her daughter benefited from child care. "I think I can pick out the children who were in day care. They tend to share more. They had to learn to do that. They tend to be better socialized," she asserts. The evidence doesn't support her ideas, but she remains confident, nonetheless, of these benefits for her child. She has also come to see just how much her ideas about child care have been shaped by cultural biases. When her second daughter started child care, one of the children in the center was from India. "The family told me the day care situation reminds them of India, where the extended family takes care of children. They really like it," Jacobs says.

This family thought it odd that Americans expect women to raise their children all alone, in isolation from the larger community. They did not think of the staff at the day care center as strangers. They didn't worry that their child would be neglected or emotionally damaged. They had a basic trust that the community of adults could share the care of the community's children.

"They just didn't struggle over the decision to put their child in day care the way I did. It made me realize how much my ideas are more a reflection of my culture," Jacobs says. And that, she says, "really took me aback."

In the Care of Strangers

Day Care's Enduring Stigma

VANESSA SILVER never dreamed her nanny, Jeannette, would discover the video camera that she and her husband had hidden away in the cluttered wall unit in the living room. Vanessa acquired the camera to record Jeannette's behavior as she cared for the Silvers' infant son, Alex. At the time, Vanessa felt she desperately needed a window on what happened at home while she and her husband were at work.

They decided to install the camera after watching a television exposé of child care on ABC-TV's *PrimeTime Live*. "We were watching TV and suddenly I see these horrible scenes with this baby-sitter hitting a child with a telephone," recalls Silver. "It made you feel so vulnerable. No matter how wonderful I thought Jeannette was, I needed to know for sure. The show just forced you to think that way."

The first day, the camera didn't record. But within a few days, the Silvers did get a tape to view. And what the camera revealed was an affirmation of Silver's judgment when she hired Jeannette. "The tape showed how wonderful she was with my son, singing to him, playing with him," Silver says.

The shock, it turned out, was when the Silvers saw, about a half hour into the tape, that Jeannette had discovered the camera. They watched, horrified at Jeannette's image captured on videotape as she peered back at them, full-faced and forthright, for a few seconds. Jeannette then adjusted the camera slightly and went on with her day as if no one were watching. "I felt so lousy. I figured we had ruined what had been a perfect relationship with Jeannette."

Jeannette never said a word to Vanessa about the tape, but Vanessa knew she had to make amends. Trust is at the heart of any intimate relationship, and few relationships were as intimate for Vanessa as sharing the care of her infant son. She decided to take a day off work to talk over the incident with Jeannette. "I told her that I was sorry I hurt her feelings," Vanessa recalls. "But I also told her I was not sorry about trying to take the best care of our son. I explained I had to know what was going on, and what I found out was that she was wonderful."

Four months later, as she recounts the story, Silver says she is convinced there was no need for the secret filming. "I'm a veteran parent now," she jokes. "I know better."

By then, she had learned to trust her son's behavior as the best barometer of his care. She'd learned that lesson the hard way, via her first experience with child care. Prior to hiring Jeannette, she'd enrolled Alex in a family day care home. But there were signs of trouble almost immediately. "In one week, I could see the difference in my son. He was being neglected. He was nervous and not getting enough sleep," she says. When she spoke to the woman caring for her son, she was told that the staff sometimes got too busy with the toddlers to make sure Alex was getting a regular nap. She took him out after a week and started searching for a new arrangement. With Jeannette, "there was no sign of anything wrong whatsoever," she says. "Every day, when I came home, Jeannette gave me back exactly the same child I left her with in the morning—happy, alert, responsive.

"The point is, I've learned that you can tell when something's wrong. Even though Alex was such a small baby, I could see something was wrong," says Silver. "But when you see those exposés, it makes you wonder."

INDEED, it's easy to tap the collective discomfort Americans feel about day care. The anxiety sits at the center of public and private conversations, shadowing working moms every day. Media stories, parents, politicians, and policymakers describe day care as putting children "in the care of strangers," in care that is frequently painted as "custodial" or "institutional."

Day care's poor image arises in part from the power of scientific theories and the still-sturdy prejudice that women belong at home once they have children. But these disturbing and negative pictures demonstrate another powerful force at work: class bias.

Day care still carries the freight of its past, the taint of its long history as a service for the poor. Unlike the citizens of other industrialized nations, Americans have been reluctant to embrace child care as a universal service, one that benefits all families. Instead, day care services have long been earmarked for the helpless and unfortunate, a badge of shame overseen by social workers and health professionals. And that creates a stigma that undermines public support for child care funding and causes parents unnecessary worry. It also hampers efforts to upgrade the quality of child care in this country. Who, after all, wants to spend their hard-earned tax dollars on what have been called "kiddie kennels" or "kid factories" where children suffer?

At times, the bias against child care even informs sensitive decisions in child custody cases. Michigan family court judge Raymond Cashen made headlines across the country when he ruled against giving Jennifer Ireland custody of her three-year-old daughter, Maranda, back in 1994. His reason? Jennifer had put Maranda in day care. And day care, he wrote in his official opinion, amounted to leaving little Maranda "in the care of strangers."

Cashen, like so many other Americans, had a tainted image seared into his psyche, and it turned out to be even more powerful than reality. The three-year-old had been attending a well-regarded day care program for some time and knew her caregivers well—they were certainly not strangers to her. Further, court-appointed psychologists found Maranda to be well-adjusted, happy, and thriving. At the same time, Maranda had hardly ever seen her father. He had not visited her at all during her first year of life. His plan for Maranda's care if granted custody? He would leave her in the care of his own mother while he attended college. Yet his mother was a virtual stranger to Maranda. They'd met only a few times, and then only briefly.

A higher court eventually reversed Cashen's ruling. But his opinion reveals the strong prejudice that so many Americans harbor against child care. In Cashen's case, the bias was so profound that he sanctioned taking a child from her mother.

THE PREJUDICE against child care is so pervasive in American culture that for most employed moms, it's simply the stuff of daily life. "When I picked up my daughter from her dance lessons, I would hear comments from the other mothers about how they would never put their children in day care," says Nancy McConnell, a marketing executive in East Moline, Illinois. "They'd make blanket statements, say that day care is like a warehouse where you stick kids, where kids get ear infections all the time. I even heard one mother call it 'orphanages from hell.'"

Gail Luttrell, the insurance adjuster in Louisville, Kentucky, says having children in day care made her a target for neighbors and relatives. "People showed us articles about abuse in day care. They asked us how we could allow our children to be raised by strangers," she says. Coworkers put her on the spot after yet another exposé of day care aired on television, this one of a private day care center. "I go into work and they ask me, 'Did you see *PrimeTime Live* last night? Wasn't that terrible?' I felt like they wanted me to defend every day care in America. But I didn't. I just said, 'I'm glad mine's not like that.'"

Such constant questioning can only raise the anxiety level for working moms. What caring parent would leave a child with total strangers, especially an infant or toddler who is helpless to protect himself against abuse and neglect? What caring parent would allow a child to be left in a cold institution, with no one to cuddle and stroke him? Employed mothers live with these concerns each day as they struggle to see that their kids are safe and well cared for.

To tamp down their fears, to feel assured that they are doing the right thing, many, like Vanessa Silver, spend hour upon hour investigating the options, talking to friends, trying to banish the doubts. The shortage of high-quality, affordable child care in this country makes the quest all the more difficult; the Families and Work Institute reports it takes parents an average of five weeks to find reliable child care. Parents in focus groups conducted for the Child Care Action Campaign reported they tried two or three different arrangements before they found one they were comfortable with. Silver called thirty day care providers and visited ten before she enrolled Alex in the first program. Before she made the final decision, she spent several days there, observing the caregivers and the children. And even then, sometimes parents have a bad experience, as Vanessa did with Alex's first caregivers.

INDEED, an exposé like the one Vanessa Silver saw on *PrimeTime Live* has remarkable power. "We received literally thousands of phone calls the morning after that show aired. It's unbelievable how much impact a story like that has," Barbara Reisman, executive director of the Child Care Action Campaign at the time, said a few days after the show aired. She and her staff were busily putting out "alerts" to the media and answering media calls to quell the widespread anxiety.

At times, the uneasiness about child care workers can run so deep that the public, the media, and even prosecutors are willing to believe child care workers capable of hideous crimes on the basis of scant evidence. Stories of day care workers participating in satanic cults and sexually abusing children take on credibility a little too quickly. In a few cases, child care providers have even been sent to prison and had to fight for years to secure their freedom. That is not to deny that cases of abuse do take place. Rather, such cases illuminate the fact that the American suspicion of day care runs so deep that it colors the perception of cases once the charges have been brought. The collective imagination is too ready to embrace the worst-case scenario.

The facts show that parents' and policymakers' fear of abuse and neglect in child care is wildly exaggerated. Indeed, the truth is that the incidence of such problems is rare in day care settings—under 1 percent, according to national studies. The sad truth is that children are far more likely to suffer mistreatment at the hands of people they know well—probably because the relationships between parents and their children are so intense and complicated.

Nor are children much more likely to come down with terrible illnesses in day care, even though the image as a germ factory still persists. "My image of day care is twenty-five children in one room, sneezing and coughing on each other," says a lawyer who lives in Little Falls, New Jersey, as she anticipates her first child. "Your child is sick a lot and around others who are sick a lot."

Most outbreaks of disease in child care settings are mild and can be controlled by measures as simple as hand washing and requirements that all children be immunized. Although parents and pediatricians often assume that child care centers breed illness, there is serious debate about how unhealthy they actually are. Some of the nation's most prominent pediatricians contend that the dangers have been overstated. "The data just does not support the commonly espoused idea that kids in day care automatically get more illnesses," says Dr. Susan Aronson, a consultant on day care to the American Academy of Pediatrics. She does not deny that children do suffer a higher incidence of illness in *some* child care programs, especially those that don't practice good hygiene. But, she quickly adds, "that's no reason to disparage *all* child care. The point is, we have to solve the problems as they arise. We didn't close down the public schools when we had an epidemic of measles. We invented a vaccine."

Finally, most American kids don't attend "institutional" day care. By most official counts, "family day care"—the type of care offered in private homes by neighbors—is the most popular form of out-of-home care for the youngest children in this country. In these settings, children are often cared for in very small groups, much like a family. Although the quality of such care is widely uneven, it's not hard to find parents who characterize their children's caregivers as friends or extended family. Indeed, the intimate experience of sharing the care of their children can lead to deep bonds. Melissa Stevens, a marketing executive who has two children and now lives in Woodinville, Washington, remembers all the time she spent with Audrey Atkins, her children's first child care provider. "We talked about our children and our husbands," Stevens says. "We were really close." The families even spent a Christmas together. After four years together, the children treated each other as siblings. "If the people watching my kids are my friends, then I know they're going to give my kids good attention," Stevens says.

Families that use child care centers also tend to describe a warmer, friendlier experience than cultural stereotypes would allow. "My biggest fear about putting Zach in day care was what I had absorbed from media stories. I'd picture him strapped to a car seat with twenty-five other kids. I was afraid he'd just be left by himself all day," says Kristen Storey, the human resources manager who lives in Ann Arbor, Michigan. "But day care turned out to be wonderful." Storey chose a local center, near her house, sponsored in part by the university. "When I got there, I was surprised and pleased with what I saw. The staff was great. Child development was their profession. The kids were active and involved. There were no harsh disciplinary actions." Not only that, but once her son started, she found it to be an enriching experience for both of them. "At ten weeks old, he was coming home with artwork, with his fingerprints on paper. It was really amazing. They helped him explore textures and colors. They did a lot of things I never would have thought of."

And for Storey and her husband, the day care center also became a source of friendships, something akin to the relationships that an earlier generation might have struck up over a backyard fence. That is not surprising, given that the number of children in child care quadrupled between 1976 and 1990, according to a report from the Committee for Economic Development. For many moms, the day care center or a family day care home now provides a similar experience, a community of parents to commiserate with and socialize with as they raise their children. Storey's son is now in elementary school, but she remains friendly with some of the families from the day care center. "Our children played together and we would call each other in a pinch to drop off or pick up each other's kids." The term "extended family" pops up in Storey's description of the relationships, as it does so often in situations where families believe they have found high-quality child care.

But the most striking fact about child care in America today is that no stereotype could accurately describe it. Child care is so truly diverse that it is impossible to come up with a single snapshot that illustrates what most children experience each day. Nonetheless, Americans persist in talking about day care in terms that might have come straight out of a Charles Dickens novel. "Today, we shuffle millions of middle-class children off to day care settings duplicating the sort of deprivation that used to be suffered only by the poorest and the most disadvantaged," a writer for *Progressive* magazine asserted in 1988. The article was reprinted in the *Utne Reader* in 1993, as if it were a fresh idea, under the title "Day Care: A Grand and Troubling Social Experiment."

THAT DAY CARE still carries a strong stigma is widely recognized as a problem by experts in early education. "Public ambivalence" about child care for young children is cited by the Zero to Three, the National Center for Clinical Infant Programs as a key barrier to securing public support for improving and expanding child care services in this country.

Even the most ardent social conservatives concede that it would be possible to fund broad-based child care if Americans did not hold day care in such low esteem. "The money presents a serious problem, but we could probably raise it if we agreed about the value of what it was to be spent for. We do not," wrote Elizabeth Fox Genovese in her widely publicized book *Feminism Is Not the Story of My Life.*

Starting in the mid-1980s, the Child Care Action Campaign began a conscious effort to change the negative perceptions of child care in order to win more public support for funding and other measures that could improve the quality of care across the country. Some of the nation's leading authorities on child care, such as Bettye Caldwell at the University of Arkansas, have even proposed rechristening care for young children as "educare," to get away from old prejudices. To date, however, such ideas have yet to fully take root in the popular imagination.

That is not to say that Americans do not value early education. Many upper-class families vie for spots at local nursery schools, to give their kids a running start on school. But many affluent moms, who pay up to $5,000 a year for part-time enrichment programs, assure anyone willing to listen that their children are going to "school," rather than day care. "I would never put my child in day care," says one as she stands outside her child's nursery school in suburban New Jersey. "It's just too long a day." And not, she adds, educational or enriching. She spent months looking at nursery school programs and had to get on a waiting list to win admittance to this one.

Like many other Americans, she'd never bothered to visit a child care center and see what it's like. If she had, several would have fit her stereotypes. Underfunded, they struggle with high turnover among the staff and with limited and uninviting quarters. Most are in churches, often squeezed into basements or other space that would otherwise go unused. But there are also some truly excellent programs that have won the steadfast and unconditional loyalty of parents. Just a few miles down the road at the time—in Verona, New Jersey—Children's Playhouse offered a nurturing and stimulating program, on acres of land. At this program, three- and four-year-olds did exactly the same things her child did as those at the nursery school. Indeed, on a casual visit, it would be virtually impossible to distinguish which was a "nursery school" and which was "day care."

Of course, the difference in the hours children spend at the program would be profound. But the latest research doesn't show the number of hours a child spends in child care predicts much about his adjustment, unless, of course, the program is a poor one, according to psychologist Carolee Howes from the University of California, who has conducted some of the most in-depth and innovative studies of child care programs. What she does find wouldn't surprise most moms. Spending long hours with adults who are hostile or unresponsive, or having to deal with a constantly changing array of caregivers, can upset a child. But time spent with responsive, sensitive caregivers is something akin to having a day with extended family.

"In some ways, it's just common sense, isn't it," says Peggy Sradnick, director of Basic Trust Infant and Toddler Center, a child care center in New York City recognized nationally for its excellent care. "You have these standards for yourself and for your children. There's a standard of interaction between adults and children that's important, a standard of caring. Sometimes children staying at home don't get that; sometimes a caregiver at home just can't provide that. And some day care is bad. Children just don't get what they need. But the point is that there's good child care and it's good because there is that level of caring."

At the core of it, Sradnick explains, children develop either a trust or a mistrust that adults will meet their needs, keep them safe, and make them feel loved. "You need a basic trust in life to continue on, to feel that the world is a safe place, that you can get what you need from it. If the world always feels erratic, if the adults in a child's world aren't consistent, then that child won't know what to expect, and will be mistrustful."

After decades of providing care to hundreds of children, Sradnick concedes, however, what most studies show. "There is plenty of bad care out there, that's for sure. Parents still don't have good choices. But part of the problem stems from the fact that day care's identity is so poor. It's at the bottom of the barrel, struggling for a positive identity."

THE FIRST day care centers in America opened in the middle of the past century, mostly to serve the children of poor immigrant women who went to work in the factories. After the Civil War, the centers' numbers grew as the need increased. There were now the many children of war widows who needed care, as their moms were forced to go out and work. These early institutions operated as charities, "to feed the starving, clothe the naked and lighten the soul of half-orphaned mothers who were forced to seek employment." Early on, families had to submit to scrutiny of the kind that few middle-class families would choose to undergo. Home visits, for example, were used to determine "the degree of poverty of the family and its morality" before a child could qualify for care.

That these day care programs were meant expressly for the poor, the helpless, and the unfortunate was never a subtle fact. The first day care program in New York City was simply called Nursery for the Children of Poor Women. Located in a small, wooden house and run by New York Hospital, this day nursery was established to care for the children of wet nurses and working mothers in dire straits. Until then, many wet nurses' children starved to death because their mothers did not have enough milk to sustain both the children of their employers and their own biological children.

As a refuge for the poor, few of these nurseries had a cheery image. Known for their dark color and institutional feeling, many were described as shabby and depressing. "Their gloom was often accentuated by the customary dark brown color of walls and woodwork. When parents complained occasionally about the poor care their children received, or offered criticism of any kind, they were considered ungrateful and their children often dropped from the rolls," one day care historian notes. Babies were lined up in cribs, with plaques naming the donors who paid for their care.

The notion of child care as a service that can socialize and "fix" lower-class children who are suffering a deficit is long-standing, evident in the earliest writings about the day nurseries. Upper-class matrons rallied to start these charitable institutions as a way to rescue immigrant children from poverty and chaos in the late 1800s. At the time, stories abounded of children tied to the bedpost or running wild in the streets when their mothers went off to work, and these women set out to save them. "Children should be removed from the unhappy association of want and vice and be placed under better influences," read the mission statement of one nursery in Boston. Some of the commentary on the state of children in the 1840s sounds strangely current. Today, for example, child care advocates promote Head Start and other early education programs as early "intervention" that can prevent crime, teen pregnancy, and other social ills. Proponents of the first day nurseries likewise justified funding as a way of stopping "a great multitude of ignorant, untrained, passionate boys and young men . . . who become the 'dangerous class' of our city."

At the same time, the nursery school movement arrived in America. Borrowing from the ideas of German educators, upper-class women began to see nursery school and kindergarten as important and enriching experiences for young children. Unlike the custodial care and training offered in day nurseries, the new kindergartens and nursery schools aimed to guide and mold a child's learning and development through structured play activities. While some day nurseries adopted some of the same principles, by and large, the distinction between nursery schools and day care was sharp, right from the beginning. Nursery school was education—the staff were teachers and the aim was to stimulate learning and growth for the child. By contrast, day nurseries were tolerated as necessary institutions to rescue poor children. "The word 'care' became associated in the minds of many with the need to supplement inadequate parental care in poverty families requiring welfare aid. The term 'school,' on the other hand, became associated exclusively with those half-day programs having education as a major focus."

The fact that day nurseries were expressly created for poor women stigmatized the service, of course. What American wanted to be branded as poor and helpless? In 1882, one Boston donor, Puling Agassiz Shaw, even suggested that the Boston kindergartens avoid using the term "charity" in their titles or fund-raising because it demeaned those who used the service.

Those who supported the day nursery movement also found that they had to rigorously defend against charges that child care would undermine the family and challenge women's proper place. Much as social conservatives of the 1990s argue that government-funded child care will lure women out of the home, social conservatives of that time contended that day nurseries might undermine the family. "To counter the charge of aiding and abetting the breakdown of the family, the day nursery adopted as its first principle the 'preservation and maintenance of the home.'" At the turn of the century, one leader of the day care movement defended day nurseries as a temporary phenomenon that would not disrupt family relationships. "The Day Nursery is only a make-shift. The great issue is the family and the proper place for development is the home. Any system that permits the breaking up of home surroundings must be make-shift."

Starting in the 1920s, however, the social stigma associated with child care became a matter of formal policy. In 1919, the topic of day care became a "regular topic of discussion" at the annual conference of social workers, according to Margaret O'Brien Steinfels, one of the few historians to study and write about the development of day care in America. The result? A new conception of day care emerged, one that conceived of it as a formal service for "problem families." "The view of the professional social worker came to dominate thinking in the day care field . . . and projected an image to the public of the day nursery as a custodial and undesirable service for women and families who were not normal." A woman who used day care "found herself labeled a 'problem mother' with a maladjusted family." Indeed, the Child Welfare League was founded in 1920 to promote better standards for child care. At the time, nursery schools were recognized as an educational service, but day nurseries were identified as a "service for families with some sort of social pathology."

In the 1930s, the Federation of Day Nurseries issued articles proclaiming that the day nursery child "represented a social problem" and that the "day nursery ought to be the last choice in the care of children." In Philadelphia, the local day nurseries began to ban all group care of young children. As with all the recurrent debates over child care, this renewed attack on child care also coincided with a major push to drum women out of the workforce. During the Great Depression of the 1930s, married women were banned from most workplaces; there was general agreement that a married woman who worked was simply robbing a man of his job.

By the 1940s, women rarely found a day care slot without expressly taking on the identity of society's most desperate and pathological mothers. Many states and towns adopted formal criteria, drawn up by social workers, to decide who would be entitled to government-sponsored day care. New York City's feisty mayor

Fiorello La Guardia instructed the city's social workers to carefully review every mother who applied for a day care slot and counsel her to stay home rather than work. Not surprisingly, many women balked at the idea that using day care made them a bad mother. One day care historian found the following record of one mother's reaction to the overbearing treatment: "Leaving the office after an intake interview with the day nursery caseworker, Mrs. Santo sputtered, 'I guess I know my own business best. She can refuse my baby if she wants to, but telling me to stay home is too much!'"

During World War II, the federal government did fund many day care centers, a fact that has received more publicity and attention from scholars and women's historians in recent years. At times, this period is even celebrated as a sort of golden age of day care, a time when working women had day care centers at their disposal, even for swing shifts. By August 1943, there were some 53,000 children in government-sponsored child care centers. During the war, many employers also provided other services for time-pressed working moms, including prepared meals to take home to their families after work.

But the truth is that even in that desperate time, when the nation relied on women to see it through the war, Americans' ambivalence about day care and mothers working still reigned. Women with children under the age of fourteen were actively discouraged from working; day care was still characterized as a service with the potential to disrupt a well-functioning family. "Experience has shown that the surest and quickest way to disrupt a family is to take the mother out of the home," one trade-union chaplain argued at the time, in documents found by historian Alice Kessler-Harris. She also found that the government-funded day care centers were short on money and short on staff, had limited hours, and therefore couldn't serve all the children of the women who had begun to work. In addition, the centers were generally "spottily and inconveniently located" and fees for the service were often prohibitive. Mothers of very young children were still counseled not to work and it was openly stated that day care programs were "not intended as a substitute for the home, but rather as an aid to parents who face unusual problems arising from the war emergency." Even advocates of day care at the time were apologetic about lobbying for the service. "Whether we like it or not, mothers of young children are at work . . . so we do need care centers," said Florence Kerr, who was then head of the Women's Bureau. Such statements could only serve to mark the moms who relied on such services as dysfunctional and to marginalize day care as a service.

After the war, of course, women were urged to return home, as has been powerfully documented by so many authorities, starting with Betty Friedan in *The Feminine Mystique*. At the time, the best-selling book *Modern Woman, the Lost Sex* advised women to "recapture the functions in which their home demonstrated superior capacity. Those are, in general, the nurturing functions around the home." If they failed to follow this advice, mothers were told, they risked not only the censure of adults, but of their children. The child "realizes instinctively that his mother prefers her job to him, often hates her with a passionate intensity," insisted one author in the *Atlantic* in 1953. The idea that children experience day care as a rejection is not far from Penelope Leach's modern admonition to parents that a child will experience every separation as a terrible loss, that "chasm of your absence."

Across the century, one sharp distinction persisted: nursery schools were for the upper classes and day care for the poor. And increasingly, the only way to win funding for child care was to emphasize its "educational" value. It is a strategy that continues to be potent in the 1990s, with so many parents anxious to see that their children get off to a good start and get a good education. The overwhelming majority of 1,700 working moms polled in 1993 by the Child Care Action Campaign and *Working Mother* magazine described day care as a valuable educational experience. "My older son knew how to write his name. He knew his numbers, letters and shapes. He had been on field trips and done lots of artsy-craftsy projects," Jill Richardson, a Dayton, Ohio, mom and corporate manager, said as she mulled over her first child's experiences in a day care program.

•   •   •

IN TRUTH, of course, the best care for young children is both nurturing and educational, just as life at home should be. And there is virtually unanimous agreement on the qualities that make a child care program both safe and educational. Most important of all, the same conditions that lead to children's emotional health also contribute to their physical well-being. Keeping groups small ensures children get enough attention, and also ensures they are exposed to fewer illnesses. Each new person in a child's environment provides a new avenue for germs and possible infections. Studies show that children enrolled in programs with enough adults on hand to properly supervise and play with the children and with little turnover among the staff run about the same risk of falling ill as kids raised at home.

The best programs also understand that "education" for young children is usually hands-on learning, geared to their ever-increasing physical abilities. At Basic Trust, for example, kids play with sand, water, clay, and paper and even do some cooking to learn about how the world works. The warm, homey atmosphere, the comfy couches, and the engaged and upbeat caregivers all help to create a nurturing environment.

But such care comes at a steep price—about $1,200 a month for full-time care. Manhattan prices are higher than most in the country, but there is no escaping the high cost of high-quality care. Staff salaries run to 80 percent of any good program, and staff salaries are linked directly to high quality. Without a decent paycheck, turnover runs to as much as 40 to 50 percent a year in many programs. Many family child care providers—the neighbors and friends who offer care in their homes—earn only about $1.50 an hour per child.

"A lot of people would like to buy better quality care, but they simply can't afford it," says Nancy McConnell, mother of two in Illinois. "I know a lot of people who just aren't able to pay what it takes to get a good program. I feel we're very lucky to be able to afford it."

Indeed, a San Diego mom describes her search for child care as "about as easy as doing the two-step with one leg amputated."

Faced with few good options, it's hardly surprising that many parents describe child care in negative terms. "At the center where I leave my five-month-old daughter each day, they supply nothing but a body to change and feed the babies. The room is bright and colorful, but I refer to it as the baby jail. All the cribs are lined up against a wall with nothing in them except what the parents provide to stimulate their children," another San Diego mother explains.

Another says, "I can't afford a caregiver whom I consider a suitable substitute role model. If I find something affordable, it is not always ideal. When I have advertised for child care, applicants have included illegal aliens, teenagers, illiterates."

The core problem, obvious to anyone who has bothered to look closely at funding child care, is figuring out how to pay the gap between what most parents can afford and what it costs to run a high-quality program. "Other countries have embraced the idea that they need to create environments for children that are stimulating and safe," says Barbara Reisman, longtime child care advocate and former executive director of the Child Care Action Campaign. America still stands alone among the industrialized nations—except for South Africa—in refusing to fund child care for any but the most desperate families, and under welfare reform plans, even that assistance may disappear for many families. A mother or father in Europe can take a paid leave and then use child care that is subsidized by the state. But Americans still lack the political will to do what is right and make sure all children get decent, loving care.

Americans are apparently willing to sentence so many young children to such poor care because of their deep questions about whether mothers should work at all. "There's this fundamental ambivalence about whether or not child care is a good idea," says Carol Kamin, executive director of the Children's Action Alliance in Arizona and a veteran child care advocate. In all the battles over child care funding in the past twenty years, she's sensed one consistent theme. "There's a worry that somehow if we make child care too attractive, too affordable, then more women will go to work."

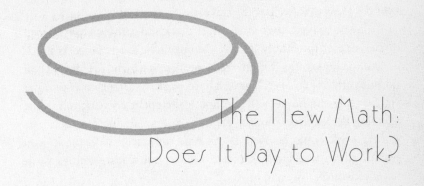

The New Math: Does It Pay to Work?

The Myth of "Choice" About Working

CATHERINE SELIGSON spent the summer of 1996 trying to come to terms with the true value of her paycheck. Did it really pay for her to work outside the home? As an accountant, she certainly had the skills for the task. She'd spent years combing the books for her employers, calculating profit and loss.

But as the mother of two children under the age of three, she found this particular math more daunting than any other. She had enjoyed her past few months at home with her kids and wasn't sure she wanted to plunge back into full-time work. Her decision about how much to work, or even whether to continue to work at all, hinged on her calculations. But how should she set up the terms of the equation? Increasingly, she had come to see the problem as one that required comparing the "costs" of working with the benefits of staying at home.

By July, after months of conversations with her husband, she had

reduced the formula to a fairly simple algebra. "When my husband
and I talk about me working or not, it always comes back to whether
I get paid less than we pay for child care," she says.

Seligson did not question the fact that child care expenses landed
on her side of the family ledger. "My husband earns twice as much
as I do," she says as if that fact stood on its own, the product of
nothing other than his talent and hard work. The truth was that her
work inside the home—all the hours she spent cooking, cleaning,
washing the clothes, running errands, and arranging for child care
during work hours, as well as the time she put in with the kids at
night and on weekends—allowed him to boost his earnings while
simultaneously lowering hers.

Still, it did not seem odd or unusual to either her or her husband
that her household work never got a price tag, except as an expense
against her paycheck. It was simply a given of life that her labor was
worth less than her husband's, that child care was her concern and
responsibility, not his.

LIKE MOST Americans, Seligson had no way to place her dilemma in
context, to understand that her private conversations with her husband were part of social history, a continuation of the struggle
women began 150 years ago to have their labor fairly valued. Only
recently have feminist scholars unearthed the voices of women at the
dawn of the industrial revolution, as the economy lurched out of the
home and into factories. They have set out a record of how women
fought in the courts and state legislatures to have their work recognized and valued, just as men's was. It was then that judges and state
legislators first insisted on giving a different value to men's and
women's work. It was then that it was decided, after heated debates,
that most women's work—most especially child care and housework—would go without pay, while most men's work would earn a
wage. In other words, the economic value of men's work would be
recognized and rewarded, while women's would not—based on their
roles in the family. Over time, men's roles as "providers" and "breadwinners" grew sacrosanct, a reason to pay men more than women.

Over the past century, unions, businesses, and even the U.S. Congress and courts have bargained and argued over the relative value of men's and women's labor. The debates reveal that paychecks are as much the product of social values as the pressures of the market-place. Gradually, working women have made gains. But at each new juncture, they had to fight the notion that their salaries were sec-ondary to men's, that they didn't need as much income as men. Most often, women's roles as wives and mothers were used as an excuse to keep their wages lower than men's, even as many working women protested that they were truly the breadwinners for their families.

THESE DAYS, the issues lurking at the core of Seligson's decision making have become the stuff of research and public policy debates, as economists, historians, sociologists, and psychologists all take a closer look at how value is assigned to men's and women's work.

Most interesting, a growing number of social scientists have begun to see the link between women's domestic labor and men's higher earnings. "I call it the dry-cleaning effect," jokes social scientist Jane Waldfogel, "the boost workers get when they have someone at home to pick up the dry cleaning and do the other chores at home." She notes that many women struggled in the 1980s, as Seligson did, to hang on to their earnings once they became mothers.

But the new debates have had hardly any airing in the popular press and virtually no publicity at all, outside of academia. So it is that many middle-class mothers are left with little perspective on the pressures that drive their paychecks down and rob both them and their families of a decent living. Most often, women's predicament is pre-sented in terms of women's "choices," as if women freely set the terms at work and at home. The fact that women's earnings are lower than men's is treated as simply the natural order of life, the fall-out of men's and women's preferences, even the natural outcome of sex differences. A widely cited report from June O'Neill, the conservative economist who headed the Congressional Budget Office in the mid-1990s, for example, concluded that the remaining gap between men's and women's earnings was due to women's "choices," and most par-ticularly the "choice" to work less once they had children.

Without historical context or an alternate way to frame the economics, women continue to see their problems as Seligson did, as deeply personal ones, to be resolved in the privacy of their own homes, in conversations with family and friends.

For most, the decisions about whether and how much to work after they have children surface gradually, as pressures mount both at home and on the job.

SO IT WAS for Seligson. Her summer of reckoning crept up on her slowly, an outgrowth of the day-to-day balancing act of home and family she'd begun three years earlier, with the birth of her first child. The fact that she took primary responsibility for the children led almost inevitably to this crossroads.

Indeed, she'd already cut back her hours and pay by 20 percent to keep up with child care and the household duties. "I was exhausted trying to fit in all the errands and chores, even with a nanny to help me," she recalls. "So after I had my second child, I cut back to a four-day week at work."

That decision cost her far more than she expected, however. That winter, her annual bonus at work was slashed—from $18,000 to $4,800. That was $200 less than the bonus she received her first year on the job, eight years earlier. "I was stunned when I heard the figure," she recalls. She knew that she still produced almost as much work as she had on a five-day schedule, by working through lunch and skipping breaks. But her department head only seemed to notice the time she spent with her family. He justified the low bonus as the price of "three-day weekends" with her baby. He also noted as a reason for her low bonus the fact that she had taken a six-week maternity leave. When she took her case to the general manager at the bank, she was told she "no longer had a future" there. Her reduced hours revealed a lack of commitment to her career, he said. "I knew it was risky to go on a flexible schedule," she says. "I was the first. But I didn't expect this treatment after already taking a pay cut."

Unlike the many women who suffer ill-treatment in exchange for a more flexible schedule, Seligson had some recourse. She knew that it was illegal for the bank to penalize her for taking a maternity leave, and hired a lawyer. "Even our human resources people were amazed that he mentioned maternity leave. They knew that was illegal. I didn't want to go to a lawyer, but I couldn't let them do this to other women," she says angrily. She won an out-of-court lawsuit—nine months of full pay and benefits. But now that money was about to run out and she had to make a decision about whether to look for a full-time job, continue to temp, or simply quit working altogether.

By then, her earning power was so compromised—standing at 40 percent of what it was when her first child was born—that the idea of quitting altogether grew ever more appealing. If she did, her story on all official records would look like a "choice" she had made. Indeed, even many of her former coworkers at the bank believed that she quit her job to stay home with her kids. Seligson had taken a pledge of secrecy in exchange for her out-of-court settlement. "The day I left my job, I just told everyone I was going to stay home with the kids," she says. "Most of my coworkers had no idea of what I had been through." Nor will most of them ever know, since she asked that her name be changed for this book.

As Seligson's salary was driven down by attitudes at home and on the job, her husband's soared. With the birth of their first child, he began to increase his hours, boosting his paycheck. Still, the idea of deducting any child care costs from his paycheck struck her as absurd. Since he refused to take responsibility for the children, that cost was hers. "He'd never stay home with the kids," she explains. And, of course, she enjoyed the time she now had with her children.

Over time, then, Seligson could expect that her earning power would likely decline, as she worked in ever more marginal jobs, at the edges of her profession. That summer, she conceded that she was not entirely comfortable with this situation. "I can't really imagine not working, because I'm an accountant and I've always worked," she says. Indeed, when she was interviewed just six months earlier, her concern about being dependent on her husband was palpable. At that time, before she was forced out of the bank, she confidently asserted that "for me personally, I feel I should be sharing the weight of supporting the whole family. I don't want to be totally reliant on my husband for income."

But in the intervening months, she'd gradually come to make

peace with the idea of quitting work altogether, at least for a while. Her husband was now on the verge of launching a new business, one that would involve a lot of travel. "He'll be away a lot. He'd love it if I were at home," she says. The only reason to continue working now, she says, is for the health benefits. "I guess my decision depends on how well his business does," she says.

And, she adds, no one—not friends, family, colleagues, or neighbors—offered much support for her to keep on working. If anything, she felt a constant pressure to quit working. In her part of the world, a privileged upper-class suburb outside Chicago, many couples fell into "traditional" sex roles. She'd been unusual until now, staying with her professional job for more than three years after her first baby was born. Most of the women in the affluent tract houses in her neighborhood were married to executives and professional men, and many stopped working after they had kids. "When I ride the train, I see mostly men. My friends in my town always say to me, 'Oh, too bad you aren't home; we could have so much fun together,'" she says.

And her days at work also led her to think about quitting. Most of the men at the bank had wives at home to take care of the kids and domestic duties, a distinct advantage in her mind. "They don't go home in the evening, fix dinner, give the kids a bath, and get them into bed," she says. "They go home and expect to be taken care of." To fit in, she believes, "you do have to pretend you don't have a family at home. If I brought up something about how hard it is to do both, they'd say, 'Oh, she's just whining and complaining.'"

In such an environment, it's easy to see why Seligson often questioned her commitment to work and increasingly described herself as "lucky" to have a "choice" about working or not working. From a sociologist's point of view, Seligson's conclusion was a predictable one—the attempt to make peace with what sociologists call "structured ambivalence." That is, work and family life are organized around a core set of social customs and beliefs that men are the breadwinners and women the caregivers. The assumptions are not always spelled out explicitly, but rather incorporated into both the formal and informal rules of success at work and at home. Those rules are constantly revealed and reinforced in the fabric of everyday life—to such an extent that they come to seem inevitable. Seligson's experience of seeing mostly men in positions of power, for example, and mostly women at home is not an uncommon one for women in management and professional jobs. Many are married to highly educated men, live in affluent neighborhoods, and still see plenty of couples in traditional roles.

"Many women talk about being torn. They don't realize it's an ambivalence fed by the structures around them, of the way work and family life are organized, rather than their own personal decisions. They see expectations in both arenas—at work and at home—that are legitimate, but contradictory," says sociologist Cynthia Fuchs Epstein from City University of New York's Graduate Center. "But few have the perspective or the history to sort out why they feel that way." Hamstrung between competing imperatives on the job and at home, they "often feel marginalized or have a sense of not knowing what to do about their situation." Making peace with the attitudes in the workplace and at home, as Seligson did, often seems the most sensible way to proceed.

But the truth was that Seligson's new equation, which made child care her exclusive expense, could put both her and her children at risk in the years to come, making her ever more dependent on her husband's earnings and the stability of their marriage. Her own earning power could be seriously curtailed and her career options limited if she took even a relatively short break from work. Research by the Urban Institute shows that women who work continuously make 40 percent more by the time they are forty than those who work intermittently. Women who take a break from work to raise their kids are often frustrated and angry at the reactions from employers when they try to start working again. "I am thirty-one years old and am afraid I'll never work again. I have sent résumés out and gone to employment agencies, and apparently everything I did prior to staying home is erased in any employer's mind," said one mom in 1995. With a college degree and several years of experience as an office worker, she had expected reentry to go smoothly. She had even kept her computer skills up to date. But she now found that the best she could do was make slightly above minimum wage. She'd been advised to put "volunteer" on her résumé for the years at home, so there wouldn't be a gap in her work history. "I have been busy raising the children and really do not have a lot of volunteer experience to put on my résumé," she said.

Like many moms, she felt betrayed by the lack of appreciation for the job she was doing at home with the children. "I honestly believe that the only people who can relate to the extreme work it takes both mentally and physically to raise children" are other people who've done it. That, of course, did not include most employers. So even though she'd been a good worker in the past, she found she was now treated as though she were "fresh out of high school." Such treatment is common even in supposedly "mother-friendly" careers such as teaching. "I am very anxious to get back into my career," says a mom who taught for nearly a decade, then took several years off while her children were young. "I find employers unsympathetic to my 'hiatus' spent raising my kids. What's the answer? Go back to school for yet another degree? I'm forty years old and don't want to start at the bottom of the food chain!"

But from Seligson's vantage point, the risks of dropping out of the workforce seemed minor at the time, if they existed at all. She did not anticipate getting divorced—who does? When asked if she had considered the long-range consequences of dropping out of the workforce for a while, she replies, "No, my husband and I haven't really talked about it." But, like most working women, she knows that as a practical matter, it's far from easy to slip in and out of the workforce without penalty. After a moment, she adds, "I guess I'd have to take a pay cut when I go to a new job, but I'd hope that I could make it up quickly. I have a lot of good skills."

Social scientist Jane Waldfogel notes that Seligson's situation was hardly unique. In the 1980s, married women with children did make more than moms in the past—their earnings grew from 60 percent of men's to 75 percent in just one decade. But that progress lagged far behind that of women without children—who pushed their earnings from 72 percent to 95 percent of men's pay.

Indeed, Waldfogel's research and that of other social scientists indicates that much of the remaining pay gap between men and women is due to penalties imposed on working women once they have children. This is not a matter of women volunteering to quit and stay home, not a matter of simple "choices" that women make.

Rather, Waldfogel and other social scientists have identified what they call the "family gap" in earnings—the direct and indirect pay cuts associated with motherhood. The lack of maternity leave benefits in so many workplaces, for example, means that many women must leave their jobs, lose seniority, and return to work at a lower rate of pay. Those who can't find child care quit their jobs or choose lower-paying part-time work even when they'd prefer to work full-time. And discrimination also plays a role—in terms of the money women lose when their bosses view them as unreliable or uncommitted workers.

Further, Waldfogel and others found, the portion of the wage gap that could be explained by motherhood zoomed over the 1980s. That was so even though women as a group had grown better educated and more experienced than any generation before them. Those assets had boosted the earnings of childless women. But not those with children.

Other researchers also took note of the enduring earnings gap between men and women. What they found was equally intriguing. While the earnings picture for most men was better than that of most women, there was one group of men who also suffered an earnings penalty in the 1980s: men with working wives. Dual-earner dads made 20 percent less than other men, even though they worked nearly as many hours. Indeed, the men from two-paycheck families put in an average of only one or two hours less on the job per week—not enough to explain the gap. Researchers remain uncertain about exactly how to explain the pay difference, but there seems to be a good case that the lower pay derives as much from psychic realities of the workplace as the concrete issues of productivity. Social psychologists note that there are subtle signals that managers look for in the employees they supervise, signs of career commitment. When a man has a stay-at-home wife, it may signal to his superiors that he is more available for work—he fits the expected mold for most executives today. Therefore, his bosses may find it easier to relate to him and to reward him than a man with a working wife.

All of this makes it clear that the nation has much to do to make parenthood and the right to earn a good living more compatible. A full 46 percent of the workforce is now female; some 60 percent of workers are dual-earner couples. That means that vast numbers of them are paid less than they are worth, simply because they violate the old social mores of the workplace. Certainly, more voices have pressed the case for practical change. By the early 1990s, the Conference Board, a think tank for the nation's largest corporations, had established an annual conference on work and family issues for the nation's largest companies. *Working Mother* magazine's annual list of family-friendly companies generated widespread media interest—hundreds of millions of mentions in newspapers and on television and radio shows. The term "family-friendly" had even crept into popular culture. In 1993, President Clinton signed the Family and Medical Leave Act, the first bill that gave men as well as women the right to take a leave from work for family reasons. "It's true there's been remarkable progress for women on many fronts. There have never been so many opportunities for women," says Epstein. "And the nature of change is profound in many areas—for instance, the number of women entering the professions and managerial jobs.

"But the change is not happening in every sphere at the same rate. What hasn't changed much is the allocation of child care to women," she adds. And that makes it possible for the new math to take hold.

BY THE early 1990s, the old idea that women must bear total responsibility for child care was translated into a new vernacular: Now women were told "it didn't pay to work once they have kids." A whole raft of media stories began to appear, urging women to do just what Seligson had done—that is, reduce the question of whether to work to a simple mathematical equation. Half a century ago, women might have heard their paychecks referred to as "pin money," extra money they brought in to buy jewelry and other small family luxuries. This new spate of coverage was simply a new way to dress up those old arguments about women's work—that it is unimportant and secondary to men's.

New York Times reporter Tamar Lewin was one of the first to take the plunge, on April 21, 1991, by daring to ask what she called the "prime postfeminist question" in print: Does it really pay for women to work after they have children?

"Financially, the answer may be no—at least for professional women, and at least for the short run."

Like many other articles that followed, this one counseled women to add up all the "costs" of paid work—including child care, clothes for work, commuting, lunches, and even the price of morning coffee and a bagel—and deduct them from their paychecks. To make her point, Lewin laid out the math for a woman making more than most in America: $50,000. Such a woman would be making more money than most men, even more than most dual-earner couples, according to the labor statistics at the time.

But this woman's earnings nearly vanished via the *Times*'s accounting system. After subtracting all the "expenses" associated with working outside the home, she was bringing home just $5,909. The conclusion: she might as well quit working.

"Soul-searching about whether the second income really makes the family better off has become a staple of playground talk," Lewin reported, encouraged by articles in women's magazines. That very month, *Redbook,* for example, carried a piece entitled "I Couldn't Afford My Job," which included a similar cost-benefit analysis of women's work. The cost of child care, clothes, commuting to work, buying timesaving foods, and taxes whittled a woman's paycheck down to practically nothing.

Lewin did acknowledge there were problems lurking beneath the surface of this analysis. "Men and women alike may question why it should be the mother who considers leaving her job," she noted. She went on to quote several feminists, including Heidi Hartmann, who had won widespread attention for conducting a study that put a dollar figure on the wages women lose the first few years after they have children. Her research and many studies since then demonstrated that thousands upon thousands of women face dilemmas similar to those Seligson faced: lack of child care, lack of flexible work policies, pay cuts. Taken together, Hartmann and her associates estimated that women's lost pay due to motherhood amounted to nearly $8500 in the first two years after the baby was born because they must quit, search for a new job, and frequently accept a new post at lower pay. Waldfogel's studies, as well as research by others, show that things have not gotten much better for moms.

But rather than pursue the question of why child care and other "expenses" of work are seen as women's expenses, Lewin dismissed the feminist logic as simply impractical. "As a practical matter, working women earn 68 cents for every dollar men earn, and are therefore the obvious candidates for child care, another poorly paid job."

This type of analysis marked a stark departure from the media themes of the 1970s and 1980s, which exhorted women to value themselves more highly. In those years, reporters urged working women to see if their pay truly reflected the value of their labor and seek a remedy if they felt underpaid. Only a few years before, many reporters eagerly covered campaigns to improve women's pay, and ran story after story exposing how a person's gender affected pay scales in the workplace. They also presented the long-range consequences of dropping out of the workforce in vivid detail, following the plight of "displaced homemakers"—the women of an earlier generation who had chosen to drop out of the workforce or scale back their ambitions once they had children, only to find themselves destitute in their later years.

But by the early 1990s, the new impulse had taken hold. Rather than challenging the assumptions that held women's pay in check, Lewin joined the "soul-searching" of the playground, feeding the forces that marginalized women's earnings. The facts that women's work was paid less because it was done by women and that women had primary responsibility for child care were no longer topics for outrage. Now they were subjects to be made palatable, the inevitable facts of life.

Her argument was buttressed by an imposing chart, produced by the prestigious accounting firm of Price Waterhouse. Under the title "To Work or Not to Work," the *New York Times* presented the accountants' numbers, lending an aura of science to the analysis. The subtext of this presentation was that the *Times* had arrived at a dispassionate way to answer the question of whether women should work. Who could quibble with the numbers, especially when they had been compiled by one of the Big Six accounting firms?

That this argument appeared in the pages of the *New York Times* is no small matter, since its influence extends far beyond its pages, frequently setting the agenda for other media. Lewin's thesis was prominently featured in the *Times*'s Sunday Op-Ed section, under the heading "Ideas and Trends"—a weekly feature that is well read by policymakers and journalists. When contacted five years after the article, Lewin said it was an article she remembered well, although she refused to elaborate on the themes or the reporting she did to put the story together. "My work in print speaks for itself," she said. She did confirm that she hired Price Waterhouse to run the numbers. "It was hard to figure out just which expenses to include and which ones not to." And she did confirm that the article was her own idea, not one thrust on her by her editors. It was an idea that grew from her own personal experience as a working mother, from talking to friends, and from her own reporting.

It's a sure bet that many working moms read this article closely, since it touched the core issues of their lives. Indeed, in a brief discussion of the story, Lewin did recall that her story "tipped the balance" for one of her neighbors in New York City, persuading the woman to quit her job in financial services. "She told me she realized her job was just pushing them into a higher tax bracket," Lewin recalled.

The *Times* was one of the first major media outlets to take this view of working mothers' earnings. Many other reporters and editors ran similar stories, turning the devaluation of women's paid labor into a virtual science, replete with charts that women could use to do the math. In 1994, *Barron's* asserted that "many women are working for nothing."

The argument was aimed mostly at professional, educated women—the ones most likely to be in jobs previously dominated by men. "It's always the case that when you have movement toward greater participation in some endeavor—in this case, more women wanting to participate in the workplace—it's going to create resistance from people who see it as a threat to their stake," says Epstein. "Whether consciously or unconsciously, those in power will always cling to the reasoning that helps them undercut the people who make the breakthrough. In this case, it's mostly men holding high-paying jobs who see women as the threat. What better argument to use than ones that valorize motherhood and make it seem a positive value for a woman to give up and go home?"

Single moms and working-class women were generally exempt from the new math. The argument that many women worked "out of necessity" had gained ground. That may have been partly because of the perception that working-class women were helping their men, rather than competing with them. And single moms on welfare, scapegoated as a drain on taxpayers, were exhorted to work, no matter what the consequences for their children. These women also posed little threat to male dominance of the workplace. Many were poorly educated and had checkered job histories. They were unlikely to challenge male authority or earnings. The welfare "reform" bill pushed thousands into the workforce, even though nearly every policy paper on the topic showed they had no one to care for their children. This dilemma received periodic lip service in the press and from policymakers. In the fall of 1997, Hillary Clinton even held a summit at the White House on child care, trying to put the issue on the media's agenda. But reporters paid the meeting little mind. The headlines lasted barely a day. Instead, the media focused on the trial of a British nanny who was accused of murdering a Boston couple's baby.

In a way, the new logic that "it didn't pay to work" amounted to an intriguing and innovative assault on women's progress, playing subtly on the power of gender in American society. The charts and graphs put the message in a new package, but the bottom line remained what it always had been. "Hey, gals, once you think it over, you'll realize you shouldn't challenge the status quo. You really belong at home."

Such stories persist in the media, from CNN to *Parents* maga-

zine, much to the detriment of working moms. They not only reinforce the idea that child care is exclusively women's work, but also
the idea that women's earnings are still supplementary to men's—an
argument that keeps women's wages down. "When I went for my
performance review, my boss told me I didn't need a raise because
my husband has a good job," says one female executive at a major
bank. "He asked me why I needed more money when my husband
was already making a good living."

THE SUPREME irony of this logic is that it surfaced just as the economics of family life had taken a dramatic turn in the opposite direction. By 1990, married women brought in an average of 40 percent of
their family's income. One in three women working full-time earned
more than her husband.

So while Lewin justified her point of view as simply acquiescing
to "practical" matters, by the time she wrote the story, the "practi-
calities" of life had convinced a growing number of women that
their incomes were essential to their families' well-being. Women
themselves began to actively claim the title of "breadwinner" and
"provider." In 1995, the widely heralded study by the Families and
Work Institute showed that women today consider earning money
simply to be one way that they care for their families. And for many
married women, the idea of dropping out of the workforce is little
more than a pipe dream, a fantasy that few could afford.

"I'm a breadwinner. I make nearly as much as my husband. I
count just as much as he does," says Sheri Rose, an executive secretary in Fair Lawn, New Jersey. "If I don't work, we lose the house.
It's as simple as that. It's the times. It doesn't matter if you rent or
buy. It's one thousand or twelve hundred dollars a month to live
somewhere. The only people at home have husbands who are doctors or lawyers, or they bought their houses a while ago and have
mortgages of four hundred to six hundred dollars a month. If you
buy a house now, it's one thousand to fifteen hundred dollars a
month. That's the market, and there aren't that many men making
enough on their own to cover that."

Two paychecks also means far more security for a family. "I

know it's worthwhile for me, my husband, and my children to have me working," says Gail Luttrell, the insurance adjuster who lives in Louisville, Kentucky. "All you have to do is look at the cost of a college education. I don't think it's fair or makes sense to have one person trying to pay for all the bills, plus retirement for two people. And what happens if he gets laid off? With me working, he doesn't have the pressure of being the sole breadwinner."

The truth is that the model of male breadwinner, female homemaker has historically worked only for a fairly small proportion of American families. Many working-class women, immigrant women, and women of color have always worked outside the home. Over the past two decades, men's wages have dropped, divorce rates have soared, and nearly every family with children feels the pinch. It is true that the top fifth of Americans are doing better, but most are staying even largely because of the second paycheck, as Luttrell points out. It is absurd to insist that it "doesn't pay" for women to work. Instead, many polls of working women show that their families need the money and they want to earn more. The problem is not that their work has no value, but rather that it is *devalued*, both at home and at work.

Nonetheless, the idea that it "didn't pay" for women to work caught fire. Indeed, the new calculus has become practically a national sport among working moms.

TERRI HARTMAN sat at her desk, calculator in hand. She didn't know Catherine Seligson. She lived thousands of miles away. Nonetheless, she examined her life through a similar lens, at the same time, in the summer of 1996. It was her first week on the job with the Allegheny Health, Education, and Research Foundation, a nonprofit health and educational foundation in Philadelphia, and she had made up a list of the expenses she incurred just to show up on the job: child care, commuting, clothing, parking, and several other items landed on the "expense" side of her ledger. "I looked at everything—even the money I'd spend on lunch instead of fixing my tuna fish sandwich at home," she says. She then subtracted these expenses from her take-home pay.

Her conclusion? "It was pretty much of a wash. I was in the black, but not by much." Hartman says that she and her husband often engage in this exercise that working mothers know so well, a constant cost-benefit analysis of the choices they make about work and family. "For me, it wasn't really part of the decision-making process in terms of working or not. I really wanted to work," Hartman says. "But I decided to see if this job was really profitable or not."

One of her colleagues recalls the amount more precisely. "Terri said she was only bringing home one hundred dollars a month," says Sharon Jacobs, the mother of two who had gone through so much soul-searching over child care. That number stayed in Jacobs's mind because, by then, she had heard so many other women walking themselves through similar calculations. "We talk about these issues every day. It's just something you live with as a working mother," she says.

"I know women in secretarial positions who say it's just not worth it to work. They end up quitting because child care in the Philadelphia area is so expensive. Good care can easily run to nine thousand or ten thousand dollars a year. Even not-so-good care costs a lot. They say it's just not worth working after they figure in taxes and commuting."

At the time, Hartman said she felt fortunate that the math worked out in favor of paid employment, if only by a little. "I love to work. I need the psychic rewards of bringing home a paycheck. I need to have my contribution to the family have economic value. I like getting paid for my work," she said. In the summer of 1996, she found her life to be nearly perfect. "I know I have a great life," she said. "I am financially secure. I have three wonderful kids." The fact that her husband made far more than she did was not an issue in their marriage. Indeed, his hefty salary allowed her to be more bold at work, to take risks. "I'm very aware that we could live without my income at this stage, and that frees me up and makes me a better performer on the job," she said.

Still, she added, there was one issue that bothered her. "Why doesn't it occur to women to subtract the cost of child care and not men? Why is there the assumption that child care is a woman's cost and not the couple's?"

HARTMAN was surprised to hear that this assumption had roots in history and law—that even today, her husband has the right, under law, to demand that she do the housework and child care for free. It is part of her "wifely duties," part of the marriage contract, under law, even in the 1990s. Not so long ago, her husband would have owned both his and her earnings, and she would have had to ask him for an allowance. Just a few decades ago, he could have had her arrested and thrown in jail, divorced and disgraced her, for taking a few dollars from his pants pockets to pay the household bills. He could have done that had she worked outside the home or not, whether their joint income was the result of his inheritance or hers.

But how could Hartman have known this? Until recently, women's struggle to have the economic value of their work fully recognized, both inside and outside the home, was lost. Now that the record is found, it illuminates why women's wages still lag behind men's. The roles of breadwinner and homemaker, provider and dependent, did not happen by accident. Rather, these roles were purposely written into law and economic agreements—often over the loud protests of working women.

10

Women's Puny Paychecks

How They Got So Small

LEGAL SCHOLAR Reva Siegel thrilled at her discovery. It was 1989, and Siegel, a professor of law at Yale University, had begun to read her way through the six-volume, 6,000-page *History of Women's Suffrage*, put together a century before by Elizabeth Cady Stanton and Susan B. Anthony, the leaders of the women's movement in the past century. Stanton and Anthony had collected the papers for future historians and academics interested in the feminist movement. Many scholars had studied the papers, but none had yet looked at them from Siegel's perspective. She wanted to know exactly how women of the time felt about the value of their household labor.

And what she discovered was that women had petitioned to have the economic value of their work in the home recognized in the law. That would be something akin to wives today demanding their husbands pay them for doing the housework and raising the kids. The hope was to make the value of women's work visible and valued, and to put it on an equal footing with men's, as the nation moved to a market economy.

Such a proposal was nothing short of revolutionary, rightfully perceived by legislators of the past century as a threat to the nation's economic order. "I began to realize that this amazing set of arguments had been made over a century ago, that this history had been ignored and no trace remained. I wanted to pull it together again so that there was some known record that these conversations ever existed," Siegel says.

The fact that these women failed to win their battle goes a long way toward explaining why women's pay still lags so far behind men's. Siegel is one of the latest feminist scholars to begin to tell the story of women's pay from women's perspective. "The importance of knowing history is that it provides a framework for thinking about working women. The ways people have thought historically about women and households and who's a breadwinner are all part of an explanation as to why so many women are trapped in particular kinds of jobs today," says feminist historian Alice Kessler-Harris, a leading scholar on working women. "It's important to know where you came from, if you want to change things, change the framework in which women are forced to operate."

What the record shows is that women's pay was explicitly and routinely kept below men's, out of a widespread cultural belief that women belonged at home, not the workplace.

In the early 1900s, one economist noted that higher wages would be "a great gain for women" because work tends to "develop their faculties." Yet, he added, paying women as much as men would also be "an injury in so far as it tempts them to neglect their duty of building up a true home, and of investing their efforts in the personal capital in children's character and abilities."

Sixty years prior to that, a writer for the *New York Post* asserted that "the only way to make husbands sober and industrious was to keep women dependent by means of insufficient wages."

·   ·   ·   ·

IT TOOK Siegel several years to piece her part of the history together. Starting back in 1989, she simply began to read her way through the 6,000-page feminist papers.

She began this project after discovering other fascinating references showing that women had tried to lay a claim to the work involved in child care and housework as property within a marriage. This was an intriguing argument, one that had never been raised before, as far as Siegel knew.

The hodgepodge of documents in the collection did not make the research easy. "None of this was indexed. These volumes were basically what they kept in their attic. It was all the petitions, all the speeches from conventions, everything they had." Siegel laughs. "I had to just read my way through it to understand what it was that women were asking for."

What she found was startling, and finally published in the *Yale Law Journal* in March of 1994. She has dubbed her work a "political history of housework," but it is much more than that. Indeed, she shows how the bargains struck at the dawn of the industrial age set the stage for many of the dilemmas women face today. The separation of men's and women's work, the higher value assigned to men's work, coupled with the devaluation of women's, doomed women to lower wages, along with the "second shift."

"There are many ways that work could be organized and valued, so that women could be equal to men," notes Siegel. "What this record shows is that what we have today is not a given, natural arrangement."

Indeed, it is one that a cadre of early feminists bitterly disputed. As far back as the 1850s, women protested that women's work was unfairly treated as inferior to that of men. "The ignoramus who feeds the pigs or cattle is paid for his labor in proportion to his toil, the wife and mother who rears the family is not considered self-supporting . . . [even] though she is doing two-thirds of the work of the world," the editor of *New Northwest Journal*, a women's journal published in Portland, Oregon, wrote in the early 1870s.

These women fought for a broader definition of work, one that recognized the value of all the work women do, including child care and housework. "They pierced the veil of sentiment about work inside the family," says Siegel. "They understood that the work they did in the home had economic as well as emotional value." Some were even prescient enough to understand that without a dollar value attached to the work they did, the value of their labor could be discounted and even slip into obscurity. Only paid work—men's work—would remain visible and valued.

In speeches, petitions, and protests, they also insisted they were not dependent on men, nor did they want to be. Instead, they asserted that it was the unfair laws and social customs that forced them to depend on men. Women's work, they contended, was equally valuable to a family's economic survival and should be recognized as such. "It takes three, and sometimes four women to get a man through from the cradle to the grave, and sometimes a pretty busy time they [women] have of it, too. It is time we stated facts and called things by their right names and handled this subject without kid gloves," one woman wrote to the *Woman's Journal* in 1875.

Women understood then, perhaps with even more clarity than women do today, how their roles as wives and mothers were used as an excuse to discount the value of their labor—while boosting the value of men's. "If you had paid for the cooking, baking, washing, ironing, sweeping, dusting, making and mending of clothes, would your wages have kept you, your wife and five children as comfortably as you have lived?" one woman angrily asked New York State legislators in the late 1800s. "Certainly not!" she answered herself.

Their clarity of vision grew out of their situation in the last century, a time when "work" and "home" were one and the same for most Americans. Most families still lived on farms, raising their own food, making their own clothes. Many households operated on the barter system, trading goods and services for the necessities of life. Fights over whether the nation should even have paper money—and how an economy with money at its center would be organized—were yet to come. Most men and women still worked side by side, making an equal, if different, contribution to the family and community economy.

That is not to say that men and women were equals. Quite the opposite. Under property laws at the time, husbands owned title to all their wives' property, including a wife's inheritance and any wages she might earn at a job outside the home or any other money she might make. But most notable of all, men owned the right to their wives' labor inside the home, including child care, housework, and any other duties that kept the family going. Under marital laws of the time, women's work in the home was considered part of their "wifely duties," service due their husbands. The Iowa Supreme Court, for example, concluded that "a husband is entitled to his wife's labor and assistance in the discharge of those duties and obligations which arise out of the married relation." A man might even divorce his wife if she refused to help care for his extended family.

The fact that at least some women saw this as an injustice was what so fascinated Siegel. They argued that the work of child care and housework should not sit outside the mainstream economy; they predicted that treating it differently than other work would only serve to marginalize women's labor and make women dependent on men. At the time, they did not ask for pay for it, but property rights to its value. At the time, such a claim would have made them equals in marriage. It would also, of course, have kept women's work visible. Their arguments eerily foreshadow current arguments in favor of "comparable worth" and "pay equity" for women, which assert that while men and women do not always do the same work, women's work should still be valued at least as highly as men's. It was especially notable that these women saw the work of rearing children as a job with economic as well as emotional value. Without someone at home to raise kids, they saw that men could not earn wages.

"The power of Reva Siegel's work is that she brings child care into the frame, so we can see it. Most of the time, we leave the work of child care out of the frame, out of sight. It's made into a personal issue," says Joan Williams, law professor at American University who studies the way property rights play out in marriage. She notes that many women today drop out of the work force or earn less because of child care problems. And they see such problems as their

domain, not their spouse's. "Women will say, 'It's not worth working. Life is too crazy when I work,' instead of seeing that the stress
they feel comes from the pressures of a set of social rules, from the
way work is organized and valued."

Some early feminists compared women's situation with that of
slaves, a comparison that seemed apt to many women at the time.
The abolition movement was vibrant, and many women saw a parallel between their situation and that of slaves in the South. "Wives
have too soon discovered that they were the unpaid housekeepers
and nurses and still worse, chattels . . . to be used and abused at the
will of a master," wrote Sarah Grimke, one of the leading lights of
the early women's movement. "Let us own ourselves, our earnings,
our genius," argued another woman before the New York State leg-
islature. Yet another, Antoinette Brown Blackwell, argued, "The
wife owes service and labor to her husband as much as and as
absolutely as the slave does his master." And, she added, "the reason
that our women are paupers is not that they do not labor right
earnestly, but that the law gives their earnings into the hands of
manhood."

Again and again, they asked state legislatures to grant women an
ownership right not only to any earnings outside the home, but also
to the work they did at home. "As I was researching this, people kept
saying to me, 'No one would ever have thought to emancipate household labor,'" Siegel recalls. "But as I read these papers, I began to see
that, lo and behold, married women were making that argument.
They wanted to lay claim to the economic value of their labor as
property in their own name. They saw that what was being set up
was a distinction between market labor and housework."

They saw that that distinction was a crucial one. The value of
the work they did in the home was simply disappearing from view
and they saw that could easily put women at an economic disadvan-
tage as the nation moved to a market economy. Women would have
to purchase things they'd made or bartered for in the past. Yet they
had no right to their earnings and no value attached to the work
they did in the home. "The value of things," wrote Helen Jenkins,
editor of the *New Northwest Journal,* "as the world goes is increas-

ingly its money value. Law and society say this home work need not be paid in money, therefore, society and law value the work of the mothers of the nation at how much?" Her answer? "Nothing." She suggested husbands pay their wives so the work would become visible and women become "an equal partner" in marriage. Another woman suggested that women refrain from doing housework until its economic value was recognized. "I feel like advising every woman not to do another day's labor unless she can be the owner of the value of it."

By the late 1800s, after protest and petition, women did win some expanded property rights. Finally, in some states, women had the right to control the money they earned outside the family. Up until then, men owned their wives' wages; they were considered men's property. But even this concession came grudgingly, often in response to arguments that women were the weaker sex, in need of protection from husbands who were drunkards or gamblers.

Judges and state lawmakers refused to concede the larger argument—that women's and men's work were equally valuable. Above all, they refused to recognize women's household labor as having any economic value. Instead, any work done on behalf of the family was considered a labor of love and caring—romanticized and put on the proverbial pedestal.

By the late nineteenth century, the Victorian cult of domesticity, the notion of separate spheres for men and women, was widely accepted among the middle class, washing away any remaining hope women had of winning title to the work they did at home. A few women continued to protest the way sentimentality was used as a hammer against them, to discount the value of their labor and make them dependent on men. "This work of the home, this mother work, which men poetically praise (praise is so cheap!) is not recognized as having any value whatever. Neither does society recognize a value in it," wrote Helen Jenkins in *New Northwest Journal*. So it is that Americans have evolved what some sociologists and economists have come to call a domestic economy of "gratitude." Women selflessly care for the family's needs and the family is grateful to them. It is an emotional, rather than a financial, currency. "Starting in the nine-

teenth century, we began to define the domestic economy very differently than the rest of the economy. It was decided that the home
existed outside the rest of the economy, that you don't pay people in
the family to do things. It was the first great separation of home and
work," says Viviana Zelizer, chair of the department of sociology at
Princeton University and author of *The Social Meaning of Money.*
"Home becomes the oasis in contrast to work."

That separation carried the force of deep cultural assumptions—
about money, work, men, and women. Caring for the family now
existed in its own protected realm, as women's work with its own values, increasingly isolated from the world of commerce. Men, on the
other hand, were to immerse themselves in the larger world, as
providers. "Men's wages became a badge of honor," Kessler-Harris
noted in her book *A Woman's Wage.* Women's paychecks, on the other
hand, signaled profound shame—a sign that the man was not able to
provide for his family. "For his wife to be earning income meant that
the husband had failed," she wrote, which helped to "isolate men in
an endless search for upward mobility and financial success." Indeed,
she noted, a "quintessentially American presumption" exists that if
"a man cannot work, he is a rather worthless individual."

It's hard to overstate the power these beliefs exerted over women's
earnings. The core notions of masculinity and femininity—built on
men's and women's roles in the family—were incorporated into ideas
about which jobs would be available to men and women. Gentility,
neatness, morality, cleanliness, support, and service were the qualities associated with women's fields. Indeed, domestic service was one
of the first and only fields open to women, followed by such careers
as nursing and teaching. "Such distinctions confirmed women's place
in the home, even while they worked for wages," Kessler-Harris
added.

Yet most important of all, men's jobs always paid more than
women's. And that lower pay for women was usually justified by
their family roles. "The belief that women belonged at home per-
mitted employers to pay wages that were merely supplemental,"
Kessler-Harris noted.

·   ·   ·

THE IDEA of a "family wage" first emerged at the opening of this century, as factory workers struggled to improve their working conditions and standard of living. More than anything, this early fight for better pay defined the proper roles for men and women, for the family wage was to be paid to men only, to reinforce their socially sanctioned roles as breadwinners. "It was a fight for social order in which men could support their families and receive the services of women," Kessler-Harris wrote.

On average, women earned one-half to two-thirds of what men earned—and this situation was endorsed by popular opinion. Indeed, employers even felt comfortable paying less than subsistence wages to women—on the assumption that it was only right that women depend on men. One box manufacturer, for example, readily admitted that he felt no compunction about paying young women less than subsistence wages. "We don't pay the girls a living wage," the businessman asserted, since their income was purely supplementary to their fathers' or husbands'. In 1912, the head of Sears, Roebuck and Company asserted that his company "made it a point not to hire girls living at home for more than $8 a week," because a "girl's wages" were simply a family supplement. In 1905, trade unionists argued that "the great principle for which we fight . . . is opposed to taking . . . the women from their homes to put them in the factory and sweatshop. . . . We stand for the principle that it is wrong to permit any of the female sex of our country to be forced to work, as we believe that the man should be provided with a fair wage in order to keep his female relatives from going to work. The man is the provider and should receive enough for his labor to give his family a respectable living."

This was the case despite the fact that one-quarter of the factory workers were female and many the sole support of their families. Indeed, Kessler-Harris found the wages of even the most highly skilled women in mills rarely matched the lowest wages of men—and that situation persisted into the 1950s. Men earned three dollars for every two paid to women.

In the 1920s, many corporations kept separate pay scales for men and women. "Our theory was that women did not recognize the responsibilities of life and were hoping to get married soon and would leave us," the president of Westinghouse explained.

At General Electric and Westinghouse throughout this decade, Kessler-Harris discovered, men's benefits included a 5 percent bonus every six months, pensions, and paid vacations. Women, on the other hand, were offered dances, cooking classes, secretarial instruction, clubs, and summer camps. She noted that historian Stephen Meyer III found that Ford Motor Company shut women out of its profit-sharing plan. Ford "considered all women, regardless of family stakes, as dependents, and therefore ineligible for Ford profits."

During the same era, a wave of "protective" legislation swept the country—laws that limited women's hours and the types of work that they could do also had the practical consequence of lowering women's pay. The laws were enacted and justified on the grounds that women needed special protection because they were the ones who gave birth to and reared children. In 1908, for example, an Oregon court ruled that women's "physical stature and performance of maternal functions" was justification enough to bar them from certain jobs. By 1920, about half the states had such laws on the books.

In the 1930s, working women faced the most serious hurdles of all, however. In the grips of the Great Depression, with unemployment running at 30 percent, married women were drummed out of the workforce. State after state passed laws specifically barring married women from work—with so few jobs, only one adult per family was to be employed and that was the man. In those tight economic times, the rhetoric grew fierce, scapegoating mothers for the downfall of the nation.

Indeed, the arguments of that era sound much like the current cultural debate over family values. Working women were derided as selfish and greedy, neglectful of their children, as evidenced in the letters to Franklin Delano Roosevelt unearthed by Alice Kessler-Harris.

One letter writer of the time complained to Roosevelt, for example, that women rushed back to work after having babies, ignoring their family duties. "All over the country, women marry and immediately return to their jobs, instead of endeavoring to live within their husbands' income," and taking the time to "build a home." This irate citizen insisted that working women "consistently dodge motherhood" and "go home after their work is done with a paper carton in one hand and a can opener in another." Another complained that a woman and her husband used her wages to "purchase a new auto," then hired domestic help, leaving their children to "go around the streets and grow up and not be reared by parents." These kids, the writer predicted, "would grow up to become candidates for houses of correction."

"A male would spend his income to support his family, while the woman spends for permanent waves, lipsticks. But those things do not pay the grocer and all the other bills that the father is expected to pay," one outraged citizen wrote to Roosevelt. Another insisted that men used their paychecks to buy a home, a car, a radio . . . while a "girl" used hers to buy "cosmetics and finery." An attorney in Washington echoed those sentiments: "I do not believe these women are making as good use of the money they receive as would be made of it if it was paid to the husbands of other women who are desperately in need of employment and whose wives are staying at home looking after home and children."

Then, as now, much of the rhetoric aimed at working women stemmed from a perceived threat that women would take men's jobs. In 1939, writer Norman Cousins noted there were about 10 million people out of work, "and there are also 10 million or more women who are jobholders. Simply fire the women, who shouldn't be working anyway, and hire the men. Presto! No unemployment. No relief rolls. No depression."

Working women of the time angrily protested they needed the money as much as any man, and further, they argued that the restrictions on the jobs available to them kept them from being a threat to any men. After all, women then, as now, worked mostly in female-dominated fields. "Do men pine to slave in somebody else's kitchen, to work in beauty salons?" one asked. But such protests fell on deaf ears. The marriage bars stayed in place for years. So did the yawning pay gap between men and women. In most workplaces, the highest-paid women earned only as much as the lowest-paid men.

Throughout the century, working women protested this situation to public officials, to union leaders, to employers. And social activists periodically documented the impact of women's low wages on both women and their families. In 1910, *McClure's* magazine reported that "girls" working in factories made such paltry salaries that many "ate no breakfast, lunch was breakfast and a roll." Some social activists went so far as to argue that women's low wages would drive them into prostitution.

But it was not until after the second World War that American opinion began to shift about women's wages.

THAT CHANGE grew out of the raw injustice women experienced during the war. Recruited to help the war effort, 5 million women poured into the nation's defense plants and factories to replace the young men fighting overseas. Yet even though they did exactly the same work as men, most employers paid them less. One explained that he set women's wages five cents per hour lower than men's to keep women's pay "somewhat in line with other women's rates."

The inherent unfairness of paying millions of women less to do exactly the same jobs was too obvious for most working women to ignore. Kessler-Harris reported that one widow protested, "What do you think of all these women working in defense plants, doing men's work and only receiving children's pay? . . . At Studebaker's . . . men make as much as $15.00 a day. In two days, these men get more than I get for six days and I have a family to support and rent to pay."

Just as galling, women began to measure how their lower earning power translated into lower buying power. "Grocery stores do not have double standard price tags, one for men customers and one for women. A loaf of bread is just a loaf of bread and sells for so much. It makes no difference whether a woman pays for it or a man . . . there are no male or female tax rates."

By the end of the war, policymakers and legislators took an active interest in the pay gap between men and women. In 1945, the first equal pay act was introduced into Congress. Such a law would seem to be a matter of simple justice from the vantage point of the

1990s. Why would two workers doing exactly the same work be paid different rates? But it took legislators another eighteen years to pass the bill.

Yet the great irony of the debate was that the bill finally passed in part because trade unionists came to see it as a way to protect men's wages. By 1963, with the most recent wave of feminism coming into its own, there was fear that troops of women would invade male-dominated fields—and drag down men's rate of pay. Indeed, feminists learned to use this argument to sell the bill. "I appealed to their [male workers'] selfishness in terms of preserving their own jobs. I said, 'There will be competition for jobs; then the employer will hire the cheapest workers,'" Mary Anderson, head of the Women's Bureau at the U.S. Department of Labor, said as she lobbied for the bill. "While I am interested in getting work," she added, "I am not interested in women being exploited and used to lower the standard of living."

By the mid-1950s, the argument had won plenty of advocates at the state level—one-third of the states had adopted equal pay laws. But the bills in the U.S. Congress still languished. And once again, a good deal of the resistance stemmed from deeply rooted ideas about women's proper place. It was nothing short of an "indisputable fact that women are more prone to homemaking and motherhood than men," one senator argued. As such, women weren't worth investing in.

Business groups built on that argument, saying they had to pay women less because women simply cost more to employ. "Women's . . . attachment to the home and their responsibilities to families justified a lower wage" because family responsibilities caused them to be absent more, quit jobs more quickly, take longer to train, and be harder to supervise. In addition, the business groups argued, they had to add toilets and lunchrooms for women at considerable expense.

By the 1960s, however, the resistance to the bills was on the wane. The vibrant civil rights movement was also in full flower, riding a new national passion for justice and equality. As feminism took root across the country, trade unionists saw a real danger in women flooding into male-dominated fields and bringing men's pay down. A broad coalition of women's and labor groups rode the crest of these new sentiments and pressed a bill into law.

The Equal Pay Act of 1963 helped many women, of course. But it was far from a total remedy. The core issue was that such a law did nothing to raise the wages of the 80 percent of working women who still worked in fields dominated by women. For them, the slogan "Equal pay for equal work" meant little. "Part of the wage gap results from differences in experience or time in the workforce. But a significant portion cannot be explained by any of those factors," says Susan Bianchi-Sand, executive director of the National Committee on Pay Equity. "Certain jobs pay less because they are held by women and people of color." In 1996, the cost to women was estimated to run to about $120 billion in lost wages.

IT IS ONLY recently that this problem—putting a price tag on women's work that truly reflects the value of women's labor—has begun to move toward a conclusion that might satisfy the feminists who fought so valiantly 150 years ago to see that women's work was properly valued. The ongoing fight for "comparable worth" laws—as opposed to equal pay—directly addresses the assumptions of gender that lower so many women's paychecks.

Starting in the early 1980s, labor and women's activists began to press this new remedy through lawsuits, union agreements, and legislatures. The argument was fairly simple. Every job should be ranked according to the skills, education, and experience needed and paid accordingly. These laws recognize that far too much of women's labor—the work women do as child care workers, clerks, secretaries, and nurses, for example—is devalued simply because it is done by women. Even advanced degrees do little to raise women's pay in these fields. One study, for example, showed that staff nurses in Denver earned about $24,000 a year, less than the average hospital maintenance worker. Broad-based studies across occupations show even more insulting and injurious differences. Electricians, for example, whose duties include fixing refrigerators and air conditioners, earned nearly $9,000 more than registered nurses—who had to make life-and-death decisions about critically ill patients. Messengers earned about $305 a week in one survey, compared with $203 earned by day care workers.

Those are the facts that fired the movement for "comparable worth"—a new generation of laws to remedy discrimination against women. In a growing number of workplaces, every job is now reviewed and salaries adjusted in line with the skills, experience, and education required. By the early 1990s, twenty states and hundreds of cities across the country had adopted "comparable worth" or "pay equity" laws, to raise women's wages in jobs that have been traditionally female. This new approach has dramatically improved life for many working moms.

Just consider the progress Karen Foreman, a single mother of two in Mankato, Minnesota, has made over the past fifteen years, as such a law took effect in her state. With two children under the age of eight and no support checks from her ex-husband, she remembers how difficult it was to make ends meet on her salary of $4.35 an hour as a clerk-typist at Moorhead State University in Minnesota back in 1980. Even working full-time, she depended on several government-sponsored assistance programs to get by, including the school lunch program, food stamps, and fuel assistance.

"I used to have to take some of my vacation days to stand on line for commodities for the month," she recalls. She, along with hundreds of other people, many of them women earning low wages, would wait outside a warehouse to pick up food at a state-sponsored giveaway, known as the "commodities" program. Those who qualified could pick up cheese, rice, and dried milk and sometimes even fresh fruit and vegetables bought up by the government to keep farm prices stable. "It was degrading, standing there, waiting for charity. A lot of times, they weren't ready at ten o'clock, when they were supposed to start, so it took a lot longer than it was supposed to," she says.

But it stretched her food budget and in those days, every penny counted. Indeed, she still has stinging memories of the time when her son came home and wanted to go with the other fifth-graders on a ski trip that cost fifteen or twenty dollars. "That cost had a real financial impact. I remember the three of us, my son, my daughter, and I, had to sit down and talk about what we were going to give up in order for him to afford to go," she says. And not allowing him to go meant inflicting a deeper hurt on her children. Not to go, she recalls, would have meant marking him as poor. "Just being in the school lunch program already meant that people thought of them as poor and there's a stigma that goes with that. The teachers try to make things equal, but there's a stigma. And you try to avoid that. You don't want your children marked that way. And you don't want them left out of things their peers are doing."

By the time Foreman's daughter made fifth grade a few years later, however, the ski trip was no problem—Karen was earning twice as much, thanks to Minnesota's pay equity law, which took effect in 1982. Under the new law, all jobs performed by state workers were reviewed, and women's wages rose, on average, by 10 percent. In cases such as Foreman's, where the disparities were even more notable, salaries doubled. By 1997, she had tripled her salary. "It's amazing to me the difference that law made. I don't have to go in a big panic when something breaks down. I can remember one time when the washing machine broke down and not having enough money to fix it. I had to load up all the laundry and go to a Laundromat with fifty inches of snow on the ground.

"The tough times made us strong," Foreman adds. But earning a decent salary makes life a lot happier. "I'm now making in the thirty-thousand-dollar range, and for me, that's like a million dollars. I have a car. I have the house. I have money in retirement accounts. I can even take a short trip every once in a while."

By the early 1990s, however, such victories were fewer. The momentum for "comparable worth" stalled as attacks on working women and feminism were renewed. Bills pending in the U.S. Congress went nowhere. When Eleanor Holmes Norton introduced the Fair Pay Act in 1996 and 1997, there was hardly a word in the media about it. Efforts to rally women's magazine editors in the spring of 1997 produced very few stories. The political climate of the 1990s left little hope for such initiatives, despite polls showing broad support for them.

11

It Does Take a Village
to Raise a Child

The Myth of Personal Responsibility

O N APRIL 17, 1991, David Prickett learned he had three days to solve a problem—or lose his job. That was the ultimatum from his supervisor at Circuit Science Incorporated in Minneapolis.

Or so it seemed to Prickett on that fateful Friday morning. Shortly after he showed up for his regular shift as a maintenance mechanic, Prickett was told that as of Monday, he'd be required to work new hours. Instead of showing up at about 7:00 A.M., Prickett would need to report for work in the midafternoon and stay until nearly midnight.

The change did not seem like a big deal to company officials. It was only a temporary reassignment, meant to last about two weeks, while another worker was being trained. Besides, managers at CSI saw no alternative to changing Prickett's hours. Union agreements required that such shift changes take place according to seniority.

Switching Prickett's hours on short notice simply occurred as part of the normal chain reaction of hiring and training new employees.

But the change created a crisis for Prickett: Who would care for his three-year-old son, Kyle, while he worked?

Prickett had taken temporary custody of Kyle so his ex-wife could attend to a family crisis in Iowa. Until now, Kyle's care was not a problem. Prickett had entrusted him to a neighbor. But she could not take Kyle in the evenings, because of her own family responsibilities.

Prickett explained his dilemma to his boss, but to no avail. The company could not bend on this schedule change; Prickett had to show up or be reported for an "unexcused" absence. On Saturday and Sunday, Prickett searched desperately for a solution. First, he asked his own mother if she could take time off her job to care for Kyle. Then a sister. But neither was able to help out. Nor were friends or neighbors he approached. Panicky, Prickett called his supervisor over the weekend, from his mother's house, to say he still had not found care for Kyle and that he didn't think he could work the new shift. Still, his boss insisted there was no alternative.

When Monday rolled around, Prickett decided it would be better to show up for his old shift than not come in at all. He took Kyle to his neighbor's and reported to work. After further conversations with his supervisor, he was granted the day off to continue his search for child care. But Prickett still came up dry—as he did over the next three days. He contacted five local, licensed child care centers, but none stayed open after 6:30 P.M.

On Thursday, Prickett met with company officials and a union representative to discuss his dilemma. During the meeting, one CSI official suggested that Prickett leave Kyle with family friends who also happened to work at CSI, the Voights. But that situation would have been taxing on everyone, most especially Kyle. The three-year-old would have had to come to CSI, wait for two hours until the Voights got off work, and then be picked up from their home at 1:00 A.M. each day. No one, except for one of the company's officials, seemed to think that was a good idea.

On Friday, just a week after he learned about the schedule change, Prickett was suspended from work for "unexcused absences." He continued to miss work the following Monday and Tuesday.

On Wednesday, April 29, Prickett called CSI to say he still could not make it to work. And that day, CSI fired Prickett.

But, as Prickett would soon learn, things could get worse.

A few days later, the state of Minnesota informed Prickett that he was ineligible for unemployment benefits. The reason? His "unexcused absences," which were deemed to be "misconduct." Under Minnesota state law, workers fired for misconduct cannot collect an unemployment check—as is the case in most states. As this book went to press, some thirty-two states still refused to recognize lack of child care as a legitimate reason for a parent to miss work. Lack of child care is conceived of as a "personal" problem workers must solve themselves. In this case, however, Prickett challenged the decision, only to be told by a state hearing officer that CSI had provided him with a child care option, one that Prickett should have embraced—leaving Kyle with the Voights.

That was when Prickett contacted Tim Thiesen, an attorney specializing in employment law. It took Thiesen two years, but eventually, he won an important precedent—one that brought employment law in Minnesota into the 1990s. "We managed to change a forty-year-old precedent," Thiesen says, "one which said that a parent's domestic duties could not be used as a reason to miss work."

The winning argument? "We kept pointing out that there is no night care for kids—the reason day care is called day care is that it is offered during the day, when parents usually work," says Thiesen. "It simply was not possible for Prickett to find care for his son on such short notice."

Justices with the Minnesota Court of Appeals recognized that fact, and finally, in 1993, two years after that fateful Friday morning, ruled that Prickett was eligible for unemployment benefits. Indeed, they found Prickett's case to be a bit Kafka-esque. "If Prickett had left his child without supervision, he would have been subject to criminal sanctions. He also could have been sanctioned for failure to support Kyle," they noted. "Prickett seemed to have no choice but to do as he did."

PRICKETT'S case was just one of a growing number showing up on court dockets around the nation in the early 1990s. These cases offer a window on the ways that working parents are hamstrung by hostile work practices, outdated public policy, and lack of child care. At times, it is simply impossible to function as both a good parent and a good worker.

Cases such as Prickett's are extreme, of course, illuminating the most painful choices thrust on working parents. Prickett had to choose quite literally between his job and his child's welfare. But such a scenario is not so rare, either. Many other working parents— the cashiers at supermarkets, workers on factory floors, clerks, secretaries, and nurses—face situations daily that compromise their ability to earn a living and still ensure the safety and well-being of their children. As Prickett's case so vividly illustrates, even a temporary change in schedule can put a child's safety at risk or dramatically reduce a family's income. At times, desperate parents make harrowing choices. One recent study by the U.S. Department of Labor found that parents at a factory in Idaho were leaving their children in their cars outside the plant at night, because they could find no one to care for the kids during the graveyard shift.

Not surprisingly, most cases involve women rather than men, since women still shoulder primary responsibility for child care. And not surprisingly, with the workforce now half female, many attorneys expect the number of such cases to skyrocket in the future. "If there's a trend, it's that there will be more of these cases," asserts Abby Cohen, managing attorney at the Child Care Law Center in San Francisco. "I've heard so many stories from women of having to work mandatory overtime and not having child care arrangements. With downsizing in the workplace, work is tight and the demands on workers are growing. The attitude of employers seems to be 'If you really wanted to keep the job, you'd do anything we'd ask.'"

These cases also reveal just how much families can be battered by the policies and practices built around traditional gender roles. "The unemployment insurance system was not designed with the realities of women workers in mind, but rather accepts the male breadwinner as the 'normal' worker," wrote Richard McHugh, an employment law attorney in Ann Arbor, Michigan, who has followed the trend. In researching the case law, in fact, McHugh discovered that the architects of unemployment insurance specifically designed a system for families with mothers at home. One of the original drafters of the Social Security Act—which included provisions creating unemployment benefits—described the "ideal family" in 1934 as one where the father worked and the mother stayed home. And for the most part, the law has not been updated to reflect the changing nature of workers' family lives.

Today, such bias is so ingrained in the law, in the rules of work, and in the assumptions of American culture as to become nearly invisible. Rather than describing the ideal worker explicitly as a "breadwinner dad," for example, most states' unemployment rules require that a person be available for full-time work to qualify for benefits. That rule has meant that women who work part-time or part-year because of child care have traditionally been denied the right to collect unemployment insurance when they are laid off work. And, of course, most employers have also constructed their work practices around such assumptions. Anything less than full-time work is considered marginal, often lacks benefits, and is unlikely to lead to advancement. "As I began to look at these cases, I had one of those 'Aha! experiences.' I began to see that this was a very male standard. The pattern of full-time work ignores family responsibilities," says Deborah Maranville, lecturer and supervising attorney who specializes in employment law at the University of Washington. "Any issues related to home life were considered 'personal' issues."

Thus, Prickett's failure to show up for work was treated as a "personal" failing, "misconduct" that could lead to dismissal. In the past, women were forced to accept such rules, whether they liked it or not. Their claims for unemployment were denied, their child care issues treated as "personal" ones they should solve on their own. "The challenge of attorneys representing women," wrote attorney

McHugh, "is to adapt, bend or break the existing legal guidelines in order to assist clients and move the unemployment insurance system closer to the realities of the 1990s workplace as they are experienced by women."

So it was that Prickett's case—and a number of others—broke new ground by recognizing the intimate connections between work and family life. In effect, the judges in Prickett's case made visible what had long been denied by the business community—workers cannot show up for the job without support at home. The pretense that home and family are separate has been shattered.

Just as important, these cases shatter the myth that individuals can resolve conflicts between work and family duties on their own. Alone, these parents cannot change companies that frivolously change work schedules. Nor can they create a system of reliable child care by themselves. "These problems are beyond the control of a single worker," one judge declared in a recent ruling. "These problems are endemic to our society and must be addressed by policymakers and business leaders." The Minnesota justices who heard Prickett's case ruled that treating child care as a personal issue ignored the reality of today's family life. To call Prickett's behavior "misconduct," they argued, "would be to ignore significant facts about the world today. In 1990, almost 60 percent of the children in Minnesota lived in families where both parents worked outside the home." Many more were headed by single parents, like Prickett.

Indeed, these cases put a lie to the popular belief that families today would thrive if only parents would take "personal responsibility" for their children. That new slogan, bandied about by elected officials from Bill Clinton to Newt Gingrich, plays to Americans' fierce romance with individualism. Starting in 1997, across America, new welfare laws required women and men to sign "personal responsibility" contracts to remain eligible for aid, job training, and child care benefits. The rhetoric is powerful because it calls up deeply held American values and traditions; indeed, there are few values more sacred to Americans than the value of individualism. "The triumph of the individual is a powerful story in American culture. We have the history of the immigrants, of pioneers," says Helen Blank, a veteran child care advocate who has worked for the Children's Defense Fund in Washington for decades. "Americans have accomplished things under unspeakable conditions and amazing odds. There's a romance with the individual. It's an 'I can do it' kind of country."

But urging working parents to solve the problems that bedevil them all by themselves borders on the barbaric, as Prickett's case so vividly demonstrates. Most ironically, it puts children at risk, even though many advocates of "personal responsibility" often claim to be speaking in favor of family values and children. "It's cruel the way the term 'personal responsibility' is being used in public policy debates, because it's really a way of saying, 'Solve it yourself!' when people can't. They don't have the resources. They can't create a system of child care. It's like telling someone with cancer to cure themselves. It's used in situations where individuals are facing social problems they can't solve all by themselves," says Marcy Whitebook, executive director of the National Center for the Early Childhood Workforce, a group that works to improve the wages and working conditions of child care workers.

Yet Whitebook—along with sociologists and other experts— notes that Americans are migrating through a major social transition, where institutions have yet to catch up to the needs of today's families. Most people have not caught up psychically to the concrete realities of their lives. "There are still a lot of us who were raised to think that women's primary role was to be a mother. I know that I was definitely raised to grow up and be a mother. I might be a schoolteacher, but that would be on the side," Whitebook says. "So the idea of child care as a social issue is still relatively new to many people. It's easy for them to just say that women should be home and that would solve the problem. Or that taking care of a child is a personal responsibility. It's hard to break apart this idea of responsibility and see what parts of it they can really do. It confuses people that we need services today that we didn't need in the last generation. They don't know where to draw the line between personal responsibility and social issues."

In addition, child care is held to be a fiercely private issue. Unlike most other countries of the world, there is no notion of very young children as a social responsibility, the literal lifeblood and future of our society, young people to be cared for and nurtured by the community at large. In America, that concept does not take hold until children reach school age. Instead, each parent—and most especially each mother—is held responsible for every aspect of her child's life and well-being. And because of the strong attachment most parents feel for their children, they willingly take on this responsibility. Indeed, most women take on their new roles with pride, ingenuity, and love—which adds great heat to the debate over whether they should work and whether their children can thrive in the care of others while they are at work. The issue is not that they don't take responsibility, but that, too often, they shoulder responsibility for issues they can't solve themselves.

Most women conduct an excruciatingly private search for child care and for jobs that will mesh with raising children. On a deeply human level, thinking of child care and choices about work as personal problems makes perfect emotional sense. What could be more intimate, more private, for a mother than making a decision about who will care for her child and where her child will spend his days? "I am always struck by women's carefulness and concern over child care arrangement," says psychologist Lisa Silberstein, who counsels many dual-earner couples. "They spend so much time thinking about it, investigating it."

The core issue, then, is not that women shirk their responsibility, as social conservatives so harshly charge, or that they are self-absorbed and materialistic, but that institutions, policies, and attitudes still lag behind the profound social change that has taken place. Until now, of course, millions of working-class women have faced stark choices between their jobs and children. With no support and few good choices, they have done the best they can, waging guerrilla warfare with the expectation that somehow they could be two places at once—at home caring for their children and at work doing their jobs.

And most remarkable of all is that women have risen to the challenge of finding ways to see that their children are cared for when they go to work. Americans now have a vast underground system of child care, one largely created by women to serve women's needs. Ask any working mom, and she can point to the system in her town for finding care for infants, toddlers, preschoolers, and school-age children. "I have people calling me all the time with new babies, asking me about baby-sitters," says Deborah Brooks McDaniel, a teacher in Mansfield, Ohio. "I put them in contact with other people who have baby-sitters or ask moms who have small children at home. They know other stay-at-home moms and eventually you find someone who wants to care for babies. That's how people get infant care. They don't use the newspaper."

But this system is fragile at best, resting as it does on the best of intentions, but the poorest of financing.

Money Is the Problem

In the spring of 1996, Maureen Bennett began to grow concerned about the quality of care at her son's child care center, in Grosse Pointe, Michigan. The experience had been a good one until recently, when there seemed to be a new teacher in her son's room every other week. "Parents were very upset," she recalls. "We began to worry about the kids. Did they know all these new faces coming in?"

Bennett decided to join the board of the child care center and soon learned that turnover was indeed soaring among the staff— running as high as 70 percent in certain months that year. She also learned the source of the problem. "Some of the caregivers had only been making $4.75 an hour, and getting no benefits. They could have done better at McDonald's!" she says. In January of 1997, the center increased wages to seven dollars an hour. In the six months that followed, turnover dropped from 70 percent to just 10 percent.

But Bennett knows that it's going to be hard to keep the staff's wages at an acceptable level. "Of course, we all want a qualified staff. But funding the center is such a problem. Most of the parents have no idea how difficult it is. Most are paying as much as they can afford in fees—or even more than they can really afford," she says. "But it's still not enough to keep things running smoothly. Many of the programs housed in Y's have pools, and that gives them a profit to support their child care centers. But we don't have a pool. So we're always struggling. We ask parents to give us their old Little Tikes toys and other things for the children. And we have fund-raisers all the time just to keep the supplies current."

The saga in Grosse Pointe is played out in countless other child care centers and family day care homes across the country. The teaching staff in child care centers averages $12,058 annually for full-time work, and only one in five has health care benefits. Many hold second jobs, live with their parents, or depend on their spouse's income to make ends meet. And many have degrees in higher education. On average, child care workers earn $5,238 a year less than they could in other jobs, given their education, gender, age, and ethnic and racial status.

Family child care providers who care for kids in their own homes—that legion of women who have created an extended family for working parents, the ones whom parents tend to find by word of mouth—earn even less, about $9,528 a year.

It's no wonder, then, that turnover runs to about 33 percent in most child care centers—and many national studies put it at about 50 percent. Even more disturbing to many advocates of quality child care is the fact that many workers leave the field entirely, despite their desire to stay with it and deep feelings of affection for the kids they care for. But spending time in a child care center makes it easy to understand how the poor pay and lack of benefits conspire to drive even the most dedicated workers from the field. In this case, the names have been changed, but the story line is one that is painfully familiar to most anyone who's bothered to investigate the reasons for the high turnover rate and poor quality of American child care.

Suzanne Pliny's voice is tired, edgy, as she answers the phone at the church-sponsored day care center in Jersey City. She doesn't have time for an interview with a reporter this week, she says, since she's just had two of her four staff people quit on her. She's having trouble finding replacements, so she'll have to fill in herself with the kids. "This time, I didn't get many replies to my newspaper ad. And most of the ones who called weren't interested after I told them the pay was one hundred thirty-five dollars a week before taxes," says Pliny. "It works out to one hundred to one hundred twenty-five dollars a week for demanding, full-time work."

She pleaded, she says, with church officials to upgrade the pay— even by five dollars a week, just to get the salary above minimum wage. "I was told, 'We've always gotten people at minimum wage, and that's what we'll continue to do,'" she recalls.

She does manage to get staff. But mostly, these days, it's high-school girls who see the job as a way to pass the time until they get married. Many quit soon after they start. "They think working with children will be a breeze, an easy way to make one hundred thirty-five dollars a week," says Pliny. "But they soon find out it's exhausting, demanding, to be with young children all day."

To make matters worse, she has no list of ready substitutes to fill in when a staffer is sick. She must fill in, and the entire staff sometimes sacrifices breaks. In her recent crisis, she called up a good friend who was going to school and the mother of a child who once attended the day care center and asked them to help her out.

Pliny says she's lasted five years as director of the center because she has a dedicated head teacher, Amy Smith. Smith has lasted more than a decade at the center and has moved up from a student helper to become assistant director. But at the moment, Smith's future with the center—and the child care profession—is precarious. "The pay is the pits. I don't even tell people what I make. I wouldn't dream of it. I'm too embarrassed," says Smith. Not only that, but benefits are nonexistent. That makes things tough, considering she is the main support for her eight-year-old daughter and her disabled husband. A couple of times a year, she works as a cashier for a few months to make ends meet.

Both Pliny and Smith would like to stay in child care as a career. "I can't imagine myself behind a desk or doing anything else," says Smith. "I'd really be torn if I couldn't work with the children."

"The children are the blessing, the redeeming factor," she says. Each day, there is some little thing they do that lifts her spirits. Like the day when she was blue over her staffing problems. Thomas, a four-year-old, told her, "I like you a lot, Amy." At least something was going right, she told herself, if the kids were feeling safe, loved, and well cared for.

Pliny's center—like so many in America—stayed afloat not only because of the generosity of the staff, but also because it was housed in a church. Low rent kept overhead down and allowed the center to keep the rates it charged parents low. A working parent could still get full-time care here for less than $300 a month in the early 1990s.

Not only was this center affordable, but it also offered another valuable service to parents and children. It was reliable. This is not the case with much of the child care in America today.

INDEED, Maureen Bennett originally turned to the day care center at her local YMCA only out of desperation, a few weeks after her second child was born. Like so many Americans, she would have preferred to have her tiny baby cared for in a private home. And that was what she'd done with Jimmy, her oldest son. She'd found a local woman who cared for children in her home, and Jimmy stayed with her for three years. When Bennett learned she was pregnant a second time, she called the woman and arranged to have her care for the baby. But two weeks before she was to report back to work, Bennett got a shock. "She called me to tell me she decided she wasn't going to do child care anymore," Bennett recalls.

Such a revelation sets off seismic tremors in the life of a working parent. But Bennett was lucky. The local Y had space for her new son, and she breathed a sigh of relief. "I knew how lucky I was. In most cases, you almost have to tell the day care you're going to have a baby before you tell your husband. Otherwise, you can't get in," she says, laughing.

The fragility of child care casts a shadow over the lives of both parents and their children. Bennett's saga is a familiar one to experts on child care. According to the best estimates, as many as a third of the kids in day care under the age of three are in family day care homes, one of the least stable forms of child care. "So many of the women who decide to do child care as a living do it because they have children themselves or they've been home and find it difficult to get back into the workplace. What they've done best for five or six years is care for children," says Kay Hollestelle, executive director of the Children's Foundation, an advocacy group dedicated to improving this type of child care. "But many of them don't stay in business long. They find it stressful or they just find it's not what they want to do. So they close down suddenly."

The state of Oregon has recognized this problem to be so widespread that officials there set up an orientation session for people who want to start child care businesses, to educate them on what it takes to succeed in the business. "The idea is to put the brakes on anyone who might enter the profession who thinks it's an easy job, and then close up shop and leave parents in the lurch—a fairly common scenario," according to *Working Mother* magazine.

The shortage of affordable high-quality child care affects the day-to-day lives of today's families, keeping many parents on edge about whether they can even make it into work. Infant care is particularly difficult to find. Many centers will not take children under six months old, even though employers often require parents to be back on the job much sooner and many parents can't afford to take much time off because they need the paycheck. One study by the Department of Education found that only 10 percent of the nation's day care centers had openings for children under the age of one.

Finding part-time care or care for odd hours can be especially hard. Margee Krebs Haynes from Virginia reports that it took her two months to find a reliable caregiver for her second child. "I decided upon and hired six people. Sometimes I got a week before they quit. I was pulling my hair out. I kept telling my boss I was coming back to work, but I kept having to call back and say I still didn't have child care."

And the quality of much of the care available leaves parents anxious and disturbed. Regulation of child care is largely a state responsibility, and few states do much to ensure the health and safety of kids in child care. Although child development experts, pediatricians, and fire safety officials have developed a consensus—and even written extensive guidelines—on what it takes to prevent kids from harm in child care, most state governments still do little to see that such standards are adopted. In 1997, for example, Mississippi's top child care licensing official admitted that she had personally come across a situation where one woman was trying to care for seventeen children at once in her private home. And that was perfectly legal under the law in that state.

Although that situation was extreme, myriad reports over the years have painted a dreary picture of much of the nation's care. Most recently, a national report found that 86 percent of child care centers provided mediocre or poor-quality services. At about 12 percent of the sites, researchers declared the care "so poor as to compromise children's basic health and safety needs." Turnover among the staff ran to about 37 percent.

A study of children in family child care found the picture there to be even worse. Only 9 percent of the sites were considered to offer good-quality care; the majority were considered "adequate or custodial"—and a full third were described as "inadequate." Interestingly, this report did show that the caregivers who considered the work to be a career offered the best-quality care. And relatives pressed into service by desperate working parents provided the worst.

Informal reports from parents certainly give life to these dry statistics. "When I started calling people, I was amazed at the number of kids one woman would watch. A number of them were watching eight or twelve kids," says Beth Forbes, who works in public relations for Purdue University in Indiana. "Most people I called didn't have a limit. Most weren't licensed, so they could do whatever they wanted."

The lack of quality, affordable, reliable child care also undermines family stability and keeps many moms on edge. When parents are forced to settle for care they know is not the best, they react exactly as one might expect them to—they worry about their children, think about quitting their jobs, and experience more symptoms of stress and depression, according to a study of 300 dual-earner couples conducted by Wellesley's Center for Research on Women. Men were likely to have similar feelings if they were actively involved in their children's day-to-day care.

• • •

THE CORE problem is well known and well documented. Because child care is considered a private family expense, caregivers can charge only what parents can afford to pay. And, of course, that is very little in most cases. The slack is taken up by child care providers who work for low wages. "In child care, we have no third-party payer, no insurance, no government support. It's a totally private family expense. What you end up doing, then, is asking people doing the work to subsidize the service. They work for low wages because that's what parents can afford to pay," says Marcy Whitebook. A median-income family in America earns $32,000 and spends about 11 percent of its income on child care. A family earning $15,000 spends nearly a *quarter* of its household income on child care, but that is still just $3,600 a year in fees—or about $75 a week to a child care provider.

Most working moms understand the dilemma, of course. "A lot of people just can't afford the kind of child care they'd like to select," says Vicki Brett-Gach, a bank manager in Ann Arbor, Michigan. "We feel lucky that we can afford the care we have for our children. But it costs three hundred dollars a week, and lots of families can't pay for that." "In Philadelphia, if it's a good day care center, and a lot of them are now, it's quite costly, about eight hundred seventy-five dollars a month," says Sharon Jacobs, the mother who came to love her daughter's day care center. "That's out of reach of most families I know." Sandee Mackey-Trombler paid $1,400 a month for infant care at a local child care center in Marin County, just outside San Francisco. "It was top-notch. At times, I asked myself how I could afford this," says Mackey-Trombler, a single mom at the time. "But I felt I just couldn't compromise on child care. It was just too important to me."

By contrast, child care advocates note that there are many other services, such as higher education, health care, and highways, that Americans have come to see as a collective responsibility. These days, for example, families pay only about a quarter of the actual cost of a college education, with the balance picked up by government grants and support and private scholarships. That is the case even though most families also have even more income from higher earning power by the time their kids enter college. "In child care, we don't ask everybody to make a contribution to a fund, to insurance or through taxes, to pay for this service as a community," Whitebook says.

THE MOST frustrating part of the problem, however, is that it is so clear that solutions exist. "Just recently, President Clinton noted that the military has solved the child care problem—and that's true," says Whitebook. The U.S. military now has one of the most extensive and best-run systems of day care. With the help of government support, the staff are paid decent wages and, unlike most child care workers, they receive benefits, such as health insurance. "But if you look at that example, you have to acknowledge an important fact— the military stepped in and picked up the slack between what parents can afford to pay and what good-quality care costs."

There are other examples of communities that have begun to raise funds for child care and improve its quality. Just recently, the Pew Charitable Trusts issued a report on dozens of new projects across the country that offer new strategies for funding child care, from a Families and Education Levy in Seattle to Georgia's state lottery, which funds a universal prekindergarten program for families who reside there. Colorado recently added a checkoff on its state income tax forms allowing its residents to direct a portion of their taxes to child care programs.

The most striking feature of these programs is that they recognize child care as a collective responsibility, which needs a community response. That has yet to happen, however, at the federal level. Grassroots conservative groups have made sure of that.

12

Whose Family Values?

The Politics That Devalue Working Mothers

THE HOMEMAKER IN America is nothing less than the "very heart and soul of a modern and free society, the absolutely essential profession that secures true social and economic progress," Allan Carlson, president of the Rockford Institute, told several hundred conservative activists gathered in Saint Louis in 1988.

The conference, held at the Marriott Airport Hotel, had been called by none other than Phyllis Schlafly, that tireless opponent of equal rights laws for women. At the time, more than 100 child care bills sat before Congress. One in particular, the Act for Better Child Care, or the ABC bill, looked very likely to pass, thanks to a broad-based coalition of child care advocates, as well as women's and labor groups, all led by the Children's Defense Fund. It was the first time in nearly twenty years that politicians and policymakers began to talk seriously about child care funding and even a federally supported system of child care.

And that prospect galvanized social conservatives, who now gathered to map a strategy to defeat the bill. "It was a raging battle over making day care a new entitlement for middle-class women," Schlafly reflects in a phone interview nearly a decade later. "We had all the media against us, the Children's Defense Fund, [U.S. senator] Chris Dodd, who wanted to be the Big Daddy of day care, all lined up against us. We were fighting the government bureaucrats, the marshmallow politicians, and all of their so-called experts and we won. We beat them."

Indeed, by the time the bill passed in 1990, many of its strongest provisions to expand and improve child care in this country were gutted. Basic standards to assure children's health and safety, for example, were dramatically weakened. But most important, funding levels were kept low, so that in the end, most states would have long waiting lists of families qualifying for child care assistance, but not enough money to serve them all. And that accomplishment is the one that Schlafly seems most proud of. "The fight was to make sure that day care was not going to become a middle-class entitlement," she says a second time, "and we won."

But Schlafly did far more than that.

She played an early and crucial role in changing the public dialogue about family policy in America. As a grassroots activist, she understood the critical importance of controlling the terms of the debate. With the right messages, social conservatives could defeat initiatives to improve and expand child care, as they had so many times in the past. In 1971, President Nixon vetoed a comprehensive child care bill, saying that it would promote "communal approaches" to child rearing and thus "Sovietize" America's children.

Schlafly would soon be eclipsed by a new generation of conservative activists. The sleepy Family Research Council was getting a new leader—Gary Bauer, who served as domestic policy advisor in the Reagan White House—and new money that would take it to the forefront of Republican politics. Focus on the Family was just beginning to organize a network of state organizations to promote its version of Christian family values. David Blankenhorn and Barbara

DaFoe Whitehead were gearing up their Institute for American Values in New York City.

But at this critical moment in the development of child care policy, it was Schlafly who had the contacts, the organization, and the notoriety with the media to mount the assault. And so she did. The meeting in Saint Louis where Allan Carlson so idolized homemakers was just one of the opening salvos in the renewed battle over child care. It would be followed by other conferences, books, rallies, media appearances, and plenty of lobbying, backed up by letters and phone calls from her conservative base. Working in concert with other influential groups, such as the Heritage Foundation, the American Enterprise Institute, and Carlson's Rockford Institute, she could make real noise. And by the late 1980s, she knew this fight needed considerable firepower.

A Turning Point?

At the time, she was right to fear that child care was on the verge of becoming a middle-class political issue. The need for it was so broad, the options for working parents so limited, that families of every income bracket and background were desperate for solutions. More than 100 national groups, from the Child Welfare League to the AFL-CIO, signed on in support of the bill. A 1986 poll commissioned by the Service Employees International Union showed that 73 percent of Americans were even willing to pay higher taxes to get better child care programs.

Ed Zigler, a man respected on both sides of the political aisle, proclaimed federal action was not only necessary, but almost inevitable. "Asking people to solve this on their own is like asking people in the late nineteenth century to set up and pay for their own schools," he asserted at the time. "It just doesn't make any sense. It's a societal problem that society must address."

And much to Schlafly's dismay, the mainstream media seemed to agree. "I came home one evening in 1988 and my son told me that *MacNeil-Lehrer* had named child care the issue of the 1980s. That disturbed me," she says. In fact, her son's comment was a wake-up call, the moment, she says, that decided it was time to fight back.

Liberals might have demographics on their side, she knew. But she also knew that majority opinion doesn't always lead public policy. Political victories go to those with the best organization, the best funding, and the most effective message. That was abundantly evident in fights over abortion, the Equal Rights Amendment, and child care. Indeed, the dynamics behind Nixon's veto revealed just that. Arch-conservative Pat Buchanan, then an aide in the Nixon White House, wrote the veto speech warning of "communal" child rearing. Even Buchanan is said to have conceded, in policy debates with other White House aides, that the language was extreme. But he correctly calculated that Nixon needed only mobilize his natural base of conservative support. Liberals had already written the president off as "Tricky Dick." And then, as now, the Republicans willingly conceded domestic policy issues to social conservatives to keep them voting for the party. In fact, the child care veto has been described by some as the salve for conservative angst over Nixon's opening of Red China at the time. Without such a bone, many right-wingers might bolt from their camp.

It was certainly smart politics. The argument forced child care advocates not only to respond to the idea that day care might undermine traditional families, but also to defend themselves as patriotic Americans. "When the veto came, it was a shock. It had tremendous impact for years afterward," says Barbara Willer of the National Association for the Education of Young Children. "It took a long time to recover."

Given this history, Schlafly saw the opportunity to transform the debates over child care into a referendum on the future of the family, the role of government, tax policy, and women's roles. "Stronger Families or Bigger Government? The Challenge of Child Care" was the headline for her specially prepared lobbying materials for Congress.

And, of course, she played on child care's lingering stigma. In public forums, speeches, and policy papers, she and other conservatives used Jay Belsky's warnings on infant care to brand day care an unmitigated disaster for children's social, emotional, and physical development. Allan Carlson, who so vaunted homemakers, had published hundreds of articles in his institute's newsletters about the supposed dangers of day care. One speaker on the agenda, Bryce Christensen, had penned a front-page article for the institute's newsletter just a few months before, declaring day care "the thalidomide of the 1980's."

In the course of the fierce struggle that ensued, child care advocates—most notably Ed Zigler—put forth some extraordinarily innovative proposals to fund child care. Zigler suggested, for example, that families be allowed to take a loan against future Social Security benefits when they had young children, as a way of creating a paid leave from work to care for their new babies. Most other industrialized countries provided not only paid leave for childbirth, he noted, but also family allowances, health care, and other benefits to help defray the high costs of child rearing. Well aware that Americans loathe paying taxes, he made sure the plan would be essentially tax-neutral. Families would pay back the loan over the course of their working lives.

He also put forward a creative proposal for using public school buildings as a hub for all child care services in a local community. The idea has since been adopted, with some success, by a number of state and local governments.

Zigler had also been the prime mover behind a set of federal guidelines on quality in child care, standards that were part of the legislation that Nixon vetoed in 1971. Based on consensus among fire and safety officials, as well as health and child development authorities, the proposal would have set forth basic protections for children—such as limiting the number of children one adult could care for. "There's a hue and cry every time there's a terrible accident in child care. The whole nation watched in horror when that poor young girl, Jessica, fell down a hole and got trapped a few years back. She was in a family day care home," says Kaye Hollestelle, executive director of the Children's Foundation. "But still, the nation has no consistent standards to protect children in child care."

Indeed, within a decade, ideas such as Zigler's largely faded from the national scene. Child care would no longer be a vibrant political issue, except as a footnote to the welfare debate. The rhetoric of the right—from distrust of government to an embrace of "personal responsibility"—would dominate the public conversation about family policy. The idea that families suffer from a moral and cultural malaise would dominate both policy debates and media coverage in the 1990s. The old ploy of "states' rights," used so effectively in the past to derail civil rights and other progressive movements, was even revived, only now it was marketed as the "devolution" of government.

Under this new "devolution," states were handed broad new authority to set child care policies and funding, even though some states, such as Louisiana, Mississippi, and Idaho, had miserable records in protecting young children. At the time the law passed, for example, Idaho allowed one adult to care for up to twelve infants at a time. Shamed by bad publicity, state lawmakers finally revised the rules in 1996. One caregiver is now limited to caring for six babies at once—still way too many to assure basic safety. Fire safety experts suggest that no one ever try to care for more than three babies at once, since it's so hard for one adult to carry even three out of a building in an emergency. Only five states met that standard as this book went to press, a fact widely known to child care advocates and presented repeatedly to Congress.

Most stunningly, a Democratic president, Bill Clinton, followed the new sentiment created by the conservative politics, signing a bill that entitled the Personal Responsibility and Work Opportunity Reconciliation Act, which would drive thousands of mothers with young children into the workforce with scant funds allocated for their children's care. As part of the legislation, former welfare recipients all across the nation were required to sign "personal responsibility" contracts as a condition of receiving temporary grants as they searched for jobs.

"Ironically, the very families that were the poster children for health care reform just a few years ago are now being scapegoated as the undeserving poor," Joan Entmacher, policy analyst with the Women's Legal Defense Fund, says. "We have women who gave up working because their children have serious disabilities. Now they're on welfare and get Medicaid. A couple of years ago, these women would have been trotted out as examples for why we need national health insurance. Now they are under attack, their cases are being investigated, to see if their claims for assistance are fraudulent." Indeed, over 100,000 claims for federal disability insurance, many of them for families with children, were under review in the mid-1990s.

Women in the front lines of the "reform" most certainly felt the heat. "Some of us are not fortunate enough to have a family member help out," says one Connecticut mom, who took a job at a local department store after she was pushed off that state's welfare rolls. Not that she was adverse to the proposition that she find a job. She says that she prefers working to "sitting around waiting for a check once a month."

Nonetheless, her quest for self-sufficiency quickly ran aground. Not long after she started work, her child's caregiver quit. "My baby-sitter decided she couldn't watch the kids anymore." She shunted the children "back and forth from one sitter to another" because she worked an evening shift, when it was hard to find care. "Soon it became very difficult to find adequate night care because the neighborhood I live in has a majority of people I wouldn't leave my cat with," she says. With the child care arrangements constantly shifting, she says, her "children started complaining about not want-ing to go here or there and they became irritable and spiteful. No one seemed to have the time or wanted to be bothered with helping them with homework."

Initially, she solved her problems by moving to a day shift, although she lost two weeks' pay waiting for the new assignment to take effect. But soon she faced a new problem—both she and her daughter came down with strep throat. When she called in sick, her boss advised her to simply take some Tylenol and report for work, since it was a busy time of year. "I was asked to come in with a fever and possibly find someone to watch my sick child, which is very hard," she recalls. "Who wants to watch sick kids for fear of their own family's health?

"I would think welfare reform is to benefit the children. But in the past year, I found it very difficult to handle," she says. In the end, she decided to cut back her hours and change shifts, a move that would affect her benefits. "Now I face the threat of losing part of my benefits because I decided to do what was in the best interests of my children."

Such stories are nothing new to Helen Blank, who has spent decades documenting the difficulties families face trying to find child care. "You have to ask yourself why this is so, why we still don't have decent child care in this country," Blank says wearily.

It is the spring of 1997, and for the past three years, she's spent most of her waking hours at the center of the congressional debate over welfare. No one has lobbied more passionately to see that mothers forced off welfare under the new law have care for their children when they go to work. It was Blank and her charismatic boss, Marian Wright Edelman, who shamed, cajoled, and reasoned legislators into conceding that child care has to be an integral part of welfare reform.

But as the ink dries and the policies take effect, Blank sees a daunting future for working mothers. More women will be forced into the job market, creating new demands for child care. Yet federal funds for child care are not slated to grow much after 1998. Already, it's evident that former welfare recipients and low-wage workers are vying for the few child care subsidies now available.

By now, Blank realizes it's a cliché to point out that every other industrialized country, with the exception of South Africa, provides child care assistance to working families. That is an argument she has advanced tirelessly over the years. She is also rightfully proud of the progress made on child care in recent years. The version of the ABC bill that did pass has modestly expanded the supply of child care across America. And after so many years in the fray, she is nothing if not realistic. She understands the struggle to win decent child care will last many more years.

Still, the response is so small compared with the need.

And in the spring of 1997, Blank sounds almost defeated. "When you ask yourself why we still don't have decent child care, you have to answer that the status quo is attractive to business. Child care as it exists is affordable enough. After all, millions of women somehow show up for work every day," she says. "If we make a serious attempt at making child care better, if we try to change the health and safety rules, if we pay child care workers more, then it will cost more for women to go to work."

She pauses, as if she wished she hadn't conceded this truth. "We in the child care community don't like to talk about it that way because we know the kinds of choices parents have now aren't very good ones."

Further, she adds, the resistance to serious funding for child care in America is far more profound than it was in the days when Phyllis Schlafly led the charge against the ABC bill. "Now we don't talk about child care per se, we talk about the role of government a lot. The conservative positions are now mainstreamed," she says.

Another veteran of the battles over child care concurs. "We no longer debate child care as such. Instead, we talk about everything as tax policy. We talk about tax credits and tax breaks, usually for business," says Nancy Duff-Campbell of the National Women's Law Center, a veteran child care advocate. "Essentially, the conservatives have changed the nature of the debate. Now we say, 'We're going to make social policy through the tax code.' It's brilliant strategy because people like the idea of tax cuts and it's easy to disguise who benefits from tax policies."

In 1998, President Clinton proposed new child care initiatives in his State of the Union address. Yet the bulk of the new child care proposals relied once again on tax credits and incentives. Conservative groups, cheered on by the editorial page of the *Wall Street Journal,* immediately attacked the initiative as unnecessary and a burden on taxpayers. It would be better, the *Journal* argued, if moms stayed home to care for the nation's kids.

Just as important, social conservatives created an environment where it was possible to stall—and possibly even derail—progress women were making in the workplace. Their antigovernment rhetoric and attacks on feminism helped to make attacks on affirmative action acceptable and to water down the Family and Medical Leave Act and stall its passage. The U.S. Chamber of Commerce, for example, was able to float ridiculously inflated figures on the cost of providing even an unpaid leave for workers after childbirth by arguing the bill would create a hideous government bureaucracy and costly rules. Now that the law is in effect, research shows that it has actually cost employers very little.

More recently, social conservatives have backed an effort by corporate America to mount an assault on such a basic protection as the hard-won forty-hour workweek. In 1997, new bills were introduced into Congress that would give employers the right to ask workers to put in overtime without paying overtime wages. Instead, workers would be granted "comp time," a practice that many labor activists feared would be abused. Far from helping today's families cope with stress, the "family values" crowd has thus helped clear the way for employers to make the workplace even less hospitable to parents. With their extreme rhetoric, they serve as convenient cover for the business lobby.

As always, ambivalence over women's roles sits at the center of the debate. For the right wing, protection of the breadwinner dad and homemaker mom remained central to the debate over social policy, even when those roles had long been abandoned by most Americans. Schlafly has long characterized funding for child care as "discrimination" against traditional families. By "traditional," of course, she means families where Mom stays home. At the Saint Louis meeting, Schlafly was slated to present a "Full-time Homemaker Award" right after a speech from Oliver North.

THE BIRTH OF FAMILY VALUES

Indeed, it is instructive to look in detail at Schlafly's work in the late 1980s to understand just how the conservatives changed the debate over family policy. It took nearly a decade for the arguments to win popular appeal. Their arguments were often fallacious, but they spoke to the gut, to populist fury at taxes, and to a growing anxiety about women's changing roles.

In three conferences dedicated to fighting the ABC bill in 1988 and 1989, Schlafly assembled the conservative thinkers and activists who would come to put "family values" and "culture wars" at the top of the nation's political agenda. There was William Bennett, once the U.S. secretary of education and later the best-selling author and speaker on cultural values. Dick Armey, who went on to become House majority leader under Newt Gingrich, was on the agenda. George Gilder, the father of supply-side economics and critic of feminism, spoke. President Ronald Reagan delivered a special videotaped message. Representatives from leading conservative think tanks, including the Heritage Foundation, the American Enterprise Institute, and the Rockford Institute, also spoke.

Distrust of the government was predictably a dominant theme of the forums and lobbying efforts, often delivered with the fiery oratory meant to stir conservative ire. "The same people who paved the road to hell in America's inner cities want to take care of your small children," George Gilder warned. Publicly funded child care was nothing less than an arrogant attempt by social workers and day care providers to create jobs for themselves and weaken traditional family life, he charged. "The more the state subsidizes the breakdown of family responsibilities, the more families will break down."

Not only that, it was big government forcing so many women into the workforce. Women were abandoning their children to child care centers only because families had to pay such extraordinarily high taxes. Without those onerous taxes, women would stay home and there would be no need for child care. Douglas Besharov, resident scholar at the American Enterprise Institute, urged the crowd to "start now in recasting" the debate over child care as a part of "major tax reform."

But the issue that trumped all others, the one that sat at the center of the speeches, was the one that Allan Carlson of the Rockford Institute articulated, the question of women's proper place.

Mothers working outside the home gnawed at the very heart of civilized society, these speakers argued. "The woman's role is nothing less than the hub of human community," Gilder insisted. "The success or failure of civilized society depends on how well the women can transmit values to the men." Making child care available would only disrupt the critical bond between children and their mothers, which in turn would lead to widespread social disruption. "The prisons, reformatories, foster homes, mental institutions and welfare rolls of America already groan under the burdens of children relinquished to 'society' to raise and support." Other speakers trotted out references to John Bowlby's research on infants in orphanages and Jay Belsky's warnings on the dangers of infant care.

Schlafly even had a day care director on hand who left the business because she believed children suffered inevitable deprivation when mothers worked. "What we truly cannot afford is a society of day care children, a society where the problems of violence, drugs and divorce increase," asserted Wendy Dreskin, who once ran a preschool in the San Francisco area. "The phenomenon of children feeling unwanted is the crisis of day care in our time. Only the family unit can give children a sense of belonging and of being valued."

Dreskin said her center had the latest equipment, great teachers, and wonderful projects. "The books and articles on helping your child adjust to day care say that if a child isn't happy in day care, there's a problem with the center or it isn't the right center for that particular child. Nowhere do they say that day care itself is the problem. And yet after two years of doing day care, that is exactly what we concluded." She added that "I will not be surprised if in the next five years research shows that the stress of full-time day care is measurable even if a child begins day care at three or four."

Other speakers blasted working mothers as self-absorbed and materialistic. "It's a myth that it now takes two incomes to maintain the standard of living that Ozzie and Harriet had on one," argued Robert Rector, a policy analyst from the Heritage Foundation, who remains one of the most influential conservative thinkers on family policy in Washington. "The median income of husbands today, adjusted for inflation, is 40 percent higher than the median income of traditional families in 1955."

This argument was a particularly curious one for a scholar to make, given that Ozzie and Harriet were, of course, themselves the stuff of mythology. There was further irony in the fact that Harriet Nelson was a professional actress herself, making a living by working on television. It's also true that the show never made it clear exactly what sort of work Ozzie did. Their life simply had nothing to do with the real lives of real people. Like Martha Stewart today, they were the stuff of fantasy that could be used to market consumer products from laundry detergent to cake mixes.

Not only that, but any close examination of families' economic situation in the 1950s reveals that the relative prosperity of the middle-class family then, along with the fact that so many more women were home full-time then, was largely the result of the force that conservatives so derided—government programs. "One of the most successful and widespread affirmative action programs of all times were veteran's benefits that were made available after World War Two. It helped many families join the middle class," says Stephanie Coontz, family historian at Evergreen College and author of *The Way We Really Are: Coming to Terms with the American Family*. By her accounting, a whopping 40 percent of young men eighteen to twenty-four were eligible for veteran's benefits and many used them to go to college and to buy houses. Indeed, the GI bill paid directly for 20 percent of all private homes purchased in the 1950s and fueled a new housing market. According to Coontz's research, the majority of new homes in 1950 were directly or indirectly financed via government programs at the time.

That translated into an economy where a thirty-year-old man could buy the median-priced house on 15 to 18 percent of his income. Today, the figure is about twice that, which is why the American Association of Home Builders reports that dual-earner families are the ones buying most of the nation's single-family homes. "It's so amazing that conservatives think of the 1950s as a model and that they attack government programs. It was government programs that allowed and undergirded the male-breadwinner, female-homemaker family. And the economy was thriving then mostly because our major economic competitors lay in shambles after the war," she says. "There was no global competition."

She understands the appeal of the 1950s, however, and why the fictional characters of Ozzie and Harriet have become what she calls "stand-ins" for better times. "The idea that there was a time when people had more of a choice about working resonates now, in an economic environment where more and more people feel they have less choice about working," she says.

Perhaps that is why Robert Rector of the Heritage Foundation and other conservatives persisted in bashing dual-earner couples. It is most certainly a familiar theme in Rector's attacks on the ABC bill. "Over 80 percent of young children using day care come from affluent two-parent/two-earner couples."

Whatever the motive, such rhetoric does prove to be good politics for the conservative cause. Framing the argument that way divides voters and undermines support for government-sponsored family leave and child care. Why should working-class and middle-class voters pay taxes for child care for families who don't truly need it?

Those who lobbied for working women took pains to lay out the true economics. "The tendency to label families with two earning parents 'affluent' is growing," feminist economist Heidi Hartmann, executive director of the Women's Policy Institute, noted in testimony before Congress in support of the ABC bill. By Rector's accounting, she figured, family income of more than $25,000 had become "upper income"—a ludicrous idea for most Americans. "'Upper income' used to be a term that referred to the top one-fourth or perhaps the top one-third of the income distribution. It hardly makes sense to refer to the top three-fourths of an income distribution as upper income."

But the image of working moms as "career" women interested only in their own advancement and material wealth persisted through the debate over the child care bill. It also proved to be powerful fodder in the war waged against the Family and Medical Leave Act, branded a "handout for yuppies" by some of its opponents in the business lobby. It was the theme invented by and cherished by social conservatives. The "chief beneficiaries" of family leave "would be relatively well-to-do parents," argued Gary Bauer of the Family Research Council. More pointedly, he called the proposal a "boon only for upper-income two-earner families" when he testified before Congress in 1989. Two years later, William Mattox, who had by then taken over the lead in lobbying on work-family issues for the council, charged the family leave bill appealed only to "fast-track careerists who are eager to resume employment soon after the birth or adoption of a child." He added the law "fails to address the priorities of parents (particularly mothers) who would like to stay home with their children for more than three months."

George Orwell would have appreciated this logic—blaming supporters of the bill for the demise of its most valuable benefits. It was the business community—led by the U.S. Chamber of Commerce and the National Federation of Independent Businesses—that demanded the leave be unpaid and short. All along, the bill's supporters lobbied for a more extensive leave—one that covered more workers and for a longer period of time. The original bill, introduced into Congress in 1985, would have provided eighteen weeks of leave and covered businesses with just five employees. The length of the leave, the number of employers covered, and any attempt to win a paid leave were surrendered as a compromise to win *some* minimal protection for workers, and most especially women. "Of course, we would love to see paid leave, a longer leave, and to see both men and women use it!" says Donna Lenhoff, general counsel for the Women's Legal Defense Fund, who led the coalition fighting for the law. By 1997, she and other women's groups were, in fact, lobbying for proposals for a paid leave. "But at that time, we had to consider what we could realistically win."

As with child care, the role of government grew central to the struggle. "The language of this debate was very important. It was absolutely a battle about what's important," says Lenhoff. The business community bitterly fought the proposal as a "government mandate," an unwarranted intrusion that would saddle American employers with unnecessary and costly paperwork, as figures floated by the Chamber of Commerce so vividly illustrated.

Early on, the Chamber argued the bill would cost businesses $27.2 billion a year, because of the cost of hiring temporary workers to replace those on leave. A few years later, with serious questions raised about these estimates, the Chamber reduced the price tag to about one-tenth of that original amount—to $2.6 billion. The Government Accounting Office found even that estimate too high, and put the cost at $340 million.

Now that the law is in effect, the record shows that family leave policies are basically cost-neutral or even save employers money. Even before the law was enacted, Aetna Life & Casualty reported it saved $2 million a year by extending its existing leave—the savings accrued from the company's ability to retain experienced workers who would have left the company without it.

There were also costs of not having a family leave that the business lobby ignored altogether—those borne by women workers and the taxpayers. Without a job guarantee, many women were fired or quit their jobs to stay with their new babies. On average, that cost them about $3,000 in lost wages the first year after the birth of a child. That is because it took them an average of twelve weeks to find a job once they started looking, and they often had to accept a pay cut in a new position. In addition, many collected unemployment at taxpayers' expense. The total tab: about $600 million a year. "The debate often goes on as if the only costs that exist are the ones to employers. That's just not the case. Not having a leave costs women and their families money," economist Heidi Hartmann argued at the time.

Still, the rhetoric used by the business community to taint family leave as yet another onerous "government mandate" proved potent in a nation that loves free enterprise, hates taxes, and is suspicious of bureaucracy. "That language put us on the defensive for a long time," recalls Lenhoff. Indeed, it took a decade of struggle to pass the bill that President Clinton signed into law in 1993. More workers now have the right to take time off after the birth of a child, to care for a sick family member, or to attend to their own illness and still keep their jobs. But the final version of the bill, the one that became law, reduced the leave to just twelve weeks with no pay and covers only large employers, those with fifty or more employees.

That means only 60 percent of all American workers are covered. So while it does offer some progress, it's still miserly when compared with policies adopted by other industrialized countries decades ago. Most of Europe offers parents a nearly fully paid leave the year after a baby is born. By law, workers there are also entitled to an average of about six weeks' paid vacation a year, a benefit that could put a dent in the "time famine" that America's social conservatives so lament. Most American workers have just two weeks' paid vacation a year, and many moms use part of that time to tend sick children or go to school events—leaving them very little real vacation time to spend with their children.

The lack of such support in public policy is a point of anger to many American women. "I think government and business have never truly adapted to working women and their families. I think they must live in the Stone Age and I don't understand why. They are blind to the fact that mothers work and there's a need for these things. I can't believe it took an act of Congress for me to get more than my six weeks' maternity leave," says Kelly Hogan-Lewis, the registered nurse in Wilton Manors, Florida, and mother of four. Indeed, she, like so many other women, found herself limited to medical disability leave of just six weeks after her children were born. "If I didn't report back to work, I would have been fired."

Many women, especially those working for small employers, still face such treatment. And those most at risk are, of course, working-class women, the ones most in need of the paycheck. Yet the conservatives succeeded in dramatically shifting the terms of the debate. "There's such a drumbeat from the right about working mothers. Anything that tries to address their problems is attacked as antifamily," says Nancy Duff-Campbell. In addition to opposing the ABC bill, for example, many conservative groups lined up against expanding the child care tax credit, a relatively small benefit available to working parents that allows them to deduct some child care expenses from their federal income tax. Current tax policy gives an advantage to families with only one spouse working. "All we ever fought for is to make working mothers equal in the tax code. The truth is that some families have child care as an expense if they are to go out and work and others do not. The child care tax credit is simply a way to make the two families equal in the face of the tax code. That's all we were fighting for—to make working mothers equal," says Duff-Campbell.

But instead, conservatives have fought for a tax break for home-makers, as part of their campaign to support the "traditional" family. Interestingly, however, the family that social conservatives so ardently defend has been long abandoned by mainstream America, out of both necessity and choice. Indeed, the model that the so-called "family values" crowd worked so hard to protect—the bread-winner dad and homemaker mom—existed only in a few notable places in America. The U.S. Senate and Congress were certainly members of that crowd, with most lawmakers themselves married to stay-at-home wives. In other words, those at the top of the nation's power structure, the ones with the authority to set public policy, often do so with little or no firsthand knowledge about what it means to be a working parent. "I look around at a committee hearing and I'm often the only one with color in my suit," says U.S. Senator Patty Murray, laughing. Indeed, she was one of just eight women in the Senate in the spring of 1997. She was instrumental in winning family and medical leave as a state legislator in her home state of Washington before she was elected to the U.S. Senate. That spring she was leading a fight to expand the Family and Medical Leave Act to allow parents time off work to attend school events and conferences. But, she says, it's not easy to sell the idea. "The problem is, when they vote or talk about it, it doesn't come from their hearts. They don't have the personal experience to create the passion for the issues."

And as the "devolution" of power flows to the states, it turns out that the picture there is very much the same. A survey commissioned by the Mailman Institute found that child care rarely got a serious hearing in part because of the demographics of state legislators. About 90 percent of them are white males with virtually no personal responsibility for the daily care of their children. That is largely left to the women in their lives. There is no conscious conspiracy, of course. Instead, there is a sort of blind spot, as consultant Fran Rodgers would say, about the need to improve and expand child care options for working parents.

New Grassroots Networks

Now that social conservatives have a considerable power base, they are fond of exercising their muscle by flooding lawmakers with faxes and phone calls. Many learned their tactics as they fought abortion. Indeed, many were, and still are, keenly energized by the abortion issue. "When you stop to look at the evolution of the debate over family policy, the antiabortion movement really was the mother's milk for the family values crowd. That's where their grassroots organizations came from," says Andrea Camp, an aide who served Congresswoman Patricia Schroeder during the 1980s and 1990s and thus had a front-row seat on the unfolding drama as the conservatives swept into Washington. "They radically changed the climate in Washington." Schroeder herself, an outspoken liberal and feminist, decided not to run for reelection in the wake of the conservative takeover of Congress in 1994.

It's a fact the new generation of social conservatives takes pride in. "Many of our state policy councils are really organizations that were originally set up to fight abortion, and have just taken on other conservative issues by default," says Sheila Malloney, policy analyst for the Family Research Council. Starting in the late 1980s, the council worked closely with Focus on the Family to set up organizations in every state. The Family Research Council now claims a loose network of thirty-five such state-based groups. Each one gets "calls to action" when there is an important bill pending in Washington, and members of congressional staffs confirm the ability of these groups to "light up" the switchboards and fax lines when they care about a piece of legislation. "They have fantastic networks. Our Georgia Policy Council can generate twelve hundred phone and fax messages in an hour!"

A quick check with Randy Hicks, executive director of the Georgia group, reveals this to be a huge exaggeration. "We're not that well organized," he says, laughing. "But we hope to be." Abortion issues remain a hot button for members of his council, he says, but the agenda is now much larger. Fatherlessness, marriage, family breakdown, are at the top of their agenda. So is the "family-friendly" workplace. Indeed, the latest bill put forward by corporate America, one that could gut the forty-hour workweek for many Americans, was on the agenda of "calls to action" Hicks and other state activists received.

Hicks says that similar issues top the agenda at other state policy councils, and he is an authority on that score. He was hired back in 1989 by Focus on the Family to travel the country and "start organizations at the state level to address some of these family issues, to start shaping the message at the state level to be the same as the one coming out of the Reagan and Bush White House." Gary Bauer, who had just left the White House as a domestic policy advisor, was "key" to all these efforts, he recalls. The general idea of "family breakdown" was a big concern, coupled with the notion that the problems were "cultural" ones not easily addressed by any government policy. There was plenty of momentum at the time, generated by the fights over abortion and the Equal Rights Amendment. "I'd love to tell you that we were geniuses, but we didn't have to do much," he recalls. "There were a lot of people just looking for an organization to be a voice on the family and family values."

Still, he concedes the conservative positions had not won the hearts of mainstream voters in the late 1980s and early 1990s. "Dan Quayle was laughed at in 1992 when he tried to talk about family values," he says. The turning point came in 1993. "Everything changed when Barbara DaFoe Whitehead published her piece and she and David Blankenhorn started making the same arguments that we were."

Whitehead's "piece" was a cover story for the *Atlantic* titled "Dan Quayle Was Right," and is cited by liberal and conservative commentators alike as a critical juncture in the debate over family values. What was needed, Whitehead asserted, was not new government policies, but a reworking of cultural attitudes, especially toward marriage. "It was so powerful to have their voices saying the same things we were," says Hicks. "The idea that what we needed was a change in cultural values and not more government programs suddenly got more credibility."

The Family Research Council plans to eventually have one "policy council" in every state. The affiliations are loose—there is no lockstep march. Each council sets its own priorities and decides when to rouse its membership. None take any government funding, as a matter of principle. Most seek to influence state and local policies as much as federal ones. Indeed, with the new "devolution" of power and money to the local government, the Family Research Council and Focus on the Family apparently see the need to devolve as well to the local level, where real money will be spent and real impact on social policy is likely to take place in the coming years.

But they still make considerable noise in Washington. With a web site on the Internet, faxes, and phone calls, the Family Research Council communicates regularly with its grass roots, keeping them apprised of important bills in Congress and sending along any new research or studies that support their point of view. "We also call Focus [on the Family] to let them know," says the council policy analyst Malloney, "and very often, Dr. Dobson will say something on his radio show."

The syndicated radio show reaches several million listeners every day. Dobson is well known among many congressional staffers, who receive calls from his listeners. "I used to hear from them all the time when I worked for Congressman Applegate from southeastern Ohio and Congresswoman Louise Slaughter in New York. Those districts were more conservative, and Dobson's show was broadcast there," says Ann Grady, who now works for Senator Patty Murray on women's issues. "They came out in force against child care."

Dobson himself has declared a "'civil war of values' is raging across North America" in a 1993 brochure to members. "We believe that only a full-fledged return to Biblical concepts of morality, fidelity and parental leadership in the home will halt the disintegration of the family."

The Family Research Council now serves as the "voice" for Dobson's organization in Washington, D.C., according to spokespeople for both groups. Malloney goes to great lengths to point out just how separate the two organizations are. "We have to be careful of the IRS rules," she says. As a nonprofit organization, Focus on the Family is limited in terms of the time and budget it can spend on public policy issues.

These days, the Family Research Council is a potent political force, with Gary Bauer recognized on the front page of the *New York Times* as a power broker in the last presidential election. Other lesser-known conservatives wield considerable influence as well.

A full decade after Allan Carlson's speech, the Rockford Institute also remains in the forefront of conservative think tanks—and still promoting the idea that women belong at home, in newsletters, research papers, congressional testimony, and conferences that go out to journalists, policymakers, and grassroots activists.

His embrace of homemakers springs as much from a clear-eyed and unflinching critique of the economics of women's roles as anything. Carlson understands quite clearly how women's unpaid labor and underpaid labor fuels an industrial economy. "Women's labor usually isn't counted; it's kept invisible and undervalued, almost as if there's a conspiracy among economists not to count it," he says. Most certainly, no worker could show up for a job without someone at home to care for the kids and tend the home front.

Yet in 1997, Carlson concedes the vision he offered of homemakers back at Schlafly's meeting sounds a little off-key, even to him. "The model of the 1950s and 1960s homemaker just isn't a good one anymore," he says.

Does this mean he recognizes the need and desire for women to work outside the home? Quite the contrary. If anything, his vision of women's place has become ever more radical as the grassroots conservative movement gains momentum. "Something far more countercultural is needed," he says. Homemakers of the past simply became consumers rather than women truly dedicated to strengthening families. "The old homemaker was just a handmaiden of market production, a consumer supporting market production." Instead, he argues, women need to be at the center of a vital new home-schooling movement. "Women could bring education back into the home—that would refunctionalize the family" and make "mothers the pivot of family renewal."

Carlson sounds strangely out of touch with American families today, of course. But in 1997, as in 1989, he sits at the center of a movement that has proved its muscle in shaping social policy. Several congressional staffers and academic researchers who follow family policy have noted the vibrancy and political power of the new home-schooling movement in America, which has flooded the Washington switchboards with phone calls on the issue several times. While no one predicts that women will realistically take up Carlson's call, those watching the debate evolve note that the goal of conservative activists is to expand women's child care responsibilities—now to embrace children's education—rather than support for the real lives of real families.

Indeed, his institute's ardent opposition to working mothers and child care has not changed over the years. His public relations liaison, Christopher Check, sends along over seventy-three separate articles indicting child care as the cause of disease, emotional distress, and behavior problems among children. The headlines for the press releases begin to run together as one long indictment of child care, starting in the mid-1980s: "Day Care Centers Breed Disease," November 1988; "Day Care Germs," April 1991; "Day Care Epidemics," February 1992; "Day Care Diarrhea," July 1993; "Day Care Disease," July 1994.

Others highlight studies that claim mothers suffer extreme tension and unhappiness when they work. One is a familiar one, conducted by researchers at Boston University. It is ironic for the Rockford Institute to choose this one for its newsletter, since it revealed moms were stressed not by their jobs, but by the lack of support when they did work. One key finding, in fact, was that married women did a few more hours a week of housework than single moms. The conclusion of the Boston research team? Men create work for their wives instead of sharing the load at home, a key source of anger for working moms.

Nonetheless, the Rockford Institute newsletter reported the study as evidence that women's jobs created the stress. "The average working mother" was more likely to suffer depression, dissatisfaction, low energy levels, than homemakers and often missed work because of these problems. "All of which makes one wonder just why

Americans gave up on the one-earner household," the newsletter concluded. "Some of the alluring claims of feminism, heard so often in recent years, deserve skeptical reassessment," another article concluded.

Given such outdated and unsupportive attitudes, it's easy to wonder why Allan Carlson and William Mattox at the Family Research Council have gained such influence. The answer is that they do understand one key fact about modern life and it is an important one: they are deeply sympathetic to the way that jobs intrude on family time. They talk increasingly about the "industrialization" of family life—a shorthand for describing how the demands of work distort family life. Mattox's widely circulated tract on the "time famine" had such power because it struck that chord.

As this book was being prepared for publication, they took up the cause of a bill promoted by major corporations to amend the labor law. The new proposal, floated as the Family-Friendly Workplace Act, contained provisions that could easily wreak havoc with many workers' lives. Employers would no longer be required to pay overtime rates when hourly workers put in more than forty hours a week. Instead, they could award "comp time" for the extra work. The version of the bill most likely to pass also included a proposal that would create a new two-week, eighty-hour standard to replace the standard forty-hour week that exists now. That would mean that employers could ask an employee to work sixty hours one week and twenty the next—or any other combination that suited business needs.

In principle, this could be promoted as a way to give workers more flexibility and "family time." But unions lined up in bitter opposition to what they saw as an attack on the one remaining protection workers had against arbitrary demands on workers' time. "When the Republicans first won back Congress, one of the first initiatives that began to be discussed as a business agenda item was getting rid of the forty-hour workweek," charges Karen Nussbaum, head of the women's department at the AFL-CIO. "The only mandated benefit that still exists for workers is that employers pay mandatory overtime when workers put in more than forty hours. This bill is just a way to reduce costs for business."

Of course, it is polemics to say that the forty-hour week is the only "mandated benefit" employees still retain. But it is no exaggeration to say that it is one of the few protections that hourly workers have against employers laying claim to ever-increasing amounts of their time. And it is most certainly of grave concern to working parents. And in April 1997, *USA Today* reported that "off-the-clock" time, that is, work done beyond the forty-hour week, had emerged as a serious labor problem. A fast-food chain, a grocery chain, and a major discount department store company all stood accused of asking employees to work through lunch, skip breaks, and even do work before punching their time clocks—all possible violations of labor law.

Sponsors of the bill and lobbyists from the business community argue such incidents are rare and contend this legislation would simply allow employers to create more flexible work schedules. "There isn't a week that goes by when workers don't ask for time off," says Sandy Boyd, lobbyist with the Labor Policy Association. Despite its name, the association does not represent unions or even workers. Instead, Boyd serves as the hired gun for 250 of the nation's major corporations. She is fond of noting that 35 of them have made *Working Mother*'s list of best companies. "We need to change the Fair Labor Standards Act. It was written in 1938 and it's simply outdated. Under that act, employers simply can't be flexible. They can't allow employees to bank time. With the change we want, employers will be able to be more flexible." Of course, employers can be as flexible as they want, as long as they pay time-and-a-half when workers put in more than forty hours a week.

"I know the unions say that employers want this change because employers just don't want to pay overtime costs, that it's going to save employers money," Boyd says. "But I have not talked to anyone in a company who thinks that's true. They'll still have to pay for comp time. This is not a proposal to save money. It's a proposal to allow employers to be more flexible."

Not surprisingly, the unions were not buying such a benevolent vision. "It's absolutely true that working parents are desperate for more control over their hours. Many families are at the panic point. Working mothers in particular are desperate," says Nussbaum. "But this bill would put more control of time in the hands of employers. The point is that parents need time when they need time—not just when employers feel like giving it to them."

Asked about this issue, Boyd says, "Well, Karen and I just have different views of the world. Her view is that it's the exceptional employer who would do the right thing. Our view is that we're moving into the next century and we need a law that will allow us to do that. I still think most employers value their employees and will do what's right."

This bill was not yet a major item on the agenda of the Family Research Council network of state action groups in late 1997. But Malloney said it would soon become more of a priority, because she expected the council to issue a "call to action" in support of the bill. "Government should let businesses and workers decide these things themselves," she says.

A New Veneer for an Old Argument

The new generation of social conservatives frames the issues in polished and careful language, research that carries the imprint of scholars, and a tone that mostly keeps their more radical agenda from clear public view. William Mattox, for example, always suggests it's best one "parent" is at home, rather than engage in a debate over women's roles. In fact, Mattox has managed to escape heavy scrutiny in the media precisely because he—along with Blankenhorn and Whitehead—has learned to frame his arguments in a way that sounds almost liberated. "You don't have to agree with me on gender roles to agree with me on the issues," Mattox asserts.

But when his guard drops, there is very little doubt about his view of women's proper place. "You can really paint me out to be all kinds of terrible things," he joked over coffee at an Au Bon Pain store, just below his offices in Washington, D.C., in November 1995. Traditional roles for men and women suit him just fine, he admitted.

But he also knew conservatives were ridiculed for idealizing the 1950s. "When you ask me, 'When were the glory days?' it's not the 1950s." He added, however, that "if you ask me, 'Was that better than today?' You bet. If that's the best we can do, I would say let's move in that direction."

But the real glory days for Mattox occurred way before that. "To me, the heyday, the model, comes from Colonial Williamsburg. That's when Mom and Dad were both involved in productive, creative work which did not typically take them away from their children," he said. There "was a very sharp division of labor" between men and women then, he conceded, but there was also a "great deal of creative opportunity for both genders."

Colonial Williamsburg has its charm as a destination for modern tourists. But in real life, the colonial period was a remarkably difficult time for women. They had virtually no economic autonomy and few property rights. Their money, their children, and their inheritance were all controlled by men—their fathers, husbands, or a brother if no other man was available. As for "creative opportunities," women's domestic duties allowed little respite. With no birth control and large families, women endured a grueling daily grind, along with a devastatingly high rate of childhood disease and death.

Such nostalgia does have a way, however, of seeping into popular culture, almost by osmosis, as Americans try to grapple with the enormous changes in family life. With a workplace eating up more and more of their time, nearly everyone longs for a simpler life. Even sociologist Arlie Hochschild, for example, can be found embracing a vision that mimics Mattox's. She argued, for example, that women's work in the home once embodied the work of caring, a value lost to modern life. She romanticized the times when families made their own candles and other household goods. This from the author of *The Second Shift,* who a decade earlier maintained that women's main problem stemmed from having responsibility for too many domestic chores. The same month Hochschild's book came out, a syndicated Martha Stewart column suggested families make their own soap for Mother's Day.

Yet in the end, nostalgia and ideology simply cannot trump reality, even within the conservative ranks. "The issue of working mothers is one that we have really struggled with," Glen Stanton, policy analyst with Focus on the Family, confesses. "We have a lot of single mothers and mothers who work full-time right here and we've even had the discussion internally about whether we would like to entertain day care for the employees here. As you can imagine, it was pretty hotly debated." What was the decision? "We ended up not doing it."

He pauses and adds, "I'm not comfortable with that being mentioned in your book." But after some coaxing, he continues. "Employees themselves were taking it on to discuss the issue. This issue is problematic in the sense of getting a good balance between ideological beliefs and what is reality."

He says he has sympathy for women who "have to work to support their families because of the economy and the taxes." He feels fortunate that his own wife is at home, he says. He adds, however, that at the headquarters of Focus on the Family, it's plain to him that he is the exception. "Most of the times, the second spouse has to work just simply to make ends meet. There's no arguing with that."

And what about single mothers? That is a real problem, he concedes. His answer? "My bias is toward marriage. It's difficult to talk about individually. I'm not saying that every single mom just should be married. But culturally, I think marriage is the answer to that problem. Marriage provides a very nice division of labor. We, as a society, can esteem marriage more than we currently do. I think more people should work at marriage, that marriage is a solution to many problems."

13

Yes, Families Are Changing—

For the Better

WHEN LAURA KOENIG arrives home from work in Stoughton, Wisconsin, she often finds dinner on the table, the dishwasher empty and waiting for a new load of dishes. There may even be a load of clothes already in the wash. All of this is done by her husband, Kurt, who gets home a couple hours ahead of her. "It's awesome, isn't it?" Laura says. "My marriage is better than it's ever been. I couldn't be happier."

Koenig, an occupational therapist and mother of two, still sounds a little surprised in early 1997 as she recounts this homecoming scene. "It sure beats the heck out of being angry all the time," she says, laughing. Five years ago, she thought their marriage was over, largely because Kurt did so little child care and housework. "All I used to think about was how could I screw him over. Now I look for things to make him feel good. It's so different."

Her husband, Kurt, sounds equally awed by the change in their marriage. He now uses the same words as Laura to describe it. "It's better than it's ever been," he says. "We couldn't be happier."

Not only that, but Kurt says he's much closer to his children. "It's been a gradual evolution. Taking part in the day-to-day rigors of life has helped my relationship with the kids." That means the children now turn to him for solace and support. "The kids don't go to Mom for everything now; they have confidence that I can meet their needs. My daughter will ask to do things with me, to read and draw with her. It's much more comfortable now."

But the road to this marital bliss was a remarkably bumpy one. It was not so long ago that Laura issued Kurt an ultimatum: "Either come to marriage counseling or move out." The issue? As for so many dual-earner couples, his lack of participation in child care and domestic chores. Kurt's new engagement at home grew directly from the insights he gained in counseling as a way to save his marriage. Both he and Laura learned that it can be far more dangerous to resist change than to embrace it.

Indeed, the Koenigs show just how much family life in America has changed over the past two decades—all in response to the growing numbers of mothers who now have jobs outside the home. Between 1975 and 1993, the number of two-paycheck families in America swelled from 43 to 63 percent of all families, making them the solid majority today. As that happens, life inside the average household is shifting, with Americans reinventing what it means to be a husband or wife, mom or dad, son or daughter.

"Having women work after having children changes everything. We now have a new family form," says Rosalind Barnett, scholar at the Murray Research Center at Radcliffe College and coauthor, with Caryl Rivers, of *She Works, He Works: How Two Income Families Are Happier, Healthier, and Better Off*. And contrary to the hand-wringing from social conservatives, this new kind of family turns out to be quite a vibrant one, with benefits for men, women, and children. Women's new earning power offers both men and women more flexibility about the way they pursue their careers and family life. With two incomes, families are more secure economically and better able to weather a recession or downsizing at work, which has had savage effects on family life in the past. There is also plenty of evidence that women's new economic clout has the effect of encouraging a new intimacy between men and their children, as Kurt is discovering.

To be sure, the mere fact that a woman has a job outside the home does not automatically guarantee a happy life. Marriage is one of the most complicated human relationships; so is the one between parents and children. The effects of women's employment on a marriage and family life are as various as the jobs they hold, the husbands they marry, the children they bear. Nor is the fallout from a job on family life some static phenomenon. Rather, the effects vary over time, as circumstances change both at work and at home. And there is a growing body of research that shows that the attitudes a woman or man has about male and female roles matter as much as anything.

Sociologists and psychologists also report that the best marriages today are those forged between equals, much like the one Kurt and Laura have achieved, where responsibilities for home, children, and breadwinning are shared. Such a union breeds a sense of reciprocity, empathy, and affirmation for both mates that deepens intimacy, trust, and respect in a marriage. "People are more willing to be direct, to reveal themselves and be themselves when they feel like equals," says Janice Steil, professor of psychology at Adelphi University's Derner Institute of Advanced Psychological Studies and author of *His and Her Marriage from the 1970's to the 1990's.*

That this message is still a faint one in American culture, that there is still a deep ambivalence about mothers working, is not surprising to researchers, however. The truth is that American families are caught in the cross fire of change as society moves ever so slowly to accept the new family roles. Today men and women live in what sociologists call a "transitional" phase; that is, the daily realities of individual families have changed, but the nation's institutions and social expectations lag behind. Most still follow rules created for families of another era. "We're in the middle of an evolution," says James Levine, head of the Fatherhood Project at the Families and Work Institute. "These patterns just don't change overnight, because gender roles are so overdetermined. The scripts that women and men have internalized growing up, the economic realities, the continuing differential between men's and women's earning power, all conspire to keep men and women in the old roles."

Nonetheless, there is a louder call than ever from social conservatives for a return to old-fashioned "family values," when men earned a living and women stayed home with the kids. "One Breadwinner Should Be Enough," conservative economist Jude Wanniski headlined in the *Wall Street Journal* in early 1996. "When both husband and wife must work full-time to make ends meet," he insisted, "children are more likely to become unruly, communication between the spouses breaks down . . . the divorce rate increases and so does abortion." At about the same time, the right-wing Rockford Institute featured a picture of the 1950s Cleaver family, from the sitcom *Leave It to Beaver*, under the headline "Ward and June Were Right" on the cover of one of its 1996 monthly newsletters. Social conservative David Blankenhorn at the Institute for American Values asserts that "marriage is the most fragile institution in society today," and calls for a return to the old ways. "Feminists are constantly talking about wanting to reengineer sex roles, that men should do more nurturing. But it would be better to accept the premise that fathers are different from mothers. Men still see their primary responsibility as breadwinning and protection. And both men and women like it that way."

Certainly, there are some men and women who prefer those roles. But the evidence shows that many families are thriving today as they adapt to a changing way of life. Men want more expansive roles, more involvement with kids. And what Blankenhorn and other social conservatives miss is that the core problem in many marriages today is not that men's and women's roles are changing. Rather, the real threat to marriage and family life often lies in the inability or resistance to change those roles. Further, it is not some feminist plot or liberal ideology that inspires men and women to reinvent their family life. Rather, it is the day-to-day realities of home life today, transformed by women's new earning power, that drives couples to alter the terms of marriage and parenthood.

· · · ·

FOR LAURA Koenig, it took a full five years after the birth of her first child, Danny, for the tension in her marriage to build to a crisis. By then, she had had a second child, Alexandra, who was eight months old. And by then, fights over housework and child care had become the stuff of daily life. "I felt such a lack of support and appreciation. I began to feel it would be easier to be with my children by myself. It would mean one less person to clean up after."

That truth came hard to her. "I went into marriage thinking I'd be married for the rest of my life," she says. When she found herself pregnant at twenty-two, she knew raising a child would be demanding. But she trusted that she and Kurt could do a good job. She never expected to be overwhelmed by the duties of raising the kids and keeping the house running.

But at twenty-six, with a job and two kids, housework and child care were foremost on her mind. Because of their different work schedules, Kurt generally arrived home a few hours ahead of her, with the two children. Back then, she recalls, "I'd typically arrive home and the kids' stuff would be all over the floor in front of the door. The kids would be hollering for something to eat. And Kurt was there reading the paper, hanging out and watching TV. I always wondered how he could do that," she recalls.

After dinner, the scenario was no less frustrating to Laura. Kurt would again retreat into his own world with a newspaper or watching television, while she cleaned the kitchen, gave the kids a bath, and got them into bed. "Kurt never used to take responsibility for the kids. He saw it as my job and only helped if I asked him to. If he gave them a bath, he'd tell me it was for me. If he put on their pajamas, he'd say he did it for me."

His attitude infuriated her. "I blew up. I asked him, 'Why is it always my job? Don't you enjoy these children? Aren't they your children, too?' "

At the time, this was hardly a new question in the Koenig household. Over the years since the birth of their first child and then their second, she had tried to get Kurt to take more responsibility for the kids. "We went through stages of trying to negotiate this. I remember sitting down and saying, 'These are all the things that need to get done around the house above and beyond my job. We have to get meals, clean up, give the kids baths,' and so on," she recalls. "I'd ask him, 'Which items will you do, will I do? Which do you never want to do?' These talks would change things for a while." But, she recalls, "it was never a sustained effort. It would work for a couple of weeks or a couple of months. Then it reverted back to the old scenario. He always paid the bills and took care of the cars. But otherwise, I did everything else. It was like I had two full-time jobs."

And this, she came to see, was corrosive to the marriage. "My anger was biting his head off. I'd swear and stomp my feet," she says, to prompt the talks about chores. Otherwise, she retreated into her anger, withdrawing from Kurt. "The anger went into every depth of our life. I remember feeling he didn't do this and didn't do that, then I'd be damned if I'd cuddle with him. I would just be cold," she says. "If he was watching TV, I'd just find anything to do besides go down and watch TV with him."

Such a situation is a familiar one to psychologists who deal with two-career couples. While the external trappings of their lives are dramatically different from those of earlier generations, many still inhabit the psychic landscape of the past. Kurt, for example, says that he didn't sense there was a truly serious problem in the marriage, even after the repeated talks about housework and child care. He'd grown up as an only child; his mom took care of all the household chores. The stress that Laura was experiencing was invisible to him. "I was off in my little world, assuming things were fine," he says. That is, until Laura gave him the ultimatum to get out or go into marriage counseling.

Such a situation is also a common one to family counselors. With few role models and no real system for assigning duties in the marriage, many couples wage war over the minutiae of daily life. "It's a new structure for marriage, so questions arise all the time about the extent to which expectations match in the marriage. Who's going to stay home with a sick child? Who's going to do the housework?" says Lisa Silberstein, a clinical psychologist in New Haven, Connecticut, and author of *Dual-Career Marriage: A System in Transition.* "The success in the marriage and marital satisfaction depend on how much a couple can keep those issues on the table and talking about them."

The conversations the Koenigs had in marriage counseling over the course of a year helped them arrive at new roles at home. Kurt began to take more initiative with the children and household chores. Not only that, but Kurt says he now views his wife as his true equal. "It was never an issue what my wife earns. I've never been the type to have a wife who sits home and takes care of the nest. I just never felt real strongly about that, that I needed a stay-at-home wife taking care of my kids," he says. On the other hand, he adds that "there maybe was a time when I was working and Laura was still in school, when I didn't see her as equal. But now we split everything fifty-fifty and there are a lot of benefits from that."

And that is exactly what the research on marriage shows. Dual-career couples who manage to share child care and housework tend to describe their marriages as far more satisfying than others. Such give-and-take in all aspects of family life makes both men and women feel valued and supported, and allows an intimacy that is otherwise hard to achieve, according to sociologist Pepper Schwartz, who has conducted broad surveys of marriage in America. The "mutual friendship"—the shared values and shared sense of responsibility for all aspects of family life—is the most gratifying aspect of their lives, Schwartz asserted in her book, *Peer Marriage*.

Part of the reason for this is that such marriages are so liberating to both men and women; such a relationship allows couples to play to their personal strengths and preferences rather than be boxed into expectations based on traditional gender roles. "We moved from California to the Midwest because of my career," says Nancy McConnell, marketing coordinator for LinguiSystems, an educational publisher in East Moline, Illinois. Her husband, a Methodist minister, supported her decision wholeheartedly. "It was exciting and scary when I got this job. It meant that I was becoming the primary breadwinner for our family, but that didn't bother him. I was proud that I actually had a partner, a man who was willing to be a real partner and say this is what's best for our family."

Indeed, the move meant that the McConnells could adopt what

Nancy describes as a "kinder, gentler life" in the Midwest, where housing was more affordable and the neighborhoods safer and schools better than where they had lived in the West. "It actually turned out the way we expected. We were able to buy a house, which we couldn't afford to do before in California. And the kids are happy here."

Melissa Stevens, a marketing executive with an advertising agency in Seattle, Washington, has also found that a marriage built on flexibility and equality has made both her and her husband happier than they would have been otherwise. "I've always been the aggressive one in our family. I've always thrived on the competition of business," says Stevens. Her husband, Russell, on the other hand, wasn't too happy in his job as a salesman in a sporting goods store when Melissa learned she was pregnant with their first child, Jeanne. When Jeanne was born prematurely, both she and Russell felt it was important for one of them to be home during her first full year. So he and Melissa decided it just made good sense for him to be the one at home. During his year at home, Russell began to plot a career change—he decided to study to become a registered nurse. Melissa encouraged the decision, because she knew it would make Russell happier and give him a lifelong, satisfying career. "I guess I've never really questioned my working because I've been the primary bread-winner all along," Melissa says. "And it makes me happy that Russell is going to have work that makes him happy."

Was this the way she anticipated her life to turn out? "I guess I thought I would have a husband who supported me. My work would be just for fun and extra income. But I've always been the primary breadwinner and now the only one. And the truth is, I never would have been happy with a traditional marriage. Neither would Russell."

And even though the institutions around them still largely fail to support working moms, a growing number say that equality is simply becoming a core assumption in life. "Working moms are now the norm in many places, so that changes the way women feel about their roles," observes psychologist Barnett at Radcliffe. Stevens, for example, notes that she is surrounded by other working moms, who face the same issues as she does. "I've been in the working environment as long as I've had children. I suppose if I spent more time with people who stayed home, someone might try to put different values on me, but most of my friends have made the same choices I did."

Part of her ability to be happy in her role, she adds, is the ability to exchange responsibilities with her husband. "It did feel really important that my husband be home during the first years of our children's lives," she says. "If he hadn't been able to do that, I might feel differently about going off to a job. But I'm happy we've been able to work things out the way we have."

Other moms echo Stevens's sentiments. "I've always worked in my marriage, so there was never any question about that," says Barbara Brazil, assistant to the chief counsel for the school district in Kent, Washington. "We give and take. We have real good open communication in our marriage. We share just about everything—he even does some clothes shopping for me." Even more surprising, he selected their younger son's latest day care arrangement. "I know women usually do that, and I am the one who usually does the legwork for day care. But the last time we made a change, I just couldn't get the time off work, so he went and checked places out, interviewed the lady we chose, and made all the arrangements.

"I just don't think I could be home full-time with the kids," she adds. "I don't have the personality and I don't think my kids would be happy, either." Her current job makes it easy to be involved in the kids' lives, she says, with the flexibility to take time off for school events or to care for a sick child. Her husband's job as a telephone lineman for U.S. West starts early, and allows him to be home with the boys after school lets out, to shuttle them to soccer and baseball practice. Barbara takes time off work for school conferences and parties. Overall, she believes they have a full and happy life. "We have our struggles, who doesn't?" she says. "But we're happy; we're content."

Still, marriage counselors and sociologists who study dual-career couples concede that such easygoing acceptance of the new expectations, roles, and responsibilities in marriage is far from a simple task for many couples. The questions that Laura Koenig put to her husband, Kurt, at the flash point in their marriage—Why was child care always her job? Didn't he enjoy their children? Weren't they his children, too?—reverberate through American culture. "Who Takes Care of the House and the Kids?" asked the headline of the *Newark Star-Ledger* in February 1997. That story covered a survey by *American Baby* magazine that found a majority of moms wished their spouses would do more around the house. By now, no one has to explain what is meant by the term "second shift." Survey after survey shows that women still put in far more hours than men do at home. Women managers at the nation's major corporations put in thirty-three hours a week on housework and child care, compared with eighteen hours a week for men, according to a study by Rodgers and Associates, the research arm of Work/Family Directions. That means the average woman manager puts in a total of eighty hours a week between duties at home and on the job, compared with sixty-seven hours for a man. It also means that a man is typically putting in a couple extra hours a week on the job, a powerful reinforcement of traditional roles for men and women. Strategies for getting men to share housework and child care are now regular topics for women's and parenting magazines.

Why, then, is it so hard to arrive at equity on the home front, given the benefits for both men and women? More than anything, the answer seems to lie in a deep-rooted cultural allegiance to old-fashioned gender roles. Although family life is clearly changing, the cultural attachment to the old ways is deeply internalized and hard to shake.

WHEN ELLEN Galinsky and Dana Friedman, then copresidents of the Families and Work Institute, released their research in mid-1995 showing that married women were now true breadwinners, bringing in half or more of the income in the majority of American families, their research made news for weeks, reaching millions of Americans.

But even before the findings were released, there was one inconsistency in the raw data that intrigued Friedman. While the new numbers left no doubt that women were now true providers, women still insisted that men's careers were more important than women's.

Almost two-thirds of the married women polled said their husbands' jobs provided more financial security for their families. "Their opinions just didn't jibe with reality; they didn't reflect what women were bringing into the family," Friedman recalls. Unfortunately, neither she nor Galinsky had anticipated the response, so they had no way to explain the inconsistency. Still curious, Friedman decided to pursue the issue in small focus groups. What she found was illuminating. "Women are in a sort of collusion with men in making men feel that their work is more important than women's."

Women confided, for example, that they understood the need to "preserve the natural order" between the sexes. "Women told me men would just be too threatened if women said their careers were as important as men's," says Friedman. "They said maybe women devalue what they do to make men feel more important."

This finding comes as no surprise to Janice Steil, professor of psychology at Adelphi University, who has devoted her career to exploring how men and women work out equality in the context of intimate relationships. And increasingly, she has come to see that the psychic reality of men and women, the way they define what it means to be a good husband and father or a good wife and mother, is key in predicting marital happiness. "The more I looked at the research, the more it led me to think about the importance of the way men and women internalize their gender roles," says Steil. Indeed, many social scientists now describe "sex role ideology" as a key factor in predicting how well or how poorly people will fare in modern marriage. Such beliefs are among the most powerful and most deeply held ideas people have, since gender is such an important part of a person's sense of self. And the notion of femaleness, of what it means to be a woman, is very closely bound up with being a mother. "When you listen to the stereotypes of what you say a mother is and what a woman is, they're very, very similar," says psychologist Kay Deaux, who pioneered research on gender stereotypes. Words such as "nurturing," "warm," "sensitive," "caring," for example. And those ideas are so powerful because they are instilled and reinforced from birth. "Gender is something that is part of nearly every interaction we have in life, and the stereotypes are reinforced over and over again." Such ideas can be comforting in that they maintain the status quo. "Part of gender identification has to do with power issues," says Susan Fiske, the social psychologist who took her arguments about stereotypes all the way to the U.S. Supreme Court. Although Fiske has focused primarily on how gender identity plays out in the workplace, her ideas about the interplay of gender and power certainly have relevance for marriage. "People do understand the function that maintaining a certain identity has in maintaining power. It can happen without it being conscious. It's not intentional, but it's comfortable to hold a set of beliefs because it maintains things as they are."

That certainly goes a long way toward explaining why most American men and women still insist that men's work is more important than women's. Indeed, Steil found that one consistent, powerful fact turned up in studies on how couples achieve equality in marriage, the same one that Friedman and Galinsky stumbled upon in their research. When asked to rank the importance of men's and women's careers, both men and women described men's careers as more important than women's. It did not matter how much a woman earned, how accomplished she was. Indeed, if a woman earned more than her husband, recognition of that fact was often grudging and incomplete. "The most a husband would say about his wife's career was that it was equally important to his—even when his wife earned more than he did," Steil says. "On the other hand, the least a wife would say about a husband's career was that it was equal to hers, even if she earned more."

This is no minor fact, given other major findings on marital happiness among dual-earner couples. "The best predictor of a woman's psychological well-being in marriage is how important her career is relative to her husband's," Steil says.

"When a woman doesn't feel equal, she may not feel she has as much influence in the relationship. Then she may not feel that she can be as open, that she can say what she wants directly and bargain for it." When that happens, women—and sometimes men as well—resort to indirect tactics, such as withdrawing from their mates. Or they may be reduced to begging or crying for what they need. That sense of dependency and powerlessness can feel humiliating, erode self-esteem, feed resentments, and eventually threaten the relationship.

Conversely, earning a paycheck often contributes to a woman's sense of well-being by giving her a sense of entitlement in the marriage. "What you see when you look at the studies on power in marriage and the studies of psychological well-being in marriage is that power and psychological well-being parallel each other. They tend to happen together," says Steil. Studies show, for example, that couples are more likely to share important decision making when a wife has a job. That, of course, only makes sense in a society where money is the currency of power. And while women are often portrayed as indifferent to money, surveys reveal they are keenly aware of its importance in marriage. In one survey of 2,000 women by the Families and Work Institute and *Working Mother* magazine, for example, more than half of the women polled reported that earning a salary made them feel more at ease about spending money. "If I didn't work, I'd feel guilty about what I bought, or I just wouldn't buy anything," one mom told the magazine. Intuitively, she understood how such inhibition could hurt her marriage, because, she added, "I think that would cause tension in our family."

Indeed, while women may "collude" in saying that men's jobs are more important in public survey data, economists and other social scientists note a very different phenomenon playing itself out in the privacy of American households. A woman's paycheck does play a very pivotal role in the bargaining that goes on between husbands and wives. Indeed, in the past five years, a new body of economic research has come to illuminate—and even quantify—the way a woman's paycheck, or lack of one, impacts family life. "Economists used to treat the family as a little factory run by one person," says Joan Lundberg, professor of economics at the University of Washington and a leading expert on the economics of family life. Under that model, economists assumed the "factory" was run by the male breadwinner, and family members simply pooled resources and acted in the common interest of the group. The idea that women stayed home was perceived as a simple choice, for example, based on women's lower earning power outside the home. "But we came to realize [that] that really trivialized the way family life works, especially since couples now have to contemplate the fact that they may be divorced," Lundberg says. "We have had to look at how individuals operate within the family, not just the family as a unit."

Indeed, women's economic stake in marriage is profoundly changed by their relatively new ability to earn a good living—and that changes the terms of marriage. Not only that, but most will have fewer children and live longer, and so work will play a larger role in their lives than it did in previous generations. "No young woman in her right mind today would think she could specialize in the profession of homemaking as women did in previous generations," says Lundberg. "They can't count on that as a reasonable lifetime possibility anymore."

Nor is it one that particularly appeals to most women, even after they have children. "I believe more women are working today not just because they 'have' to, but because they are choosing economic autonomy," says Heidi Hartmann, economist at the Women's Policy Institute in Washington, D.C. "Work does change power within the family. It means that if a woman finds herself in a bad situation, it's easier to get out of it. Basically, I think it's great that women are moving toward economic self-determination. It's empowering for them."

Indeed, it's a sentiment that a growing number of women express quite openly. "It's important for me to support myself. I think a lot of women are willing to put up with the stress they feel between work and family because it's important to know they can support themselves," says one communications executive in the Southwest. Kristen Storey, the human resources manager in Ann Arbor, Michigan, doesn't have any concrete reason to worry about her marriage. Still, she says in passing that holding a job is important, just in case something happens to her husband or the marriage sours. "I need to feel I'm pulling my weight in the marriage," she says. "And what always goes through my mind is that if anything happens to my marriage, a divorce or death, money is a big point. I don't want to have to move back in with my mother." Besides, she adds, "it helps my self-esteem that I help provide for my family, that I can take care of myself if anything happens."

Having that sense of control is certainly one reason why women generally fare better in marriages when they earn a paycheck. But, of course, the formula for women's well-being is not quite so simple as all that. It's not the mere existence of a paycheck that empowers women. Were that the case, Americans would have reached marital bliss by now. "If chores in the home were divided on a *purely* rational basis, husbands and wives who were employed equal numbers of hours would do equal amounts of housework," wrote sociologist Catherine Ross in one of the earliest and most important studies of how couples divvy up the chores.

What she found in 1987, and other researchers have confirmed since then, was that relative earning power is often at the heart of domestic relations. It is the difference between a husband's and wife's income that is often the deciding factor in how a couple divvies up child care and housework. The larger the difference between the two paychecks, the wider the disparity between the spouses. "The more money the wife contributes to the family, the greater leverage in getting her husband to help around the house," wrote Ross. Part of the reason is related to the way that housework and child care are valued in America, of course. Ross noted that "if housework is devalued, unrewarded, onerous and menial, the spouse with more power should be able to delegate it to the other." Which is precisely the conclusion that Steil finds in a review of the literature in the mid-1990s. The economics, combined with the power of gender roles, make for a potent mix in marriage, setting the terms of work and intimacy, of power and dependency, and, most of all, of who owns which work. Once again, it is the association of certain types of work with gender that takes center stage in the relationship. "There is a sense that men shouldn't have to get stuck doing female tasks, that it's somehow denigrating to men, that doing 'women's work' will hurt their self-esteem," she says.

Conversely, some women feel driven to do "women's work" to prove they are "real women," that is, good mothers. That urge can be especially acute when they earn more than their husbands; a situation that obviously upsets the usual assumptions of power between men and women. Their career success calls into question their femininity, their ability to fulfill the traditional expectations of women. One female executive and mother of two children in Fort Worth, Texas, vividly recalls the days not so long ago when she hurried home from her job to cook dinner, supervise her son's piano practice, clean up after the meal, and get him to bed. "I rushed home to make dinner, set the table. Then we'd eat, and I'd drag my son to the piano to practice. We'd spend a half hour at the piano. It was excruciating pain for both my son and me. And I was exhausted by trying to do all this after work," she says. She says she felt compelled to keep this grueling evening schedule to maintain her own esteem. "I had to prove I was a good mother, and cooking dinner every night was part of that."

As she grew more confident in her abilities as a mother, she gave up the routine. "I can't believe I did that to myself," she says, laughing. Now that her children are nine and fourteen, she no longer needs or wants to keep up the grueling schedule. And unlike many women, she can afford to buy her way out of this situation if her husband doesn't pick up the slack. Both are professionals and live a comfortable lifestyle, and these days, she is just as likely to order takeout at a local restaurant or go to a restaurant. They also have a cleaning service to lighten the load of housework. Interestingly, the services she buys to keep her life on track also incorporate assumptions about gender. Both the housework and child care have always been done by women.

She does recall when she looks back, however, one other aspect of the bad old days. Her husband never seemed to notice the work she did in the evenings. "He never said, 'Gee, honey, you must be tired; why don't we go out for Chinese tonight?' He was usually sitting on the bed reading during this whole time." Yet she didn't get angry at him. Indeed, she was grateful that as a college professor, he had a more flexible schedule than she did and ferried their son around after school. "I think he does as good a job as you can expect, if not better. He probably does better than what you could expect from a typical man. He takes a lot of responsibility."

Such reasoning—that she has nothing to be upset about because her husband does more than a "typical man"—demonstrates an important principle, according to sociologists who study issues of social justice, and shows just how central gender is to family dynamics. Most anyone trying to decide what is fair looks around to see how others are doing in similar situations, a process known as "social comparison." So it is when working moms get exhausted from doing the lion's share—or more accurately, the lioness's share—of child care and housework, they compare themselves with other moms and their husbands with other husbands. Such a lens is self-protective, of course. Women doing twice as much as their husbands, in addition to a full-time job, might fly into a rage if they did a straight comparison with their mates. And most feel the need to assess the costs and benefits of bringing that anger into the marriage. "Women have to ask themselves, 'What am I going to achieve by protesting this situation?'" Steil notes. "They have to believe that they will gain something. Otherwise, they believe it's not worth the fight."

If their discomfort grows large enough, however, women may threaten to leave the marriage. And when men refuse to change, the marriage may be doomed. One mom in Arizona, for example, explained how her marriage disintegrated back in 1992. "I had a new baby, I was nursing, and I had a full-time job. My husband didn't help around the house at all," she told *Working Mother* magazine. "I was too hostile to have sex and I knew he resented it. If I hadn't finally hired outside help, I would have been too angry even for that." Eventually the couple did divorce. Indeed, therapist and author Lisa Silberstein says the most hopeless cases in her marriage counseling practice are the ones where one partner has given up hope for change. "The success of a marriage depends on how much a couple is able to keep these issues on the table," she says. "In some cases, however, women feel worn down, that they just can't raise the issue. That can be even worse than open conflict. If the issues can't even make it to the table, a marriage is in deep trouble."

It's also true that women who feel conflicted about working suffer more conflict than others, for obvious reasons. If a woman is deeply invested in the old gender roles, if those values sit at the core of her very identity, it's hard to be happy. The tension of being at odds with deeply held beliefs every day that she leaves home for work can inspire conflict and guilt for both her and her spouse. "I still wish I were at home, even though I've worked since the kids were born," says a mother of two boys in Summit, New Jersey, who works full-time as an executive secretary. "My husband and I had a fight about that yesterday. It got heated and I made some comments. I told him when I was growing up, my mother was home baking cookies and we had family dinners. I am very envious of those times, and he feels guilt that I have to work."

The research shows the payoff from working outside the home is muted for such women. "While the research shows that working women often score better on mental health than homemakers," Steil says, "the benefits of work will be less if a woman really doesn't want to work."

Perhaps more surprising—given the professed American attachment to the provider dad, homemaker mom model—is that women tend to be less happy even when they consciously choose the traditional role of stay-at-home wife. It's not hard to understand, once one pierces the surface of such relationships. "My husband isn't home much. He doesn't come home until after the children are asleep at night. They really only see him on weekends," says Susan Brown, mother of two young boys who gave up a job as director of marketing at a small company in Manhattan to raise her sons full-time. "I feel levels of frustration that he's not around more. I do think he should be more interactive with me and the children.

"One thing that is extremely disconcerting to me is that I'm living the life of a 1950s housewife," she adds. (Susan asked that her real name not be used.) "I'm not too thrilled about that aspect of my life." Why? "There's a lot of jobs related to being home that I don't want to do, but they have to get done. If my husband is not getting home until eight at night, he's obviously not going to cook dinner. He's not going to pick up the dry cleaning. He's not there to give the boys a bath. But it all has to be done."

How did she and her husband decide on this division of labor? "He earned a lot more money than I did. He could carry us. I couldn't." And now, with a high-powered job, he feels very little flexibility about the way he does his work. "With his job, he's not in a position to work flexible hours. He's in the corporate world and the corporate world doesn't care whether he has a family or not." Did she miss earning a paycheck? "Money rarely comes up between us," she insists. But she also says that a year ago, she tried to find a part-time position that she could do from home, to no avail. "There's not much in my field except full-time work." So she gave up the idea, at least until the boys are older. "The way I look at the money is that his income is just what we live on. I do all the finances. I don't ever ask him for money. It's not like I have to go to him for money."

Still, she adds a very strong caveat: "I do feel an insecurity that I'm not earning any money right now. I am out of the job force and the job market is not the greatest in the world." And in the end, she is very direct about how it feels to be so dependent on her husband. Her sense of vulnerability is palpable. "I guess there's an underlying thing when you don't earn your own money. There is a sense of not having some control over my life that is scary. If divorce were to happen, I would really be up the creek. We're not talking about divorce. But you read about it. How common it is. There's always that lingering thought; it's always out there in my mind."

Her admission reflects another truth in research on marital happiness: historically, men have been the emotional beneficiaries of marriage. When married men and women are compared, men always score the highest on mental health, showing the least symptoms of depression. Homemakers with young children usually score the lowest. Perhaps it is time to drop the idea that the old-style roles are good for everyone. Clearly, they are not in women's best interests, economically or psychologically.

AND THAT IS why the growing numbers of women in the workforce is such a hopeful sign. Women's growing economic clout can only enlarge the possibilities for men, women, and their children. Freed from the shackles of old gender roles, they can explore their options in life as they see them.

Most notably, there is a new cultural expectation that men will

be more involved fathers. "The idea that men will be active participants in raising children is still relatively new. But it's so evident;
when you walk around any major city, you see young men carrying
their babies and pushing baby carriages," says Lois Hoffman, professor of psychology at the University of Michigan and one of the
nation's leading experts on how women's employment affects
today's families. "You just wouldn't have seen that even a decade
ago." Indeed, psychologist Faye Crosby notes that it's not so long ago
that men were derided as "henpecked" when they did household
chores. Now, she and others note, the men who are actively involved
with their children are "heroes," making a distinct change in the culture. "Of course, we all know that women still do more than men at
home," Crosby adds. "But the point is that the public dialogue is
changing, and men's resistance to participating at home is less than
it once was."

That sentiment is one that Jim Levine, head of the Fatherhood
Project at the Families and Work Institute, hears quite frequently in
seminars he runs for corporations on how workers can balance their
jobs and personal lives. With working wives, many find themselves
cast in the role of involved father, whether they initially choose it or
not. Surveys show that male workers under the age of forty suffer
just about the same level of stress between their work and family life
as women their age.

That, of course, is what most often drives men and women to
their new roles. It's even possible to find men who have taken a paternity leave—something unheard of a generation ago. Such a scenario
is still rare, of course. "My husband was only the fourth man of
twenty thousand employees to take a leave after our son was born,"
says Elizabeth Raynor, a human resources manager at Barnett Bank
in Jacksonville, Florida. In the case of the Raynors, Jeff decided to
take a three-month leave for very practical reasons. Elizabeth had
had a tough pregnancy with their second child, Sarah, and used up a
good deal of her family leave even before Sarah was born. "It was
wrenching for me. I had Sarah in August and I had to come back to
work in six weeks. The only way I could have done it was knowing
my husband was at home with Sarah. We both felt she needed a par-

ent in those early months," she says. "I had been home with our first for a whole year. I think I would have quit my job if Jeff hadn't worked out a leave."

And even with Jeff at home, Elizabeth felt enormous conflict, at first, about not being the one at home. She had cherished the days at home with Joshua, her first child. "I could feel the benefit in that, how close we became. I was the only one who could read his cries, his body language. I could verbalize what he was trying to say. People witnessed that and would joke that they never wanted to play charades with Joshua and me on the same team. We'd win." So when she went back to work and left Sarah at home with her husband, she worried at first. "I went through this whole thing, 'Will she know who I am?' When I got home and she started crying and I didn't always know what to do right away, I'd wonder, 'Does she hate me for going to work?' I felt like I was not always able to deliver what she needed."

Over time, she grew more confident and also saw that her daughter had something that her son had missed—an intimate relationship with Dad. "He could be in another room and she could hear his voice and she'd do everything to get to him, twist all around and look for him. She's his biggest fan," she says, laughing. She concedes that "there's that smidgen in me that wants to have that place of honor," a place traditionally reserved for mothers in most American homes. But she quickly adds, "What a glorious life she's got. Her dad is wrapped around her finger and her mother is so involved."

As she reflects on her decision to return to work, she sees other changes in her family life as well. "I had been offered a promotion when I was pregnant, but on the condition that I come back to work one hundred percent. I couldn't have done that without Jeff's decision to stay home, of course." That, in turn, meant that her earning power is greater now than it would have been had she taken a break after Sarah's birth. Their paychecks had become roughly comparable, giving them new security and flexibility—especially since they were so careful about their spending. "We didn't want to feel dependent on both of us working, so we try to pretend we only have one salary and the other is gravy. I'm not saying we always do it, but we try."

These economics have changed life for both the Raynors, providing them both wider options. Jeff even dreams of starting his own business someday, a risk that he couldn't afford to take if the family were dependent on his paycheck alone. "When he had the higher earning power, we were thinking along the lines of putting all our ducks in his basket, of me staying home," Elizabeth says. "But now we say, 'This is great. This gives either of us the chance to step out of the workforce if we want to or have to.'"

There is also evidence the "new male," the one driven by his own desire to be a deeply involved father, does indeed exist and his ranks are growing. "Men are still as concerned as ever about providing for their families, but they are also concerned about having a close emotional relationship with their kids," Levine from the Fatherhood Project says. "They see the old role of father as provider as just too narrow. They understand that that role meant that women took care of the emotional lives of families. And that's not what they want."

Such a view is not yet sanctioned in the culture, he quickly adds, and what he hears most from men working in corporations is that they need a "safe place" to talk about what it means to be a father today. "Their emotional conflicts are different from women's because they don't feel as comfortable about their conflicts. They don't feel they have permission until they hear another guy talking about it," he says. "And they have a great fear that they're going to be considered uncommitted to the company if they talk about their families and explore how to be an involved father."

When men do break through the constraints of their traditional roles, studies show, they achieve an intimacy with their children—even with tiny babies—that is very similar to what moms describe. In one breakthrough study, Kyle Pruett, a psychiatrist at Yale University, looked at the dynamics in seventeen families in which the fathers were the primary caregivers for their children. The family situations varied widely: Some of the men were unemployed; the incomes of the rest ranged from $7,000 to $125,000. Some were at home full-time for quite an extended period; in other cases, the men returned to work after a paternity leave. Yet despite all these different circumstances, virtually every one of them reported feelings that paralleled those of new moms—including a reluctance to leave their new babies in anyone else's care, even their wives'. In one case, for example, a father called home repeatedly his first day back on the job—just to make sure that his wife knew how to properly care for their infant.

Men's attachment to their children grows from those same rewards that women have always known come from caring for a child. The drudgery of diapers and whining is worth enduring once a close bond is forged with a child. Indeed, Mike Downey sounds very much like the stereotype of a proud mother as he describes his eight-month-old son. "Davis smiles with his whole face and body. His little legs kick. Nothing could be more exciting," he croons. "Right now, he's just this lump of happiness."

Downey, a technical writer at the University of Texas A&M, insists that "nothing is better or more important than being a dad." And he is true to his word. He took a six-week paternity leave after the birth of their first child, Chelsea. He remembers the days after Chelsea was born as the most special. "I had a reclining chair, and I'd sit in it with Chelsea resting on my cheek and both of us sleeping." After Davis was born, he took a three-week paternity leave. If he had his druthers, he'd cut back to part-time work to be with the kids even more. He is not overly romantic. "I don't think I could do this full-time. I think everyone needs a balance." He's had to learn how to deal with temper tantrums and days that just get plain wearing. Still, he insists, "There's no other job like this. The rewards are instant. You always know when you're doing well, and when you're not. It's hard when you're not. But there's this instant gratification when you do it right. There's nothing else like it, having your child in love with you," he says. "It definitely keeps you wanting to come back the next day."

Rebecca Downey delights in her husband's involvement with the kids. "I think he was sorry he couldn't breast-feed Chelsea," she says, laughing. "But he shared everything else. I think he changed more diapers than I did, took her to half the doctor's appointments, and knows everything about the kids that I do." Part of Mike's devotion, she concedes, is that this is his second marriage. "I think he thought a lot about what it takes to make relationships work," she says.

She believes both her children benefit from the two of them sharing the care. "We both feel that it's good for the kids to have two involved parents, instead of only one or one and a half. We want them to grow up to have a good sense of themselves, that both parents care about them."

At home, the Downeys also divvy up the household chores. "He does his share of the housekeeping, his share of the laundry, and he cleans up after big meals," says Rebecca, a human resources manager. This is a conscious decision, worked out in advance of having children. "He and I chose to share it all, so I have the luxury of pursuing a career and not neglecting my children. I love going to work and coming home."

There is an important lesson in this for their children, Rebecca adds. These kids are growing up seeing that men and women need not be constrained by their gender. Many women feel especially strongly about the expanded options for their daughters. "Chelsea is bright. I want her to believe she can do anything she wants, whatever she's good at," says Rebecca. "She sees Mike doing the chores and assumes men do that. I want her to have that expectation when she gets married someday."

Thousands of miles away, in Kent, Washington, Barbara Brazil, the assistant to the chief counsel in her local school district, echoes similar hopes for her children. With two boys, however, her hopes are to instill a sense of equity on the domestic front. "In our house, our kids know both of us work. They see Dad do the wash and the cooking. I think that's very important. I want them to see men and women sharing the work and treating each other with respect," she says.

Some research bears out Brazil's belief. Kids raised in dual-earner households do tend to be more flexible about men's and women's roles when they become adults. But there are still few wide-ranging, long-term studies of how children turn out when they grow up in such new-style families. The truth is, of course, that most families are still wrestling with the practical and psychological fallout of the changing terms of marriage, making it hard to gauge just how today's kids will react to their parents as role models. Open conflict over the household chores could, for example, turn a girl off from wanting to fight for equity at home. A cultural pessimism, fanned by the conservative backlash, can undermine young women's confidence that men can and will change. As the article "The Death of Supermom" in the widely circulated Long Island newspaper *Newsday,* for example, quoted earlier in this book, shows, young women may be fearful of pressing for equality. "Young women find that after they get married, they don't want to 'poison' the atmosphere with their husbands by an 'overinsistence on equality,' " according to Teri Apter, a social psychologist.

One can only hope that such pessimism won't be allowed to take root in the hearts and minds of today's children. Equality in both work and home life is clearly a winning proposition for everyone. "Women tell me that their kids are proud of them. They feel that one of the gifts they're giving their children is a new model for a different type of life, one where women can do anything they like," says therapist Lisa Silberstein. For that to happen, Americans need to broaden their idea of possibilities for both men and women.

14

Not Guilty!

From Angst to Anger

EVEN IN THE rarefied air of communication over the Internet, the anger comes crackling through. "Do you readers want to know how much money I have spent on professional counselors and psychologists to tell me that I am my own person, that it's time for me to take care of my needs and return to work, if that is what I want to do?" writes Karen, a mom participating in an on-line forum about work and family issues. "Just think how much money I would've saved my husband if I had actually returned to work outside of the home!

"Please forgive my ranting," she continues, "but for crying out loud, if what you are doing is working, then so be it. Guilt is a very misused word in my opinion. Guilt feeds off of others and it's our job to stop it in its tracks."

Indeed, writer Mary Cantwell once described guilt among

women as a bacteria gone wild, one that eats away their pleasure and ruins their lives.

Studies by sociologists and psychologists bear her out; most women tend to feel guilt more often than most men. Research shows that women are more at risk for what they call "false" guilt, that is, taking responsibility for situations even when they are not to blame and may have little or no power to solve the underlying problem. "Often the guilt is inappropriate, de-energizing, even paralyzing," the late psychologist Grace Baruch of Wellesley's Center for Research on Women wrote. Indeed, self-blame is corrosive to women's esteem and sense of power.

Part of the reason stems from women's lower status and socialization; they are raised to read others' emotions and take responsibility for the well-being of everyone around them. In essence, then, women are literally trained to take on an extra burden of guilt. When there is a problem, they are encouraged to take personal inventory, to improve themselves. It's a habit so familiar to women as to be a joke.

"I read somewhere that the guilt gene is passed from mother to daughter," jokes Nancy McConnell, who works for a software company. "I try not to waste my time feeling guilty. I know I shouldn't. I feel guilty sometimes about feeling guilty. But you do want to do a good job at work; you don't want to let anyone down. You try to be all things to all people, to be the best mom, the best wife, the best housekeeper. And then we ask each other, 'Why do we do this to ourselves?'"

McConnell and her coworkers briefly set up a phantom "guilt chamber" for anyone suffering undue guilt. "When someone was feeling guilty about something they shouldn't, we'd send them to the guilt chamber. Humor helps to relieve the stress," she says. "But the messages come from everywhere. And on top of everything else, you're supposed to fit in thirty minutes of exercise a day to relieve your stress for feeling guilty. That's after you fill your day up, go to work, spend time with your kids. Oh, and by the way, did you smile at everyone today?"

When asked if the men in her office ever visited the "guilt chamber" or shared the same stress as women, she laughs. "I don't think the guilt gene is passed from father to son." Indeed, research shows that men don't indulge much in self-blame. Indeed, they are more likely to blame others for their problems. In one classic study, a man blamed his wife when he left his wallet at the grocery store. Why? Because she had sent him to the store to buy milk for the family. Interestingly, there is also some research showing that men tend to blame their wives for stress arising from a conflict between job and family duties. "Men tended to blame their wives for poor allocation or management of time and for other role conflict problems. Women, in contrast, tended to blame themselves for putting their husbands and children in a difficult situation," Baruch observed.

Women's propensity for self-blame turns out to be very bad medicine. Self-blame, after all, is corrosive to women's esteem and sense of power. Even worse, it masks the real social issues that stand in the way of today's families. With women scapegoated, Americans need not examine the core premises of work and family life that undermine the well-being of men, women, and children.

Nonetheless, women's guilt habit is one that is aided and abetted by the society around them, from coworkers to teachers to pediatricians to relatives. As so many of the women in this book reveal, accusations of wrongdoing are a constant undercurrent in their lives, arriving both in the way of casual conversation and in the subtext of formal rules and policies of nearly every institution in their lives. In the most extreme cases, they are used as a blunt instrument, a weapon to keep women in their "proper" place, to justify discrimination and block change. An official at the insurance company of Olde & Company, for example, told a woman that he was denying her a raise and a promotion ostensibly to help her become a better mother. "You need to be closer to home to spend more time with your daughter," he allegedly told her.

And, of course, once women become mothers, they suffer from the mother of all guilt, taking the blame for most everything that happens to their children. For some, it is even a badge of honor, proof they take their role of mother seriously. "Mothers continue to be a convenient missing link in germ theory," joked social worker Janna Malamud Smith in an article for the *New York Times Magazine* a few years back. "If it is not viral or bacterial, it must be maternal."

And for working mothers, guilt is often said to come with the territory. That is because the roles of worker and mother are still treated as mutually exclusive. The message that mothers do something wrong when they work outside the home is transmitted casually and constantly, through the social fabric of everyday life. Indeed, the rewards and punishments on the job and at home create a blueprint for what it means to be a good parent and good worker in America today. So it is that both men and women absorb the idea that a good mother works only if she "has" to, that a good worker puts the job ahead of all other commitments, that children cannot thrive outside the exclusive care of their mothers, that men are the providers and women the nurturers.

These notions persist, even though many of these assumptions are dead wrong and have outlived their economic and social usefulness. They served an old order, the economy created by the industrial revolution, a revolution that separated home and work, that created separate spheres for men and women, separate and unequal spheres that rendered much of women's labor undervalued and even invisible. These old rules, which deemed men the "providers," bestowed power upon men in the world of work, but also separated men from their children. Yet the old rules live on and still inform workplace policy and practice, as the women in this book and study after study now demonstrate.

And so it is today that women often describe themselves as guilty, as "torn" between two worlds. Trapped between the competing expectations, stressed by the lack of support, many women feel somehow responsible for letting everyone down at home and on the job.

Or so it used to be.

Increasingly, women, like Karen on the Internet, are finding the guilt give way to anger.

* * *

"I LET OTHERS, including my husband, influence a decision I never should have made. I stayed home for three years and now I cannot command the same salary I had when I left the workplace. I find myself in a bit of a pickle. Should I settle for a low-paying position, or worse yet, an entry-level position," Karen asks the others in her chat room. "I want to scream! The real reason I stayed home was because my husband (who makes more money than I do and has a degree) felt there was no justification for my return to work because of the amount of money it would cost to put two children in day care.

"I am irritable, resentful, and above all tired of being low man on the totem pole in my relationship," she writes. In a phone interview, Karen reveals that her husband is a management consultant, with a bachelor's degree. She has no college degree and earned far less as an office manager. "I let him talk me into staying home. I take that responsibility. I didn't stand my ground," she says. "But now I'm so angry. And he doesn't change. He keeps saying my role in the marriage is to take care of the family, the kids, the house. His is to be the provider.

"Of course, I love my kids. But I'm not good at home full-time," she says. "I tried play dates. I tried going to the playground. I tried Gymboree. It's just not my style. And I want to go to work. I want to contribute financially to the family. I find that I've changed now that I don't earn money. I'm not as forthright as I used to be. I don't feel equal in this marriage anymore." Further, she adds, she is jealous that he "wakes up on Saturday and reads his book. He can jump in the car and go to the store when he feels like it, all because I'm there, taking care of the kids."

Karen's situation, more than most, illuminates the sheer power of social expectations based on gender. The fact that she had a choice about working, that her husband made enough money to support the entire family, that she could not proffer up the "excuse" of economic necessity, was what left her in such an emotionally untenable position. She was one of the "lucky" women, who, according to the current cultural folklore, should have been grateful for the opportunity to be home full-time.

And that was exactly what she was told by some of the other participants in the forum on America Online. "I did stop working to raise my children," one of the other moms told Karen. With palpable indignation, she added, "I know why women go back to work," she said. "It's EASIER!" Working moms leave the truly "thankless job at home with their kids to fulfill their own selves and leave their babies/kids in someone else's care. Is that really care?" Her answer was obvious in the tone, but she went on to list the ways she believed children suffer when women work. Kids are "overweight, lazy and bored" because mothers work, and many now experiment with drugs, have sex, and are violent because their mothers are at work instead of at home, she charged. In a follow-up e-mail, she even suggested "If parents choose not to take the time to be with their kids, they should see about giving them up for adoption!"

Karen is not shocked by this suggestion, nor should she be. Polls and survey research show that most Americans have selective vision about working women; they pay attention to and absorb the information that supports their own deeply held beliefs. And the most predictive attitudes are the ones related to gender. In most cases, women are quickest to defend their own choices. Working women tend to think that it's fine for mothers to be employed, while those at home defend that choice. And not surprisingly, most do so with a great deal of passion, given the sacrifices that women make, whichever role they choose. "When you look at the way society treats mothers, you have to say that none of them have it easy," says sociologist Faye Crosby. "They're all told that they should be guilty about something."

Yet increasingly, working women see they have little reason to have guilt heaped upon them. Many, like Karen, have seen with their own eyes that their children can thrive when they work. Karen placed her oldest daughter in day care when she worked, and it was a great experience both for her and for her daughter. "The next time you feel guilty about leaving your child while you work, phone or stop by unannounced at your provider's and see just how happy and active your child is! My four-year-old is in preschool right now and every time I come early to pick her up, she tells me to leave and come back later. She has more playmates, friends, from this school than she did when we were part of a parent co-op."

So, given the evidence of her own life, given her desire to work, she concludes, "Yes, you might say I am angry! I am angry that the more I want to return to work, the more I am pushed down, either by prospective employers, friends, or family." Her counseling, she says, has evolved into creating a "game plan for my return to work and being able to accept that I'm okay if I want to work, go to school, and put my children in others' care."

She is far from the only working mom eager to vent her frustration and anger at the attitudes that suppress her voice, limit her choices, and depress her earning power. Between 1992 and 1996, the Center for Policy Alternatives and the Ms. Foundation found frustration about problems combining work and family life to be growing. In survey research and focus groups, women reported an anger at what feminist pollster Celinda Lake called "false choices" about blending motherhood and paid work. "Women agree that they have more choices in principle, but they see few true choices in their own lives," Lake concluded. Without child care, without husbands who shared child care and domestic duties, and with low pay on the job, women reported they felt hamstrung between work and family obligations. "Regardless of their economic circumstances, these women struggle with the competing demands on their time and feel that men do not carry an equal load."

Indeed, many feel betrayed and angry at the way their choices are circumscribed by gender, both at work and at home. The fact that women's work is still more poorly paid than men's, and that women are still expected to put in a second shift at home, remains a flash point for many. "We are all slaves. Meaning that we have to work; we clean the house; we raise the children; we have to please the husband," says one Latina woman. Another white-collar woman has similar complaints. "You still have to be the mom and you still have to do all the house stuff; even if you work, you still have to do all that when you come home."

And while the issue of fairness is plainly visible to women, many report that their mates remain stubbornly blind to it. "My husband comes home and when he comes home, that's it. He's done. He's worked. That's it. I work. I come home. I have a two-year-old that doesn't quit. Dinner, straightening up," says one woman. A young African American woman describes a similar scenario. "After work, I go to two or three grocery stores, come home, cook. And then he goes to work, comes home, and plays video games."

In a survey of a quarter of a million women in 1994, the U.S. Department of Labor's Women's Bureau also found working women disturbed and irate at the lack of support for their dual roles both at home and on the job. "The number one issue women want to bring to the President's attention is the difficulty of balancing work and family obligations. They report that problems with child care are deep and pervasive, affecting families across the economic spectrum," the report concluded.

Market research tells a similar story of women's changing attitudes. "Our study verifies most women, including moms, need and want to work. More than that, employment is empowering," said a 1995 report from Grey Advertising after polling a nationally representative sample of 400 women. And, the survey showed, women were growing weary of stereotyped advertisements and commercials.

Just as they are tired of gender stereotypes in other areas of their lives. Women's growing impatience with such treatment should be seen as definite progress. As any mental health professional can attest, anger is a sign of strength, a signal that the self has been violated, that something needs to change. If the anger is not turned outward, to spark positive change, there is a danger that it will be turned inward, on women themselves.

Yet it is also true that women's guilt is more easily tolerated than their anger. Indeed, only the powerful dare to express anger without restraint, for anger is a call to change, a signal that someone else is to blame for the problem. Those with less power dare not challenge the status quo unless they can tolerate the consequences or win a reasonable victory.

Instead, they live with the problem and absorb its consequences, at great personal cost.

• • •

INDEED, even as women like Karen vent anger, there is also plenty of evidence that many others still internalize the message that they are doing something wrong. "More and more women are coming forward presenting symptoms of depression and I think the problems are often bigger than the individual women I see. After you talk to them, you realize the reason they are stressed or depressed is because of inflexibility on the job or poor child care," says Mary Ellen Romano, a psychologist who runs workshops on work-family issues for many employers on Long Island.

Romano also observes that many employers are not open to this message. "We can spot trends and can make recommendations to the human resources department to help employees with work and family issues. But the reality is that many corporations are not receptive to hearing about those larger issues—and mental health professionals don't have the power to change workplace policies," she says. So Romano does her best to fashion individual solutions for women she sees—helping them form an informal network of other working mothers for practical tips and advice, for example. "My responsibility is to the individual client, so that's how I have to focus my energy," she says.

Romano is far from the only mental health professional observing the explosive growth in the number of women thrust into psychic turmoil by conflicts between job and family. Employee assistance programs, now in place at 80 percent of the nation's largest companies to help workers deal with emotional issues, are increasingly seeing a new type of client: women stressed by the competing demands of their jobs and families. "Work-family stress" was officially identified by the Employee Assistance Professionals Association as one of the most common workplace problems of the 1990s.

This fact, however, raises serious questions about the way Americans continue to frame women's problems. Most programs are staffed by social workers and psychologists, trained to spot and diagnose mental health problems. In the past, that made sense, given that such programs helped employees with alcoholism, depression, and drug abuse. But one has to wonder if such professionals are offering the right kind of "help" to working moms. Are moms, for example, being offered psychological therapy as a "cure" for what ails them, when the root of their stress is a work environment hostile to their needs? Are such programs encouraging women to take personal responsibility for issues that only the community at large can solve? Are women being subtly stigmatized as dysfunctional, and their problems dismissed as personal failures?

"The assumption of many people in the helping profession is that when someone comes in to see them, there is an underlying psychological problem to be treated," says consultant Fran Rodgers, who is concerned about the trend of employee assistance programs taking on work-family problems. "Don't get me wrong. I have great respect and belief in therapy, when it is appropriate. But what I see is that what many women need is just to feel normalized. I worry that women's problems might get medicalized, treated as abnormal.

"Sometimes what people need is just sound advice, some tangible assistance, such as flexible hours, and—most of all—a sense that what they are feeling is normal." A few decades ago, she notes, many women got that over the backyard fence, talking to neighbors and friends. But now, with more moms in the workplace, they may not have the same access to other parents to share concerns and problems and learn what is normal and what is not. "Working women need to know, for example, that separation anxiety is perfectly normal when their children start a new program," she says. "When they leave a toddler crying, it is very distressing if they don't know that."

Which is why Rodgers set up her consulting business the way that she did. A big part of her business is providing on-the-spot advice over the phone to working parents, finding them concrete solutions, and working with companies to set up child care, elder care, and other programs that support working families. One of her most innovative contributions is helping the American Business Collaborative on Dependent Care, a loose-knit organization of more than 200 companies, get off the ground. This group now works together to create child and elder care projects for their employees. "People are dealing with enormous change, and in many cases, there are not basic support systems in place. Women sit at the center of that change because they are the ones who have always managed family change," says Rodgers. "So what they often need is a new support system, help managing the tremendous change that is rippling through American society."

Yet it still takes a great act of will for Americans to clearly see that fact. The old ways, the traditions, have been in place for so long that they seem like the natural order of things. Often, it is only when a man or a woman steps outside the conventional roles that the power of gender becomes evident.

WHEN BILL Galston decided to resign from his White House post in 1995 as a domestic policy advisor to spend more time with his son, he met with instant disbelief in the media. "A reporter from the *Washington Post* called me and said she'd heard I was leaving and wanted to know why. When I told her it was to spend more time with my son, she paused and said, 'Really, why are you leaving?' In effect, she was saying, 'I don't believe you. Men don't leave their jobs to spend time with their children,'" he recalls. And, in fact, he noted that the story reporting his departure dedicated several paragraphs to possible political reasons for his leaving. "I'll never forget the headline. It said 'A Family Spin on a White House Departure,' " he says. "I don't blame the reporter. Reporters don't write headlines. But I have to confess I was annoyed. It suggested that I was lying, using my son as an excuse to cover up some political motivation for leaving," he says.

In fact, Galston had been the primary parent for his ten-year-old son for years. As a university professor, he'd had more time than his wife. But when he started working for the president, life changed. "The job at the White House was demanding. Most of the other people working there were single or had grown children or wives at home. The hours were long. People worked all the time, sixteen hours a day. You couldn't start at eight and leave at six; you worked all the time and my son missed me," he says. "Not only that, but I would never have dreamed of asking my wife to put her dream job in jeopardy. She was up for tenure and I knew her job as a law professor was what she longed for, what she ardently wanted to do. It was very competitive and meant she had to work long hours for a while. There was no way I was going to tamper with that at all. So I quit my job."

He did not quit working altogether. He simply returned to the job he'd had at the University of Maryland before he joined the Clinton White House. Yet his second surprise arose after the *Washington Post* article appeared. Several other stories followed, most notably one in the *Wall Street Journal*, detailing his decision to leave his high-profile job to spend more time with his son. "It was remarkable. I was invited to become a poster boy for the fatherhood movement, to write columns, to write a book," he says. "I said no to all of it. I left the White House to become a real father, not a professional father."

But he understood, since he'd long been studying family issues, that his notoriety arose from the fact that he'd violated the rules of gender. "I don't want to hold myself out as a role model. That would be absurd. My situation is not typical at all. But I'm not sorry that it really helped spark discussion of the issue that fathers are affected by work-family conflicts as well as mothers," he says.

Galston's story is worth pondering because it illuminates the power of gender roles in the debate over work and family. Research shows that conflicts between work and family are still largely perceived to be women's problems, and that the guilt women carry with them is often a product of the view that they have somehow violated their proper roles.

At times, women speak poignantly of how they struggle with that guilt. "I had a lot of depression about it at first, but I am at peace with my decision to quit work now," says Kari, a woman in her mid-thirties who had worked as a market research analyst in Florida before her first child was born. The family moved to Portland, Oregon, when her daughter was four months old, and she found a job initially at a local hospital. But her boss refused to allow her any flexibility with her hours, and the work was not very satisfying. Her husband was working longer hours than ever and refused to do any housework or child care. "He takes his role as provider very seriously," she says. "I got frustrated not having any help with even small things, but talking about it always meant a fight. For a while, I contemplated having just one child." But instead, she had a second child and she also stopped working.

She says she is now at peace and can pinpoint the moment that gave her solace. "I was lying on the floor, reading Penelope Leach. That helped me get clear. I didn't read the whole thing, but my sense of her argument was that there are some things that are inherently female, that there are roles that automatically happen as a result of being female and being a mother, and that's not necessarily bad," she says. "That came as a relief. I said to myself, 'Well, I don't have to fight these battles anymore. I can just stay home and be a mom.'"

Kari may continue to feel at peace in her role, or she may find herself as furious as Karen down the line, when she tries to reenter the workforce at a lower salary, or if she finds herself divorced and in need of a good income. She may find, eventually, that her options are constrained, that giving up the fight was not the right choice. Only time will tell, of course.

But sociologist Cynthia Fuchs Epstein voices hope in the fact that a growing number of men and women are openly facing the tension between the roles of parent and worker. "As the number of people who experience those problems grows, there is far more possibility that we will begin to understand that what we are facing are social issues rather than personal problems," says Epstein. "And that means we can start talking about real solutions."

There is no one answer for all families, for all workers, for all men and women. In some cases, what both men and women need is some flexibility on the job. As stories in this book reveal, even a matter of fifteen minutes can make a huge difference in a parent's life. The ability to find and pay for high-quality child care could make a dramatic difference for many working families today. Half the women on welfare in the mid-1990s reported that they would work if only they could find decent care for their children. Many new parents would love to have a paid leave to care for their newborn babies. And many women and men say they work just for health benefits. But with the right support, it's most certainly clear that working women and their families can thrive.

CHRIS STASIO sounds genuinely surprised as she reveals a core truth about her life. "What I've found since I started working full-time is this: No one suffered. I have greater respect for myself than ever before," she says. "My family needed help after my husband was laid off, and I went out and got that help. My two youngest children have thrived in day care."

In fact, some days, she says, she thinks her oldest son is a little deprived, since he never went to day care. "My younger children are much more comfortable with other children. I think if he'd had the experience they did in day care, he'd be less shy."

This is quite an admission for Stasio, given how she felt a decade ago, when her first son was born. "Back then, I just felt I couldn't possibly go back to a full-time job because no one could care for him like I could and I would just miss him too much," she recalls. Not that she ever saw herself as much of a homebody. She says she always liked working and enjoyed working two days a week as a secretary at John Hancock Insurance Company in Boston. It was a perfect balance, she thought. Then, the very same week her third child arrived, Stasio's husband was laid off, after eleven years with the same employer. Not only that, but it was the same employer his own father, uncle, and brother worked for.

It was quite a shock. A graphic artist, he'd never held another job. For two years, he searched for a new job, but to no avail. Stasio knew she could apply for full-time work at John Hancock, but resisted. "I hemmed and hawed about coming back. I thought my children would suffer and my life would fall apart." She believed her children would wither in day care. "I pictured them crying in a corner of the day care center. I thought they would never get individual attention." But finally, she says, money grew so tight for the family that "I realized that we were out of choices and that we were in a desperate situation." She took a full-time secretarial position and enrolled her children in day care. Her husband eventually landed a job as a teacher, but she remained on the job and moved up. "I have a lot of responsibility and I work for one of the higher-level executives, so I learn a lot."

And now she marvels at the way things have turned out. "I never pictured my life this way. I enjoyed the children. I enjoyed staying home with them. I never dreamed I could even be strong enough to work full-time and handle three young children," she says. "I surprised myself."

Not that every moment is wonderful. "I have my days," she says, "like today! One of my children is home sick today. I had to wait until my mother came home from her job as a school bus driver to take him home with her."

Nonetheless, life has changed for the better in Stasio's mind. "We set a good example for the boys. They see us both working hard for a better life." They are certainly not rich, she says with a laugh. "We still struggle quite a bit. But we do put some money away. And we have money to do those little extra things on occasion—to see a movie once a month, go to McDonald's here or there."

Most of all, she says, "it's important for my daughter to see that women don't have to be dependent on a man to take care of them, that she can be anything she wants to be. It's very, very important for me to see her grow up with that idea."

STASIO'S good feelings about work stem from getting the kind of support that most working moms—and dads—say they need in the 1990s. John Hancock is one of the nation's most family-friendly employers, with an impressive on-site child care center, programs for older kids when schools are closed, and flexible work programs. She describes her boss as "awesome" about meeting her family needs. "I'm lucky my boss is very understanding when I need time for family. He works with me." And the company also benefits, she says. "It goes both ways. If he would need me to come in for a weekend and I had someone to watch the kids, I'd obviously come in." Happily, she clarifies, she is not called upon for Saturday duty much—another reason she is happy to be working. This job does not normally spill over into weekends.

More women, of course, could use the kind of support that Stasio found on the job. So could so many men. But it won't happen unless women start to speak up. "It's time for women to confront the system, to raise issues on the job, to confront policymakers and people with power to make changes," says Deborah Lake, the diversity manager at SC Johnson Wax who organized that company's eye-opening training on women's issues. "Women do have a critical mass in the workplace now and it's time to speak up. It's risky, but without speaking up, there will never be change."

And it's not, psychologist Kay Deaux insists, a matter of finger-pointing and blaming men. "It's not like you can lasso a couple of guys and get rid of these problems. These are deeply entrenched attitudes that everyone shares." It will take broad-based activism, something akin to the women's movement of thirty years ago, to stir change in the workplace, at home, and with policymakers in government.

"There's no substitute for an organized power base. Hoping someone will respond to you because you are needy does not work. You have to organize and demand change. There is power in numbers," says Karen Nussbaum, head of the Women's Department for the AFL-CIO and founder of Nine-to-Five, the National Association of Women Office Workers. "Until women create more conflict over these issues, government is not going to change. The workplace is not going to change. Nothing is going to change. If we don't speak up, nobody else is. Nobody is going to change the world for us. We have to do it ourselves."

Endnotes

INTRODUCTION

19. Dr. Spock referred to day care as "baby farms" in his book *Dr. Spock's Baby and Child Care* until his 1976 edition. See page 564 in the 1968 edition. There, he put "the working mother" under the heading "Special Problems" and opined: "A day nursery or a 'baby farm' is no good for an infant. There's nowhere near enough attention or affection to go around. In many cases, what care there is is matter-of-fact or mechanical rather than warmhearted. Besides, there's too much risk of epidemics of colds and diarrhea." Even these fears, as discussed in Chapter 8 of this book, turned out to be quite exaggerated. By the 1976 edition, Spock, chastened by the women's movement, had revised the book to endorse working parents. Spock confirmed that he changed the book largely because of the influence of feminism during a phone interview with him for an article I wrote for *Working Mother* in 1986.

20. Hochschild's book *The Second Shift* was published in 1989 by Viking Penguin, New York, New York.

20. Criticism of working moms came most predictably from arch-conservatives such as Congressman William Dannemeyer. For example, in April of 1991, he argued that society had been "devastated by working mothers who put careers ahead of children and rationalize material benefits in the name of children." He linked working mothers to divorce and drug abuse, among other

social ills, on the floor of the House in a proclamation on family. . . . Congressional testimony pertaining to child care and proposals for family and medical leave characterized the bills as "handouts for yuppies" and for "careerist" moms who cared little about their children's well-being. For more specifics, see Gary Bauer's testimony on the Family and Medical Leave Act of 1989, then Senate Resolution 345, submitted to the U.S. Senate's Subcommittee on Children, Family, Drugs and Alcoholism on February 2, 1989. See pages 266–72 of the *Congressional Record*. William Mattox testified before the same subcommittee on the 1991 version of the bill on January 24, 1991. See the prepared statement submitted on page 67 of the *Congressional Record*.

20. For news stories, lengthy chronology, and discussion, see Chapter 2.

20. In October 1991, *New York Woman* ran the cover line "Trophy Kids: Children of the Rich and Busy." The story inside, by Sue Woodman, was titled "Bye, Bye, Baby." The theme of the article was that "career" women neglected their children. See pages 67–68, for example, where she suggested that "hardworking committed career women" had children as part of the "acquisitive Eighties," but then virtually ignored the children, turning the kids over to a "bevy of nannies and baby-sitters." A "terrible byproduct of the gains so doggedly fought for through the Seventies and Eighties" was neglect of children. One pull-quote compared the children's situation with domestic violence, but said, "There are no screams through the walls of neighboring apartments, just the cry, 'When will Mommy be home?'"

20. The custody disputes included Jennifer Ireland, a student in Michigan; Sharon Prost, a prominent Washington attorney and an aide to Orrin Hatch; Ruth Parris, a realtor in North Carolina; and Marcia Clark, the prosecutor in O. J. Simpson's case. For more on these cases, see Chapters 4 and 8.

21. Hochschild, Arlie, "Work: The Great Escape," *New York Times Magazine,* April 20, 1997, cover story, starting on page 50. An excerpt from Hochschild's book *The Time Bind: When Work Becomes Home and Home Becomes Work* (New York: Metropolitan Books [Henry Holt], 1997).

21. "The Myth of Quality Time: How We're Cheating Our Kids," *Newsweek,* May 12, 1997.

21. Brownlee, Shannon, and Miller, Matthew, "Lies Parents Tell Themselves about Work, Kids, Money, Day Care and Ambition," *U.S. News & World Report,* May 12, 1997, cover story, starting on page 58. The photograph of the woman carrying packages is on page 59.

21. "How a Child's Brain Develops and What It Means for Child Care and Welfare Reform," *Time,* February 3, 1997.

23. The "forty years of research" refers to the literature reviews and studies done by Lois Hoffman. For more details, see the detailed discussion in Chapter 4 and the endnotes for that chapter.

23. For detailed analyses and references on mothers' performance on the job, see Chapters 5 and 6 and their endnotes. Sociologist William Bielby; Fran Rodgers, chief executive officer of Work/Family Directions; sociologist Barbara Reskin; business professor Linda Stroh; and Jane Waldfogel at Columbia

University's School of Social Work are particularly persuasive on the point that mothers are just as productive and attached to the workplace as fathers.

24. For research on the difficulty of changing people's stereotypes, see Fiske and Deaux's studies, cited in Chapter 5.

24. Brazelton made this comment about the resistance to improving child care at a forum on child care sponsored by the Child Care Action Campaign.

25. The revelation that one of the Big Three automakers uses a cultural anthropologist to identify the core attitudes and change them came to me from a human resources professional who attended a seminar on women, work, and family in Wisconsin in June 1995. She asked that both she and her company remain anonymous so her competitors would not be privy to the company's strategies for changing the workplace.

26. For the satisfaction women find in multiple roles, see psychologist Faye Crosby's research as discussed in Chapter 5 and the endnotes for that chapter.

1. Supermom's Daughters: The Birth of a New Pessimism

29. The article "The Right Sacrifice" by Sheila Warren ran in the *Light-house,* vol. 6, no. 3, March 1996, a student publication of Harvard University and Radcliffe College, Cambridge, Massachusetts.

30–31. Warren, Langston, and Fausset were interviewed by phone in the spring of 1996.

32. Fran Rodgers was invited to speak at the Kennedy School of Government in the fall of 1995 for a course on women's changing roles. Some members of Harvard's faculty have also noted the change of mood among young women. Most notably, Claudia Goldin, economics professor, published a paper documenting women's continuing inability to successfully blend family and career. Goldin's paper, "Career and Family: College Women Look to the Past," was published by the National Bureau of Economic Research (Working Paper No. 5188, July 1995). It received widespread publicity, and in it, she noted that she was driven to do the research in part by what she perceived as pessimism among young women at Harvard over their ability to have both career and family.

34. Teri Apter, a social psychologist, told *New York Newsday,* November 1, 1995, in "Young Women Look for Brilliant, Balanced Careers."

34. Claudia Goldin's study is called "Career and Family: College Women Look to the Past," Working Paper No. 5188, National Bureau of Economic Research, July 1995.

35. The *USA Today* article, "Off-the-Clock Time: More Work for No Pay," ran on page 1 on April 24, 1997.

38. Daugherty, Jane, Hoover, Rusty, and DeHaven, Judy, "Educated Women Will Soar into the Next Century," *Detroit News,* May 15, 1996, page A1. In this article, the authors quoted a psychologist identified in this piece only by the last name of Greenstone, saying, "I think a lot of us women are going to limp into the 21st century if the majority of us keep trying to do it all.

Hopefully, the next generation of women will exercise more choices and have the option of mixing career and family with greater success than the current generation."

2. HOMEWARD BOUND? THE FEMININE MYSTIQUE CIRCA THE 1990S

41. *CBS This Morning,* April 16, 1996, interview. Ann Pleshette Murphy of *Parents* magazine discussed a survey by the magazine that showed that many women would choose to be stay-at-home mothers if they could afford it. The piece being publicized was Louv, Richard, "What Do Moms Really Want?" *Parents,* May 1996. The article was somewhat more evenhanded in its headline, asserting that what many women wanted was part-time jobs, not to be home altogether. But that was not the drift of the publicity, or of much of Louv's article. In a follow-up telephone interview about the publicity around the article, Louv said he was not entirely happy about the emphasis on women "going home," but refused to comment on the record.

41. About 63 percent of *Parents* readers work, about 47 percent work full-time, according to MRI Research, Fall 1997.

41. The figures on labor force participation come from interviews and data provided by Howard Hayghe, economist with the U.S. Bureau of Labor Statistics. Also see: "Married Mothers' Work Patterns: The Job-Family Compromise," *Monthly Labor Review,* June 1994.

42. Abraham's study was published under the title "Women's Labor Market Activity: A Story of Change." It was presented on May 19–20, 1995, at a Working Women Count conference that marked the seventy-fifth anniversary of the Women's Bureau.

42. Reporter Michelle Osborn's story "Women Change Career Paths: More Choose to Stay Home with Children" ran on the front page of *USA Today,* May 10, 1991.

42. "Supermom Reconsidered: Part Two," *Newsday,* January 5, 1994.

43. Martha Stewart made these comments to *Special Reports* (November/December 1993, page 35), published by Whittle Publications and widely circulated in doctors' and pediatricians' offices.

43. Books about women quitting work to go home include Sanders, Darcie, and Bullen, Martha, *Staying Home: From Full-Time Professional to Full-Time Parent* (Boston: Little, Brown Company, 1992); Davidson, Christine, *Staying Home Instead: Alternatives to the Two-Paycheck Family* (New York: Lexington Books, 1993); Dorn, Katie Kelley, *From Briefcase to Diaper Bag: How I Quit My Job, Stayed Home with My Kids and Lived to Tell about It* (New York: Times Books, 1994); Fox, Isabelle, *Being There: The Benefits of a Stay-at-Home Parent* (Hauppauge, New York: Barron's Educational Series, 1996); *When Work Doesn't Work Anymore* (New York: Delacorte Press, 1997); Krakow, Iris, *Surrendering to Motherhood* (New York: Miramax Books, 1997). Specialty small presses dedicated to conservative and Christian audiences also added to the list: Hunter, Brenda, *Home by Choice* (Portland, Oregon: Mult-

nomah Press, 1991). Hunter received wide publicity, since its publication coincided with press reports that mothers were going home. Throughout the 1990s, she has appeared often on television talk shows, bashing working moms and charging that day care is bad for children—a theme in her book. Bauer, Gary, *Our Journey Home: What Parents Are Doing to Preserve Family Values* (Dallas: Word Publishing, 1992). Bauer was once a domestic policy advisor to President Ronald Reagan and went on to head the Family Research Council, a leading think tank for social conservatives. Mills, Kathi, *Mommy, Where Are You? What Could Be More Important Than Investing in the Lives of Your Children?* (Eugene, Oregon: Harvest Publications, 1992).

43. The press release issued September 15, 1993, with the paperback version of Tolliver, Cindy, *At-Home Motherhood: Making It Work for You* (San Jose, California: Resource Publications, 1994) was headlined "More Women Are Staying Home" and claimed, "Staying home has become a major national trend. In 1991, the Bureau of Labor Statistics announced that for the first time since they began keeping statistics in 1948, the percentage of women in the workforce has dropped. The drop is primarily due to the increasing number of mothers choosing to stay home."

43. Reporter Alecia Swasy wrote a front-page piece for the *Wall Street Journal* that was widely discussed among working women: "Status Symbols: Stay-at-Home Moms Are Fashionable Again in Many Communities," July 23, 1993.

43. "Superwoman's Daughters: They Don't Want Your Job, They Don't Want Your Life," *Working Woman*, April 14, 1994.

43–44. Joanne Lublin's story "Family Values: Some Adult Daughters of 'Supermoms' Plan to Take Another Path" ran on December 28, 1995. The article was syndicated and picked up in many papers over the next month, including the *Arizona Republic, Tampa Tribune, Greensboro News & Record, Raleigh News and Observer, Salt Lake Tribune,* and *Tacoma News Tribune.*

44. Many, many other stories followed the template set out in *Working Woman* and the *Wall Street Journal.* For a sampling, see Peterson, Karen, "Twentysomethings Shun Supermom," *USA Today,* April 25, 1994; "Superwoman Losing Hero Status," *Washington Post,* January 3, 1995; Hart, Betsy, "Supermom's Daughters Kick Back," *San Francisco Enquirer,* January 7, 1996 (Hart's essay was syndicated and appeared in a number of papers, including the *Arizona Republic,* January 8, 1996); and Veciana-Suarez, "Being Supermom Isn't So Super to Our Daughters," *Atlanta Journal and Constitution,* April 5, 1996, page F1 (Veciana-Suarez was a columnist for the *Miami Herald;* this column was picked up from the Florida paper).

44. Freda Hurst's comments are drawn from an interview with her in the spring of 1996. Two other sources in the story were also interviewed for this book; neither wanted to be quoted on the record.

45. Elizabeth Fox-Genovese's comments are taken from her book *Feminism Is Not the Story of My Life,* published by Doubleday, 1996, page 215.

45. Sylvia Ann Hewlett's book *When the Bough Breaks: The Cost of*

Neglecting Our Children came out in 1991 and received extensive publicity, from the networks' morning news shows to local television stations and news-papers. Her theme, which was also a prominent one in her earlier book, *A Lesser Life: The Myth of Women's Liberation in America,* 1986, was also that the feminist movement had not served working-class and poor women in par-ticular, or women who valued motherhood.

46. The Martin Marietta case is *Phillips* v. *Martin Marietta,* U.S. Supreme Court, January 25, 1971.

47. Roiphe's essay ran under the title "The Myth of the Independent Woman," *Esquire,* February 1997.

48. Crittenden, Danielle, "Yes, Motherhood Lowers Pay," *New York Times,* August 1995, Op-Ed page.

48. The statement that "we are the gender that gestates" is drawn from an article on work and motherhood by Clair Fabian in the *Washington Times,* July 4, 1993.

49. Shari Turner's statement on motherhood comes from the *Boston Globe.*

49. These observations about workplace change are drawn from my work as an editor of *Working Mother* magazine's annual list of family-friendly employers. Over the five years I edited the list, interviewed consultants, went over entries, and attended conferences, it was clear that certain industries were more eager to look at innovations to retain mothers than others. Pharmaceuti-cal companies such as Johnson & Johnson, Merck, and Glaxo became regulars on the list. So did software and high-tech firms such as IBM, Mentor Graphics, Motorola, and Xerox.

50. The most intriguing surveys of men's attitudes about blending work and family come from the Du Pont Company. Their in-house studies of work-family stress show that men under the age of forty are quite concerned with how to balance work and family duties, especially if they are married to a working woman.

50. Kessler-Harris described the 1930s magazine article about working women on page 253 of her book *Out to Work: A History of Wage-Earning Women in the United States* (New York: Oxford University Press, 1982).

51. "Braving Backlash in the Workplace," *Catalyst Perspective,* Novem-ber/December 1994.

51. Johnston, Jill Natwick, "Of Glass Ceilings and Sticky Floors," *Wall Street Journal,* May 10, 1996, editorial page.

52. The shift in attitudes was described in the *Kansas City Star,* in an arti-cle by Gary Blonston, "A Renewed Concern for Family Values," July 4, 1991, page F1.

52. The cover story on "The Simple Life" appeared in *Time* on April 8, 1991. Inside, the subtitle told readers, "Goodbye to Having It All. Tired of Trendiness and Materialism, Americans Are Rediscovering the Joys of Home Life, Basic Values and Things That Last."

53. The article describing career women dropping out of the workforce appeared in the *San Diego Union-Tribune,* November 27, 1993.

53. Figures on working women's earnings come from the U.S. Women's Bureau, 1995.

53. Barbara Bush was quoted in *Redbook,* in an article entitled "It's Time to Bring Back the Family," May 1991.

53. The story on women in the workplace ran in the business section of the *New York Times,* October 9, 1994.

54. Marian Gormley's statement was syndicated by Knight-Ridder and can be found in Jones, Rachel, "More Mothers Are Opting to Stay Home with Kids—and Feeling Good about It," Knight-Ridder, May 19, 1996. This story was picked up across the country, running in the *Los Angeles Daily News, Buffalo News, Fresno Bee, San Antonio Express-News,* and *Tacoma News Tribune,* among others.

54. The idea of quitting work as an antidote for stress could be found in Barbara Roessner's piece "Responding to Stress: Women Shift Values from Workplace Back to Home," *Los Angeles Times,* March 10, 1991.

54. "Decline in Number of Working Women," *Dallas Morning News,* July 14, 1991. The article asserted that "a growing number of professional women are quitting their jobs and choosing a life at home with their children over the pressures of trying to manage a career and motherhood."

55. The *Parents* article that dealt with women's stress when they stay home full-time ran in May 1990 as a sidebar to an article entitled "Home Full-Time and Loving It."

56. The stockbroker was quoted in Alecia Swasy's front-page piece "Status Symbols: Stay-at-Home Moms Are Fashionable Again in Many Communities," *Wall Street Journal,* July 23, 1993.

56. Pesman, Sandra, "Forget the Porsche! '90's Moms Want Time for Family," *Advertising Age,* September 19, 1994, page 1.

56. Louis Uchitelle's story ran on the front page of the *New York Times,* on November 24, 1990, under the headline "Women's Push into Work Force Seems to Have Peaked, For Now."

56. Liz Spayd referred to the "intriguing dip" in her story "More Women Trading Paychecks for Full-Time Parenting," *Washington Post,* July 8, 1991.

57. Osborne, Michelle, "Women Change Career Paths: More Choose to Stay Home with Children," *USA Today,* May 10, 1991, page 1.

57. Richard Morin's story ran on page C of the *Washington Post* on July 14, 1991, under the headline "The Trend That Wasn't: Are Moms Leaving Work or Did the Dip Deceive?"

58. The *Working Woman* story ran in October 1991, under the headline "Trend Check: Are Women Really Leaving the Workforce?"

58. The research cited by Spiers came from data in the 1991 *Monitor,* an annual survey by Yankelovich, Clancy and Shulman, one of the nation's leading survey research companies.

60–61. The data on women's labor force participation comes from a special analysis conducted by Howard Hayghe, economist with the Bureau of Labor Statistics, in response to the *Barron's* article.

62. The research cited about men's and women's attitudes toward work was provided in phone interviews by Anne Clurman of Yankelovich, Clancy and Shulman.

64. The research by the Families and Work Institute, released in 1993, is known as "The Study of the Changing Workforce."

63. Bielby's study can be found under the title "She Works Hard for the Money: Household Responsibilities and the Allocation of Work Effort," *American Journal of Sociology,* vol. 93, no. 5, March 1988.

65. Margaret Usdansky's story "A Trend without Substance: For Women, No Rush Back to Homemaker" ran in *USA Today* on August 12, 1994.

65. The confusion over how to interpret the *Barron's* story can be seen in a series of stories, including "Superwoman Goes Home," *Detroit News,* June 19, 1994; "U.S. Working Women Still Are Trying to Have It All," *Detroit News,* August 15, 1994; "Are Women Leaving Jobs for Home? Not Likely," *Sacramento Bee,* August 15, 1994; "More Mothers Jilt Jobs for Home," *Sacramento Bee,* August 21, 1994; "Women Making Career Out of Quitting Jobs," *Salt Lake Tribune,* July 17, 1994; "Gender and Jobs: Facts Derail the Myth that Women Are Fleeing the Career Track," *Salt Lake Tribune,* August 12, 1994.

65. The idea that the predictions of women dropping out of the workforce were nothing more than wishful thinking was in columnist Jim Mulder's article "The Percentage of Working Women Drops for the First Time in Thirty Years," *Syracuse Herald-American,* April 3, 1994, page F1.

66. The *USA Today* article that claimed moms were going home, even after Usdansky's article declared the idea a false one, was Peterson, Karen, "In Balancing Act, Scale Tips Toward Family," *USA Today,* January 25, 1995, page 1. Two years before that, Peterson wrote a similar story for *USA Today,* "Many Women Say Their Place Is in the Home," September 20, 1993.

3. Marketing the Mystique: For Profit and Ideology

67. The relaunch was profiled and Browning talked about the "spiritual side" of house and garden in Reilly, Patrick, "From Soup Ladles to Hamptons Spreads: Condé Nast Bets Big on Nesting Yuppies," *Wall Street Journal,* July 30, 1996, page B1. Here, and in other interviews, she said, "I am totally unrecognizable in the home furnishing world" and referred to shelter magazines as "girls' pornography." This article was picked up around the country in many papers in the months that followed, reaching millions of readers in America.

68. Slaughter, Sylvia, "Home: Plan Your Escape," *Tennessean,* February 9, 1997. In this article about the relaunch, Browning asserted, "We're returning to our homes, to our children, our gardens."

68. Brozan, Nadine, photo of *House & Garden* publisher David Carey giv-

ing Dominique Browning the $700 vacuum cleaner at a party celebrating the first issue of the newly revived magazine, *New York Times,* August 2, 1996, page 2.

68. "*House & Garden* Reappears on a Crowded Stage," *New York Times,* July 30, 1996, page D1; Klages, Karen E., "House-Keeping: New Editor for Resurrected *House & Garden* More than a Designing Woman," *Chicago Tribune–Los Angeles Times,* reprinted in *Fort Lauderdale Sun-Sentinel,* September 13, 1996, page 3E. In this piece, Browning also referred to the magazine as "girls' pornography."

68. Susan Wyland was quoted in a cover story for *New York* magazine called "She's Martha Stewart and You're Not!" which ran on May 15, 1995.

69. The shift in status symbols was noted in interviews in 1996 with Susan Hayward, a well-known marketing executive who has worked for some of the nation's top survey research firms, including Yankelovich, Clancy and Shulman and Roper Starch Worldwide.

69. Figures on competition among shelter magazines are from Garigliano, Jeff, "Shelter Titles Square Off," *Folio,* February 1, 1997.

69. The characterization of the relaunch appeared in the *Wall Street Journal* in a story titled "From Soup Ladles to Hamptons Spreads: Condé Nast Bets Big on Nesting Yuppies," by Patrick Reilly, July 30, 1996, p. B1.

69. The sales figures for *House & Garden* were provided by the publicity department at Condé Nast in the spring of 1997.

70. Browning's statement that "making a home is an act of love" appeared in an article in the *Los Angeles Times.*

72. Laurel Cutler was quoted in a column by Bernice Kanner on page 42 of the *New York Times* on January 2, 1995. The piece was titled "Advertisers Take Aim at Women at Home."

72–73. The comments from David Blankenhorn and William Mattox are drawn from in-person interviews as well as phone interviews.

73. The Women's Bureau of the U.S. Department of Labor conducted an extensive survey of working women, known as "Working Women Count!" which was released in May 1995.

73. The article "New Women's Revolution," which quoted Hayward, appeared in *American Demographics* in April 1991.

74. The *Chicago Tribune* article quoting Hayward appeared on June 2, 1991. The *Seattle Times* piece, "Shifting Down: Yankelovich Study Charts Big Change in Attitudes on Work and Family," appeared on May 5, 1991.

75. The article by Christina D. Keen in *Human Resource News* appeared on page 7 of the May 1991 issue.

76. The figures on toys and the juvenile market are drawn from "Retailings Rule-Breakers," *Journal of Business Strategy,* March 19, 1997.

76–77. The articles on marketing to new parents appeared in *Advertising Age,* July 3, 1989, and November 1, 1993.

77. The figures on home improvement are from *Folio,* February 1, 1997.

78. Whitehead and Blankenhorn were quoted in "Polls Show Shift toward Emphasis on Motherhood and Home," in the *Washington Post* by Paul Taylor, May 21, 1991.

78. Whitehead's piece "Dan Quayle Was Right" was a cover story for the *Atlantic* in April 1993.

78. Mattox's piece appeared in the *San Diego Union-Tribune* on August 11, 1991, on the Op-Ed page.

79–80. Blankenhorn's comments are drawn from an interview at his office in New York City in late 1994.

80. Mattox's comments are drawn from interviews with him in Washington, D.C., in 1995.

81. Dobson's influence with the Family Research Council was first described by Mattox and later confirmed by a spokeswoman for the organization. A spokesman for Dobson said he was too busy traveling to be interviewed for the book, and an alternative spokesperson was provided for interviews.

81–82. For detailed citations and more extensive analysis of Mattox's congressional lobbying, see Chapter 12, "Whose Family Values? The Politics that Devalue Working Mothers."

82. For Kessler-Harris's research on attitudes during the depression, see *Out to Work: A History of Wage-Earning Women in the United States* (New York: Oxford University Press, 1982).

83. The articles that referred to the "proliferation" of groups to support dropout moms appeared in *USA Today*, "In Balancing Act, Scale Tips Toward Family," January 25, 1995, and in the *Washington Post*, "More Women Trade Paychecks for Family," July 8, 1991.

83. The information on membership was provided by spokespeople for the groups and was cited in other news articles.

83. The labor statistics come from Hayghe's *Monthly Labor Review* article, which he wrote in response to the *Barron's* article. It appeared in July 1994.

83–84. Information on the groups and their press activities was gained through material sent to me and interviews with their spokespeople over a period that lasted from 1994 to 1997.

84. Gormley is quoted in the *New York Times,* on January 2, 1995, page 42, in the article "Advertisers Take Aim at Women at Home."

85. *Discovering Motherhood* was edited by Heidi Brennan, Pamela Cornish, and Catherine Myers and published by Mothers-at-Home, Vienna, Virginia.

85. Mary Eberstadt's piece "Putting Children Last" ran in the *Wall Street Journal* on May 2, 1995. It was an excerpt from the May issue of *Commentary*. The piece was also reprinted in the Mothers-at-Home newsletter in May of 1995.

85. Yankelovich poll cited "Attitudes of Working Women Are Starting to Change," *Newspaper of the Society for Human Resources Management,* May 1991; "Major Shift in Women's Attitudes," *Salt Lake Tribune,* May 28, 1991; "New Roots for the 1990's: Survey Says Women Turn Again toward Home,"

Hartford Courant, March 10, 1991; and Roessner, Barbara, "Responding to Stress: Women Shift Values from Workplace Back to Home," *Los Angeles Times,* March 10, 1991.

86. Mattox's piece on Take Our Daughters to Work Day appeared on April 28, 1994.

86–87. The study was called "Women: The New Providers" and was released by the Families and Work Institute in New York City in May 1995.

89. The reporting on how "The New Providers" survey was picked up in the media is drawn from a review of hundreds of clippings from around the country that the Families and Work Institute graciously shared with me.

89. "About That Good News—Was That Cause for Celebration?" *Newsweek,* June 5, 1995, page 47.

90. "Mom the Provider," *New York Times,* May 14, 1995, editorial page.

4. What About Your Kids? Stigmatizing Ambition

94. Clark's case and Gordon's charges were detailed in many places, most notably in a cover story for *Newsweek,* March 13, 1995, page 54. This article detailed both the complaint and the courtroom action when Clark explained she couldn't stay late in the courtroom.

95. Keenan, Marney Rich, "Like All Moms, Marcia Clark Can't Have It All," *Detroit News,* March 4, 1995.

95. See Anthony Lewis's column on the Op-Ed page of the *New York Times* on January 25, 1993, for a review of the questions Senator Biden put to Zoe Baird.

95. *The Hillary Clinton Quarterly,* Spring 1995. The newsletter is published four times a year by Maracom, PO Box 2642, Concord, New Hampshire.

96. For a report on the custody dispute involving Sharon Prost, see Chira, Susan, "Custody Fight in Capital: A Working Mother Loses," *New York Times,* September 20, 1994, page 1.

96. Ruth Parris appeared on Jane Pauley's *Dateline* on April 8, 1993. Pauley led into the piece with the questions "How will your career look to the judge? What is the price of having it all?" Judge Donald A. Fanning of Beaufort County Family Court declared Parris "too career oriented" in a decision issued December 31, 1991.

96. Chris Woods spoke at a conference on labor issues of the 1990s at Columbia University on October 8, 1996.

98. Schwartz, Felice, "Management Women and New Facts of Life," *Harvard Business Review,* January/February 1989.

99. Both the senior partner and the younger man who felt torn after paternity leave are quoted in sociologist Cynthia Fuchs Epstein's report on law firms in New York City, "Glass Ceilings and Open Doors to Women's Advancement in the Legal Profession," which can be found in the November 1995 issue of the *Fordham Law Review.*

101. Paul Taylor's article that quotes Whitehead on the differences between women who work primarily for money and those who work for fulfillment ran on page A18 of the *Washington Post* on May 12, 1991.

101. Congressman Dannemeyer made the comments on the floor of Congress on April 23, 1991, in a speech on family policy.

101. Jane Mayer wrote one of the more cogent and thoughtful pieces on the way Clark's ambition colored the public debate in the article "Motherhood Issue: Marcia Clark Isn't the Only One Who's Got Troubles," *New Yorker,* February 1995.

102. Reimer, Susan, "Marcia Clark's Trials Have Now Begun outside the Courtroom," *Baltimore Sun,* March 5, 1995.

102. The comment from the Louisiana newspaper reader comes from Barri Bronston's article "Who's on Trial Here?" *New Orleans Times-Picayune,* March 20, 1995, page C1.

104. The section on Lois Hoffman is drawn from interviews with her, conducted between 1990 and 1995, for various articles for *Working Mother* magazine and for this book, and from literature reviews and books: Hoffman, L. W., "Effects of Maternal Employment in the Two-Parent Family," *American Psychologist* 44 (1989): 283–92; "The Effects on Children of Maternal and Parental Employment," in Gerstel, N., and Gross, H. E., eds., *Families and Work* (Philadelphia: Temple University Press, 1987); "The Effects of Maternal Employment on the Academic Attitudes and Performance of School-Aged Children," *School Psychology Review* 9 (4): 319–35 (1980); "Maternal Employment," *American Psychologist* 34 (1979): 859–65. Hoffman also published *Working Mothers: An Evaluative Review of the Consequences for Wife, Husband and Child* (New York: Jossey-Bass, 1975).

104–106. Among the most notable and widely cited studies that followed Hoffman's research is one by Scarr, S.; Phillips, D.; and McCartney, K., "Working Mothers and Their Families," *American Psychologist* 44 (1989): 1402–9. Also see: Fuligni, Allison Sidle, Galinksy, Ellen, and Poris, Michelle, "The Impact of Parental Employment on Children," published by the Families and Work Institute in 1995. This article provides an overview of the research on maternal employment and offers citations to hundreds of academic studies for those who wish to delve deeper into the issues.

106. Hoffman's book *The Employed Mother in America* was published by RandMcNally in 1963. She coauthored the book with Ivan Nye. A later edition of the book was published in 1976 by Greenwood Publishing Group.

106. The National Academy of Sciences published "Who Cares For America's Children?" (Washington, D.C.: National Academy Press) in 1990.

108. Marshall, Nancy L., and Barnett, Rosalind, C. "Work-Family Strains and Gains among Two-Earner Couples," *Journal of Community Psychology* 21 (January 1993): 64–78. Also see: Barnett, Rosalind C., and Rivers, Caryl, *She Works, He Works: How the New American Family Is Making It Work* (New York: HarperCollins, 1996); Barnett, Rosalind C., "The Good News Is the Bad News Was Wrong: Reexamining Gender-Bending Roles in the 1990's,"

Compensation & Benefits Management, Spring 1996; Repetti, Rena L., Matthews, Karen, and Waldron, Ingrid, "Employment and Women's Health: Effects of Paid Employment on Women's Mental and Physical Health," *American Psychologist,* November 1989, pages 1394–99.

108. Hock, E., "Working and Nonworking Mothers and Their Infants: A Comparative Study of Maternal Caregiving Characteristics and Infant Social Behavior," *Merrill-Palmer Quarterly* 26: 79–101.

109. The article that Brett-Gach read was Swasy, Alecia, "Status Symbols: Stay-at-Home Moms Are Fashionable Again in Many Communities," *Wall Street Journal,* July 23, 1993, page 1.

110. Ellen Galinsky has a particularly easy-to-read and thoughtful discussion of the issues new parents face in her book *Six Stages of Parenthood* (Reading, MA: Addison-Wesley Publishing Co. Inc., 1987).

111. Statistics on working women's earnings from "Working Women Count," Women's Bureau, U.S. Department of Labor, 1995.

111. From interviews with Shelly Lundberg and papers, including Lundberg, Shelly, and Pollak, Robert A., "Bargaining and Distribution in Marriage," June 1996; Lundberg, S. J., Pollak, R. A., and Wales, T. J., "Do Husbands and Wives Pool Their Resources? Evidence from the U.K. Child Benefit," August 1995; and Lundberg, Shelly, and Pollak, Robert A., "Noncooperative Bargaining Models of Marriage," May 1994; all in the *American Economic Review.*

113. For a collection of articles on how multiple-role theory has evolved and changed, see Crosby, Faye, ed., *Spouse, Parent, Worker* (New Haven: Yale University Press, 1987). Crosby has published several articles and books that take a close look at how women fare in multiple roles. Her most accessible is *Juggling: The Unexpected Advantages of Balancing Career and Home for Women and Their Families* (New York: Free Press, 1991).

114. For studies that compare the stress of homemakers and working mothers, see Hoffman, Lois, "Effects of Maternal Employment in the Two-Parent Family," *American Psychologist* 44 (1989): 283–92; and Scarr, S. Phillips, and McCartney, D. and K., "Working Mothers and Their Families," *American Psychologist* 44 (1989): 1402–9. These offer a quick summary of the large body of work that shows depression and anxiety to be more prevalent among women who stay home full-time with young children than among other groups.

115. For an in-depth discussion of the meaning of work among working-class women, see Lillian Rubin's book *Worlds of Pain: Life in the Working-Class Family* (New York: Basic Books, 1976), page 169ff.

115. Mattox, William R., Jr., "The Parent Trap: So Many Bills, So Little Time," *Policy Review,* Winter 1991, Heritage Foundation, Washington, D.C. Other versions of the study appeared under the following titles: "Running on Empty: America's Time-Starved Families with Children," Working Paper No. 6, an Institute for American Values working paper for the Council on Families in America, November 1991; and "The Family Time Famine," Family Research Council, a division of Focus on the Family, 1991.

116. Zinsmeister's comments can be found in the *Washington Post,* September 25, 1988, on page C3. The full headline read "Is Day Care Ruining Our Kids?"

117. Hewlett, Sylvia, "It's Time We Put Children First," *Parade,* July 17, 1994.

117. New York Times Magazine used the statistic in its short blurbs at the front of the magazine, April 10, 1994.

117. "Is Your Career Hurting Your Kids?" *Fortune,* April 1991.

118. Robinson's comments are from an interview with him in the winter of 1997. Also see: Robinson, John, "Time's Up," *American Demographics,* July 1989; and Robinson, John, and Godbey, Geoffrey, *Time for Life* (University Park, Pennsylvania: Penn State Press, 1997).

118. These particular figures on the hours that professional women in corporate America put in at home and on the job come from a 1995 study by Work/Family Directions, and were presented by Charles Rodgers, chairman of WFD Consulting, to a seminar on work and family issues in New York City in September of 1995. Other studies reveal a similar pattern for the workforce at large.

119. Zick, Cathleen, and Bryant, W. Keith, "A New Look at Parents' Time Spent in Child Care: Primary and Secondary Time Use," *Social Science Research* 25 (1996): 1–21; Bryant, W. Keith, and Zick, Cathleen, "An Examination of Parent-Child Shared Time," *Journal of Marriage and Family* 58 (February 1996): 227–37; Bryant, W. Keith, and Zick, Cathleen, "Are We Investing Less in the Next Generation? Historical Trends in Time Spent with Children," *Journal of Family and Economic Issues,* vol. 17, Winter 1996.

5. MOTHERS NOT WELCOME HERE:
HOW THE MYTHS FUEL DISCRIMINATION

121. The case discussed here is *Mary Quaratino* v. *Tiffany.* Records of the case can be found in U.S. Court of Appeals for the Second Circuit, *Mary C. Quaratino* v. *Tiffany & Co.,* Michael Eiring and David Wright, Defendants-Appellees, No. 94-9268, November 20, 1995. The testimony quoted is taken from the trial records on the retaliation charges. The trial was held in U.S. District Court for the Southern District, July 29, 1996, before Judge S. Martin, Jr. Attorneys representing both the plaintiff and the defendants were also contacted.

123. The conversations of the meetings of partners at a prominent New York firm were related over dinner at a restaurant in a New Jersey suburb in 1996. The attorney quoted is a junior partner with the firm.

123. The bank executive quoted was interviewed at the Plaza Hotel in the fall of 1995 and by phone several times after that. Details of her story were confirmed with colleagues.

124. Vladeck was interviewed at her midtown Manhattan offices and by phone in 1995 and 1996. Bound by confidentiality agreements, she did not reveal the names of any clients who had reached out-of-court settlements. The women who are quoted in the chapter as her clients came to me by way of other interviews.

125. Goodman was interviewed at her offices in midtown Manhattan in 1996.

128. Nancy Shilepsky was interviewed by phone in 1997.

129. The survey on women and ambition ran in *Working Mother* in the December 1997 issue.

129. The earnings gap figure for managers is taken from surveys by the Bureau of Labor Statistics and the National Committee on Pay Equity.

129–30. The most recent and most interesting glass ceiling reports referred to are "A Solid Investment: Making Full Use of the Nation's Human Capital, Recommendations of the Federal Glass Ceiling Commission," November 1995; and "Women in Corporate Leadership: Progress and Prospects," Catalyst, 1996.

130. The discussion of the "authority gap" is taken from interviews with Reskin and Jerry Jacobs, professor of sociology at the University of Pennsylvania. For more detail, see Reskin, Barbara R., and Ross, Catherine E., "Jobs, Authority and Earnings among Managers: The Continuing Significance of Sex," *Work and Occupations,* vol. 19, no. 4, November 1992, pages 342–65; and McGuire, Gail M., and Reskin, Barbara, "Authority Hierarchies at Work: The Impacts of Race and Sex," *Gender and Society,* vol. 7, no. 4, December 1993, pages 487–506.

130. Waldfogel, Jane, "The Family Gap for Young Women in the U.S. and U.K.: Can Maternity Leave Make a Difference?" October 1994; "Working Mothers Then and Now," a cross-cohort analysis of the effects of maternity leave on women's pay, a paper prepared for Gender and Family Issues in the Workplace, at Cornell University, April 1995. Both are unpublished. Waldfogel was based at Columbia University's School of Social Work and also conducted several studies for the federal Commission on Family and Medical Leave, which produced similar results.

131. Figures on the number of pregnancy discrimination cases are from the *Wall Street Journal,* May 16, 1995, in a story by Rochelle Sharpe titled, "Pregnancy Discrimination Complaints Are Up."

131. Lisa Bailey's case is reported in the *Washington Post* on October 6, 1997, in a story titled "A Mother's Settlement." Attorneys for Bailey and her employer were interviewed in the winter of 1998.

131. Stroh, Linda K., "All The Right Stuff: A Comparison of Female and Male Managers' Career Progression," *Journal of Applied Psychology* 77 (3): 251–60 (1992).

132. The figures on sex segregation can be found on page 54 in *Women and Men at Work,* by Barbara Reskin and Irene Padaric (Thousand Oaks, CA: Pine Forge Press, 1994).

132. Bielby, William, "Sex Segregation, Gender Stereotypes and the Impact of Lucky Stores' Personnel Policies on Women Employees' Opportunities for

Advancement," January 1991, expert testimony in class action lawsuit against Lucky Stores, which the employees eventually won.

132. Depositions in the case involving Home Depot are from the Declaration of William Bielby on June 23, 1995, in a class action suit brought against Home Depot in 1994, Vicki Butler et al., in U.S. District Court, Northern California.

133. The study for the Bar Association of the City of New York was conducted by Cynthia Fuchs Epstein and appeared in the December 1995 issue of the *Fordham Law Review.*

134. The figures on women in the top jobs comes from the Federal Glass Ceiling Commission.

135. Joanne Totta was interviewed for this book. Her research is available in a number of reports published by the Task Force on the Advancement of Women in the Bank at the Bank of Montreal between 1992 and 1995.

135. Catalyst Perspective, Fall 1995.

135. Epstein, Cynthia Fuchs, *Fordham Law Review,* November 1995, page 377.

135. "Presumed Equal: What America's Top Women Lawyers Really Think about Their Firms," written and published by the Harvard Women's Law Association, Cambridge, Massachusetts, 1995.

137. The Lucky Stores case was heard in U.S. District Court in Northern California. See 803 F. Supp. 253 (N.D. Calif. 1992).

137. Four out of five return to work after a baby is a figure from Catalyst, a nonprofit research organization based in New York City.

138. Report of the Governor's Task Force on the Glass Ceiling Initiative, November 1993.

138–40. From interviews with Kay Deaux and from her articles. See Deaux, Kay, and Paludi, M. A., "Gender Stereotypes," in *Psychology of Women: A Handbook of Issues and Theories* (Westport, Connecticut: Greenwood Press, 1993).

140. From interviews with Fiske. Also see: Fiske, Susan T., Bersoff, Donald N., Borgida, Eugene, Deaux, Kay, and Heilman, Madeline, "Social Science Research on Trial: Use of Sex Stereotyping Research in Price Waterhouse v. Hopkins," *American Psychologist,* October 1991; Fiske, Susan T., "Controlling Other People: The Impact of Power on Stereotyping," *American Psychologist,* June 1993; Fiske, Susan, "From the Still Small Voice of Discontent to the Supreme Court: How I Learned to Stop Worrying and Love Social Cognition," in *The Social Psychologists,* edited by Brannigan, Gary, and Merrens (New York: McGraw-Hill, Inc., 1994).

143. The women quoted here are from the Wisconsin glass ceiling report cited above.

6. YOU HAD THE BABY, IT'S YOUR PROBLEM!
JUSTIFYING THE INFLEXIBLE WORKPLACE

147. The material on the focus groups at SC Johnson Wax was gathered in on-site interviews at SC Johnson Wax headquarters in Racine, Wisconsin, and in follow-up telephone interviews with those quoted in this chapter.

155. The study on the impact of work on family life cited by Galinsky is *The Study of the Changing Workforce,* published by the Families and Work Institute in 1993.

156. A summary of Tina Miller-Silverman's case was released by the American Association of Flight Attendants on July 5, 1995.

157. A brief summary of the debate over Social Security can be found in Richard McHugh's article "Unemployment Insurance: Responding to the Expanding Role of Women in the Work Force," *Clearinghouse Review,* April 1994, which offers a quick history of both Social Security and unemployment insurance.

157. Du Pont released its latest study on its workforce on October 30, 1995.

158. The attorney quoted about working out in the gym asked to remain anonymous. He is a junior partner. The tension between men and women in law firms is described in Cynthia Fuchs Epstein's article "Glass Ceilings and Open Doors to Women's Advancement in the Legal Profession," *Fordham Law Review,* November 1995, pages 129–30.

159. The study on executives was conducted by Paul Ray Berndtson and the Center for Advanced Human Resources Studies, Cornell University. "Why Executives Look for New Jobs" was released on February 16, 1994, by Paul Ray Berndtson, an executive search firm based in Fort Worth, Texas.

160. The Merck study was conducted by Ellen Galinsky, now at the Families and Work Institute in New York City. At the time of the study, she was on the faculty of Bank Street College of Education.

161. Quotations are courtesy of Kwasha Lipton, an employee benefit consultant firm, based in Fort Lee, New Jersey.

161. The research on New York Telephone is contained in the "Final Report to the New York Telephone Joint Union/Management Work and Families Issues Committee."

162. The woman quoted as saying her managers don't want to know about flexibility is drawn from the records of focus groups conducted by Kwasha Lipton, a consulting firm in Fort Lee, New Jersey.

164. The Rodgerses released the data on the demographics of corporate managers at a seminar on work and family issues in September 1995.

165. Schwartz, Debra B., "An Examination of the Impact of Family-Friendly Policies on the Glass Ceiling." The report was funded by the U.S. Department of Labor, Glass Ceiling Commission in 1994.

166. For Wohl's comments comparing military and maternity leave, see *Summary of "Beyond Parent Tracks": Alliances for the 90's,* published by the

National Council for Research on Women, based at the Sara Delano Roosevelt Memorial House, New York, New York.

166. Du Pont corporate press release issued October 30, 1995.

166. Interviews with James Levine were conducted in 1994. Levine runs the Fatherhood Project, which started at Bank Street College of Education and is now based at the Families and Work Institute in New York City.

168. Studies that show the payoff from flexibility are gathered from my years of editing "The 100 Best Companies for Working Mothers," and the IBM, Corning, and Aetna figures can be found in reports on those companies in *Working Mother* magazine, October issues, 1991–1994. Lottie Bailyn, at Massachusetts Institute of Technology, has also conducted extensive research documenting how family-friendly policies improve productivity in companies. Extensive studies on the topic are also available from the Families and Work Institute in New York City.

169. "100 Best Companies for Working Mothers," *Working Mother,* October 1997.

7. WILL ONLY MOMMY DO? THE POWER OF SCIENTIFIC MYTHS

172. Jay Belsky set off the furor with a piece entitled "Infant Day Care: A Cause for Concern?" in *Zero to Three,* a publication of the National Center for Clinical Infant Programs, in September of 1986. It was especially powerful, given his earlier review of the literature, Belsky, J., and Steinberg, J. D., "The Effects of Day Care: A Critical Review," *Child Development* 49 (1978): 929–49, which had basically given day care a clean bill of health.

174. Diane Eyer's comments are taken from interviews with her in 1994.

174. John Bowlby, the father of attachment theory, first laid out this concern in a widely circulated paper: Bowlby, John, "Maternal Care and Mental Health," World Health Organization, 1951. In this paper, he invented the idea of "maternal deprivation," which became a core tenet of child-rearing advice in the 1950s.

175. Caldwell's comments and descriptions of her early days as a researcher are taken from interviews with her.

175. Dr. Spock's new-and-improved ideas about men's and women's roles can be found starting with the 1976 edition of his best-selling *Dr. Spock's Baby and Child Care.*

175. The statement that the Child Welfare League vehemently opposed any out-of-home care for children under the age of three is from Caldwell, Bettye, "Infant Day Care—the Outcast Gains Respectability." Caldwell took the statement from Child Welfare League of America, *Standards for Day Care Service* (New York: Child Welfare League of America, 1960), page 6.

175–76. Caldwell, B.; Wright, C.; Honig, A.; and Tannebaum, J., "Infant Day Care and Attachment," *American Journal of Orthopsychiatry* 69 (1970): 690–97.

176. The comments from Alison Clarke-Stewart are taken from interviews with her.

176. Lamb's comments are taken from interviews with him. See also: Lamb, Michael, "Nonparental Child Care: Context, Quality, Correlates and Consequences," in *Handbook of Child Psychology,* 4th ed., edited by I. E. Sigel and K. A. Renninger (New York: Wiley, 1998) for an in-depth treatment of the ideas and research.

176–77. References to the fast growth in infant care can be found in "Education before School: Investing in Quality Child Care," a report from the Committee for Economic Development, Scholastic, Inc., 1995.

177. The comments from Helen Blank are taken from interviews with her that spanned 1988 to 1997, as she lobbied for child care legislation.

177. Holcomb, Betty, "Where's Mommy?" *New York* magazine, April 15, 1987. Both Zigler and Siegel were interviewed for and quoted in that piece.

178. Eckholm, Erik, "The Good Mother," *New York Times,* October 6, 1992.

178. The Carnegie report was "Starting Points: Meeting the Needs of Young Children," published by the Carnegie Corporation, New York, April 1994, and reported in the *New York Times,* April 12, 1994: Chira, Susan, "Study Confirms Worst Fears on Children."

178. "How a Child's Brain Develops and What It Means for Child Care and Welfare Reform," *Time,* February 3, 1997.

179. Zero to Three's campaign on the brain research included an active publicity campaign that lasted for several years.

180. See Lamb's chapter on the debate over the effects of infant care, "Child Care Does Not Affect Infant's Attachment to Mother Unless Mother Is Insensitive to Infant's Needs," National Institute of Child Health and Human Development, April 20, 1996; "Is Day Care Bad for Kids? No Simple Answers," a report from the National Institute of Child Health and Human Development, *Infant Behavior and Development,* March 25, 1994. Also see two special issues of *Early Childhood Research Quarterly,* September and December 1988, dedicated to the topic of infant day care.

182. The comments from Scarr are from interviews conducted with her at the outset of the debate over Belsky's research.

182. The data on shyness is covered by studies by developmental psychologist Jerome Kagan. See, for example, his book *The Nature of the Child,* which deals extensively with the genetic components of personality.

185. Focus groups conducted by the National Center for Clinical Infant Programs, in *Zero to Three,* page 197.

185. For a brief background on Bowlby, see *American Psychologist,* April 1990.

186. Harlow's work is summarized in the 1960 *Distinguished Scientific Contribution Awards,* published by the American Psychological Association, Washington, D.C., December 1961.

187. The article that expressed the fear of children growing "hollow-cheeked and bony" in day care appeared in *Parents* magazine, "What Are Child Care Centers?" August 1944, page 20.

188. Arlene Skolnick's comments are taken from interviews with her.

190. White, Burton, *First Three Years of Life* (New York: Fireside Books, 1993), page 270.

190. Rubinstein, Carin, "What Pediatricians Really Think about Working Mothers," survey with the American Academy of Pediatrics, *Working Mother,* April 1990.

190. Leach, Penelope, *Your Baby and Child* (New York: Alfred A. Knopf, 1995), pages 274–78.

191. Ainsworth, Mary, Blehar, M. C., Waters, E., and Wall, S., "Patterns of Attachment," (Hillsdale, New Jersey: Erlbaum, 1978).

195. Belsky's comments here are drawn from interviews conducted with him at the beginning of the debate, for an article that appeared in *New York* magazine, and from an extensive phone interview with him in July of 1995. For more on the debate over his study, see Phillips, D., McCartney, K., Scarr, S., and Howes, C., "Responses to 'Infant Day Care: A Cause for Concern?'" and "Selective Review of Infant Day Care Research: A Cause for Concern!" *Zero to Three,* February/December 1987; and Belsky, Jay, "Risks Remain," *Zero to Three,* child care anthology published by the National Center for Clinical Infant Programs.

196. Belsky, Jay, "Infant Day Care: A Cause for Concern?" in the anthology version printed by the National Center for Clinical Infant Programs. There, Belsky said, "I am well aware too, that my gender and the more or less traditional nature of my family structure could bias my reading of the evidence" (page 114).

196. Zigler's comments are drawn from an interview in July of 1995.

197. Helbrun, S., "Cost, Quality and Child Outcomes in Child Care Centers: Technical Report," Denver, Colorado, Department of Economics, Center for Research in Economic and Social Policy, University of Colorado, 1995.

198. The scene at Johnson & Johnson's child care center was drawn from reporting for an article on infant care for *Working Mother* magazine. Scarr, Sandra, with Betty Holcomb, "Quality Care for Infants," July 1993.

199. Howes, Carolee, *Child Development,* 1992 and 1994.

8. In the Care of Strangers: Day Care's Enduring Stigma

202. The *PrimeTime Live* program that Silver saw aired in 1995.

204. Check, Christopher, "Our Kids Don't Deserve Day Care," *Chicago Tribune,* February 28, 1995. In this editorial page piece, he suggested the term "kiddie corral" or "kiddie kennel."

204. The decision from Raymond Cashen was issued on July 27, 1994, in Macomb County, Michigan, in the *Ireland* v. *Smith* case over custody of Maranda Ireland.

204. William Mattox asserted that it was "increasingly clear that the climate for germ exchange is ripe in group care facilities where large numbers of unrelated children spend their days," in testimony before the House's Subcommittee on Human Resources of the Committee on Ways and Means on September 26, 1991.

204. The *Utne Reader* devoted its May/June issue in 1993 to the debate over child care and working parents.

204. Keating's veto was reported in *Working Mother.*

206. The Child Care Action Campaign's study of the time it takes to find child care was conducted in 1993 as part of its "Child Care Aware" campaign.

207. For a quick and thorough discussion of how child care workers get tarred by the scandals, see "Child Abuse by Interrogation," *Wall Street Journal,* March 15, 1995.

207. Figures on abuse in child care come from the Child Welfare League of America in Washington, D.C.

207. For a summary on the prevalence of illness in child care settings, see Zigler, Edward, and Susan Muenchow, "Infectious Diseases in Day Care: Parallels Between Psychologically and Physically Healthy Care," *Reviews of Infectious Diseases* 8, No. 4 (July–August 1986).

208. The popularity of family child care has been widely documented. See especially studies by Sandra Hofferth. For a quick overview, see "The Future of Children: Financing Child Care," Center for the Future of Children, David and Lucille Packard Foundation, Vol. 6, No. 2, Summer/Fall 1996, pp. 41–61. The Packard Foundation is located in Los Altos, California.

209. Child care is called a "grand experiment" in the *Utne Reader,* May/June 1993.

209. The statement from the National Center for Clinical Infant Programs comes from "Providing Goal-Directed Technical Assistance to State Policymakers," in *Zero to Three,* Washington, D.C., 1994. The organization is based in Arlington, Virginia.

209. Genovese, Elizabeth Fox, *Feminism Is Not the Story of My Life* (New York: Doubleday, 1996), page 229.

211. Howes, Carolee, *Child Development,* 1992 and 1994. For more on the idea of sensitive caregivers, see NIMH study.

212. "to feed the starving . . ." Goldsmith, Cornelia N., *Better Day Care for the Young Child* (Washington, D.C.: National Association for the Education of Young Children, 1972), page 80.

212. "the degree of poverty of the family and its morality . . ." Goldsmith, Cornelia N., *Better Day Care for the Young Child* (Washington, D.C.: National Association for the Education of Young Children, 1972), page 80. The Nursery for the Children of Poor Women is referred to on page 80.

212. The reference to "gloom . . . accentuated" is on page 82 of Goldsmith, Cornelia N., *Better Day Care for the Young Child* (Washington, D.C.: National Association for the Education of Young Children).

212. "Children should be removed . . ." Steinfels, Margaret O'Brien, *Who's*

Minding the Children? (New York: Simon & Schuster, 1973), page 36; "dangerous class," page 38.

213. "The term 'school,' on the other hand . . ." Goldsmith, Cornelia N., *Better Day Care for the Young Child* (Washington, D.C.: National Association for the Education of Young Children, 1972), page 13.

213. "The term 'charity' . . . demeaned those who used the service." Hewes, Dorothy, *Child Care Information Exchange Newsletter,* November 1995, page 24.

214. "To counter the charge . . ." Steinfels, Margaret O'Brien, *Who's Minding the Children?* (New York: Simon & Schuster, 1973), page 49.

214. "The Day Nursery is only a make-shift." from Steinfels, cited above, page 49.

214. The idea of child care as a service for "problem families" and the founding of the Child Welfare League was covered in a chapter by Virginia Kerr entitled "One Step Forward—Two Steps Back: Child Care's Long American History," in *Child Care, Who Cares?* edited by Pamela Roby (New York: Basic Books, 1973).

214. The move by Philadelphia day nurseries to ban group care was reported in Margaret O'Brien Steinfels, *Who's Minding the Children?* (New York: Simon & Schuster, 1973), page 66.

214. For an extensive discussion about the treatment of married women during the depression, see Kessler-Harris, Alice, *Out to Work: A History of Wage-Earning Women in the United States* (New York: Oxford University Press, 1982), pages 250–75. Also by Kessler-Harris, *A Woman's Wage: Historical Meanings and Social Consequences* (Lexington, Kentucky: Kentucky University Press, 1990).

215. La Guardia's instructions to review applicants for day care can be found in Kerr's essay cited above, page 164.

215. " 'I guess I know my own business best.'. . ." from Steinfels, Margaret O'Brien, *Who's Minding the Children?* (New York: Simon & Schuster, 1973), page 64.

215. The number of children in day care in 1943 is from Kessler-Harris, Alice, *Out to Work: A History of Wage-Earning Women in the United States* (New York: Oxford University Press, 1982), page 295. The references to the nature of the care offered and opinions about it, including the chaplain's reference, are also on page 295.

216. The references to *Modern Woman* are on page 296 of Kessler-Harris's book *Out to Work.*

216. The notion that kids think moms prefer their jobs to them is from "Women Aren't Men," the *Atlantic,* August 1950, as cited in Kessler-Harris's book *Out to Work,* page 297.

216. Penelope Leach's reference is drawn from her book *Your Baby and Child* (New York: Alfred A. Knopf, 1995), pages 274–78.

216. For the poll conducted by *Working Mother* and the Child Care Action Campaign, see *Working Mother,* April 1993.

217. The information on caregiver salaries was provided by the National Center for the Early Childhood Workforce, based in Washington, D.C.

218. For a summary of policies in other countries, see Kammerman, Sheila, and Alfred J. Kahn, *Child Care Family Benefits and Working Parents* (New York: Columbia University Press, 1981).

9. THE NEW MATH: DOES IT PAY TO WORK?
THE MYTH OF "CHOICE" ABOUT WORKING

220. Alice Kessler-Harris is the most notable scholar to write about the history of fights over the value of women's work and how that valuation is related to their roles as mothers, starting with *Out to Work: A History of Wage-Earning Women in the United States* (New York: Oxford University Press, 1982) and with *A Woman's Wage: Historical Meanings and Social Consequences* (Lexington, Kentucky: Kentucky University Press, 1990). More recently, Reva B. Siegel, professor of law at Yale University, has documented how women fought to have the value of their household labor recognized and rewarded. See her articles in the *Yale Law Journal,* most notably "Home as Work: The First Women's Rights Claims Concerning Wives' Household Labor, 1850–1880," vol. 103, no. 5, March 1994, pages 1073–1217. Viviana Zelizer's *Social Meaning of Money* (New York: Basic Books, 1994) is also illuminating on these issues.

221. Waldfogel's comment on the "dry-cleaning effect" is taken from interviews with her. For her analysis of women's earnings, see Waldfogel, Jane, "Working Mothers Then and Now: A Cross-Cohort Analysis of the Effects of Maternity Leave on Women's Pay," paper prepared for the Conference on Gender and Family Issues in the Workplace, Cornell University, Ithaca, New York, April 1995; revised June 15, 1995. See also Waldfogel's paper "The Family Gap for Young Women in the US and UK: Can Maternity Leave Make a Difference?" October 1994.

221. O'Neill, June, "The Causes and Significance of the Declining Gender Gap," talk at Bard College, September 22, 1994. This paper, sent out by the Congressional Budget Office in 1995, summarized O'Neill's point of view. The paper received widespread attention in circles that follow women's employment trends and was excerpted on the *Wall Street Journal*'s editorial page.

225. Research by the Urban Institute refers to a paper by economist Elaine Sorenson, "Continuous Female Workers: How Different Are They From Other Women?" *Eastern Economic Journal,* vol. 19, no. 1, Winter 1993, page 255.

226–27. The figures on women's earnings during the 1980s are from Waldfogel, Jane, "Working Mothers Then and Now: A Cross-Cohort Analysis of the Effects of Maternity Leave on Women's Pay," paper prepared for the Conference on Gender and Family Issues in the Workplace, Cornell University, Ithaca, New York, April 1995; revised June 15, 1995. See also Waldfogel's paper "The Family Gap for Young Women in the US and UK: Can Maternity Leave Make a Difference?" October 1994. For another good study of the effects of discrimination on women's pay, see Stroh, Linda, "All the Right Stuff: A Comparison of Female and Male Managers' Career Progression," *Journal of Applied Psychology* 77: 251–60 (1992).

227. For specifics on the pay penalty suffered by dual-earner dads, see Stroh, Linda, and Brett, Jeanne M., "The Dual-Earner Dad Penalty in Salary Progression," a paper written for Loyola University on August 11, 1995, and accepted for publication in *Human Resource Management Journal.*

229. Lewin, Tamar, "For Some Two-Paycheck Families, the Economics Don't Add Up," *New York Times,* Ideas and Trends Section in Week in Review, April 21, 1991.

229. The *Redbook* article "I Couldn't Afford My Job" ran in April 1991.

230. Spalter-Roth, Roberta, Hartmann, Heidi, and Gibbs, Sheila, "Unnecessary Losses: Costs to Workers in the States of the Lack of Family and Medical Leave," Institute for Women's Policy Research, Washington, D.C., August 1989.

232. Studies that show that many of the women who receive welfare can't work because they lack child care are available from the Child Care Action Campaign and the Children's Defense Fund.

233. The figures on women's earnings are from Howard Hayghe, Bureau of Labor Statistics.

236. For the documentation on women's allowances at the turn of the century, see Zelizer, Viviana, *The Social Meaning of Money* (New York: Basic Books, 1994).

10. WOMEN'S PUNY PAYCHECKS: HOW THEY GOT SO SMALL

238. For Kessler-Harris's in-depth analysis of how social expectations of women shape their wages, see her books *Out to Work: A History of Wage-Earning Women in the United States* (New York: Oxford University Press, 1982) and *A Woman's Wage: Historical Meanings and Social Consequences* (Lexington, Kentucky: Kentucky University Press, 1990).

238. The commentary by the economist is recounted by Kessler-Harris in her book *A Woman's Wage* on pages 19–20.

238. The *New York Post* statement comes from Kessler-Harris, *Out to Work* (full citation above), page 51.

239. Siegel, Reva B., "Home as Work: The First Women's Rights Claims Concerning Wives' Household Labor, 1850–1880," *Yale Law Journal,* vol. 103, no. 5, March 1994, pages 1073–1217.

240. "The ignoramus who feeds the pigs . . ." from Siegel's "Home as Work" article cited above, page 1157.

240. "It takes three, and sometimes four women to get a man through from the cradle to the grave . . ." from Siegel, cited above, page 1160.

242. Grimke "Let us own ourselves, our earnings . . ." is quoted in Siegel's article on page 1126.

243–44. Helen Jenkins's writings in *New Northwest Journal* can be found on page 1157 of Siegel's article in the *Yale Law Journal*.

244. Kessler-Harris, Alice, *A Woman's Wage.*

245. For a discussion of the "family wage," see Kessler-Harris, *A Woman's Wage.* It is a concept she discusses throughout the book, as a way of illuminating why men's wages have been set higher than women's.

246. The reference to the head of Sears, Roebuck is from page 18 of Kessler-Harris, *A Woman's Wage.*

246. The references to Westinghouse and General Electric can be found on page 25 of *A Woman's Wage.*

247. The letters to President Roosevelt are cited on page 76 in Kessler-Harris, *A Woman's Wage.*

247. Norman Cousins's remarks, along with more elaboration on this theme, can be found on page 256 of Alice Kessler-Harris's book *Out to Work.*

248. The *McClure's* article is cited on page 13 of *Out to Work.*

248–49. For a more in-depth discussion of the views of women who worked during World War II and how those attitudes influenced their wages, see *Out to Work,* starting page 273.

249. The quote "there are no male or female tax rates" can be found on page 106 of *A Woman's Wage.*

249. Mary Anderson's worry over how women might be used as cheap labor can be found on page 95 of *A Woman's Wage.*

249. Senator Paul Findley's comments on women being "prone" to homemaking are recounted on page 111 of *A Woman's Wage.*

249. For an extensive discussion of the arguments business used against equal pay bills, see *A Woman's Wage,* starting on page 109.

250. The $120 billion in lost wages comes from figures provided by the National Committee on Pay Equity. That figure assumes that one-third to one-half of the wage differential between men and women is due to discrimination.

251. The figures on salary differentials are taken from studies done by the City of Denver in the late 1980s, when equal pay statutes were under consideration there. The other figures come from research done by the National Committee on Pay Equity and the Institute for Women's Policy Studies and presented to Congress in 1996.

11. It *Does* Take a Village to Raise a Child:
The Myth of Personal Responsibility

254. For an extensive discussion of David Prickett's situation, see decision, *David L. Prickett v. Circuit Science, Inc.,* CX-92-1985, Court of Appeals of Minnesota, 499 N.W. 2nd 506; 1993 Minn. App. In Lexis database, LEXIS 456. Filed: May 4, 1993.

257. Study on Idaho workers: "Care around the Clock: Developing Child

Care Resources before and after Five," U.S. Department of Labor, Women's Bureau, April 1995.

257. For a paper on the trend, see "Unemployment Insurance: Responding to the Expanding Role of Women in the Work Force" by Richard McHugh and Ingrid Kock, *Clearinghouse Review,* April 1994. Also see: "Feminist Theory and Legal Practice: A Case Study on Unemployment Compensation Benefits and the Male Norm" by Deborah Maranville, *Hastings Law Journal,* vol. 43, April 1992, pages 1081–94.

257. McHugh, Richard, and Kock, Ingrid, "Unemployment Insurance: Responding to the Expanding Role of Women in the Work Force," *Clearinghouse Review,* April 1994, page 1423.

257. McHugh, Richard, and Kock, Ingrid, "Unemployment Insurance: Responding to the Expanding Role of Women in the Work Force," *Clearinghouse Review,* April 1994, page 300.

261. Silberstein's comments are from an interview with her. Her book is *Dual-Career Marriage: A System in Transition* (Hillside, New Jersey: Lawrence Erlbaum Associates, 1992).

263. For figures on the salaries paid to child care workers, see "Financing Child Care," *The Future of Children,* vol. 6, no. 2, Summer/Fall 1996, Center for the Future of Children, the David and Lucille Packard Foundation, pages 75–76.

263. National studies on turnover among child care workers, see: "Making Work Pay in the Child Care Industry," a report by the National Center for the Early Childhood Workforce, Washington, D.C., 1997.

266. For a report on Oregon's approach to family child care, see Holcomb, Betty; Cartwright, Catherine; and Dreisbach, Shaun, "State of the States: A National Report on Child Care," *Working Mother,* July/August 1997.

267. Mississippi's child care official is quoted in "Child Care: How Does Your State Rate?" by Betty Holcomb, with Catherine Cartwright, Shaun Dreisbach, and Ann Fritz, *Working Mother,* July/August 1997.

267. Helbrun, S., ed., "Cost, Quality and Child Outcomes in Child Care Centers: Technical Report," Denver, Colorado, Department of Economics, Center for Research in Economic and Social Policy, University of Colorado, 1995.

267. Galinsky, Ellen, "Study of Children in Family Child Care and Relative Care," Families and Work Institute, 1991–92.

268. Mitchell, Anne, Stoney, Louise, and Dichter, Harriet, "Financing Child Care in the United States: An Illustrative Catalogue of Current Strategies," the Ewing Marion Kauffman Foundation, the Pew Charitable Trusts, 1997, page 2.

269. For a description of the military child care centers, see "Making Work Pay in the Child Care Industry," a report by the National Center for the Early Childhood Workforce, Washington, D.C., 1997, page 25.

269. The report from the 1997 Pew Charitable Trusts is the one cited above.

12. WHOSE FAMILY VALUES?
THE POLITICS THAT DEVALUE WORKING MOTHERS

270. Allan Carlson's and the other speeches from the conferences sponsored by the Eagle Forum are drawn from press kits issued by the Eagle Forum as well as the media reports on the conferences at the time. Follow-up telephone interviews were conducted with Phyllis Schlafly in the spring of 1997 and with Allan Carlson of the Rockford Institute. Carlson also had his public relations representative send copies he had kept of the speech, as well as other materials the institute has issued on child care and working mothers.

271. For a quick summary of the White House debates over Nixon's veto, see Mary Francis Berry's book *The Politics of Parenthood,* published by Viking, 1993, pages 137–41.

271–72. Information on the Family Research Council and the support offered by Focus on the Family are drawn from interviews with William Mattox as well as PR spokesperson for the Family Research Council and a Focus on the Family representative.

273. Pat Buchanan's role and the internal debates over Nixon's veto of child care legislation are recounted in Mary Francis Berry's book, *The Politics of Parenthood,* pages 137–141.

274. Christensen, Bryce, "Day Care: Thalidomide of the 1980's?" *The Family in America,* a publication of the Rockford Institute Center on the Family in America, vol. 1, no. 9, November 1987.

275. For a complete roundup on child care at the state level, see "Child Care: How Does Your State Rate?" by Betty Holcomb, with Catherine Cartwright, Shaun Dreisbach, and Ann Fritz, *Working Mother,* July/August 1997.

276. The Connecticut woman's comments come from affidavits collected by the Legal Assistance Resource Center of Connecticut and students from the University of Connecticut as part of a research project examining the effects of welfare reform, and published in an interim report in March of 1997.

279. For an examination of the Chamber of Commerce's evolving figures on the cost of offering family and medical leave, see Spalter-Roth and Heidi Hartmann's 1989 study, "Unnecessary Losses." Also see "A Workable Balance: Report to Congress on Family and Medical Leave Policies," a report from the Commission on Family and Medical Leave, April 30, 1996, which concluded that the law either had minimal impact or even a positive impact on businesses' profitability.

281. Dreskin's speech is taken from press materials provided by the Eagle Forum Education and Legal Defense Fund, January 1989. Dreskin and her husband wrote a book called *The Day Care Decision: What's Best for Your Child?* and also appeared on numerous radio talk shows to publicize their ideas, according to these materials.

282. Coontz provided her analysis of the impact of government programs in interviews in 1997.

284. Gary Bauer submitted testimony on the Family and Medical Leave Act of 1989, then Senate Resolution 345, to the U.S. Senate's Subcommittee on Children, Family, Drugs and Alcoholism on February 2, 1989. See pages 266–72 of the *Congressional Record.* Mattox testified before the same subcommittee on the 1991 version of the bill on January 24, 1991. See the prepared statement submitted on page 67 of the *Congressional Record.*

285. For Aetna Life & Casualty figures, see Moskowitz, Milton, "100 Best Companies for Working Mothers," *Working Mother,* October 1992.

285. For costs to women themselves, see the "Unnecessary Losses" study by Heidi Hartmann; see full citation above.

285. "The Economic Realities of Child Care," testimony by Heidi Hartmann, Ph.D., director of the Institute for Women's Policy Research, April 21, 1988, and May 5, 1988, before the Subcommittee on Human Resources, Committee on Education and Labor, U.S. House of Representatives.

286. For a review of policies of other countries, see Kammerman, Sheila and Kahn, Alfred J., Child Care: Family Benefits and Working Parents (New York: Columbia University Press, 1981).

287. Mailman Institute report: "State Legislative Leaders: Keys to Effective Legislation for Children and Families," published by the State Legislative Leaders Foundation, Centerville, Massachusetts, 1995.

289. Whitehead, Barbara DaFoe, "Dan Quayle Was Right," *Atlantic,* April 1993.

290. Dobson's statement on the "civil war of values" is from a glossy informational brochure on his organization, Focus on the Family, entitled "Helping You Build a Healthier Home," published in 1993.

292. The Boston University study was conducted by Bradley Googins and Dianne Burden in 1987.

293. For description and analysis of the legislation, see "Family Friendly Workplace Act," report from the Committee on Labor and Human Resources, April 2, 1997 (Report 105-11 to accompany Senate Resolution 4).

13. Yes, Families Are Changing—For the Better

299. The statistics on changing families come from the "Impact of Parental Employment" by Allison Sidle Fuligni, Ellen Galinsky, and Michelle Poris, the Families and Work Institute, New York City, 1995.

299. Barnett, Rosalind C., and Rivers, Caryl, *She Works, He Works: How the New American Family Is Making It Work* (Harper SanFranciso, an imprint of HarperCollins).

300. For a summary of the research on the evolution of sharing roles when both husband and wife work, see Steil, Janice, "Supermoms and Second Shifts: Inequality in the 1990's," in Freeman, Jo, *Women: A Feminist Perspective,* pages 149–161.

301. Wanniski, Jude, "One Breadwinner Should Be Enough," *Wall Street Journal,* February 12, 1996, editorial page.

301. "Ward and June Were Right" appeared on the cover of the Rockford Institute's 1996 newsletter.

303. Silberstein, Lisa, *Dual-Career Marriage: A System in Transition* (Hillsdale, New Jersey: Lawrence Erlbaum Associates, 1992).

304. Schwartz, Pepper, *Peer Marriage* (New York: Free Press, 1994).

304. For the survey on how couples share chores and child care that was publicized in the *New Jersey Star-Ledger,* see "Who Takes Care of the House and the Kids," *American Baby,* February 1997.

307. The information about how couples share child care and housework from Work/Family Directions was presented at a workshop sponsored by *Working Mother* magazine in New York City in September of 1995. The figures are taken from a presentation entitled "Women and Career Advancement: Mixed Results on the Business Front," given by Charles Rodgers, president of Rodgers and Associates, the research arm of Work/Family Directions, based in Boston, Massachusetts.

307. "Women, the New Providers," The Whirlpool Study, Part One, Families and Work Institute, New York City, 1995.

307. Janice Steil's work takes a long, hard look at equality within marriage. See Steil, Janice, and Weltman, Karen, "Marital Inequality: The Importance of Resources, Personal Attributes and Social Norms on Career Valuing and Allocation of Domestic Responsibilities," *Sex Roles,* vol. 24, nos. 3 and 4, 1991. Also see: Rosenbluth, Susan C., and Steil, Janice M., "Predictors of Intimacy for Women in Heterosexual and Homosexual Couples," *Journal of Social and Personal Relationships,* vol. 12, no. 2, 1995, pages 163–75; and Steil, Janice, and Turetsky, Beth, "Is Equal Better? The Relationship between Marital Equality and Psychological Symptomatology," in *Family Processes and Problems: Social Psychological Aspects,* edited by Stuart Oskamp (Newbury Park, California: Sage Publications, 1987).

310. "The Power of Work," *Working Mother,* September 1993.

312. Ross, Catherine, "The Division of Labor at Home," *Social Forces,* vol. 63, no. 3, March 1987, pages 816–33.

314. For a discussion of social comparison theory as applied to the workplace and home life, see Crosby, Faye, "The Denial of Personal Discrimination," *American Behavioral Scientist,* vol. 27, no. 3, January/February 1984, pages 371–86. Also see: Crosby, Faye, "Relative Deprivation in Organizational Settings," *Research in Organizational Behavior,* vol. 6, 1984, pages 51–93; and Major, Brenda, "Gender, Justice and the Psychology of Entitlement," in P. Shaver and C. Hendrick, eds., *Review of Personality and Social Psychology,* Sage Publications, 1987. Also by Major: "Gender, Entitlement and the Distribution of Family Labor," *Journal of Social Issues,* vol. 49, no. 3, 1993, pages 141–59.

314. Debra Kent, "Sex and Housework," *Working Mother,* September 1992.

315. For a discussion of the dynamics of marriage, see references above to Janice Steil's work.

322. Apter's observation is quoted in Bernard, Joan Kelly, "Death of Supermom: Young Women Look for Brilliant Balanced Careers," *Newsday,* November 1, 1995.

14. NOT GUILTY! FROM ANGST TO ANGER

323. The name of this mother has been changed to protect her family's privacy. The on-line conversation took place in August 1996, on America Online, in the ParentSoup chat room. The on-line conversation was followed up by e-mail and phone interviews with two of the participants, including the mom who is highlighted in this chapter.

324. Cantwell, Mary, *Vogue,* October 1982, page 154.

324. Baruch, Grace K., "Reflections on Guilt, Women and Gender," Working Paper No. 176, Wellesley College, Center for Research on Women, 1988. All references to Baruch's work in this chapter are taken from this paper.

325. The Olde & Company case is described at length in the *New York Times,* Business Section, April 26, 1995.

326. Smith, Janna Malamud, "Mothers: Tired of Taking the Rap," *New York Times Magazine,* June 10, 1990, pages 32–38.

330. "Working Women Count," survey by the Women's Bureau, U.S. Department of Labor, 1995.

331. "Venus Rising: Women on the Verge of the Twenty-first Century," *Grey Matter,* Fall 1995, published by Grey Advertising, New York, New York.

331. For a discussion of power and the ability to protest stereotypes, see Fiske, "Controlling Other People: The Impact of Power on Stereotyping," *American Psychologist,* June 1993.

331. "Stress at Home and in the Workplace," *Vital Issues in Employee Assistance,* a publication of the Employee Assistance Professionals Association, based in Washington, D.C., October 29, 1992.

333. For coverage of Galston's leaving the White House, see the *Washington Post,* "A Family Spin on a White House Departure," March 17, 1995.

335. *Women's Voices '96,* the complete report on the poll, was published by Lake Research, 1730 Rhode Island Avenue, N.W., Suite 400, Washington, D.C. 20036.

Index

94–95, 103–8, 111–12
employment discrimination suits
brought by, 121–29, 131, 132,
140, 142–43, 145–46
media promotion of supposed
retreat by, 40–93
part-time work by, 50, 71
"psychic retreat" of, 71
psychological studies on, 104–10,
112–15
questioning of motives of,
100–101
as role models, 107
typical work weeks of, 118
see also glass ceiling, corporate;
"mommy track;" promotion,
job
caregivers, 14
Carey, David, 68
Carlson, Allan, 269, 271, 273, 279,
290–91, 292
Carnegie Corporation, 179
Cashen, Raymond, 204–5
cashiers, 132, 133, 156
Catalyst, 51, 66, 130, 135
CBS This Morning, 41
Census Bureau, U.S., 61
Center for Parent Education, 183
Center for Policy Alternatives, 328
Chamber of Commerce, U.S., 278,
283–84
Charen, Mona, 90
charities, 212, 213
Charlotte Observer, 91
Check, Christopher, 291
Chicago, Ill., 82, 225
Chicago Tribune, 75
Child, 69, 77
child care, 57, 60, 73
corporate centers for, 148, 149,
152, 161, 198–99
cost of, 168, 220, 235, 264
economics of, 261–68
legislation on, 269–70
parents' shared responsibility for,
301
as private vs. community issue,
253–68, 271–72
public funding for, 24

regulation of, 265–66
work absences and, 253–55
see also day care; other-than-
mother care
Child Care Action Campaign, 160,
161, 206, 209–10, 216, 218
Child Care Law Center, 256
child care tax credit, 285
child custody, 16, 20, 94–96, 101,
102–3, 204–5
children:
community responsibility for,
200–201, 253–68, 271–72
day care's effects on brain growth
of, 21–22, 177–82
developmental influences on,
182–201
effects of mothers' careers on, 38,
43, 85, 94–95, 103–8, 111–12
"family time famine" and, 81,
115–20, 285, 292
parental anxiety over intelligence
of, 77
school-aged, 42, 51, 182, 260
second, 150–51, 184, 222, 301, 316
social skills of, 22
tending to illnesses of, 15
see also babies; girls; infants
Children's Action Alliance, 218
Children's Defense Fund, 80, 177,
260, 269, 270
Children's Foundation, 265, 273
Children's Playhouse, 210
Child Welfare League, 214, 271
Christensen, Bryce, 273
Christian right, 81, 271
Christian Science Monitor, 88
Chubb Insurance, 107
Ciervo, Lynnette, 185
Circuit Science Incorporated (CSI),
253–55
City University of New York, Gradu-
ate Center of, 25, 62, 135, 138,
225
civil rights legislation, 129
civil rights movement, 249, 274
Civil War, U.S., 211–12
Clark, Gordon, 94–95, 102–3, 104,
116

stigma attached to, 202–18, 273
see also child care
Day Care Council, 87
Deaux, Kay, 138, 139, 144, 307–8, 337
Deceptive Distinctions (Epstein), 135
depression, 38, 81, 115
Detroit News, 38, 65, 95
developing countries, 111
diaries, of time-use, 118, 119
Discovering Motherhood, 85
"displaced homemakers," 47, 230
diversity training, 144, 147–55, 163
divorce, 43, 62, 234, 241
Dobson, James, 81, 116, 289
Dodd, Chris, 270
Doherty, Jill, 58
Dolan, Donna, 162
Dole, Robert, 81
domesticity:
    cult of, 243
    media marketing of, 67–93
Downey, Mike, 319–20
Downey, Rebecca, 319–20
Dreskin, Wendy, 280
"dry-cleaning effect," 221
Dual-Career Marriage (Silberstein), 302–3
Duff-Campbell, Nancy, 277, 285
DuPont Company, 157, 161, 166
Dwyer and Collora, 128

Early Child Care Research Network, 196–97
Eberstadt, Mary, 86
Edelman, Marian Wright, 276
education, 57, 111
    birth rate and, 59
    early, 210
    earnings and, 249–50
    home-schooling and, 290–91
    of working mothers, 47, 63
Education Department, U.S., 265
Embattled Paradise (Skolnick), 188
Employed Mother in America, The (Hoffman and Nye), 106
Employee Assistance Professionals Association, 330

employee assistance programs, 330
employment discrimination suits, 121–29, 131, 132, 140, 142–43, 145–46, 223
Entmacher, Joan, 274–75
Epstein, Cynthia Fuchs, 25, 62, 99, 135–37, 225, 228, 232, 334
Equal Employment Opportunity Commission, 131
Equal Pay Act (1963), 248–50
Esquire, 47–48, 50, 67, 69
Europe, 111, 193, 218, 285
Eyer, Diane, 174, 182

"face time," 158
Fair Labor Standards Act (1938), 293
Fair Pay Act (proposed), 252
Faludi, Susan, 50
families:
    benefits from working mothers gained by, 104
    burden of working mothers borne by, 64, 155–56
    contemporary changes in, 297–321
    cultural ideals of, 33, 34–35, 157, 257, 286
    extended, 200
    Mattox's "new paradigm" for, 81
    median income of, 267
    Ozzie and Harriet image of, 64, 71, 187, 280, 281, 282
    "problem," 214
    relocation of, 97–98, 152, 166
    in "transitional" phase, 299
    two-income, 61, 76, 228, 233–34, 280–83, 298, 300
    women as breadwinners of, 87–91
Families and Education Levy, 268
Families and Work Institute, 62, 64, 86, 87, 92, 103, 106, 155, 160, 165, 181, 206, 306, 309
    Fatherhood Project at, 299, 316, 318
"familism," 78
Family and Medical Leave Act (1993), 45, 81–82, 117, 129, 228, 277–78, 282–85